Parties, Interest Groups, and Campaign Finance Laws

A Conference Sponsored by the
American Enterprise Institute for Public Policy Research

Parties, Interest Groups, and Campaign Finance Laws

Edited by Michael J. Malbin

American Enterprise Institute for Public Policy Research
Washington, D.C.

Library of Congress Cataloging in Publication Data

Main entry under title:

Parties, interest groups, and campaign finance laws.

(AEI symposia ; 79I)
Papers presented at a conference sponsored by the American
Enterprise Institute and held in Washington, D.C. Sept. 4–5, 1979.
　1.　Pressure groups—United States—Congresses.　2.　Elections—
United States—Campaign funds—Congresses.　I.　Malbin, Michael J.
II.　American Enterprise Institute for Public Policy Research.
III.　Series: American Enterprise Institute for Public Policy Research.
AEI symposia ; 79I.
JK1118.P37　　　329'.03'0973　　　79-25938
ISBN 0-8447-2167-0
ISBN 0-8447-2168-9 pbk.

AEI Symposia 79I

Printed in the United States of America

Contents

PART FIVE
CAMPAIGN FINANCE REGULATION IN INTERNATIONAL PERSPECTIVE

Major Participants

DAVID W. ADAMANY is vice-president for academic affairs, California State University, Long Beach. A lawyer and political scientist, Adamany has held numerous positions in Wisconsin state government, the most recent of which were chairman of the Governor's Study Committee on Political Finance (1973–1974), and then vice-chairman (1974–1975) and chairman (1976–1977) of the Wisconsin State Elections Board. He is the author of *Campaign Finance in America* (1972) and coauthor, with George E. Agree, of *Political Money: A Strategy for Campaign Financing in America* (1975).

GEORGE E. AGREE is director of a Freedom House study of the transnational interactions of political parties. He has been a political consultant for many candidates and groups, including the Republican Legislative Research Association and the Democratic Study Group, and was coauthor of *Political Money* with David W. Adamany.

HERBERT E. ALEXANDER is director of the Citizens' Research Foundation, which specializes in campaign finance analysis, and professor of political science at the University of Southern California. The most recent of his many books on campaign finance is *Financing the 1976 Election* (1979), the fifth in a quadrennial series that began in 1960.

DAVID BRODER is a Pulitzer Prize winning political correspondent for *The Washington Post* and author of *The Party's Over: The Failure of Politics in America* (1972).

BERNADETTE A. BUDDE is director of political education for the Business-Industry Political Action Committee.

RICHARD B. CHENEY was elected to the House of Representatives from Wyoming in 1978. He was President Ford's White House chief of staff from 1974 to 1977.

RICHARD P. CONLON has been staff director of the Democratic Study Group in the House of Representatives since 1968.

EDWIN M. EPSTEIN is professor and chairman of the Political, Social and Legal Environment Group in the School of Business Administration, University of California, Berkeley. He is the author of *Corporations, Contributions and Political Campaigns: Federal Regulation in Perspective* (1968) and *The Corporation in American Politics* (1969). He is a coauthor, with Dow Botaw, of *Rationality, Legitimacy, Responsibility: The Search for New Directions in Business and Society* (1978).

DAVID JESSUP is special assistant for the Committee on Political Education (COPE), AFL–CIO, and is a former national chairman of Front-lash, a labor-backed organization to encourage voter participation among youths.

RUTH S. JONES is associate professor of political science at the University of Missouri, St. Louis, and has served on the Governor's Commission on Campaign Reform and Official Conduct. Her paper for this conference is the first product of what will be a multiyear study of state campaign finance laws.

XANDRA KAYDEN was a member of the Campaign Finance Study Group of the Institute of Politics at Harvard University, whose report to the Committee on House Administration of the U.S. House of Representatives was made public in May 1979. She also is author of the institute's *Report of a Conference on Campaign Finance Based on the Experience of the 1976 Presidential Campaigns* (1977).

ROBERT J. KEEFE is a political consultant in Washington. He was the campaign manager of Senator Henry Jackson's 1976 presidential effort and before that was executive director of the Democratic National Committee.

CLARK MACGREGOR, vice-president of United Technologies Corp., served in the House of Representatives from 1960 to 1970, ran unsuccessfully against Hubert H. Humphrey for the Senate in 1970, and was counsel to the president from 1971 to 1972 and campaign manager of the Committee to Re-Elect the President in 1972.

MICHAEL J. MALBIN is a resident fellow at the American Enterprise Institute, a contributing editor to *National Journal,* and adjunct associate professor of politics at Catholic University. His books include *Religion and Politics* (AEI, 1978) and *Unelected Representatives: The New Role of Congressional Staff* (forthcoming, 1980).

THOMAS E. MANN is codirector of the American Enterprise Institute's Congress Project, a visiting fellow at AEI, and assistant director of the American Political Science Association. He is the author of *Unsafe At Any Margin: Interpreting Congressional Elections* (AEI, 1978).

WALTER K. MOORE was director of the Washington office of the National Committee for an Effective Congress at the time of the conference, but has since joined the Carter-Mondale Presidential Committee. Before NCEC, Moore was executive assistant to Commissioner Neil Staebler at the Federal Election Commission.

MANFRED VON NORDHEIM is director of the Washington office of the Konrad Adenauer Foundation, a research foundation affiliated with the Christian Democratic Union, with headquarters in Bonn.

WILLIAM C. OLDAKER was general counsel of the Federal Election Commission from January 1977 through October 1979, when he became counsel for Senator Edward M. Kennedy's Campaign Committee.

KHAYYAM ZEV PALTIEL is professor of political science at Carleton University, Ottowa, Canada. A past secretary of the International Study Group on Political Finance, he is the author of *Political Party Financing in Canada* (1970) and numerous related articles, including one for AEI's *Canada at the Polls* (1975), as well as articles on Israeli and Middle Eastern politics.

HOWARD R. PENNIMAN is resident scholar and codirector of the Center for the Study of Political and Social Processes at the American Enterprise Institute, professor of government at Georgetown University, and an election consultant to the American Broadcasting Company. He is the editor of seven AEI studies of elections in other countries, the most recent of which is *Israel at the Polls: The Knesset Elections of 1977* (1978).

LARRY PRATT is executive director of Gun Owners of America, Inc., and before that was executive director of the American Conservative Union. In November 1979 he was elected to the Virginia House of Delegates.

NELSON W. POLSBY is professor of political science at the University of California, Berkeley, and author of numerous books and articles on American politics, including the soon to be published fifth edition of *Presidential Elections*, coauthored with Aaron Wildavsky.

STEVEN F. STOCKMEYER is executive director of the National Republican Congressional Committee.

STEPHEN W. THOMAS is director of the Council for a Livable World.

FRED WERTHEIMER is senior vice-president of Common Cause.

PAUL M. WEYRICH is director of the Committee for the Survival of a Free Congress.

MORLEY WINOGRAD is chairperson of the Michigan State Democratic Party and president of the Association of Democratic State Party Chairpersons. He also chaired the Democratic National Committee's Commission on the Role and Future of Primaries from 1976 to 1978.

Introduction

Michael J. Malbin

When the campaign finance reforms of 1974 and of 1976 were adopted by the U.S. Congress, supporters and opponents alike predicted the new laws would have profound effects on the way elections are fought and government is run in the United States. Some two election cycles after the changes were enacted, there are now serious disagreements over the effects of the law. About the only point on which students of campaign finance all seem to agree is that the changes indeed have been profound.

On September 4–5, 1979, the American Enterprise Institute sponsored a conference in Washington, D.C., to probe the impact of campaign finance reform on interest groups, political parties, and campaign strategies. Interest groups and parties were discussed in the four panels of the conference (two on each day), while campaign strategies were the theme of its two major luncheon speeches.

The Panels

The conference started with the interest groups for two reasons: first, because curbing the power of the "special interests" was one major purpose reformers said they had in mind in advocating the 1974 law, and, second, because the growth of political action committees (PACs) has been the most widely noted aspect of the postcampaign law political environment. There were two panels on interest groups. The first, which I chaired, was composed of six representatives of interest groups of widely divergent political perspectives, and also included the general counsel of the Federal Election Commission (FEC). (The papers on the remaining panels were all by political scientists with a particular interest in campaign finance, while the commentators were journalists, current or former practitioners, or political scientists.) All participants on the first panel were asked to discuss how the law affected their own organizations, but most also took the opportunity to address the more general themes subsequently debated during the second panel, which was chaired by Nelson W. Polsby and centered on papers by Edwin M.

1

Epstein and myself. Some of the questions raised in the two panels were as follows:

• What is the connection, if any, between the law and the remarkable growth in the number of corporate, single-issue, and ideological PACs?
• Does this growth mean that the law has failed to achieve its purpose?
• Does the law help to democratize political influence? If not, and if such democratization is a desirable goal, what can be done to spread political power more widely?
• Who, if anybody, does the law favor?
• How have the law and the regulatory procedures of the FEC affected the internal operations of politically active interest groups?
• What would be the likely effect of future changes in the law on the role of private organizations in federal election campaigns and their influence over government?

On the second day, the focus of the conference shifted somewhat. The third panel, chaired by Thomas E. Mann, was on the subject of political parties. Xandra Kayden traced the centralizing, bureaucratizing, and energizing effects of the 1974 and 1976 laws on national party organizations. Ruth Jones's paper was the first of three with an explicitly comparative perspective: it presented an examination of the differential impact of seventeen varying state public finance statutes on seventeen sets of state party organizations.

The paper on state parties brought home an important point: it is not enough to talk about the effects of campaign finance "reform" or even about the effects of public financial assistance for campaigns in the abstract. Different statutes, with slightly different provisions, can produce widely divergent institutional results. This observation was deepened as a result of the two cross-national papers submitted by participants in the fourth panel, which was chaired by Howard R. Penniman. Khayyam Zev Paltiel discussed the impact of public financing abroad, and Herbert E. Alexander considered the impact of other forms of campaign finance regulation on parties and interest groups. It is hoped that the overall effect of this discussion will be to help break through the insularity that has hitherto marked most of the public debates over campaign finance in this country.

Historical Background

The ten conference papers were written as self-contained essays to be presented to an audience of politically active people. The following historical outline of campaign finance regulation in the United States is designed to make the papers more accessible to the broader audience for which this book is intended.[1] More detailed treatments of the legislative provisions affecting PACs and political parties may be found in the papers by Edwin Epstein and Xandra Kayden.

Until 1971, most federal law relating to campaign finance was codified in the Corrupt Practices Act of 1925,[2] which required disclosure of receipts and expenditures by candidates for the Senate and House of Representatives. But the law did not apply to political committees set up by a candidate, and it did not apply to presidential and vice-presidential candidates. The 1925 act put spending ceilings on "interstate committees," but presidential candidates evaded the limit by setting up more than one committee in their name. The same device was used to circumvent the $5,000 limit on contributions by individuals imposed by the 1940 Hatch Act[3] as there was no limit on the number of committees candidates could set up, each being eligible to receive $5,000.

The Corrupt Practices Act was repealed by the Federal Election Campaign Act (FECA) of 1971.[4] The new act had three major provisions: (1) it significantly tightened disclosure and reporting requirements for all candidates for federal office as of April 7, 1972; (2) it limited the amounts of money candidates could spend on media advertising; and (3) it limited the amount a candidate and his immediate family could contribute to his own campaign. At about the same time, the Revenue Act of 1971[5] allowed taxpayers to claim 50 percent credits of up to $12.50, or deductions of up to $50, for political contributions, and allowed taxpayers to check a box on their tax forms in order to place a dollar of their taxes in a fund for presidential and vice-presidential candidates. The 1971 law contained provisions directing how these funds were to be disbursed, but these were to be changed before they were ever implemented.

The FECA amendments of 1974[6] probably represented the most sweeping set of campaign finance law changes ever adopted in the United States, if not in the world. The 1974 law:

• limited the amount individuals could contribute to federal candidates to $1,000 per election (primary, general election, or runoff), and a cumulative total of $25,000 per year

---

[1] For a more complete history, see Herbert Alexander, *Financing Politics: Money, Politics and Political Reform* (Washington, D.C.: Congressional Quarterly Press, 1976). The following paragraphs are based on Alexander's account.
[2] 43 Stat. 1053, ch. 368, Sec. 301-319.
[3] 54 Stat. 772.
[4] P.L. 92-225.
[5] P.L. 92-178.
[6] P.L. 93-443.

3

- retained the 1971 limit on contributions by candidates to their own campaigns
- limited to $1,000 the amount an individual could spend independently to influence an election (such spending is termed an "independent expenditure")
- limited what candidates could spend to get elected
- amended a 1940 Hatch Act provision prohibiting contributions from federal contractors to make it clear that contractors could form PACs
- limited PAC contributions to $5,000 per candidate per election, with no cumulative limit
- limited expenditures by political parties on behalf of a candidate (over and above contributions) to $10,000 per candidate for the House in general elections, $20,000 or two cents per eligible voter, whichever was greater, in general elections for the Senate, and two cents per voter in the presidential general election
- established formulas for disbursing public funds to match contributions of up to $250 for presidential candidates in prenomination contests
- used flat grants to cover the full expenses of the conventions of the two major parties and the major presidential general election campaigns, with proportional formulas for postelection grants to qualified candidates of minor parties
- required candidates of major parties who choose to accept flat grants for general elections to forgo private financing and limit their expenditures to the amount of the grant
- created an independent, six-member Federal Election Commission (FEC)
- strengthened disclosure and closed previous legal loopholes by requiring any federal candidate to establish a single central campaign committee through which all contributions and expenditures would have to be reported.

The law immediately was attacked as being unconstitutional. Within days after it went into effect on January 1, 1975, a coalition spanning the political spectrum filed a case that came to be known as *Buckley* v. *Valeo*. The Supreme Court's decision on that case, handed down a little more than a year later on January 30, 1976,[7] held unconstitutional the limits on campaign spending, independent expenditures, and contributions by a candidate to his own campaign, along with the method by which the FEC was appointed. The court upheld disclosure, public financing, and the limits on individual, PAC, and party contributions.

---

[7] 424 U.S. 1, 96 S.Ct. 612, 46 L.Ed. 2d 659 (1976).

The court also upheld the spending limits imposed on a candidate as a condition for accepting public financing.

Since *Buckley* v. *Valeo* effectively put the FEC out of business in the middle of a presidential election campaign, Congress was forced in 1976 to pass yet another set of amendments to the FECA.[8] It could have simply reconstituted the FEC along lines suggested by the Court, but Congress decided to use the occasion to address a number of other issues. The 1976 law:

- limited individual contributions to political parties to $20,000 per year and to other political committees to $5,000 per year
- limited contributions to political parties by PACs to $15,000 per year
- increased the amount that the Democratic and Republican Senate campaign committees could contribute to Senate candidates from $5,000 per election to $17,500 per year
- limited to $50,000 the amount of their own money that presidential candidates who were publicly financed could spend to support their own campaign
- reversed an FEC ruling on PACs (described more fully in Epstein's paper) that appeared to allow labor and business PACs to proliferate in a way that effectively might have destroyed the PAC contribution limits.

This was the state of the law at the time of the AEI conference. One more development, however, bears noting. Several of the papers in this book contain references to a bill (H.R. 4970) whose principal sponsors in the House of Representatives were Representatives David Obey (D-Wis.), and Tom Railsback (R-Ill.). As originally written, the bill would have cut in half the amount PACs could contribute to candidates from $5,000 per election to $5,000 per election cycle (or $7,500 for candidates in runoff primaries). At the same time, the bill would have put a $50,000 ceiling on the amount any candidate could accept from all PACs combined. On October 17, 1979, the House, by a vote of 217–198, added a modified version of the Obey-Railsback bill to an FEC authorization bill passed by the Senate (S. 832) and sent it to conference. As amended, the bill would limit PAC contributions to a total of $6,000 per election cycle ($9,000 for candidates with runoff primaries), while limiting candidates to a total of $70,000 in all PAC contributions per election cycle ($85,000 for candidates in runoffs). As of this writing, the bill's fate is still pending.

---

8 PL 94-283.

INTRODUCTION

Format

The format of this book essentially follows that of the conference: papers, comments, replies, and general discussion. There are a few minor deviations. First, the luncheon speeches by Robert J. Keefe, and Richard B. Cheney belonged together and were therefore placed between the proceedings of the first and second days. Second, because of the pivotal role of Common Cause in shaping the campaign finance legislation of the 1970s, Fred Wertheimer was encouraged to write a longer set of comments than he could present at the conference. Most of his written comments were directed at my own paper, and so my reply was also subsequently revised and extended.

The time that elapsed between the conference and the publication of this volume has been remarkably short. Carol Rosen and Yamile Martin, editors on AEI's publication staff, and my secretary, Kathleen Long, all deserve an acknowledgment for the work they have done to make this book available in time for the 1980 elections.

Special thanks should also go to the people who attended the conference. The audience included all six FEC commissioners, as well as a goodly number of people from business, labor, and issue-oriented PACs, political activists from both major and some minor parties, and political scientists and journalists. Their contributions added immeasurably to the conference and, in turn, to this volume.

Part One

Interest Groups and the Law:
Some Perspectives from Inside

Business Political Action Committees

Bernadette A. Budde

Any discussion about business political action committees (PACs) inevitably begins with the search for a cause-effect relationship—Which came first, the PACs or the law? In regard to this "chicken or egg" controversy, many commentators have concluded that it was the law, specifically the amendments to the Federal Election Campaign Act (FECA) adopted in 1974 and the regulations drafted in 1976 that caused the "rush" to form political action committees. Those of us who have been active in the PAC movement for a decade or more are amused by the assumption, for we have watched the development of PACs over a long period.

PACs did not just happen with the changes in the 1974 law. Failure to understand this crucial factor results in faulty conclusions by those who are frightened by the growth of PACs and want to do something with the law. It might be sobering for the anti-PAC forces to realize that countless successful committees operated in a climate of pre-1970 regulations in a fashion strikingly similar to the way they operate today.

Future changes in the law may halt the formation of PACs and alter the role of young committees, but it is hard to imagine that mature groups would be forced from the electoral scene. The observation that no matter what the law, business would continue to exercise First Amendment rights may not apply to many corporate political action committees—being younger, they might be less adaptable. Unaffiliated PACs such as the Business-Industry Political Action Committee (BIPAC), may be in a stronger position. Labor union PACs or others with a membership base may be the least affected.

That, of course, is speculation based on an intimacy with the regulations and a reflection on what the "reformers" claim they have in mind. This speculation is also based on an assumption about what has so alarmed the critics—money—precisely, money going to candidates. Even Common Cause, which is without question the most frequent and intense of the PAC critics, does not deny that there is a role for individuals or groups of individuals in the political/electoral process.

9

As long as there are rights to communicate ideas and the correlate rights to pay for the cost of those communications, there will be a role for political action committees. Clipping their wings and making it more difficult to undertake multiple activities will only require that each PAC learn to master the few skills than can be performed within the law and the Constitution. Independent parallel campaigns are one attractive option to direct candidate contributions.

Roots of Corporate PACs

Going back to the "chicken or egg" analogy, it can be argued that even without the amendments to the Federal Election Campaign Act business would have some portion of the number of PACs that exist today. As of October 1978 corporations had 821.[1] The largest and most sophisticated political action committees began before the mid-1960s—American Medical Political Action Committee (AMPAC), Business-Industry Political Action Committee (BIPAC), Life Underwriters Political Action Committee (LUPAC), American Dental Political Action Committee (ADPAC), Forest Products Political Action Committee, and others. Several corporations also had programs in place during the 1960s. Those headquartered in California had a head start, given the activism of much of its business leadership, the ability to make corporate contributions at the state level, and the dramatic nuances of that state's elections. Union Oil, Southern California Gas/Pacific Lighting, Atlantic Richfield, Hughes Aircraft, Fluor Corporations, and Dart Industries all had a variety of vehicles for employees who became exposed to political campaigns.

By the late 1960s and early 1970s, other companies had in place what was often called a trustee plan, something which the current law also addresses (notably, the law did not "invent" the concept). This was a simple arrangement whereby bank accounts would be opened for employees who wished to participate in the plan, employees would designate a certain portion of their salaries to be set aside in the accounts each pay period, and the employees had full discretion over the distribution of the funds in their account. A few of the more successful of these plans were found in Republic Steel, Eaton Corporation, and Standard of Indiana. It may be recalled that something similar to this was submitted to the Federal Election Commission (FEC), in the now-famous Sun case—known as Employee Participation Accounts.[2]

---

[1] U.S. Federal Election Commission, *FEC Reports on Financial Activity 1977– 1978,* Interim Report no. 4, May 1979.

[2] U.S. Federal Election Commission, *AO 1975–23,* November 24, 1975.

This lineage puts corporate development in perspective and proves that the seeds had been sprouting before the law was passed. The desire and the need to be involved politically is deeply rooted in American industry. PAC formation was not a response to a law or a movement that began to blossom only in the mid-1970s. Naturally, there was some reaction by business and some desire to be part of the new movement, but nearly every successful PAC had an embryonic period of incubation that began before 1976.

Relationship to Government Regulation

Laws and regulations are, however, related to PAC development. It was not the Federal Election Campaign Act and the Federal Election Commission that promoted the PAC movement; it was every other law and every other regulatory body that began intruding into the business of business. A clear pattern emerges when reviewing who does and who does not have a PAC—the more regulated an industry and the more obvious an industry is as a congressional target, the more likely it is to have a political action committee within the associations or within the companies that make up that industry. As the government moves closer and closer to partnership with an industry, the result of that liaison is a PAC, mothered by industry but unmistakably sired by government.

When looking over PAC lists, is it such a surprise that railroads, utilities, oil, timber/paper, banks, savings and loan associations, drug companies, and government contractors in the aerospace industry seem to have a higher proportion of PACs than consumer product companies or retailers? (See Table 1.) Even the consumer product companies and the retailers are moving in the direction of greater PAC participation, although at a lesser pace, perhaps because government's flirtations with them are not as frequent or threatening.

Two rather recent entrants into the political process are the real estate industry and the auto industry. Both groups made a swift rise to the top of the charts in dollars raised for 1978, outspending all but the doctors. Was it the FECA that prompted that growth or was it the fact that Congress was setting fuel economy standards, emission standards, and safety standards for automobiles? Did the realtors become active because someone in the Chicago headquarters finally got around to reading the FECA regulations, or was it that the housing market became more and more a creature of government economic policy—that the home building and home selling industry became as captive of government regulation as any other industry?

If in the next two elections the food producers, processors, and distributors suddenly form active political action committees, it should

11

TABLE 1

POLITICAL ACTION COMMITTEE ACTIVITY
AMONG MAJOR BUSINESS/INDUSTRY GROUPS, 1977–1978

Category of Company[a]	Total Number of Companies	Number of PACs	Contribution to Federal Candidates[b]
Commercial banking	50	26	$140,450
Retailing	50	15	366,002
Utilities	50	35	566,359
Life insurance	50	5	30,950
Diversified financial	50	18	199,115
Aerospace	13	10	401,930
Building materials/paper/timber	52	20	704,772
Natural resources/gas/oil/coal	44	25	958,123
Transportation	46	30	597,061
Beverages, consumer products	79	34	390,524
Pharmaceuticals	20	12	225,820

[a] Industrial categories defined by *Fortune* and/or *Business Week* magazines as used in their *Directory of Industrial Companies and Corporate Scoreboard.*
[b] Calculated from Federal Election Commission, *FEC Reports on Financial Activity 1977–1978*, Interim Report no. 4, May 1979.

not be a surprise—nor should it be concluded that someone within those industries finally got the message from the FEC. The public's and government's reaction to increasing food costs and the focus on retail store prices may awaken this economic group.

Complications in FECA Provisions

Hazards for Business. Even if one argues that the FECA and the FEC had only a partial cause-effect relationship to the growth of corporate PACs, it would be impossible to deny that they had an impact on the internal operations of the committees. The detailed regulations made some reluctant corporate counsels finally give in to the public affairs officers who had wanted a PAC for years, but it had the opposite impact on some others. It would be grossly unscientific to say just how many are not in the PAC movement because the regulations wave red flags, but the sentiment is expressed by many who do not have PACs. The law, rather than offering guidelines on how to administer a system, creates all sorts of pitfalls in reporting and internal accounting that make some businesses nervous (particularly small ones without specialized staffs).

The law's most troublesome provision may be the distinction between executives and nonexecutives.[3] That division makes many companies uncomfortable, particularly those with few unionized workers. Under pre-1974 PACs, especially the trustee plans or the BIPAC solicitation programs, anyone could participate. Now, the regulations force discrimination between managerial and nonmanagerial employees, outlining different methods by which each can be solicited, communicated with, and treated when it comes to politics.[4] In a number of industries, this creates not only a discomfort by establishing an unnatural caste system, but also a confusion of definitions—in which category are salespeople, franchise holders, and all of those workers who are not unionized but are not clearly management, such as secretaries and administrative assistants, bank tellers, and a host of other job categories?

Those not willing to ask the FEC have taken the most conservative way out and have narrowed the group that is solicited to those who are clearly middle-to-top management, thus disenfranchising a large group of employees who have nowhere to go: the unions don't consider them part of their constituency and the companies don't either. The law's provisions for twice-yearly solicitation to the homes of the nonmanagerial class have not proved to be practical for companies from a logistical or philosophical standpoint. (We are unaware that any union has solicited nonmembers twice a year in their homes.)

If the law is to be amended, many business groups would like to see this section changed, giving management the right to communicate on any subject with all employees and to solicit any employee (or perhaps all nonunion employees) in the same fashion that management or stockholders may be solicited. This "fish nor fowl" category creates further problems for companies that have programs of political education or campaign management open to everyone (such as those sponsored by some Minneapolis-based companies, Alcoa, Cities Service, Atlantic Richfield, Sun, and others).

Special Problems for Trade Associations. Corporate-based trade associations have been given the short end of the stick in the FECA and FEC regulations. Many observers do not realize how limited PAC success has been in this category because of the way the FEC categorizes the committees. By lumping trade, membership, and health groups together, it would appear that trade associations are the most generous

---

[3] "Federal Election Commission, Establishment of Chapter," *Federal Register,* section 114.1(c), August 25, 1976, p. 35956.

[4] "FEC Establishment of Chapter," *Federal Register,* sections 114.3–114.6, pp. 35955–35960.

givers in the political process. Health groups, realtors, auto dealers, and a variety of others who are not corporate based "bring up" the numbers in this category. The trade associations within business and industry are unable to live with the serious restrictions in the law. Only one of the top ten contributors to federal candidates in this category is a corporate-based group—the American Bankers Association PAC—which was number nine with only $232,180.

Those who do relatively well are those with great numbers of smaller corporate or single entrepreneur memberships. The largest and most legislatively active trade associations, which many would assume should have large PACs, are not involved at all—National Association of Manufacturers, American Petroleum Institute, Grocery Manufacturers, Iron and Steel Institute.

The law requires that trade association PACs have permission to solicit the managerial personnel of member companies and that the member companies may authorize the solicitation of only one trade association PAC each year.[5] The result has been that trade association PACs cannot even ask members of their boards for contributions unless they meet the requirements.[6] They have been unable to solicit at annual meetings for fear that they might expose "untouchables" to the message.[7] They have been unable to compete with one another for permission to solicit in companies (nearly all large ones) which belong to more than one trade association.

Because of these complications, it will be increasingly difficult for trade associations to become full partners with companies in the political process. The role of trade associations may be that of encouraging PAC formation among member companies and providing tools and assistance in PAC operation, rather than that of raising large contributions. Proposed amendments to the law considered in 1978 would have loosened some of these restrictions.

Impact of FECA on BIPAC

The impact of the law on the Business-Industry Political Action Committee, an independent PAC, has been indirect rather than direct. Our founders in 1963 were amazingly farsighted in setting up an organization that required very little tailoring after the FECA and FEC came into

---

[5] "FEC Establishment of Chapter," *Federal Register,* section 114.8, pp. 35960–35961.

[6] U.S. Federal Election Commission, *AO 1977–18,* November 18, 1977.

[7] U.S. Federal Election Commission, *AO 1976–27,* September 2, 1976; *AO 1978–17,* April 10, 1978; *AO 1978–83,* December 18, 1978.

existence. We had a reporting apparatus in place and an internal method of computerizing contributors by place of business (although such refinements as middle initials and occupation were not part of our initial system). We had the experience of reporting contributors of $100 or more to the clerk of the House and Senate (some holdovers from those earlier years still contribute $99, thinking that the unreported contribution limit is the same). Except for one instance, we had never given a candidate more than $5,000 in a single race. We always had a system to charge the cost of fund raising and our administrative expenses to the political action division (thus assuring that corporate dollars could not be diverted to indirect support of candidates), although our formula has changed. We always handled our funds in two accounts in two different banks to prevent commingling of corporate and individual contributions. We were always audited by a national accounting firm: we underwent a pre-FEC audit from the General Accounting Office, and we were audited by the FEC in 1979. In summary, the direct, mechanical, and structural impact was minimal.

The biggest impact of the law (and the mere passage of time as corporations became more politically mature) was that the companies who ran BIPAC membership programs were beginning to set up their own PACs. As a result, we had to diversify our fund-raising programs. The law did not force a choice between BIPAC and the corporate PAC, but many companies were reluctant to solicit twice (although BIPAC probably had better luck than trade associations in getting dual solicitations). In some cases, we have received contributions from these political action committees, but the total dollars were usually greater when the individuals designated their dollars for BIPAC. In other companies, funds were received from a payroll deduction system or a slot on the authorization cards for trustee plans. In a cautious interpretation of the regulations, we advised all companies to stop those payroll deduction systems and suggestions that the trustee plan be used for our contributions.[8]

To supplement the traditional company program (distribution of a brochure and application card within the company), BIPAC has used some direct mail to selected business/private enterprise–oriented audiences and sponsored fund-raising events. We do not feel this changes our base of support, although it has increased our average contribution. Presumably, this is a result of the $100-per-ticket fund-raising events, although our direct mail appeals are also bringing in a higher dollar average than the traditional BIPAC membership program. Before 1976,

---

[8] U.S. Federal Election Commission, *AO 1976–93*, February 7, 1977.

the average contribution was between $20 and $30; now it is between $60 and $70.

One of our most pleasant surprises has been that as the number of PACs grows, we appear even stronger than before. The paradox is hard to explain, but candidates court us to a greater degree than ever. We think BIPAC's contributions become more important because of our reputation for entering only close races on behalf of clear choices, with early dollars in significant chunks (never less than $500 and usually $1,000 or $2,000 at a time). Over three-fourths of our dollars go to nonincumbents, and most of our early money goes to them during the summer months, to be followed by contributions later in the campaign. The peak of our giving period was the first week of July. We also tell other business groups (with action fund dollars) which candidates are receiving our strong support.

Patterns of Corporate PAC Giving

Lessons from Labor. Business PACs are anxious to learn from what they consider to be the masters in election strategies: organized labor. Labor without a doubt is more partisan in the distribution of their money, but they are not merely providing dollars to reward good labor voting records; they are engaging in political hardball by providing the most to those who need the most (if they are incumbents), searching for winning challengers, and seeking to replace retiring incumbents of all stripes with those who have a potential for a favorable voting record. As shown in Table 2, corporate and labor PACs contributed nearly the same proportion of funds to open seats and challengers.

TABLE 2

DISTRIBUTION OF PAC DOLLARS BY CATEGORY
OF SEAT AND PARTY, 1977–1978

| Type of PAC/Total Contributions | Percentage Distribution to | | | | | |
| | Incumbents | | Challengers | | Open seats | |
	Rep.	Dem.	Rep.	Dem.	Rep.	Dem.
Corporate ($9.8 million)	31.6	27.3	17.7	3.5	13.2	6.7
Union ($10.3 million)	4.7	54.6	0.3	21.0	0.5	18.8
Trade/membership/health ($11.5 million)	27.6	30.7	15.9	3.9	13.0	8.9
Nonconnected ($2.5 million)	15.9	12.9	36.7	6.5	21.7	6.3

SOURCE: Calculated from Federal Election Commission, *FEC Reports on Financial Activity 1977–1978*, Interim Report no. 4, May 1979.

To date, money has been a fixation for those who try to measure political effectiveness. It is one of our few standard yardsticks, but in the future the role of money may be less significant in determining where influence is exercised. Even now, money is a symbol that represents not so much purchasing power for the candidate's campaign manager but the endorsement, encouragement, and belief of one individual or one PAC in a candidate who is running for office. It is also true that money from some organizations generally regarded as politically savvy is worth more. Candidates want to tell potential contributors that they have received a contribution (ignoring the amount) from a local PAC just to arouse the interest of a national organization. Sometimes the process is reversed—national money will attract local support.

With an array of issues and plant facilities, business may continue to be less partisan than labor. There are too many Democrats with good records on fiscal issues or labor/management questions for business to automatically help every Republican on the ballot. Business is also likely to help even greater numbers of Democrats as they become more willing to enter primaries—often the only chance to make a meaningful contribution in a campaign. Table 3 shows the distribution of contributions for 1977–1978.

District-by-District Analysis. A form of "situation politics," in which each district is judged on the basis of its circumstances and the candidates are matched against each other, rather than with those in other parts of the country, is likely to become more prevalent.

As political decisions become more situational, they may also become more subjective, with industry groups disagreeing on the favorability of some incumbents. It is clear, however, that in 1978 the races where easily identified choices existed (as was the case with most of the incumbents who were defeated or who narrowly escaped), business would rally behind the challengers with the simple recognition that they would probably have better attitudes than the endangered incumbents and that they had a reasonable chance to win.

Focus on Fortune 500. BIPAC's study of PAC giving began with a look at the Fortune 500 companies, of which 210 have political action committees. These companies were selected because they are manufacturing units scattered throughout the country and are the most likely to cross state lines in their contributions. We assumed that banks, utilities, and transportation might be more apt to stay within service boundaries. This assumption cannot be verified until we use the same method to evaluate their contributions, although preliminary scans of the data suggest that

17

TABLE 3

CHARACTERISTICS OF TOP FIFTY RECIPIENTS OF LABOR/CORPORATE PAC DOLLARS IN HOUSE RACES, 1977–1978

Percentage Distribution of Candidates by Categories

	Party		Type of race			Result		Percentage of vote in general election [a]			
PAC Category	Rep.	Dem.	Incum-bent	Chal-lenger	Open	Won	Lost	55% or less [b]	56–59%	60–69%	70% or more
Corporate	74	26	56	18	26	68	32	48	12	26	14
Union	0	100	68	12	20	72	28	56	10	24	4

[a] Union totals do not add up to 100% because 6% of labor's top 50 candidates lost in the primary.
[b] Includes losers.

SOURCE: Calculated from Federal Election Commission, *FEC Reports on Financial Activity 1977–1978*, Interim Report no. 4, May 1979.

this assumption is correct. As the larger companies with the greatest number of employees and the greatest resources to use in PAC activity, the Fortune 500 companies were expected to produce the largest contributions to federal candidates.

The results of the study are far from complete, but there are several observations that appear valid from the data, and some that admittedly depend on one's perspective. The most obvious conclusion from the number of PACs is that the Fortune 500 companies are just as likely not to have a PAC as they are to have one. Despite their membership in organizations such as the Roundtable, the U.S. Chamber, and the National Association of Manufacturers—all of which are deeply involved in legislative matters and concentrate on motivation of business—they are not rushing to form PACs. Far from stimulating big business to leap into the arena, the political awakening of recent years is more likely to encourage nonmanufacturing or small business to form political action committees.

In fact, the most die-hard anti-PAC voices might be found in the board rooms of the companies which do not have PACs, not in the halls of Congress or in the cubicles at Common Cause headquarters. Business is not a monolith in viewing its political role, and no changes in the law, no matter how favorable, will change corporate attitudes, any more than every company will agree on management techniques or geographic choice of headquarters.

While it was true that a number of Senate incumbents received large contributions (Howard Baker and Robert Griffin), challengers such as William Armstrong and "unknowns" such as David Durenberger and Rudy Boschwitz were not shut off. This would suggest that these PACs were looking for opportunities to change the Senate by helping challengers or were aware of this risk in helping troubled incumbents.

Similar patterns were true of House races as well. Incumbents, especially those with good voting records and those on key committees, received contributions, but the large gifts also went to the open seats or challengers. Suggestions of payoffs, access, favors, and personal ties become less believable as those without voting records, assurance of being elected, and friendships with Washington lobbyists somehow managed to attract contributions. Removing House leadership (John Rhodes and Jim Wright) from the roster, there is only one winning incumbent on the top ten list (see Table 4).

Many of us on the so-called inside are amused by the strained attempts of outsiders to make judgments about our political behavior. It may be that there are few cause-effect relationships at play, that there are no controlling factors that can be studied with predictability, and

TABLE 4

Top Recipients of Contributions from Corporate PACs, 1977–1978

All Corporate PACs		Fortune 500 PACs	
Name/party/state/seat/result[a]	Contributions[b]	Name/party/state/seat/result	Contributions
House Candidates			
John Porter (R-Ill., ch, 1)	$100,334	John Porter (R-Ill., ch, 1)	$ 74,880
Garry Brown (R-Mich., inc, 1)	67,265	Garry Brown (R-Mich., inc, 1)	41,125
Bob Gammage (D-Tex., inc, 1)	56,750	John Rhodes (R-Ariz., inc, w)	33,830
John Rhodes (R-Ariz., inc, w)	54,055	Elford Cederberg (R-Mich., inc, 1)	30,450
Phil Gramm (D-Tex., open, w)	51,475	Larry Hopkins (R-Ky., open, w)	30,200
Elford Cederberg (R-Mich., inc, 1)	45,150	Ed Scott (R-Colo., ch, 1)	26,400
Larry Hopkins (R-Ky., open, w)	43,650	Jack Cunningham (R-Wash., inc, 1)	25,190
James Jones (D-Okla., inc, w)	43,650	Stan Aronoff (R-Ohio, ch, 1)	23,925
Jack Cunningham (R-Wash., inc, 1)	43,065	Jim Wright (D-Tex., inc, w)	23,560
Jim Wright (D-Tex., inc, w)	42,059	Phil Gramm (D-Tex., open, w)	23,200
Senate Candidates			
John Tower (R-Tex., inc, w)	$251,519	Robert Griffin (R-Mich., inc, 1)	$157,267
Robert Griffin (R-Mich., inc, 1)	211,312	John Tower (R-Tex., inc, w)	128,040
Howard Baker (R-Tenn., inc, w)	189,283	Howard Baker (R-Tenn., inc, w)	118,635
William Armstrong (R-Colo., ch, w)	175,021	William Armstrong (R-Colo., ch, w)	114,184
David Durenberger (R-Minn., open, w)	161,140	David Durenberger (R-Minn., open, w)	113,800

[a] Code: ch = challenger; inc = incumbent; open = incumbent retired; 1 = lost; w = won.

Source: Calculated from Federal Election Commission, *FEC Reports on Financial Activity 1977–1978*, Interim Report no. 4, May 1979.

that there are few quantifiable occurrences that take place. Outsiders sometimes fail to realize how diverse a species PAC is. Every PAC operates in a fashion that is suited to the parent organization and each committee has some resemblance to other "cousins," but it is a distinct creature of its parents. This is the case with much of the accounting, mechanics, and solicitation technique, and even more so when it comes to candidate support.

Decision Making in PACs

Collegial Decisions. Most PACs have some broad guidelines about how candidates will qualify for contributions. Most PACs also have some type of collegial decision-making body that selects candidates for support. (Contrary to the myth, this is not a one- or two-person body, is hardly ever made up of the chief executive officer, and often totally excludes the Washington office.) The more diverse the company and the more money the PAC has, the more likely its decision process is to be spread among greater numbers of people and with a greater diversity in background. Most PACs have scheduled meetings where they evaluate requests and reach decisions about which candidates to help and what amount of money to give.

Role of Individual Contributors. Individual PAC contributors retain a great deal of influence over what the committee decision makers do with their money. This is another of the practices not often acknowledged by outsiders. Corporate PACs (and perhaps local union PACs) have a day-to-day working relationship with the people making the decisions about where their dollars are spent. This is the real potential for coercion in a corporate PAC—at the distribution-to-candidates end, not the receipt-of-contributions end. The potential for coercion works "upward" rather than "downward"—the dollar givers have ultimate control over the success of the PAC by their ability to refuse contributions in the next solicitation.

This personal relationship between contributors and decision makers does not exist in any other political entity. Most political entities do not know their contributors; in most corporate PACs, the decision makers may not know who the contributors are, but the contributors know the decision makers. The need to look each other in the eye after the reports on candidate support are made public is a powerful incentive to pay close attention to what contributors think. To an insider, it is easily explained why business PACs tend to be bipartisan, unwilling to enter divisive primaries, and reluctant to get into campaigns too early when the risks might be greater that the candidates would lose. This may account for why the category of unconnected PACs has such a different pattern of contributions—they may be the most removed from their contributors.

A number of business PACs (such as those at Mead and Boeing) take the role of the individual contributor to the ultimate—no contributions are made unless the individual authorizes money to be spent for a particular candidate. The systems are difficult to administer, but they are the purest form of democracy known. A number of other companies (LTV, General Electric, and General Motors, among many) allow earmarking of specific candidates by the individual contributor. In searching FEC printouts, the PAC often gets "credit" or "blame" for these contributions because they sometimes show up on FEC D indexes, which are used by most students of PAC giving. Other companies allow a variation of earmarking by allowing designation of a party choice, or by having ample opportunities for contributors to make recommendations. Whatever the method, it complicates an analysis of why PAC decisions were made.

Allocation of Resources. Early reports from the 1977–1978 period revealed a preponderance of gifts to incumbents. Insiders reacted with a "so what" attitude because we realized that much of that money was going to incumbents simply because they were there and asking for it. An undetermined amount was also going to pay debts from the 1976 campaigns. With so many PACs waiting until 1977 to form, it was natural that a number of them might want to contribute to candidates they were unable to help in 1976. Money given in 1977 and in the first quarter of 1978 for the most part was not given with a view toward the elections.

Attendance at fund-raising events, in the mind of many PACs, is not a political contribution; it is something more akin to social etiquette than to tough political decisions. The entrance fee may be more than $100 or $150, and some PACs have allocated a portion of their anticipated treasuries for such events, which may be spent at the discretion of the Washington office. This in no way limits what the PAC may do later should the electoral situation require greater funding, nor does it foreclose the opportunity for the challenger to receive a political contribution. Some corporate PACs, to the consternation of their Washington offices, refuse to attend any fund-raising events. Others have tried to find a way to attend those they feel are important (to talk to honored guests, if not the person for whom the event is being held).

The role of the Washington offices is important in decisions on fund-raising events and political contributions, but many of the largest

PACs are administered and operated without a Washington office (Dart, Winn-Dixie), or where the Washington office serves an advisory but not controlling role (Eaton, General Motors, General Electric, Sun). This is even more likely to be the case with the three biggest givers in the nonunion field: auto dealers, realtors, and doctors. Both the doctors and the realtors are headquartered in and administered from Chicago, but they have an elaborate system whereby the requests for contributions must make their way through the districts and states before the national organization becomes involved in a campaign. Without local doctor or local realtor support, a candidate will not receive assistance. The auto dealers, while headquartered in McLean, Virginia, could not be called a captive of Washington influences, either. They have the same requirements that local and state endorsement is essential.

Timing. Beyond the "who," "how much," and "why" of contributions, "when" is also important. The time lag in getting up-to-date figures from the FEC was partially responsible for the distortion of 1978 data (with so many PACs reporting on a quarterly rather than a monthly basis). In the future, money may be spent earlier. One thing that kept most PACs out of races was the number of primaries held after Labor Day. In instances in which a candidate had a primary opponent, it was difficult for corporate PACs to become involved when the national parties had a policy of staying out of such races. There were exceptions, of course, in which the corporate PACs were active in races before the GOP could become involved. Colorado's Senate race is a good example.

The system for identifying the "good" candidates among the many making requests was not as refined in 1978 as it might be in the future. This is another reason so many candidates did not receive contributions until after Labor Day. BIPAC's list of recommended candidates, for example, was not distributed until September 1, despite the fact that most of the campaigns had received funds before that date.

Another crucial factor in the timing of contributions is the timing of receipts. Not all PACs raise their money early in the year. This was especially the case with the PACs that formed late in 1977 or early 1978, which account for at least half the total. They had no opportunity to build a bank account and no gauge of how much they could anticipate receiving. Sound fiscal policy dictated that they not spend what they might need at the end of the campaign until they could project the success of internal solicitation or estimate where they would want to make contributions to candidates. Those on a payroll deduction system have a greater degree of predictability, but even they cannot spend what is not in the treasury. (Transfers are usually made at the beginning of the month.) One inventive group (L. M. Berry PAC) calculated what it could expect in receipts at the end of the campaign period and took out a bank loan for that amount so it could use the money in the heat of the elections. The loan with interest was then repaid after the first of the year when end-of-the-year contributions came into the PAC treasury.

Acceptance of Corporate PACs

Insiders in the business community know a great deal about how far business has come in the political world, but we may be the harshest critics of how unsuccessful PACs have been. We know, for example, that the level of participation in nearly every company is disappointingly low. It is little solace to remember that only a third of the people vote, so why should a high percentage want to make political contributions? We are consoled in realizing—again one of the unquantifiable pieces of data that we know to be true—that corporate PACs have brought thousands into the process who have never made contributions before.

The strange thing about these numbers is the comparative reaction from insiders and outsiders: outsiders worry about the coercion potential with "so many" corporate executives making contributions; insiders worry about how few of their own people care about politics.

Corporations have not raced into PAC formation, nor have they taken full advantage of everything the law would permit them to do in the political process. They have been cautious in forming PACs, doing so only when there is general agreement among top executives that it will be acceptable to middle management or when the legislative and government problems of the company are so great that they cannot ignore politics and elections. They have set up countless internal safeguards, going to extremes not even contemplated in the law. Among these safeguards to voluntariness are earmarking provisions, the use of outside treasuries and treasurers (such as a bank), and maintenance of confidentiality to the point where no one in the company knows who contributes.

As business, we are impressed by our ability to get into politics without disgrace and with growing effectiveness. As business, we tend to be more cautious than other interest groups might be. As a diversified interest group, we know that the term "organized" can be only loosely applied to us, if organized means single-purpose or goal-directed. The structure of the business community means that we have to work harder to be effective than groups who have prior connections (union members who join a union before joining a PAC, doctors who join a medical society before joining a PAC). Because our interests are so diverse and

24

so timeless, it is difficult to match what can be accomplished by narrowly based groups that can attract a constituency on an immediate issue (such as the Panama Canal) or by those that can identify a coalition of individuals who have nothing in common but their views on abortion or guns.

With the disintegration of so many other institutions in American life, it is no wonder that corporations are undertaking functions not generally performed by them several decades ago. Corporations as employers provide all sorts of employee benefits and offer all sorts of optional participation programs for employees—mandated withholding of income taxes, payroll taxes, and social security taxes; health care, dental care, and legal care; parking lots; subsidizided cafeterias; recreational facilities; matching charitable and education grants; and others. The mystery is that political giving and the facilitation thereof was so slow in catching on. The theory is untested, but it would not be surprising if some pollster could show that an individual's identification with an employer was as great or greater than identification with a church, government, political party, or fraternal organization.

The last decade has produced a number of social commentators who feel that the corporation has a social responsibility. If that is the case (and most corporations behave as if they have community obligations), why is it that politics and concern for the employees as citizens are not part of that social responsibility?

Can Political Influence Be Democratized? A Labor Perspective

David Jessup

Predators of the squid often lose sight of their prey in the cloud of ink that obscures its escape. The cloud of misconception and irrelevance surrounding the election reform debate has similarly confused those who pursue the goal of democratizing political influence.

This article takes exception with most of the conventional wisdom that frames the discussion of election reform. In the following pages it will be argued that campaign contributions are not necessarily the most important source of influence over public policy, although they are the most heavily regulated; that the business community has an increasingly dominant advantage in political *resources* that is *not* counterbalanced by the resources of "big" labor; that the New Right and the Liberal Left possess unique but seldom discussed and seldom regulated sources of influence; that the issues of corruption, incumbency control, and special interest influence are the *least* relevant problems for campaign reform, although they are the most widely discussed; that the thrust of the reform movement has been to transfer influence from one elite to another, rather than to democratize influence; and that the major institution that *does* serve to democratize political influence is the labor movement, even though it is often the one most frequently under attack.

The underlying theme of these formulations is that the *resources* needed for achieving political influence are distributed unequally in society and that if we want to democratize our political system, we should avoid the distractions that take our attention away from these resources. To this end are the following observations directed.

Who Dominates Campaign Finance?

No group has had a more enduring advantage in mobilizing the resources needed to influence public policy than the owners and managers of our

The opinions expressed in this paper are those of the author alone and do not necessarily represent the position of the AFL–CIO or any of its departments. Assistance in preparing this paper was provided by Mike Ingrao, Greg Denier, Paul R. Porter, John and Jeannette Haynes, and Linda Jessup, although they bear no responsibility for its conclusions.

great economic enterprises. This simple fact must serve as the starting point for any intelligent discussion of election reform.

Business advantage begins with financial contributions to campaigns. In 1972, businessman Clement Stone's $2 million individual contribution to the Nixon reelection committee made history because it exceeded the entire amount of voluntary contributions donated by millions of union members.

The more recent and widely noted growth of corporate and trade association political action committees (PACs) has threatened to crowd everyone else off the track. The number of corporate and trade association PACs had reached 1,364 by May 10, 1979, as compared with 281 labor PACs.[1] More important, the proportion of PAC contributions coming from business and trade groups has risen from 32 percent in 1974 to 61 percent in 1978. Labor's share has fallen from 49 percent to 29 percent during the same period.[2] At the state level the imbalance is even more overwhelming, especially in those states allowing unlimited spending on ballot issues.

Registered PACs in the 1978 California campaign spent a total of $19 million on ballot issues and contributions to state candidates, of which an astonishing 77 percent came from corporate and trade association PACs, as compared with 8 percent from labor and public employees' PACs. Republican and conservative PACs outspent Democratic and liberal PACs by accounting for 10.5 percent and 2.0 percent of the total, respectively.[3]

For people disturbed by this imbalance, contemplation of the future potential of business PAC growth concentrates the mind as wonderfully as the prospect of hanging. One author has pointed out that most large corporations have not yet established PACs and that the potential for increase is almost limitless, compared with that of labor PACs.[4] This advantage becomes even more awesome with the realization that *most business money does not even arrive through the PAC mechanism.* The point is underlined here because press reports based on figures released

1 Federal Election Commission, "FEC Releases Year-End 1978 Report on 1977–78 Financial Activity of Non-Party and Party Political Committees" (press release), May 10, 1979.

2 Michael J. Malbin, "Campaign Financing and the 'Special Interests,'" *The Public Interest* (Summer 1979), p. 25.

3 Compiled by COPE Research Department, from State of California Fair Political Practices Commission, *Campaign Contribution and Spending Report, November 7, 1978, General Election,* May 15, 1979.

4 Edwin M. Epstein, "The Emergence of Political Action Committees," in *Political Finance,* ed. Herbert E. Alexander, Sage Election Studies Yearbook, vol. 5 (Beverly Hills and London: Sage Publications, 1979), p. 185.

by the Federal Elections Commission (FEC) or by Common Cause tend to obscure the true extent of business domination of campaign financing.[5]

The largest source of campaign contributions is the individual giver, and the proportion of funds coming from this source has remained rather constant at 58 percent for House campaigns and 68 percent for Senate campaigns. (The percentage coming from nonparty PACs has also remained fairly constant—25 percent in the House and 15 percent in the Senate, although the PAC share is likely to grow.)[6]

The occupation of individual contributors is listed in the FEC reports only for those giving in excess of $100, and without a sizable research effort there is no way to show the exact proportion of individual contributions coming from businessmen. But the proportion is probably large, as is shown by the following examples.

Listed on an early 1977 FEC report of Colorado Senate candidate Bill Armstrong was a $1,000 contribution from Coors Industries, along with $3,600 in additional funds donated by nine Coors executives contributing *as individuals*. Oil and gas industry PACs were listed for $2,700 in contributions, while 103 *individual* executives from the same industry put in an additional $17,700.[7]

In Table 1 are categorized the occupations of all individual contributors giving $100 or more to three California assemblymen and two candidates for state attorney general, winner George Deukmejian (R) and loser Yvonne Brathwaite Burke, for the 1978 general election. The proportion of such funds coming from businessmen ranged from 13 percent to 69 percent, compared with a 1 percent to 16 percent range for white-collar, blue-collar, clerical, and public employees.

Gifts and loans made by wealthy candidates to their own campaigns constitute the next category of campaign financing, one that accounts for 8 percent of the total.[8] Such wealth is not likely to be accumulated by years of work on the assembly line, and it must therefore be entered on the business side of the ledger.

The final source of campaign money is political parties and "no-connected organizations," which donated $6.5 million and $2.5 million, respectively, in 1978. Since eight of the ten largest nonconnected PACs are conservative, outspending their liberal counterparts $11,981,333 to

---

[5] Federal Election Commission, "FEC Year-End 1978 Report" (press release), May 10, 1979; Common Cause, "Analysis of Campaign Contributions by Registered Political Committees in 1972 Congressional Elections" (press release), November 30, 1973.

[6] Malbin, "Campaign Financing," p. 9.

[7] COPE Research Department, based on analysis of reports filed with the FEC by candidate William Armstrong.

[8] Malbin, "Campaign Financing," p. 26.

TABLE 1

INDIVIDUAL CONTRIBUTIONS OF $100 OR MORE BY OCCUPATIONAL
CATEGORY, CALIFORNIA, 1978
(percentage of candidate's receipts)

	State assembly			Attorney general	
Occupation of Contributor	Conservative (Ellis-R)[a]	Liberal (Bates-D)[a]	Prolabor (Alatorre-D)[a]	Deukmejian-R[a]	Burke-D[a]
Businessmen	69	13	37	51	19
Professionals	17	61	39	21	33
Public employees	1	11	16	2	1
White-collar, blue-collar, clerical employees	—	3	1	1	—
Undetermined (retirees, housewives, nonlisted)	13	13	6	25	47
Total	100	100	100	100	100

[a] Total receipts of individual contributions of $100 or more were: $8,593 (Ellis), $5,539 (Bates), $29,480 (Alatorre), $281,784 (Deukmejian), $293,171 (Burke).
SOURCE: Compiled by Committee on Political Education (AFL–CIO) Research Department from State of California Fair Political Practices Commission, *Campaign Contribution and Spending Report, November 7, 1978, General Election,* May 15, 1979.

$1,566,720,[9] it would be safe to assume that the contributors to these organizations—even the smaller givers to direct mail appeals—include a substantial number of businessmen.

More precise figures are available for the political parties: national Democratic party committees received $1,946,337 from nonparty PACs, of which 61.3 percent came from corporations, cooperatives, and medical and trade associations, 36.3 percent came from labor unions, and 2.4 percent came from "no-connected organizations." The Republicans received $786,567 apportioned as follows: business and trade, 97.2 percent; labor, 2 percent; and no-connected organizations, 0.8 percent.[10]

[9] Federal Election Commission, "FEC Year-End 1978 Report" (press release), May 10, 1979.
[10] U.S. Federal Election Commission, *FEC Reports on Financial Activity, 1977–1978,* Interim Report no. 4, *Party and Non-Party Political Committees,* vol. 1— Summary Tables (Washington, D.C., May 1979), pp. 41, 53.

Both parties received substantially larger amounts from businessmen contributing as individuals.

The remarkable conclusion suggested by these data is that *it makes little difference whether campaign funds come from individuals, PACs, parties, or the candidate himself; the advantage is clearly in the direction of business wealth.*

This crucial fact is overlooked by those who seek to increase the proportion of campaign funds coming from nonorganized sources by lifting the limits on individual contributions. Such a strategy not only misses the point; it may serve merely to obscure the source of influence.[11] After all, campaign checks are not known to arrive in a candidate's mailbox by magic; they have to be solicited by someone. That someone may be a businessman who hosts a fund-raising reception in his home, a well-connected lawyer who telephones his contacts, or a fund-raising expert like Richard Viguerie, who is able to carry a candidate's financial burden for months at a time while awaiting the arrival of the hundreds of small contributions that come in response to direct mail appeals. Are we to assume that these solicitors will wield less influence than the PAC directors simply because the results of their efforts appear on the FEC reports as "individual" contributions? The opposite assumption is more compelling.[12]

Adding all these sources together, it is difficult to avoid the conclusion that business increasingly dominates the realm of campaign finance. This fact may not come as a surprise to most people, and its extensive documentation here may belabor a point that most Americans agree with intuitively.

But the obvious does not always penetrate the hearing rooms of the U.S. Congress, where pages of testimony are offered purporting to show that big labor and big business are equal in their capacity for exercising undue influence on campaigns—or worse, that labor actually holds the advantage. This notion is put forward not only by business sources but

---

[11] The most recent proponents of this strategy, a prestigious study group from Harvard University, acknowledge this obfuscation in a highly revealing (and disturbing) sentence: "If one of the original intentions of campaign finance reforms was to limit the *appearance* of special interests in the political process, the law has, in practice, had the opposite effect." [Emphasis added.] U.S. Congress, House of Representatives, Committee on House Administration, *An Analysis of the Impact of the Federal Election Campaign Act, 1972–1978*, The Campaign Finance Study Group, Harvard University, May 1979, pp. 1–8. The group apparently does not object to the reality of undue influence as long as its "appearance" remains hidden as individual contributions.

[12] This lesson was learned the hard way by presidential aspirant Phil Crane, whose widely reported policy struggles with Viguerie have drastically weakened his campaign.

by many academic and neutral observers striving to achieve an even-handed approach.[13] To examine their argument more fully, one must look beyond a discussion of campaign finance toward other sources of power.

Beyond Campaign Finance

Contributing to campaigns is not the only way to influence public policy, nor is it necessarily the most important. The election law now explicitly permits corporations and labor unions to communicate politically with their stockholders and members, respectively, and to finance nonpartisan registration and get-out-the-vote drives aimed at these same constituencies. This can be done with treasury money, thus bypassing the need to raise voluntary funds.

Much has been written about labor's supposed advantages in this area of competition, and the 1976 FEC report on communication costs would seem to confirm this view.[14] Moreover, this advantage is being used as an argument in the Republican National Committee's suit to challenge the fairness of public financing of presidential campaigns, on the grounds that labor's membership activities give the edge to the Democrat.

The advantage begins to disappear under more intense illumination. The constituency that tends to support labor's candidates is less affluent, less educated, and less apt to participate in elections than is the business constituency. The fact that labor must spend substantial sums merely to raise its supporters' turnout to a level that remains several points behind Republican turnout is more a liability than an advantage.

---

[13] "We can see the political system taken out of the hands of big business, big labor, the rich, and the superrich, and put in the hands of the voters, where it belongs." Russell D. Hemenway, National Director, National Committee for an Effective Congress, testimony before the U.S. Congress, Senate, Subcommittee on Privileges and Elections of the Committee on Rules and Administration, *Hearings on Public Financing of Federal Elections of the Committee on Rules and Administration, S. 1103, S. 1954, S. 2417,* 93rd Congress, 1st session, September 19, 1973, p. 204.

"These special groups do not consider broader concerns. Under the current system, over five hundred business and labor political action committees are active. . . ." James MacGregor Burns, statement by the Committee on Party Renewal, in testimony before the U.S. Congress, House of Representatives, Committee on House Administration, *Hearings on Public Financing of Federal Elections,* 96th Congress, 1st session, March 22, 1979, p. 392.

[14] In 1976, labor reported spending $2,014,326, compared with business and membership organization expenditures of $132,573. The 1978 report is incomplete. Federal Election Commission, *Index of Communication Costs by Corporations, Labor Organizations, Membership Organizations, Trade Associations, 1976 Campaign,* FEC Disclosures Series # 5, p. 4.

Nonetheless, such expenditures are important. In addition to contacting its members by word of mouth, the trade union movement sends mailings, sets up telephone banks, mounts door-to-door drives, leaflets factories, and holds rallies. Labor leaders are justifiably proud of this effort and do not demur when columnists or conservative journalists exaggerate its cost. Labor's strength does indeed rest with its membership communications.[15]

But is the business world lacking in such internal communications? There are more than 4 million business establishments in the United States, 186,547 of them employing fifty or more persons.[16] (By comparison, there are 60,000 local unions in the country, representing about one-quarter of the work force.) These enterprises in turn are grouped into countless industry and trade associations, as well as geographic aggregations like the chambers of commerce. This vast in-place organizational network must surely disseminate political ideas at least as widely as the system of officers and shop stewards does with union members. In addition, there are hundreds of times more business and trade journals currently in circulation than there are labor publications.[17] (This does not include the commercial media, sustained largely through business advertising.) It taxes one's imagination to believe that these publications do not contain at least as much information about elections, candidates, voting records, and public issues as the labor press does.

It may be that individual business organizations do not make endorsements, print flyers, set up phone banks, or mail letters calling expressly for the election or defeat of candidates to the same degree that labor does. Corporate PACs may be choosing more cautious means to communicate, especially in view of the fact that no mechanism is available for stockholders to participate in endorsements as union members do through democratically constituted conventions that begin at the local level. But it requires no great intellectual leap to deduce that candidate X is "the business candidate" if one reads an "objectively" worded feature story in a trade journal that avoids a direct endorsement. Reporting such stories to the FEC is not required if the publication is a regular one with a primary purpose (as represented by at least one-half

---

[15] According to figures compiled by the Ohio AFL–CIO from precinct returns, labor's efforts have a significant impact, resulting in a 15–20 percent higher turnout among registered union members than among the regular precinct electorate.

[16] U.S. Department of Commerce, Bureau of the Census, *County Business Patterns, U.S. Summary, 1976* (Washington, D.C.: U.S. Government Printing Office, August 1978), p. 3.

[17] *The Standard Periodical Directory*, 6th ed., 1979–1980 (New York: Oxbridge Communications, 1978). This directory contains twenty-two pages of labor publications, in comparison to hundreds of pages of business and trade publications.

of the copy) that is devoted to matters other than advocating the election or defeat of federal candidates. Labor PACs tended to overreport this type of communication in 1976.

So the relative absence of *reported* expenditures on corporate internal communication may mean simply that business is getting along quite nicely without it. Or it may mean that the corporate PACs are so new that they simply have not yet gotten around to the task of activating their stockholders and employees directly. There is some evidence that this situation is changing.

A recent issue of *Campaigning Reports* claims that corporate PACs soliciting stockholders as well as employees may soon increase beyond the current figure of 10 percent, a trend suggested by favorable response to the program of the two-year-old National Association of Business PACs, which has developed newsletters and training seminars that "include overviews of this potentially huge source of new PAC revenue." [18]

Another issue of the same newsletter describes how a growing number of corporate PACs are developing programs to keep their members busy during nonelection years:

> One example is Atlantic Richfield Co., which makes sure all of its PAC members receive a newsletter, month in and month out. For employees really interested in the political system, a veritable smorgasbord of programs is available. . . . Seminars have been held on issues ranging from better communication techniques and how to write Congress members through the nuts and bolts of canvassing a neighborhood.[19]

Regardless whether an "internal communications gap" is real or imagined, its significance shrivels when compared with the importance of the newer and even more innovative methods of influencing public policy that are analyzed below. This array of mammoth political weapons makes the Republican attack on labor's internal communications seem like so much overkill.

The Expanding Frontiers of Political Influence

Business lobbying has always overshadowed campaign contributions as a method of influencing policy. Corporate funds for this purpose are growing, as lobbying becomes increasingly styled on the grass-roots model. Traditional lobbying—that is, communication with Congress by

---

[18] "Percentage of Corporate PACs Soliciting Shareholders May Increase," *Campaigning Reports* (July 11, 1979), p. 10.
[19] "Corporate PACs Coming Up with Programs to Keep Members Motivated in Off Years," *Campaigning Reports* (June 6, 1979), p. 10.

a paid representative in Washington—has suffered a decline in legitimacy in recent years. In its place has grown the idea that the government should be directly in touch with "the people." Thus lobbying tactics that create the appearance of grass-roots pressures have found a responsive audience in Congress. There are several reasons why this is so.

Large-scale demographic shifts have created many new suburban congressional districts that lack a tradition of strong local organization, whether party, labor, or otherwise. Meanwhile, party organizations in the older districts have weakened as their patronage and casework functions have gradually been assumed by the civil service and welfare bureaucracies.

Partly out of necessity and partly out of an impulse toward greater individual autonomy, many congressmen, with the newest in the forefront, have tried to increase their independence from *any* system of organized influence, including that of their own party leadership. Much of what is called reform needs to be analyzed in light of these developments.

Individual congressmen and senators now have enough staff, budget, computer services, and franking privileges to create their own personal political parties able to manage everything from precinct canvassing to ward heeling. They have replaced the congressional seniority system with a caucus system, dispersing power and privilege from a small number of large committee chairmanships to a large number of small subcommittee chairmanships. They have fractured the power of party leadership but increased their dependence on those organizations most able to mobilize the passions of the moment in that relatively narrow segment of the district electorate with the affluence, leisure time, and education to become involved in public issues, and the ability to translate those passions into media coverage. They have bolted from the longer-standing party coalitions held together by traditional loyalty and programmatic consistency, and run headlong toward the shifting alliances of constituency groups overwrought by single-issue fads and media hyperbole.

The stampede to the grass roots has added an important new dimension to the electoral process.

Organizations like the AFL–CIO and others with a stake in public policy are forced to spend increasing amounts of time and money in outside lobbying activities. The process takes on the character of a continuous campaign. First, labor must spend a lot of time and money mobilizing its members to register and vote, then it must continue spending time and money to mobilize its members to persuade the newly elected representative to vote for the things they thought they elected him for. Gone are the days when the union movement could simply elect a candidate and be done with it. Neither the leaders nor the rank and file know what to expect any more from the people they help elect; their legislative behavior seems to be up for grabs.

While some may welcome this shift as a means of increasing citizen involvement, it often produces the opposite effect. It used to be that voting for the Democrat or the liberal meant choosing a known set of policies: increasing employment and economic growth, improving the climate for labor, strengthening the national defense, and defending democracy abroad. As those labels lose their meaning, or in some cases come to mean the very opposite, many labor voters are left with the kind of doubt and uncertainty that leads to further abstinence at the polls.

Thus the shift to grass-roots lobbying is not likely to mean an increased advantage to labor, even though a large number of union members reside in each congressional district. The advantage will go to the group with the most money and the most easily activated constituency—namely, business.

Corporations have by no means abandoned their traditional lobbying structure, which overshadows that of all other groups by a large margin.[20] But the new action is clearly back in the home district. In the recent battle over labor law reform, for example, most accounts agree that the business community spent on the order of $5 million, nearly equaling the amount corporate PACs contributed to all candidates for the entire 1976 election.[21]

The Chamber of Commerce, the Business Roundtable, the associations, individual corporations, the right wing PACs, and the "single issue" organizations—everyone got into the act. Their funds released a downpour of letters, telegrams, phone calls, postcards, office visits, and even planeloads of businessmen, all flowing from the districts to Washington. The AFL–CIO, with an $800,000 budget, was able to generate its own blizzard of grass-roots messages.

Such activities have an obvious impact on elections, especially when the congressman's vote is publicized in full-page ads purchased in the local newspapers. Moreover, many of the groups engaging in these pursuits accumulate a voting record, or rating; its publication at a later date is obviously designed to influence how people vote. In recognition of this fact, the FEC has restricted the distribution of such ratings, when printed by nonprofit, tax-exempt organizations, to the groups' members.

---

20 Charles E. Lindblom, *Politics and Markets* (New York: Basic Books, 1977), p. 195.
21 Malbin, "Campaign Financing," p. 38.

Yet the true extent of resources generated for this relatively new method of influence remains hidden. There are no disclosure requirements for grass-roots lobbying, and all attempts to draft legislation that would bring this rapidly expanding effort under greater public scrutiny have met with solid resistance, even from many liberal groups traditionally associated with reform.

The second new dimension in election contests is the "independent expenditure." According to a ruling of the Supreme Court, no limit may be placed on the amount of money spent by a group or individual to influence elections, as long as it is spent independently of a candidate or his campaign. That is, the outside group may not consult with, or act at the suggestion of, a candidate's committee.

Quick to recognize the new opportunity, the U.S. Chamber of Commerce began touting the independent expenditure in its 1977 PAC manual:

> Independent expenditures provide the potential for the greatest dollar participation in politics by political action committees. To date it has been the least utilized method of participation by the business community.[22]

Business leaders are frank in their determination to use this new vehicle, especially if some form of public financing becomes law:

> If HR 1 would become law, greatly narrowing the parameters of, say our activities and the activities of all PACs, the area of independent expenditures would be a legitimate area for us to look to very strongly.[23]

But the boldest innovator in the field of independent expenditures is Terry Dolan of the National Conservative Political Action Committee (NCPAC). According to an article in the *Conservative Digest*, NCPAC's "independent expenditure" ads attacking the senators from Iowa, Colorado, and Kentucky for their support of the Panama Canal treaties ultimately contributed to the defeat of Clark and Haskell. The article goes on to say that "early independent campaigning against a supposedly popular incumbent . . . can bring the man's rating down to a point where

---

[22] Fred Radewagen, "Organization of a Political Action Committee," *Guidelines for Corporate Political Action Committees* (Washington, D.C.: U.S. Chamber of Commerce, 1977), p. 20.

[23] Joseph Fanelli, President of Business-Industry Political Action Committee, testimony before the U.S. Congress, House of Representatives, Committee on House Administration, *Hearings on Public Financing of Congressional Elections*, 96th Congress, 1st session, March 1979, p. 335.

top caliber opposition will be attracted."[24] Dolan claims that NCPAC plans to spend about $700,000 on such campaigning for the 1980 elections.

The Role of the New Right

NCPAC is near the center of an expanding network of conservative PACs and "single-issue organizations" that collectively have come to be called the New Right.

Although many social-issue activists may sincerely believe that they are engaged in a "single" cause—to stop the Equal Rights Amendment, retain the Panama Canal, fight gun control, bring prayer back to the classroom, or send homosexuals back to the closet—they are in fact linked, often by Richard Viguerie's computer, to a loose association that might best be described as a new (and still informal) conservative political "party."[25]

New Right leaders are frank in their view that the social issues serve only as a means toward establishing a broader network, raising funds, and building political power:

> To imagine that the New Right has a fixation on these issues misses the mark. The New Right is looking for issues that people care about, and social issues, at least for the present, fit the bill.[26]

The New Right has branches that specialize in various party functions: donations to federal and state candidates, campaign management and training, precinct organization, grass-roots lobbying, fund raising, state legislative initiatives, recruitment and ideological instruction of youth, compilation of voting records, publications, tax-exempt research and education, legal services, liaison with church, campus, senior citizens and other groups, and hatchet work on the opposition. The New Right has its own congressional contingent, which in spite of its small size is committed, vocal, and growing. New Right leaders meet informally to discuss legislative strategy, development of issues, marginal districts, and recruitment of new candidates, more or less as the leaders of any other political party do.

---

[24] Anonymous, "Terry Dolan: Conservative Point Man," *Conservative Digest,* vol. 5, no. 1 (January 1979), p. 27.

[25] Most conveniently, the *Conservative Digest* published a special issue on the New Right that described this network in some detail. "The New Right: A Special Report," *Conservative Digest,* vol. 5, no. 6 (June 1979), pp. 9–22.

[26] "The New Right: A Special Report," p. 10.

The relationship between this new "party" and the more established Republican-business constellation within the Republican party is a complicated one.

Some businessmen are, of course, heavy contributors to New Right candidates and organizations. Others are said to take part in the weekly strategy sessions of the "Kingston group" that meets in Viguerie's office.

But many businessmen undoubtedly cringe at the stridency of tone and the ideological zeal injected into the political debate by the New Right. Its social-issue causes probably divide businessmen as much as any other group of Americans.

Some corporations must react with alarm to the New Right's support for decreasing regulation of the noncompetitive industries in transport and communications, while others must feel equally upset at the New Right's support for increasing regulation of the highly competitive industries that are trying to sell America's leading technology to the Soviet Union.

Although the New Right is deeply involved in the Republican party, it also supports conservative Democrats and competes with the GOP for funds, issues, and volunteers. Viguerie has publicly attacked the Republican party as being an obstacle to conservative victory, and Republican Chairman Bill Brock has had to flog his cadres mercilessly to keep them in the running.[27]

Still, there are many points of convergence between the old and new parties. Underneath the New Right's social-issue superstructure rests a foundation of free enterprise ideology that enables the two forces to collaborate quite productively on many of the great class-related issues that periodically wrack the nation. Central to this ideology is the old-fashioned notion that business leaders should be allowed to decide such momentous issues on their own, without interference from the rest of us, and that without such freedom they will simply lack the confidence to perform the investment and production functions essential to society's well-being.

So the New Right, while it lasts, serves to augment corporate power in spite of the tensions it creates within the older GOP coalition. Proof of this contention is nowhere better expressed than in the Chamber of Commerce congressional voting record on business legislation: the eleven congressmen most closely associated with the New Right voted correctly, from the chamber's point of view, an astounding 97 percent

---

[27] Brock has done well in this regard, outstripping the Democratic party in contributions to candidates $8.6 million to $2.1 million. Federal Election Commission, "FEC Year-End 1978 Report" (press release), May 10, 1979.

of the time.[28] Additional confirmation is provided by the revealing list of congressional legislative victories claimed by the New Right—the defeats of situs picketing, labor law reform, and voter registration reform—battles which were led primarily by business. On issues that are not directly attached to corporate coattails, the New Right has difficulty winning on its own.

On the election front, the New Right provides the early artillery to soften up marginal districts in preparation for the arrival of major business forces. The successful campaigns of Senators Roger Jepsen and Gordon Humphrey are the most notable examples of the importance of this division of labor. The New Right's advantages in this role are its commitment and fervor, its ability to bypass the predominant media and cultural institutions, its opportunism in exploiting the frustrations of many people fed up with a decade of cultural revolution and anti-Americanism and, above all, its mastery of the new technology of mobilizing small contributions. The ten largest conservative PACs raised $11.6 million and contributed $1.5 million to candidates in 1977–1978, far more than liberal PACs were able to do. These figures reveal that conservative PACs spend about eight times as much on other functions, mostly fund-raising expenses, than they do on direct candidate contributions. PAC directors chafe under a Federal Election Campaign Act (FECA) restriction that forces them to pay such overhead costs from their voluntary collections, while union and corporate PACs are allowed to use treasury money. In return, however, the noneconomic PACs are permitted to solicit from and communicate with the general public, whereas corporations and unions are restricted to their shareholders and employees or members. Some conservative PACs get the best of both worlds by setting up sister organizations that have tax-exempt research and education functions. Such organizations are permitted to accept corporate funds, which can then assume part of the burden for rent and overhead. Moreover, direct mail fund-raising costs are not really "overhead" in the same sense as office and equipment expenditures. As Viguerie so frequently points out in defending his substantial fee (as much as 70 percent of his client's receipts), *direct mail fund raising is itself a form of political communication.* And at this point in time, the New Right constitutes another weapon, albeit a somewhat unpredictable one, in the overall political arsenal commanded by business.

---

[28] The list of congressmen comes from "The New Right: A Special Report," pp. 18–19. The voting records were published by the Chamber of Commerce, *How They Voted, 95th Congress, 1st session,* June 1979, pp. 99–111.

Above the Electoral Battle

In order to comprehend the full extent of business political dominance, one must look above the day-to-day battles about legislative and political matters.

Secure within the ivory tower of the University of Southern California there exists an organization called the Center for the Study of Free Enterprise, headed by Arthur Laffer. As is well known, the "Laffer Curve," developed in this pristine setting, became the intellectual underpinning for the tax revolt that dominated the 1978 election debate.

Less well known is the fact that the financial and organizational impetus for the center came from Justin Dart; Dart Industries PAC was the third largest corporate campaign contributor in 1978, with 92 percent of its $119,300 going to Republicans.[29]

The center is but one of a myriad of business-funded research institutes, university programs, foundations, television documentaries, and think tanks that help formulate the agenda for public discussion. To these resources might be added several billion dollars' worth of tax-free business advertising, some of which is explicitly political, like the Mobil ads.

Finally, let it be recalled than many important economic decisions, as well as the vital information on which these decisions are based, *are not part of the public political process at all.* Many of the large multinational firms with global empires exceeding the reach of most nation-states are able to remain largely aloof from open political involvement. It is therefore not surprising to discover that a large percentage of the corporations on *Fortune*'s "500" list have not yet bothered to establish PACs.[30]

More curious is the virtual explosion of PAC activity among the lesser corporations. Some observers wonder whether the election reforms themselves lit the fuse, especially the FEC's decision (in the case of Sun Oil's PAC) legitimatizing corporate solicitation of employees by means of a checkoff system.[31] It is probably true that some additional activity resulted from this dubious new procedure, in which an employer is given a green light to use his economic leverage over an employee to

---

[29] Information based on telephone conversation with the Center for the Study of Free Enterprise, July 27, 1979, and on Federal Election Commission, Interim Report no. 4, *Party and Non-Party Political Committees,* vol. 1, p. A-66.

[30] Edwin M. Epstein, "The Emergence of Political Action Committees," *Political Finance*, p. 185.

[31] Malbin, "Campaign Financing," p. 25. The law has since been changed to limit business solicitations of nonadministrative employees and to extend the checkoff mechanism to unions.

"request" political assistance. According to one account, a tire and rubber company went so far as to inform its managers that "grass-roots political activity has become part of their job, to be included in future appraisals of their performance."[32]

But there are other reasons as well for the sudden burst of activity. Businessmen themselves say the reason is increased government regulation. And after eight years of veto protection by Presidents Nixon and Ford, business faced the unhappy prospect of a newly elected Democratic president and a newly reelected Democratic Congress preparing to deal with major economic and labor legislation. Regardless of its degree of activism in *direct* political involvement, however, business shapes the world we live in by its independent economic decisions and its indirect influence over the ideas that constitute our political culture.

Is Real Reform Possible?

If business holds such an awesome advantage in the *resources* needed to attain influence, why doesn't business always prevail? The reason is partly because business is not a monolithic force. Although corporations may unite on the class issues, they often divide over others. Still, the argument of business divisiveness loses its force when it is remembered that labor is plagued with its own sources of internal disagreement.

Another reason may be that business does not concentrate its campaign resources to the extent that labor does. Trade associations tend to finance incumbents having committee jurisdiction over their industries, while corporate PACs, which compete for the same financial base, tend to spread their funds more broadly to "business candidates."[33] Discomfiture is caused in Republican party headquarters when too much business money finds its way to Democrats, and much gnashing of teeth occurs in New Right circles when too little is channeled to marginal districts.

It could be argued, on the other hand, that business distributes its funds more widely because it has more to spend, and this happy circumstance merely enables it to have the best of both worlds. It can maintain access to the Democrats and the incumbents while its interests are being advanced in the marginal races and open seats at the same time.

The principal explanation of why government policy does not *always* reflect business priorities is simple: the business constituency is

---

[32] Ann Crittenden, "Study Finds Corporations in Broader Political Role," *New York Times,* May 31, 1979.

[33] Michael J. Malbin, "Labor, Business and Money—A Post-Election Analysis," *National Journal* (March 19, 1977), pp. 412–417.

not a majority. There simply are far more voters who work for wages than there are voters who earn their living from executive salaries, dividends, interest, and professional fees. This wage-earning majority is not necessarily antibusiness, of course, and its interests are often diversified in surprising ways. When its interests are unified in opposition to the perceived interests of those who control our economic institutions, however, business does not automatically win, in spite of its overwhelming advantage in resources.

The reason is organization. As individuals, working people can wield no influence except by the act of voting. Beyond that, they will be represented only to the extent that their small contributions can be pooled and their individual efforts can be organized into a collective force. Labor has won the legal right to organize these wage earners democratically into such a force. The legal environment is not as favorable to labor as it is in many European countries, but it has been sufficient to make possible a significant advance. Many observers think our election laws should encourage this development:

> Public subsidy will undoubtedly have a differential impact on different interest groups. Groups, chiefly those representing business and the highly paid professions, which have derived their influence from the large quantities of wealth which they could place strategically in election campaigns, will find their influence considerably diminished. Groups which have derived their influence *in part from numbers of people,* such as labor, minority groups, and other broadly based organizations of citizens, whose influence has depended more on votes which they would cast in elections than on funds which they could contribute to campaigns, will have their influence considerably increased. *This shift of influence from money-based interest groups to people-based interest groups seems likely to be entirely salutary, and most appropriate in a democracy.*[34]

But in spite of their advantage in numbers, the "people-based interest groups" end up having far less influence than their size would warrant. The reason is partly due to shifting public attitudes and changes in the types of issues that periodically divide working people along nonclass lines. In the long run, however, the level of influence of the wage-earning majority is significantly related to its low level of resources. Therein lies the crux of the problem: the fundamental bases of democracy, rooted in the concept of "one man, one vote," is distorted by the unequal distribution of the resources necessary for influencing public policy.

[34] Professor Joel L. Fleashman, Director of the Institute of Policy Sciences and Public Affairs, Duke University, in testimony before the Senate Subcommittee on Privileges and Elections, September 20, 1973. Italics added.

Labor PACs serve to redress this imbalance, and they operate in a way that is basically different from that of business PACs. Business PACs serve as just one additional vehicle for promoting the interests of a relatively small number of wealthy individuals who can also influence policy in countless other ways. Business PACs are not democratically accountable to the stockholders of the corporations that pay their administrative costs.

In contrast, labor PACs rely on a greater number of people giving a smaller average contribution than does any other type of PAC. Furthermore, labor PACs are run by *elected* leaders who are ultimately accountable to their constituency in a way that is often more democratic than the accountability existing in party committees.

Once this essential distinction is grasped, many of the issues that dominate the debate about election reform seem largely irrelevant. For instance, there is a notion that the politicians have formed an entrenched "incumbency party" that eliminates congressional competition. But incumbency advantage is more closely related to congressional perquisites and gerrymandered district boundaries than it is to campaign funds, and where marginal districts exist, the challenger usually finds plenty of willing givers. *The more basic problem is that the givers to both incumbents and challengers come disproportionately from the business world.*

Proposals for Reform. The fundamental question for reform is: *can the resources of political influence be democratized?*

Public financing is one way to achieve this purpose, although in its present limited form it may simply shift private resources from the general election to the primary and from the organized PACs to the direct mail experts. If private financing could be eliminated, however, one important source of influence would be equalized.

Another proposal worthy of consideration is the voucher system, through which each individual would receive an equal number of publicly redeemable coupons that could be donated to the candidates, party, or PAC of his choice.

The most important reform would be a further reduction in the limit on individual contributions, including contributions to PACs. Business PACs are able to raise large donations from a small number of executives, whereas the average contribution from a union member is less than $5 per year. Professionals give in the $100–200 range. Reducing the limit to $100 would go a long way toward restoring the principle of "one man, one vote" to the realm of campaign finance.

Such limitations may exacerbate the problem of raising enough funds to meet inflationary campaign costs, but this problem may best be solved by making available some form of public subsidy.

Another important change people ought to consider is whether corporations should be prohibited from soliciting their employees. There is an unavoidable element of coercion in the employer-employee relationship that ought not to figure in a political contribution that is supposed to be given freely. Legally, corporations are supposed to be creatures of their shareholders. Let the shareholders, then, be the recipients of PAC solicitations, rather than the subordinate administrative personnel who are expected to be "team players" in order to advance in the organization.

On the question of disclosure, the FEC should be required to revise its method of categorizing contributions so that the fact of business dominance will no longer be obscured. It is misleading to divide business-related PACs into four separate categories, while lumping all the labor PACs into one. It is equally unhelpful to place most ideological PACs under the "no-connected organization" roof, while placing the Gun Owners of America and the Conservative Victory Fund under another.

The FEC should also try to provide a breakdown of the occupation and business of all large individual contributors and more accessible information about the proportion of smaller donations coming from fund solicitors like Viguerie.

Direct mail firms are often able to ignore contribution limits by extending sizable credit to campaigns for many months before their fund appeals begin to pay off. Strict limits should be placed on such loans, making them subject to the same standards as those that apply to any other commercial lending transaction.

Finally, Congress should enact a comprehensive lobbying disclosure bill dealing with both the traditional and the grass-roots varieties. There is no reason for allowing this important source of influence to remain hidden.

Prospects for Reform. Democratizing political influence will not be easy. Like the elephant dancing among chickens, the business community will resist all such changes with the cry "let everyone fend for himself."

The elephant will be aided by a Supreme Court decision that more or less rules out the quest for equality as a rationale for reform. In *Buckley* v. *Valeo*, the Court stated that the elimination of corruption was the only legitimate governmental interest that could justify the provisions of the federal election law.[35]

But corruption is the least of the problem. No matter how the law is reformed, there will be those who choose to disobey it. And whether

---

[35] Brice W. Clagett and John R. Bolton, "Buckley vs. Valeo, Its Aftermath, and Its Prospects: The Constitutionality of Government Restraints on Political Campaign Financing," *Vanderbilt Law Review*, vol. 29, no. 6 (November 1976), pp. 1327–1383.

corporate funds are transferred above or below the table, the fundamental logic of reform will remain rooted in the need to change the basic inequality these resources impose on the electoral system.

The Roots of Reform and the Liberal Left Network

There is another reason needed reforms may fail to pass: equalizing resources may not be the primary goal of the reform movement! To understand why this is so, it is necessary to examine the origins of the reform mentality and the political movement in which it is rooted.

Money has not been the only target of the reformers. A few examples will make this clear:

• California's Proposition 9, the earliest and most famous of the state reforms, contained no provisions for contribution limitations or public financing, the two reforms most central to the money question. Instead, it tried to force membership organizations to choose between lobbying and campaigning, while "graciously bestowing upon the rich man and the average man the equal right to lobby and engage in political action *as individuals*." [36]

• The model legislation first developed by Common Cause, the premier reform organization, called for an outright prohibition on the pooling of small voluntary contributions by organizations.

• An early disclosure law in the state of Washington required organizations to list the intended recipient of each voluntary contribution, even though many groups receive such donations on a year-round basis, far in advance of the announcements of candidates.

• A reform law in Arizona tried to abolish the use of membership dues money for internal communication on political endorsements.

More recently, the focus of attack seems to be the PAC system, without regard for the distinction between the "profit-oriented" and the "people-oriented" organizations.

> Congress Watch believes that reform of the campaign spending laws must include . . . strict limitations on special interest PACs. [37]

> We think we're headed for a system of government of, by, and for the PACs of America unless the system can be changed. [38]

---

[36] Max Mont, *Against Proposition 9, Labor's View—a Handbook*, L.A. County Federation of Labor (AFL–CIO), April 30, 1974, p. 5.

[37] Mitchell Rofsky representing Public Citizens Congress Watch, in testimony before the House of Representatives, Committee on House Administration, *Hearings on Public Financing of Congressional Elections*, p. 441.

[38] Fred Wertheimer, representing Common Cause, in testimony before the House of Representatives, ibid., p. 295.

Common to all these illustrations is a bias against organizational representation in politics. Along with money, this has been the most frequent target of the liberal reformers.

To grasp the significance of this thrust, it is helpful to examine the types of influence that take on increased importance as money and organizational representation become more strictly limited.

• Grass-roots lobbying. A citizens' lobby can investigate the financial backing and voting record of congressmen, release its findings to the press using a catchy phrase like the "Dirty Dozen," and thus materially affect the outcome of elections, *without ever having to register and report as a political committee.* Ralph Nader, among other liberal reformers, has strongly resisted attempts to require greater disclosure of funds spent on this type of activity.

• Access to the media. The creative skills needed to achieve media exposure become increasingly significant as political weapons.

• Knowledge and education. Increased power gravitates to that segment of society having the capability to investigate complicated issues and master the complex technology of political communication. (Incidentally, the liberals may soon begin to close the direct mail technology gap through the efforts of Richard Parker.[39]

• Individual commitment. Citizens with the leisure time, affluence, and the kind of class-instilled self-confidence that encourages them to "get involved" possess a resource that gains in relative political weight.

• Celebrity status. Media glamorization takes on new political meaning. An appearance by a single individual such as Jane Fonda becomes more important to the launching of a cause than a press conference by a less fashionable organizational leader representing thousands of people.

• Cultural symbols. The tone of public debate is increasingly set by the "moral" preoccupations of the intellectual and cultural elite, thereby diminishing the importance of economic self-interest as a legitimate basis for political involvement.

In reviewing these sources of power, it becomes immediately apparent that much of what passes for "reform" will not equalize political resources at all. It may serve instead to shift power from an old elite to a new elite.

The new elite has been called the "New Class," the "technostructure," the "New Politics" movement, and more simply, the Liberal Left. Author Paul Porter has christened it with the provocative name "the nonprofit sector of the managerial class."

---

[39] Maxwell Glen, "Richard Parker—The Liberals' Answer to Richard Viguerie," *National Journal* (March 31, 1979), pp. 513–515.

Regardless of its label, the Liberal Left network includes an impressive array of specialized organizations from the "liberal" Common Cause to the leftist Institute of Policy Studies. Like its counterpart on the Right, it takes on all the trappings of a political party, in everything but legal status.

Although the Left has suffered a decline in recent years, partly as a result of the moral dilemma posed by the disastrous consequences of its "success" in Vietnam, it remains a major contender for power and influence in American politics.

The Liberal Left has been the crucible within which a unique version of campaign reform has been concocted. This particular reform mixture is catalyzed by a curiously potent ideology that, like the Shadow, seems to have the power to cloud men's minds. It is the ideology of the "public interest."

A cartoon featured on several Common Cause brochures depicts two irate lobbyists labeled "Labor" and "Big Business" looking askance at the entry of the third figure labeled "Common Cause—The People's Lobby." This idea—that big business and big labor are the twin evils of political corruption, pursuing their narrow goals at the expense of the public interest—has come to dominate the discussion of reform.

So pervasive is this notion that the people holding it sometimes have difficulty in acknowledging labor's efforts on behalf of reform. On one occasion, the *Congressional Quarterly* omitted the AFL–CIO from a list of organizations backing the 1974 reform legislation and even implied that labor might be opposed to the bill:

> Candidates were dependent on big givers—big business interests, big labor committees, and "fat cats" (wealthy individuals)—often with a direct stake, certainly with a special interest in who won elections and in influencing their policies after they won.[40]

Upon reading such accounts, labor leaders must react with bemused wonder at their elevation to a position of influence equal to that of big business. They must also wonder why their status as the elected representatives of 30–40 million people—union members and their families—does not qualify them for at least some consideration as spokesmen for the public interest.

But as the founder of Common Cause, John Gardner, points out, the idea of the public interest is a "tricky concept."[41] According to

---

[40] "Campaign Financing: Growing Pressure to Go Public," *Congressional Quarterly,* March 30, 1974, p. 797.

[41] John W. Gardner, *In Common Cause* (New York: W. W. Norton & Company, 1972), p. 81. Most of the summary of Gardner's views comes from this same reference.

Gardner, the public interest consists of "purposes we all share and must pursue together." He contrasts this idea of shared purposes with the "interest-group pluralism" school of thought, which holds that the public interest emerges only out of the political conflict of competing interests and countervailing power.

As defined by Common Cause's early lobbying efforts, the public interest seemed to consist of ending the Vietnam War, stopping the supersonic transport (SST), ending the congressional seniority system, extending the vote to eighteen-year-olds, passing the Equal Rights Amendment, protecting the environment, and promoting a number of other liberal causes.

In reviewing this selection of issues, it becomes obvious that many of Gardner's causes are not really so common. Many people supported the development of the SST as being in the national interest; others, just as sincerely, did not. "No-growth" environmentalists have one view of the common good, advocates of economic development have another. More recently, Common Cause campaigned against the Cargo Preference Bill as being a boondoggle for Maritime Union members. But apparently it was not felt that the child care bill was a boondoggle for babysitters, nor was it effectively demonstrated that people who argued in favor of reviving our country's enfeebled cargo fleet might not have their own version of the common good. Which view represents the public interest?

Gardner recognizes the pitfall and concedes that "there will be various conceptions of the public interest and how it may best be served."[42] To escape from the conceptual trap (and to avoid divisiveness within his own membership), Gardner increasingly steers away from substantive policy matters and focuses instead on the *procedures* of government: the seniority system, open public meetings, voter registration, lobbying regulations, and, most important, regulation of campaign finances. But to the extent that such changes shift power from one elite to another, even the procedural reforms are difficult to wrap in the flag of legitimacy associated with the appealing notion of the public interest.

Even more complicated is the task of identifying *who* represents the public interest. According to Gardner, the impulse to set aside selfish concerns comes from enlightened individuals "who have the wit to perceive and the courage to act in behalf of the public interest. . . . They are to be found in every social class and every segment of society, . . . a housewife here, a union member there, a business entrepreneur, a salesman."[43] The problem faced by these citizens of good will is that

---

[42] Ibid., p. 96.
[43] Ibid., pp. 94–96.

they are, in Gardner's words, an "unassembled constituency." "Everybody's organized but the people."[44]

It was to remedy this lamentable situation that Common Cause was founded. It was to be a national lobby for public-minded citizens—those with "the time and energy to worry about the community and the nation, . . . so that those extraordinarily valuable men and women will have access to the channels of influence and decision."[45]

But Common Cause's own membership is not so widely representative. According to its recruitment manual, the organization's "typical" member is

> middle class; has an above average income; has an above average education. He tends to live in the suburbs; he subscribes to magazines with an intellectual or quasi-intellectual appeal, and he supports and joins groups devoted to social reform.[46]

One could add "likely to be Caucasian" to this list of characteristics.

Common Cause is not the only organization working in the public interest, we are assured. It is instructive to note which other groups receive Gardner's good citizenship seal of approval and which do not. Nader's Raiders qualify. So does the populist movement. So does the *early* labor movement, before it achieved organizational clout. The peace movement gets good marks, but not the hard hats who marched for their version of the national good. Civil rights organizations, environmentalists, the population control movement, student activists, feminists, and the poor get favorable mention. But the anti-busing activists, the pro-lifers, the religious fundamentalists, and the gun owners are apparently disapproved.

Gardner reserves his harshest attacks for the major institutions in American life—big business, big labor, government, the legislature, the political parties. He believes there is a widespread lack of confidence in these institutions because they resist change and stifle the "surging creativity" of the gifted and concerned individual acting through the mechanism of "popular movements."

> Only on the rarest occasions are significant new directions in public policy initiated by the legislature, or by the bureaucracy, or by the parties. They are initiated by the people—

---

44 Ibid., p. 80.

45 Ibid., p. 94, and Elizabeth Drew, "A Reporter at Large, Conversation with a Citizen," *New Yorker* (July 23, 1973).

46 Common Cause, *Handbook for Membership Building, Action through Membership* (Washington, D.C.), pp. 3, 10.

not "The People" taken collectively, but by vigorous and forward-looking elements within the body politic. Or they are initiated by the special interests.[47]

Are institutions as useless as Gardner claims? There is much evidence that they are not. It was, after all, a Supreme Court decision in 1954 that helped spark the civil rights movement and the federal government that helped carry out the mandate to abolish discrimination. It was the administration and Congress that launched the Great Society program, without the impetus of a massive movement by the poor. It was the business sector that developed the productive capacity that is the envy of the modern world. It was the trade union movement that sparked the drive for national health security, aid to education, the voting rights act, unemployment insurance, occupational health and safety legislation, and a dozen other innovative changes. Even the Watergate episode revealed the deep-seated capacity of American institutions to withstand shock, react appropriately, and adapt to momentous changes and challenges.

There is no doubt that many Americans *have* lost confidence in major institutions in recent years. But the "popular" movements on the Left do not appear to be more noticeably beloved. In fact, much of the conservative backlash is fueled by public anger at the extent to which the Liberal Left has scorned middle-class values, weakened American institutions, and in some cases turned those institutions into instruments of Liberal Left power.

Moreover, the widespread dissatisfactions recorded in public opinion polls are fundamentally different from the Left's antagonism toward American institutions. Most Americans want a decent job with good pay, a house in a nice crime-free neighborhood, good education for their children, efficient transportation, adequate health care, respect for their values, and the freedom to live their lives as they see fit. They become dissatisfied when society's institutions fail to deliver, undermine their dignity, or become too intrusive.

While these mundane concerns evoke concern among liberals, the deeper reason for their anger is the failure of institutions to provide more elevated kinds of gratification:

> There is in all segments of society an undercurrent of hostility toward institutional life, toward impersonal efficiency, toward organization, toward the endless small indignities of an administered age. . . . There is a longing for wholeness, for authenticity, for immediate experience, for the emotional, symbolic, non-rational elements of life that do not automati-

---

[47] Gardner, *In Common Cause*, p. 77.

cally flow from the functional efficiency of large scale organizations.[48]

These heady concerns, it will immediately be perceived, are the preoccupation of that fortunate and privileged stratum of the population whose material needs are largely satisfied, the very same stratum that forms the social base of the liberal reform movement.

Like their counterparts in the Progressive era of the early 1900s, the new generation of reformers is made up primarily of upper-middle-class professionals—doctors, lawyers, academicians, journalists, consultants, and technicians—many of whom find employment in the rapidly expanding nonprofit sector. These occupations provide most of the financial backing for the candidates and causes of the Left.

For example, it was estimated that professionals gave 56 percent of the $371,000 budget for the Proposition 9 campaign, while businessmen gave another 38 percent. Only 6 percent was raised from individuals in white-collar, blue-collar, and student occupations.[49]

To take another example, the Ripon Society revealed that professionals replaced labor as the second-largest source of financing in the 1972 presidential election, supplying nearly 50 percent of McGovern's funds and 14 percent of Nixon's.[50]

Finally, the figures shown previously in Table 1 reveal that professionals provided 61 percent and 33 percent, respectively, of the campaign contributions given to the liberal candidates for the California Assembly and for the office of attorney general.

The professional occupations carry their own unique burden of special-interest concerns that are not without their materialistic aspects. In recognition of this fact, one wit has sought to retitle the campaign reform bill the "lawyers' and accountants' full employment act."

More important than material well-being, however, is the recognition, status, and power that mass institutions fail to confer on America's "public citizens" in the amount that their selflessness, creativity, and high moral purpose would seem to warrant. It is therefore not surprising to discover that organizational influence is often the target of the liberal reform movement, that newer, more individualized forms of influence gain in its place, or that a "public interest" ideology serves to transfer legitimacy from the former to the latter.

---

[48] Ibid., pp. 105–106.

[49] This information is based on figures compiled by "Frontlash," a nonprofit youth voter registration organization, from data provided by the secretary of state of California.

[50] Clifford W. Brown, Jr., "The Gap in GOP Campaign Funds," *Wall Street Journal*, May 28, 1971.

Recognition of this fact does not disqualify the liberals from pursuing their often worthwhile goals, be they motivated by high-mindedness or by self-interest or (as is usually the case) by both. But it does deny the usefulness of the concept of the "public interest" as a basis for reform.

To repeat: Reform must deal with the *unequal distribution* of influence, not with the presumed motivation of those who try to wield it.

Labor as a Political Party

One much-lamented consequence of reform, according to some, has been the destruction of the political party system.

In testimony before Congress, a group of political scientists headed by James MacGregor Burns offered its rationale for attempting to revive the moribund victim:

> The Party serves as an intermediary between a host of special interests and the making of public policy. [As the Party declines], special interest groups grow in importance, pressing their narrow goals rather than the broader public good. . . . It is the ability of the two parties to pull out of a medley of interest groups something that represents a national program for the benefit of the people, and to present those two programs to the people, that we think is very impressive about the potential of parties.[51]

However useful these conciliating functions may be, it is unlikely that the parties will soon be able to perform them.

For one thing, the elected officeholders will probably not permit it. After years of successful maneuvering to increase their independence, our congressional representatives are not to be expected to make themselves accountable to a party structure they do not control. Nor are the presidential candidates, at least on the Democratic side, likely to turn away from a primary system that allows them to name the delegates on their slates and instead relinquish the nominating process to a quota-dominated national convention that fails to represent the party's voting base.

Second, the continuing polarization of American politics will not easily give way to the conciliatory functions prescribed for the parties, even if they were to somehow be revived. The problem here is not the "special interests," which are by nature subject to compromise in the

---

[51] James MacGregor Burns, in testimony before the House of Representatives, Committee on House Administration, *Hearings on Public Financing of Congressional Elections*, pp. 392–405.

give and take of the legislative process. The polarization derives from the moralistic crusades of the Right and the Left.

Like it or not, there are really four political "parties" operating today, only partly within the confines of the two older parties: business and the New Right on one side, and labor and the Liberal Left on the other. To herd these disparate forces artificially into a two-party corral will not necessarily lead to harmony and may well lead to the reverse, as happened in the bloody Democratic party miniconvention of 1974. To increase the funds, patronage, or nominating powers of the formal parties at this time may only create one additional battlefield on which these forces can contend. To the extent that any institution can currently play an intermediary role between the citizen and the government, it will have to be performed by the four "parties" analyzed here.

Perhaps the one best suited for the role is the much-maligned labor movement. More Americans now participate in collective bargaining than in any other organizational activity save religion. Through their union's involvement in collective bargaining and public policy, members advance their "narrow" interests as well as a broader conception of the common good. The union movement drafts legislation, coordinates lobbying activities, recruits candidates, mobilizes for elections, and even writes platforms for presentation to both national political parties.

There are differences within the union movement on matters both great and small, but conciliatory mechanisms seem to restrain passions to a greater extent than seems possible in the more ideological parties, enabling the labor movement to achieve a remarkable degree of programmatic consistency, at least most of the time.

Labor is also a profoundly democratic institution, notwithstanding the increasingly hysterical attacks mounted against it by the New Right. In one recent blast, the Right to Work Committee charged that labor's "fearsome" influence is based on "captive wage-earners who are required, as a condition of employment, to pay money to the unions and to lend support to political policies and candidates chosen by the union leadership without regard for the wishes of the rank and file."[52] Although such vitriolic outbursts, however entertaining, are not normally taken seriously enough to merit a response, the argument presented here will be served by taking the time to answer some of the points:

1. Labor's candidates are endorsed by representative conventions, starting at the local level, for which every member is entitled to run as a delegate.

---

[52] Statement by Reed Larson, Chairman, National Right to Work Committee, submitted to the House of Representatives, Committee on House Administration, *Hearings on Public Financing of Congressional Elections*, pp. 496–497.

2. Except in those remaining states allowing treasury funds to be used for contributions to nonfederal candidates, donations to all candidates and parties are made from *voluntary* funds.

3. Democratic procedures in unions are mandated by law and are more heavily regulated in unions than in any other institution. The decision whether to have a union at all is usually made by majority vote, as is the election of officers, the acceptance or rejection of contracts, and the decision whether to go on strike.

4. Any time a disgruntled member chooses, he can begin the process of decertification and, with the majority backing of his co-workers, have the union promptly thrown out.

5. It is ironic that of all the "conditions of employment" that a person must accept when choosing a job, the one most vilified by the Right-to-Workers is the union shop, which is the only condition that the employee can seek to change through democratic procedures. The other conditions imposed by management, which sometimes include such things as the requirement to work under unsafe conditions, are not subject to majority rule, except insofar as they become subjects for collective bargaining. For those employees who object to these management-imposed conditions, the Right to Work Committee offers the "freedom" to seek employment elsewhere!

To argue these points is not to claim that labor is a perfect democracy or to ignore labor's warts and blemishes. Labor has its share of narrow-mindedness, authoritarianism, and corruption, although it would have to go a long way to equal the Watergate record of the business community in the last instance.

But even labor's critics might agree that unions are at least as democratic as society's other political institutions and far more so than the institution of business. So, it is not too much of an exaggeration to say that labor performs many of the beneficial functions of a political party. It has managed, over the years, to ameliorate many of the harsh conditions that would prevail if business were to reign unchallenged and the market were to function with unrestrained impartiality, redistributing income forever upward. In a sense, labor has saved capitalism from devouring itself.

Labor's ability to perform this role is today being seriously weakened by attacks from the other centers of political power. Those conservatives who yearn for its demise ought first to consider what is likely to replace it. The alternative may not be a return of unbridled control to the private sector, with all the social tensions such a change would entail. The more probable outcome is an assumption of labor's functions by the public sector.

If "big government" is a thing to be avoided, especially one dominated by the overzealous reformers of the Liberal Left, then ways should be found to encourage labor's ability to carry out its political mission. Democratizing the sources of influence through carefully crafted election law reform is one such way.

The Case of an Independent Political Action Committee

Walter K. Moore

When Congress began the process that led to the enactment of the Federal Election Campaign Act (FECA), as amended, and the founding of the Federal Election Commission (FEC), it did so as a reaction to abuses of campaign ethics, rather than as a solution to the problems of campaign finance. This paper examines the effects of the FECA and the FEC on small, independent, ideological political action committees (PACs), like the National Committee for an Effective Congress (NCEC). In addition, it defines what is regarded as the major problem of campaign finance and its regulation—the underfinancing of campaigns for public office.

This paper also presents a historical perspective for the current law and examines the FEC as an institution, describing various strategies delivered by PACs and campaigns to deal with the law and the FEC, and highlighting some innovations attempted by PACs to cope with the legislation. The study is intended to lead us to face the problems with the current political finance system for candidates, potential candidates, political action committees, and citizens generally.

Implications of the Law

Although one cannot be certain of it, it is highly unlikely that either Common Cause or Representative Wayne Hays was trying to destroy the National Committee for an Effective Congress when the FECA amendments were passed in 1974. It is a sad irony that a reform movement, which began at the turn of the century with passage of the Tillman Act, and continued through the Smith-Connally and Taft-Hartley Acts to limit the untoward influence of both business and labor, should yield a federal election law in 1979 that gives an advantage to both of these economic interests, at the expense of groups of ordinary citizens, whose resources are much more limited.

Both corporate and labor PACs have the ability to pay legal, accounting, and administrative costs out of the treasury of the parent corporation, association, or union. Small citizens' groups such as NCEC, however, are required to raise these funds, under the contribution limits, merely to pay the staff salaries and rent. Before any contribution can be made to candidates, these costs must be met.

The importance of the problem can be seen in the fact that the NCEC has allied itself with the Committee for the Survival of a Free Congress (CSFC), whose positions are often quite different from ours, in order to decry this situation in House and Senate hearings. Our pleas, however, have had no effect in revisions proposed by either the House Administration or the Senate Rules committee regarding the FECA. Although independent, ideological committees have endorsed and contributed to members who serve on these committees, their contributions are dwarfed by corporate and labor funding.

FEC commissioners have, in the past, been particularly attentive to economic interests. The commissioners are appointed according to party, there being three Republicans and three Democrats; however, in the aftermath of the Sun Oil Advisory Opinion, the first significant advisory opinion dealing with labor-management issues, it has become apparent that the party roles must be mirrored by advocacy roles to maintain the labor-management equilibrium written into the law. The Democratic members of the commission must protect the best interests not only of Democratic party candidates and committees, but also of the labor community in adversarial questions between labor and management. Similarly, the defense of the business, professional association, and corporate interests before the commission has fallen to the Republicans.

Many disputes do fall into the labor-management, Democratic-Republican matrix; but in other disputes, there is no one to advocate the positions of independent candidates and committees. The case concerning the candidacy of Eugene McCarthy in 1976 is one such example. NCEC has brought six substantive complaints to the commission, but none has resulted in a major conciliation agreement. The problem of advocacy seems to be the central deterrent to any action. Interestingly, the most recent NCEC complaint, filed against the campaign committees of three candidates for the presidency, was followed four days later by the announcement of an FEC audit of the National Committee for an Effective Congress.

Coping with the Rules

The question stands—How does a group like NCEC cope? There are several important strategies for remaining solvent. First, NCEC, like the Committee for the Survival of a Free Congress, maintains an extremely small staff between campaigns, but it raises funds year-round. Second, the committee retains political consultants for the lowest possible long-term rates. The committee has adopted the same policy for hiring pollsters, media consultants, and other professionals. In this way the consultants appreciate the dependable, if low, income, and NCEC is able to maximize its efficiency. If NCEC can provide a $250-per-day consultant to a campaign at his or her long-term fee of $50 per day, the committee can provide more services while staying within the contribution limits. Political consultants are also placed on long-term contracts as administrative personnel, thus further reducing staff. One disadvantage to this system is that the relationship breaks down during the campaign season, when the consultants are out of town for long periods, leaving no management personnel in the political operation.

NCEC's influence and that of similar committees can extend far beyond its small financial contribution by providing badly needed intelligence to labor, corporate, association, and party contacts regarding a specific race; this information often generates contributions for endorsed candidates. By keeping costs low, and at the same time providing a credible liaison with economic interests in Washington, NCEC can have a major impact on those campaigns it becomes involved in, an effect far beyond its immediate contribution.

NCEC began its Campaign Services Project in 1974. At that time the committee was able to hire the best political talent, on a per diem basis, and send these professionals into the field. If we bought a poll and discovered that we needed new media, we simply filmed it and, if necessary, purchased additional time. NCEC was committed totally to the campaign, doing everything it could to achieve success. The situation today, however, is very different.

"No Frills" Approach. While the $5,000 contribution limit affected only a few NCEC contributors, making up for these large contributions has not been easy. Total contributions have not decreased significantly since 1974, but they have not increased in proportion to inflation, either. This can be attributed to both the law and the change in the general political climate.

Most significant is the increase in fund-raising costs, up 10 percent to generate approximately the same level of contributions. Inflation and the postage increase account for higher costs, and NCEC has been forced to seek replacements for the large contributions with direct mail solicitations, which attract small donations. The 10 percent cut in available funds, as well as the contribution limit to candidates, has caused changes in the contribution patterns from NCEC to candidates in order to maximize the effect of the committee's participation. NCEC has begun a "no frills" approach to campaign services, providing critically needed services to a campaign through in-house consultants and soliciting other individuals and groups for contributions and services of a lower priority to the campaign. Therefore, the committee assists the campaign in effectively using other funds and services that the campaign could not normally utilize.

Even with a "no frills" wholesale, rather than retail, approach to consulting, NCEC still must ration contributions, so as to remain well below the $5,000-per-election contribution limit until the final days of the campaign. The $5,000 limit also encourages as much activity as is practical prior to an uncontested primary, allowing PACs to contribute as close to $10,000 for both the primary and the general election as possible. NCEC also is taking advantage of this approach, beginning work for 1980 Senate campaigns earlier than ever before. By the end of the summer of 1979, we expect to have completed major consulting projects for no less than ten Senate candidates.

For fund-raising purposes, it is important to be able to say that the highest possible percentage of every dollar is contributed to candidates. Thus, NCEC's 1979 contributions to Senate candidates help them stay well below their contribution limits and give the committees a favorable ratio for use in fund raising. By working throughout the two-year cycle on "allocable" or "contributable" projects for candidates, NCEC spends almost every dollar on either candidate assistance or direct mail fund raising.

Legal Assistance. Often a campaign needs election law advice, which NCEC is able to provide. While the committee encourages all campaigns to retain a competent elections attorney, questions sometimes arise that can be answered only by a group such as NCEC. Because of frequent contact and experience with the FEC, NCEC has a unique perspective on the law, as well as a good and thorough understanding of the standard operating procedures of auditors, reports analysts, and public records personnel. Thus, the committee can advise a campaign on the ramifications of a specific action by the campaign committee or the FEC. NCEC is also familiar with the commission's tendency to give "nonanswer answers" to specific questions except where the legal and illegal aspects are obvious.

FEC as Legal Arbiter

The fact that candidate committees need help in their interaction with the FEC should come as no surprise to people who have watched regulatory agencies promulgate in Washington since the New Deal. Their development is predictable: a new agency is born as a legislative reaction to abuses, and it attempts to grapple with the industry on a prospective basis; the industry, however, uses the early rulings as license for actions not contemplated by the agency, so the agency makes its rulings more vague, almost ceasing to give advice prospectively, and using retrospective compliance and court proceedings to define rulings on cases with fixed actions.

Secret Deliberations. The FEC has added an additional layer of insulation from criticism of its decisions and decision-making process. It is able to pursue all compliance cases in secret, debating all issues in a retrospective fashion without public surveillance. This mode of operation began as a means of preventing the political implications of incomplete FEC investigations from wrongly prejudicing the outcome of elections; however, the lasting effect of the secret procedures is to isolate the debate, and insulate both the general counsel and the judging commissioners.

Another product of this secrecy is the fact that only those in the debate know *exactly* the state of the interpretation of the law at any given moment; this reduces the value of information disseminated by other commission offices, including the office of information, on issues raised in compliance actions. To gain access to transcripts of compliance debates, one must file a freedom-of-information request with the commission following the closing of the case. Interested but nonrespondent parties might have to wait a year to have the commission consider an aspect of their ruling. Commissioners define the law and rule on cases at times without a full understanding of the implications of their actions, while the public must operate without knowing the full interpretation of the law.

Original Intent of the FEC. Certainly no one can accuse the architects of the legislation of disinterest or apathy regarding federal election law. The interest has been, understandably, extremely strong. Federally elected officials are the only regulated "industry" in America that is able to write its own law and legislative history, veto regulations to which it objects, and monitor the enforcement mechanism. Questions do arise, however, on which even the law's architects disagree. The FEC was formed to contend with such situations.

Administrative Problems. Whether or not it was intended to do so by Congress, the legislation has constructed a commission that is strongly partisan along both party and economic lines. Although advocacy for each of the poles on the commission may be necessary, it has caused an administrative stalemate, in which no one assumes responsibility for the commission's action as a whole.

The administrative head of the agency, the staff director, must deal with a governing body whose members are suspicious of one another. All personnel at the FEC must be accepted by a majority vote of the six commissioners. Since partisan candidates may be blocked by commissioners of the opposing party, the employees of the FEC, the final arbiter of election law violations, tend to be those with little partisan experience, in effect those least interested in the political process they will be monitoring.

Further, the staff director's actions are under the scrutiny of six competing superiors. Any innovative administrative action is likely to be criticized, discouraging the search for better methods of accomplishing the commission's goals. Ultimately, even the most insignificant actions have to be cleared with all the commissioners. This, clearly, is not a path toward studied judgment and enforcement of the major issues, since the commissioners are constantly preoccupied with the minutiae of the agency.

Role of the Office of General Counsel. In the vacuum created by the commission's excessive administrative cautiousness, the Office of the General Counsel (OGC) is forced to assume much of the day-to-day definition and enforcement of the law. The OGC must issue advisory opinions, promulgate regulations, and try to answer questions from the public. Unfortunately, OGC rarely answers questions. It has found, as has the commission as a whole, that the specific facts of a particular situation are needed before an opinion can be generated.

Politics, however, does not lend itself to interpretation of the law according to different scenarios in different situations. Therefore, many opinions must be generated for similar but not identical situations. Each state is different, and each race is different from the next. Because of the administrative quagmire, response time is a major problem at the FEC. In a normal business situation, the regulation or advisory opinion could be requested, and turnaround time might be two to six months. Obviously, business opportunities would be lost and the enterprise itself discomfited, but the business would probably survive to take advantage of the ruling. A campaign is in a very different situation. The avocational nature of politics often forces campaigns and politically active groups to make decisions on a moment's notice. Facts change very rapidly in a campaign, and the ability to make decisions effectively in a fast-paced, ever-changing environment is a requirement of a good campaigner.

The result of a slow-to-respond regulatory agency in this environment is to split campaigns artificially into two categories: those that maintain sufficient staff expertise and other resources to act in a manner that is neither legal nor illegal—that is, to take a chance—and those that lack these necessary resources and are unable to take legal "risks." The necessary resources are obviously economic means that allow well-funded incumbents and celebrity candidates the luxury of taking a chance and forcing smaller, shoestring campaigns to hold back. This circumstance cannot bode well for an open, egalitarian political system.

Testing the Law. The actions of three prominent Republican presidential campaign staffs have been testing FEC regulations regarding affiliation. Previous to the campaigns, they established multicandidate political action committees to raise funds to support local Republican candidates; in fact these committees were intended to garner support for the presidential candidate. Former and future members of the presidential campaign staffs were sent out to assist local Republican candidates. "Prepresidential" committees could accept contributions of up to $5,000 per year from an individual, and presidential committees could accept an additional $1,000, so an individual could contribute $6,000 to a single candidate.

In a complaint filed in April 1979, NCEC alleged that these committees are in fact affiliated and that the $1,000 limit must be enforced. According to FEC regulations, common control is a major indication of affiliation. In all cases NCEC found a significant number of people occupying key decision-making positions for both the PAC and the Principle Campaign Committee (PCC). This allows decisions to be made not on the best interests of the congressional candidates the PAC supports, but on what will be most beneficial to the presidential aspirations of their candidate. The significance of common control is especially evident in Ronald Reagan's case, where seven decision makers, including Senator Paul Laxalt, Lyn Nofziger, and John Sears, occupied similar positions for both committees.

Regarding the other FEC requirement of affiliation, that is, a similar pattern of contributions, the significance is obvious. If within merely three months or less, 52 percent of the contributors to the PAC had also given to the presidential committee, as was reported to the FEC by the Bush committee, one must conclude that the two committees are using the same base of financial support for a common purpose.

If the FEC determines that the committees are affiliated, they could ask that all contributions above the $1,000 limit received by the presidential committees be returned. The combined total of contributions to be returned would be over $648,000. In addition, no further funds could be accepted from people who gave a combined total of over $1,000 to the prepresidential multicandidate committee and to the presidential committee.

Economic Resources and the Law. There is a similar correspondence between a committee's economic resources and its ability to force opponents to comply with the law. For example, NCEC has the resources to initiate compliance proceedings, by filing a complaint with the commission, but it cannot follow through with expensive court proceedings, as the National Right to Work Committee often does, should the commission refuse to take action.

This was the case in an NCEC complaint against the transfer of the 2-cents-times-voting-age-population spending authority in section 441a(d) of a state party to a national party. NCEC complained in October 1978 that the National Republican Senatorial Committee (NRSC) had spent over its 2-cents-times-voting-age-population limit in the Larry Williams senatorial campaign in Montana. NRSC asserted that the state party's 2-cents-times-voting-age-population spending limit had been transferred to NRSC. The commission concluded that the absence of a specific prohibition of transfer was an implicit allowance of the action. NCEC does not concur with this conclusion and is now faced with a resource allocation decision: Should NCEC spend resources on a suit against the FEC in federal district court, or save the committee's resources to affect the outcome of the election campaigns of NCEC's endorsed candidates?

Unlike groups connected with profit or nonprofit corporations, the NCEC has no funds to assist in the pursuit of the court proceedings. No one can question the large expense of suing the government, especially on a technical point that could be lost on an uninformed judge. Therefore, the NCEC has decided against pursuing the complaint in court. It is an unhappy conclusion that might well forebode the end of state party grass-roots activity in favor of the national party–coordinated expenditures. Candidates would be linked to a national party apparatus but with no bond through state parties to the grass-roots level, a result we are loathe to see.

Future of PACs

When looking to the future of political action groups, the horizons appear much brighter for PACs representing economic interests than for ideological PACs like NCEC. Business and labor groups have established over 1,300 new PACs since 1975, and two-thirds of these have been formed since 1977. Virtually all of them are sponsored by corporations and trade associations. Contributions to candidates from these PACs increased by over $16.5 million, or four-and-a-half times, over the same period. In contrast, only a few independent political action committees have been formed, and contributions have increased from less than $750,000 in 1974 to $2.5 million in 1978.

Innovations for Survival. Because independent, ideological PACs are faltering, some are attempting rather innovative methods to survive. One is the National Right to Work Committee, which has asserted that it is a "membership organization." Its membership is composed of anyone who has ever contributed to the committee. The Employees' Rights Committee, a PAC, was established by, and has its administrative costs paid by, the Right to Work Committee, which, according to the regulations, can continue to solicit contributions an unlimited number of times per year. The FEC ruled against this assertion, and the Right to Work Committee is now in court asking that the FEC ruling be reversed.

Both the NCEC and the Committee for the Survival of a Free Congress have established nonprofit foundations under section 501(c)(3) of the IRS code for the purpose of conducting research; the data gathered are not to be used to influence the outcome of any election. Because the IRS requires an arm's length relationship between the PAC and the foundation, however, this method has been less effective than had been hoped.

Finally, the American Medical Association has asserted on numerous occasions that its national association PAC is not affiliated with the PACs of its various state associations. This would allow both the AMA and the state medical society to give $5,000, thus exceeding the normal PAC limit on contributions. The AMA's assertion of independence is now the subject of a suit against the FEC's determination that the two were in fact affiliated committees. Like the matter concerning the Right to Work Committee, the issue has not yet been resolved.

Other Abuses of the Law. PACs are not alone in taking advantage of problems at the FEC. The law has been manipulated by shrewd businessmen as well as politicians. In a widely publicized case, two California businessmen set up political committees to make independent expenditures for Ronald Reagan and S. I. Hayakawa in 1976, but little campaigning was done because of the large fees the organizers of the committee paid themselves. While these commercial abuses beg for some type of regulation, none is likely to occur. Meanwhile, unsuspecting, well-meaning citizens will continue to enrich the entrepreneur rather than the candidate or cause they support.

Suggested Reforms. The NCEC has attempted, through struggles for political finance reform, to end the discriminatory treatment afforded political action committees not representing economic interests. The committee has long sought to eliminate the ability of economic interests to defray administrative costs, but this suggestion has fallen on deaf ears. The combined economic clout of both corporate and labor PACs has made the issue politically untouchable.

Therefore, in 1979, the NCEC suggested another plan as a fallback position to the Senate Committee on Rules and Administration. This plan redefines the term "contribution" to exclude contributions of up to $5,000 to a multicandidate committee for the purpose of defraying administrative, legal, and accounting costs. The Rules Committee could act favorably on this proposal. Senator Mark Hatfield, however, asked that the proposal not be included in a bill of technical amendments of the FECA, because, it is said, he fears that conservative groups will use this as a vehicle to raise more funds.

Underfinancing of Political System

The status of political action committees in politics and before the law is certainly open to debate, but this question is only one of the problems inherent to the system of political finance in this country. The main problem is the underfinancing of our political system. That we spend less on federal campaigns than on women's nail polish or garden hoses is as important an indictment of the political system as the fund-raising scandals associated with Watergate. They are, after all, merely parts of the same problem.

Discouragement of Able Candidates. The law constitutes a barrier to the goal of an egalitarian political system, a system of representative government that encourages the most able, qualified individuals to serve the public. The inability of candidates, or potential candidates, to raise "seed money" to begin their campaign for office forces too many talented potential public servants to seek other means of affecting policy. Seed money is, of course, that minimum amount necessary to gain the name identification and momentum to become a serious candidate. Throughout the current era of campaigning, the task of raising these necessary funds has fallen to a few concerned and/or manipulative individuals.

The reason for this small core of monetary support is that Americans traditionally have not given to politics. Despite tax breaks and the like, we do not give to a deserving candidate in the same way we give to the Red Cross, the American Cancer Society, or the United Way, even though political contributions are more likely to have a direct effect on an individual than any of these others. Therefore, our politics are underfinanced, and the public good has been compromised for private gain.

The able, nonrich, and noncelebrity challenger is without franking privileges, staff, or other resources to buy name identification. The position sought is encumbered with outside income limitations, much constituent contact is required at the expense of one's private and family life, under the severe scrutiny of the public. Under the Federal Elections Campaign Act, such candidates can take their case to the people only by raising enough funds to challenge the incumbent over a long period of time, while the incumbent jets home from Washington each weekend at taxpayer expense to keep in touch with his constituency. Often the only way an unknown or untested challenger can compete is to risk large sums of money—$50,000 to $100,000—to become a credible candidate. If the challenger does well, Washington PAC sources often eradicate some or all of the debt. If the challenger loses, he may be saddled with a personal debt the remainder of his life. Not surprisingly, more and more competent individuals choose not to risk their personal financial security to serve an increasingly cynical and ungrateful electorate. If we are to continue to have a viable political system, our system must be reformed to encourage able persons to serve the public.

Raising Consciousness. Much debate has raged in the political and academic communities as to how to provide adequate funding for candidates to use in campaigns, through either public financing or traditional fund-raising channels. The obvious solution to underfinancing is to encourage more people to give their money and volunteer time to campaigns, and finally, to vote.

Much has been said about the political debts built by fund raising through traditional means, but today this remains the only means by which nonwealthy candidates can gather the resources required to run for public office. It is important to emphasize that this underfinancing is merely a result of the generally apathetic way Americans view their government. This situation reduces to a vicious circle. Low voter participation and alienation beget fewer small contributions, forcing the candidate to seek large gifts. Such gifts may result in reduced confidence in both the elected official and the institution. This reduced confidence causes further voter alienation, which repeats the cycle. The public must be educated as to its role in politics generally, its responsibility to see that this country does get the best candidates to determine our future. Without this education, we cannot avoid the twin problems of low esteem of public officials and low voter participation.

In summary, this paper has outlined the ways the Federal Election Campaign Act and the Federal Election Commission affect political action committees, as well as the problems of campaign finance. Unfortunately, the law and regulatory agency have too often exacerbated the problems in the system without curbing the abuses. We must seek innovative solutions that both curb abuses and provide adequate campaign financing if faith and participation in the institutions of our government are to increase.

The New Right:
PACs and Coalition Politics

Paul M. Weyrich

When the Campaign Reform Act of 1974 was passed by Congress during the Watergate era, its backers promised that this law would give us fairer and freer elections. It is the contention of this paper that we have received quite the opposite under the Federal Election Commission (FEC), which the act established.

One of the reforms I supported was disclosure. I believe that the electorate is entitled to know, to the extent it is interested, who is supporting what candidates and in what amounts. Beyond disclosure, and criminal penalties for serious violations of the longstanding Corrupt Practices Act, I believe we do not need government regulation of elections. It is my conclusion, based on my five years as executive director of the Committee for the Survival of a Free Congress (CSFC), that such regulation is contrary to the generally honest and open system of elections we have enjoyed in this country since its inception.

Experiences with the FEC

We have had many experiences with the way the FEC can be used for ill in an election campaign, but the best example occurred in the 1976 elections. One of the candidates we backed was the senatorial candidate Orrin Hatch, of Utah. Hatch was scheduled to debate the incumbent senator, Frank Moss, near the end of the campaign. During the debate, Senator Moss charged that Hatch had accepted illegal con- tributions from a number of conservative campaign committees. Hatch was shocked; it was the first he had heard of such a charge. He called CSFC and other conservative committees, none of which had heard of it either. When pressed by Hatch during a debate, Moss said he based his charge on a complaint filed with the Federal Election Com- mission.

The media began to report these charges, not only in Utah, but also in various other states in which CSFC was involved with candidates locked in close battles with their opponents. The CSFC counsel, Marion

Harrison, tried to get a copy of the complaint, but the Federal Election Commission did not make a copy available to us.

To quote Counsel Harrison: "Thus, candidates supported by CSFC were in the Scylla and Charybdis position of being victims of denunciation for allegedly unlawful activity without knowing anything of the allegations except to the extent an opponent or the press chose to publicize the allegations."[1]

As it turned out, the complaint was filed by a liberal political action committee, the National Committee for an Effective Congress (NCEC). NCEC dated its letter of complaint October 22, but did not file it with the FEC until 10:24 A.M. on October 26, the day before its contents were used in the Moss-Hatch debate and elsewhere. This was also three days after NCEC issued its own press release detailing the complaint not only to the media, but also to all NCEC-supported candidates who were opposed by New Right PACs, such as CSFC. While the media had the story, the CSFC was unable to get a copy of the complaint from the FEC for ten days. We finally had to get a copy of the press release from NCEC.

The date of the press release, October 23, was just nine days before the election. NCEC probably knew that the complaint would not be acted upon before the 1976 elections. The complaint alleged that CSFC, the National Conservative Political Action Committee (NCPAC), and the Committee for Responsible Youth Politics (CRYP) were really affiliated PACs, mainly because they had similar suppliers and candidates.

Had the complaint been valid, candidates who accepted more than $5,000 from the aggregate of the three committees would indeed have violated the law. Because of the complaint, liberal candidates across the nation were able to hold press conferences charging that their opponents had been charged with violating the law because of their association with one of these three conservative committees. In short, the affected conservatives were on the defensive during the last few days of the campaign, a very critical time.

CSFC moved immediately to dismiss the charges, which we knew were not supported by the facts. No action was taken on the motion before the election, and, indeed, the FEC told anyone who called its public information office that the charges against the committee made by NCEC were "under investigation."[2]

---

[1] Marion Harrison, Summary of *NCEC* vs. *CSFC, et al.* case, Committee for the Survival of a Free Congress, March 6, 1978.

[2] WTMJ radio account of the Gunderson-Baldus race, November 1, 1976, Milwaukee, Wisconsin.

Just when did the FEC get around to dismissing the charges? The action was taken at a board meeting of December 15, 1977, some fourteen months after the original complaint was made. The FEC managed to inform CSFC about its action by letter on January 5, 1978, when it pronounced that there had been no basis to the complaint, and the case was closed.[3] We are not sure the FEC would have acted even then, if Counsel Harrison had not stated in early December, after months of prodding and inquiries, that the CSFC would go to federal court to force the FEC to act.

That pending case was damaging to the committee's continued operations. Between the 1976 elections and the dismissal of the charges, several newspaper articles mentioned that the NCEC had filed the complaint against the CFSC and that such charges were pending with the FEC.

Some members of Congress against whom the NCEC complaint had been used in the 1976 campaigns were apprehensive because the FEC had not acted. They wanted to settle their 1976 accounts. If the FEC had ruled against CSFC, these members would have had to return several thousand dollars, and they might have had other problems with the issue. The CSFC assured them that the issue would be favorably resolved, but there was no way to explain why the FEC was taking so long to dismiss the case if there really were nothing to it.

In 1978 we anticipated a repeat performance. Early in the year we sent our candidates a letter to help them prepare themselves: "From the . . . summarized chronology it is clear that an unscrupulous party may charge a candidate with a violation of the election laws a few days before a primary or general election, secure in the knowledge that, however outrageous the charge, the FEC would not be able to act upon it until well after the primary or general election to which the charge supposedly relates."[4]

Not everyone can file an FEC complaint with the assurance that it will not be settled until after the election, though those who represent a union or liberal point of view against conservatives apparently enjoy such confidence. In 1978, the National Right to Work Committee filed a complaint against a number of candidates who had received funds from various labor union PACs affiliated with the AFL-CIO COPE. The complaint was similar to the one filed by NCEC against the New Right committees, but unlike the NCEC action, the Right to Work complaint was based on specific points of the law itself. This complaint

---

[3] FEC Counsel Oldaker to Marion Harrison, January 5, 1978.
[4] Counsel Marion Harrison to 1978 candidates re *NCEC vs. CSFC, et al.,* March 6, 1978.

was filed on October 30, and the Federal Election Commission dismissed it on November 2, just seventy-two hours after it was filed.

When the complaint was from the Left against the Right it took fourteen months to dismiss, and then only under threat of court action. But when the complaint was from the Right against the Left, it was dismissed in less than a week.

The National Right to Work Committee, believing that it had a case, took the matter to federal court on November 3. Judge Harold Richey of the District of Columbia Federal Court ruled in favor of the National Right to Work Committee on April 17, 1979.[5] That ruling is now on appeal. Regardless of the final outcome, the Right to Work complaint that the FEC dismissed in record time obviously did have some substance to it. The complaint against the NCEC, however, was not pursued in the courts, adding to the suspicion that it was filed only for political polemics.

The point is that the FEC became the forum for legitimizing complaints during the heat of an election campaign. One can only speculate how these 1976 charges, which were aired in Denver newspapers and radio and television stations, affected the race between Ed Scott and Rep. Tim Wirth (D-Colo.). Scott lost to Wirth by only 2,482 votes.[6]

CSFC had a similar experience in a 1976 primary in Oklahoma. One of the Republican candidates for the fifth congressional district nomination, former Oklahoma Attorney General G. T. Blankenship, filed a complaint charging that CSFC had illegally given funds to his opponent, Mickey Edwards. Blankenship alleged illegality because while director of CSFC, I also served as a part-time assistant to Senator Carl T. Curtis of Nebraska. That complaint was frivolous because congressional employees do not come under the Hatch Act, as the complaint had implied. Nevertheless, Blankenship built the FEC complaint into one of the few issues between himself and Edwards. Time and again the local newspapers, which did not favor Edwards, gave it prominent attention. CSFC demanded a prompt ruling from the FEC. Counsel Harrison even contacted FEC Chairman Vernon Thompson by phone to explain to him what was happening. Still we got no action. The primary was held, and Edwards won, avoiding a run-off by only seventy votes. The FEC dismissed the Blankenship complaint eleven days after the primary saying the matter was not within its jurisdiction.

It would have been a grave injustice to Edwards if he had been forced into a run-off because of this charge. Edwards was an innocent

---

[5] Walther v. FEC, 78-2097 and 78-2193.

[6] "State Returns for Governor, Senate and House," *Congressional Quarterly,* vol. 32 (1976), p. 838.

victim, merely the recipient of our help. Even if CSFC had been violating the law, Edwards would not have had to return the money in this instance, but he received great amounts of bad publicity because of this case. The case shows again how the FEC is now used to make damaging charges during the last part of campaigns.

The FEC has had a great influence on the way candidates and PACs must operate. There were similar cases in 1978, but thanks to our experiences in 1976 we were better able to advise our candidates on how to handle them. Other committees without our experience were put on the defensive by FEC complaints raised as issues.

Role of Richard Viguerie

The Campaign Reform Act of 1974 has had another unusual effect which its proponents surely did not intend: it made Richard Viguerie a power in American politics. Richard Viguerie is the president and owner of the Richard A. Viguerie Company (RAVCO), a direct mail marketing firm in Falls Church, Virginia. He is often pictured by his political enemies as a behind-the-scenes power broker who controls nearly every conservative group in America.[7] In truth, Viguerie raises funds for only a small number of groups that can be classified as New Right. Even Morton Blackwell, who worked for Viguerie for many years, used another direct mail firm to raise funds for the Committee for Responsible Youth Politics (CRYP), which he founded. Nevertheless, Viguerie does raise funds for CSFC, the National Conservative Political Action Committee (NCPAC), and the Conservative Caucus, three of the most prominent conservative groups.

CSFC was forced to turn to an operation such as the Viguerie Company for help precisely as the result of the 1974 act. CSFC was formed six months before the Reform Act of 1974 went into effect, and the Viguerie Company did its fund raising for those six months; cash was needed for the 1974 elections, and a direct mail firm with the names of identified conservative contributors was the most expedient means of getting it. The committee's first contract with the Viguerie Company covered only the period through the 1974 elections. Had there been no act in 1974, the CSFC, after establishing its credibility, could have persuaded several major contributors to back its work in 1975 and then established another kind of fund-raising program, avoiding direct mail altogether. The act, however, took the large contributor out of the political process. Consequently, CSFC had no alternative but to turn to direct mail to seek out the small contributor. It is vastly more

---

[7] *The Right Wing Machine,* AFL–CIO film, 1978.

expensive, especially in the nonelection year, to raise funds from small contributors.

Since we had to become dependent upon small contributors, CSFC naturally wanted the firm that could produce the best results from them. At the time that was without a doubt the Richard A. Viguerie Company. The fact that RAVCO did raise a great deal of money, and did it through the use of "tough" rhetoric, gained a certain amount of prominence for Viguerie, who up to that point had not been much of a public figure. It is ironic that the election reformers who are now busy devising ways of taking Richard Viguerie out of the political process have only themselves to blame for putting him there in the first place. Their "reform" law created the circumstances that made this sort of operation the only alternative for most kinds of noncorporate or nonunion political action. Some promoters of a Kennedy-for-President write-in campaign have now turned to the use of direct mail (the columnists Germond and Witcover called it a "Richard Viguerie of the Left" operation) for the same reasons.[8]

Unrealistic Contribution Limits

The other aspect of the law that has been troublesome to the CSFC is the $5,000 limit per PAC per campaign, though, I must confess, it is often handy to invoke such a limit when pressured by friendly members of Congress to give more money to what we know to be a losing campaign. In seriousness, however, this limit is highly restrictive and should be raised or, better still, abolished altogether. The CSFC, for example, does not ordinarily give cash to candidates it helps; it gives in-kind contributions or services to a campaign. The committee begins with candidate training schools, which are a week long and have as instructors some twenty of the most skilled political operatives in different disciplines.

Impact on CSFC. The current cost of the school for the 1979–1980 season is $500. That means if the CSFC desires a candidate and a campaign manager to attend and wishes to make that a part of its in-kind contribution to a candidate, the committee will have spent a fifth of the total allotment for an election, or $1,000, just for that item. If the CSFC decides to contribute air fare, it might cost another $500.

Once a candidate has attended the CSFC school, the committee follows up with field visits. Each visit, an in-kind contribution costing an average of about $300, is designed to ensure that what has been

---

[8] Jules Germond and Jack Witcover, column in the Sunday Notebook, *Washington Star*, July 8, 1979.

learned at the school is properly implemented. Ideally, a field man should visit a campaign every ten days or so, but visits are often limited to conserve money for other essential campaign work. Five hundred dollars per month is often contributed toward a trained person to work in the campaign. If the candidate has attended the school at CSFC expense, and if there have been a number of field visits to the campaign and several more are scheduled before the election date, then it becomes obvious that CSFC can contribute at the rate of $500 per month for only a few months before reaching the maximum dollar amount allowed under the law. What is more, $500 meant one thing in 1974, when the act was passed, but it means quite another thing in 1979, when inflation is running at more than 10 percent a year.

Unlike most business PACs, the CSFC becomes heavily involved in primaries. Some primaries—in fact nearly half of them—occur before August. Suppose the CSFC supports a candidate in Illinois, which has a March primary, and is successful in helping that candidate win the primary. The committee will want to keep a trained staff person there until the general election in November. But since the staffer is subsidized at the rate of $500 per month, the CSFC must either keep field men out of the campaign, which is counterproductive, or force the candidate's campaign committee to pick up some of the additional cost for keeping the staff person in the campaign. Some campaigns, just after a primary, are not able to face that prospect.

Impact on Other PACs. CSFC happens to deal primarily in the art of organizational politics. Organizational work is one of the least expensive aspects of a campaign. Media, survey research, and direct mail promotion are three expensive parts of a well-run campaign, especially if the campaign extends over a fairly long period of time and the opponent is an incumbent whose name identification is high. Some other PACs, such as the National Conservative Political Action Committee, do a great deal of their work in some of these areas, and the $5,000 limitation hurts their ability to do creative work. It will hurt more as time goes on, since the costs of media work, especially, are rising with each election.

That is one of the reasons why some committees such as NCPAC are turning to independent expenditures for their campaign efforts. It is difficult for a bipartisan multicandidate committee such as CSFC or NCPAC to have no contact with a given candidate in a given state or congressional district, but it can be done. Where there has been no contact, a PAC (or an individual for that matter) is not bound by the limits imposed by Congress and may spend as much money in a district as it wishes for such a project. In 1976 NCPAC spent as much as

$50,000 in independent expenditures in a single race, and it plans to do so again in some Senate races in 1980.

The CSFC, on the other hand, prefers to work directly with the campaigns and candidates themselves. The committee feels that most losses are the result of poor campaign management, the failure to write a good strategy and implement it, and the failure to build a good precinct organization. Indeed, the postelection analysis conference conducted by the Free Congress Research and Education Foundation concluded that the adherence to a coherent and well-implemented strategy was perhaps the most significant difference between the close winners and close losers in 1978 House races.[9]

Most of the other New Right campaign committees give cash. An exception is the Committee for Responsible Youth Politics, which trains young people for youth campaigns and places them in the various races. The CSFC stresses that people can take the place of money and be more effective. Most congressional campaigns that have 2,000 or more volunteers working effectively on a well-conceived plan will be successful. It costs little money to recruit these people, and a lot less money to keep them working productively than it does to accomplish a similar outreach by other means.

Advantages of an Incumbent. The greatest obstacles to be faced occur when a challenger wants to run against an incumbent who is skilled in the use of his congressional perquisites. The Americans for Democratic Action (ADA) has estimated that these congressional perks are worth a half million dollars per year.[10] In a two-year term, that amounts to a million dollars working against the challenger, even *before* the incumbent has spent a dime on his own reelection campaign.

One member of the House, who represents a very compact district in a city, has six neighborhood offices; is it any wonder that, though he first won with less than 50 percent of the vote in 1976, he was reelected with more than 80 percent in 1978? A challenger candidate faces the incumbent's newsletters, district offices, mobile vans with name displays in foot-high letters, WATS lines, and a staff of twenty who represent him when he is not available, plus the news value of incumbency. A member of Congress can get constant coverage in the newspapers and on the radio with his press releases and comments on

---

[9] Susan M. Marshner, *Unity and Diversity: A Comparative Look at the Close Elections in 1978* (Washington, D.C.: Free Congress Research and Education Foundation, 1979).

[10] "Advantages of an Incumbent Seeking Re-election," staff study, Americans for Democratic Action, October 1977.

current events. A candidate, however, is seldom covered until the election is hot news, just before the primary and just before the general election.

Taxpayer Financing

Incumbents' Welfare. Those of us who adamantly oppose taxpayer financing of congressional campaigns charge that this proposal is an incumbents' welfare bill. The incumbents now have all the advantages, especially in districts where no single medium can reach all the voters, or where the single media market is New York, Chicago, Philadelphia, or some other terribly expensive place.

Just to equal the name recognition of the aggressive House incumbent now takes at least $150,000 in a typical House campaign—merely to get across the idea that the candidate exists. All of the taxpayer financing proposals so far introduced have some expenditure limit, and the U.S. Supreme Court has upheld the concept of expenditure limits for presidential candidates if they accept federal funds.

Some of the new members of Congress would not be in office today had an expenditure limit been imposed on their campaigns. Representative Martin Frost, a liberal Democrat who defeated the more conservative Representative Dale Milford in the Texas Democratic primary, has openly stated that he is against taxpayer financing for the very reason that an expenditure limitation would have denied him victory. In Frost's case, of course, the bills which have been seriously proposed thus far would not have applied, because taxpayer financing has been proposed only for general elections and not for primaries—another reason such legislation is inequitable.

The taxpayer financing proposals, although temporarily dead in this session of Congress, will be revived again soon and will remain the number one goal of the major labor unions and liberal groups such as Common Cause. Beyond their rhetoric, it is clear that such proposals seek not to "purify" the political process by diluting the strength of PACs and large contributors, but to retain those currently in power, who happen to be responsive to the point of view of the unions and liberal groups.

United Front. The New Right, although less united on campaigns and candidates than its liberal critics suggest, is nonetheless unanimous on the question of taxpayer financing. It would knock the New Right out of the political process, because candidates would probably have an incentive to take small contributions and would be penalized for taking contributions from PACs.

An additional element is the inequitable application of campaign restrictions to the activities of unions. None of the major proposals would restrict the unions' indirect contributions to candidates, such as communicating to their membership who the "good" and "bad" guys are, registering their own members to vote, and taking them to the polls. All taxpayer financing proposals thus far would restrict corporate and New Right (as well as liberal) PACs, but would have left the unions to do political business as usual, further shifting the balance of political power toward incumbents and away from challengers.

Fundamentally, however, the New Right challenges taxpayer financing on principle. It is simply not in the American tradition, and from our viewpoint it is immoral to take money out of the pockets of taxpayers who support and believe in one candidate and place it in the pocket of a candidate they oppose. It is true that all sorts of tax dollars are spent for purposes to which everyone objects. It is quite a different matter, however, to spend those tax dollars to help elect the very people who will determine how further tax dollars are to be spent.

Special Interests. The argument is made that taxpayer financing would remove special interests from politics. That would not happen under any of the current proposals, because some of the special interests, namely the unions, would remain unaffected by the bill. Only business-oriented special interests and ideological committees would be hindered. This suits the objectives of those who are pushing the legislation; it would result in leaving the liberal incumbents in power while hampering their opposition, perhaps permanently.

Federal Intervention. The worst that can be said of taxpayer-financed election legislation is that it would unfairly remove some special interests from the political process and replace them with the power of the federal government. That is a far more dangerous situation than the present one, where various groups have influence with this or that member of Congress.

What the federal government finances, the federal government regulates. The arbitrary manner in which the FEC influences elections has already been discussed. One has only to imagine the situation in which a candidate depends upon federal funds for his election. The incumbent could bring down the weight of the federal establishment on the challenger in the midst of the election for failure to comply with dozens of federal laws and regulations, promulgated by the incumbents to keep themselves in office and the challengers out. Furthermore, the incumbent has a large taxpayer-supported staff to help him cope with these regulations. The challenger, on the other hand, cannot have unlimited legal help if he conforms to the limitations imposed for accepting federal funds.

One dislikes making futuristic jokes in Washington, because the most outrageous things have a way of coming to pass five years later. It has been suggested that the day will come when an incumbent has the Equal Employment Opportunity Commission intervene against a challenger because that candidate, having accepted federal funds, failed to employ a black lesbian Episcopalian priest on his campaign staff. The example may be extreme, but the threat is there nevertheless. It is one reason the New Right, if it is united on anything, will fight taxpayer funding of campaigns to the end.

PAC "Collusion"

It was stated above that the New Right is not as united on candidates and campaigns as the opposition would have the public believe. Members of the New Right often are on different sides in primaries. Even more frequently, one or two groups will get into a primary, and the others will sit it out. Only when there is a clear-cut ideological contest in the general election do more than a few New Right groups participate in the same campaign.

The CSFC helped Democrat Kent Hance in his general election contest against Republican George Bush for a House seat in Texas, when most other conservative groups either supported Bush or did not participate. The CSFC was virtually alone in supporting Bill Royer in the primary for the California special election in early 1979 for the seat held by the late Leo Ryan; Royer was opposed by other conservative candidates, whom CSFC knew were not well enough organized to make it to the runoff. In the runoff, most other conservative groups joined in supporting Royer.

The law precludes joint decision making on the part of the PACs. However, once a decision has been made by one PAC, others are allowed to work together to carry it out. Helping to make the initial decision is considered collusion, but I know of no violation of that law. The law does permit PACs to share information. Toward that end, Morton Blackwell has for years hosted a luncheon every other week to which candidates may come and talk directly to twenty or twenty-five conservative PACs at one time. At these meetings various PAC representatives trade information regarding campaigns around the nation.

The Blackwell luncheons are particularly useful in showing us how a candidate reacts to a group situation and how he answers questions in front of the whole pack of PACs, so to speak. Candidates are skilled at telling a PAC director what he wants to hear in a one-on-one interview, but they cannot be so flexible when many PACs are representing such diverse issues such as right-to-life and gun control.

The information exchange effort is of limited value, frankly, because what the PAC directors have to share is often old, based on rumor, or the product of a partisan mind and therefore not objective. The CSFC relies much more heavily on a field team for accurate reports because those workers have been taught what to look for. In addition, under my direction the Free Congress Research and Education Foundation has inaugurated a weekly *Political Report* which has both a full-time editor and a full-time reporter. These two staff people spend their entire week on the phone, doing as many as thirty interviews per story, and consequently turning out timely, accurate, and reliable information on interesting races. The FCF publishes the information, making it available to anyone who wishes to subscribe, so it does not have the character of a private political intelligence report. There are no secrets, and the publication strives for a realistic view. To find out what is really happening in a district or state, there is no substitute for having someone on the scene to do good old-fashioned reportorial work.

Single-Interest Groups: Symptom of Party Weakness

As noted, single-issue groups play a significant role at the Blackwell luncheons. No discussion of 1980 politics would be complete without the mention of the single-issue groups and their relationship to the New Right.

Single-issue groups are not new. Throughout the 1960s and 1970s, single-issue PACs were devoted to the war in Vietnam and to environmental and consumerist concerns. Now groups have been formed around some issues that are conservative, and, suddenly, single-issue groups have become controversial. Thus, as in the case of the Richard Viguerie phenomenon, the Federal Election Campaign Act of 1974 wrought something it did not intend—a proliferation of PACs and an incentive for like-minded citizens to form political action committees on a single issue.

These groups—some of which deal with right-to-life and family matters, with gun ownership, with unions, and with energy questions—support only a candidate who is "right" on their issue and related questions. Otherwise, they may go all out against the candidate.

In my view, this development is the direct result of the decline of political parties. At one time in American politics, the parties stood for something, even if it was merely something as simple as free silver or the repeal of Prohibition. But now it is difficult to determine what the political parties stand for. The Democratic chairman of the Senate Foreign Relations Committee and its ranking Republican member are both strong supporters of the SALT treaty, as they also were of the Panama Canal Treaty. The presidents both of the freshman Republican class and of the freshman Democratic class in the ninety-sixth Congress in the House participated in the fifth anniversary celebration dinner for CSFC on July 12, 1979. In fact, the Democrat was a speaker on the program.

People no longer think in terms of parties or party position when they are looking for answers to their concerns. Consequently people who feel strongly about an issue form a group to promote their view. As the parties continue to decline, and as the party leadership continues to refuse to take positions on issues of special concern to the ordinary citizen, special groups will continue to emerge.

Since most of the newer special groups relate to conservative issues, we should watch to see whether the New Right can develop a working coalition of these groups. Thus far the New Right has been able to develop such a coalition around some candidates. As a New Right political action committee, CSFC has kept informed of the activities of a wide range of special-interest groups and special-interest PACs— which, as mentioned above, is entirely legal. Part of the committee's strategy has been to help each special-interest group attain maximum productivity among its own constituency, and within its own sphere of influence. Separate interest groups operating independently in a campaign but with a common purpose, namely the election or defeat of a given candidate, can coordinate their activities. The goal is to be sure that the activities do not interfere with the overall strategy of the campaign they support. The CSFC has been successful in Washington in getting some of these groups to form coalitions around individual issues, such as taxpayer financing.

The country could be governed much more easily if various single-interest groups formed a more-or-less permanent coalition, the way Franklin D. Roosevelt formed the coalition among the unions, the minorities, and the South. Each of these groups had a different reason to support the F.D.R. coalition, but they had enough of the same objectives to keep them glued together for decades.

Many of us in the New Right seek a similar coalition. We feel that if there were a real second party in this country, the nation would be better off, regardless whether this party were in control or in opposition. Different factions within the New Right have differing opinions on how this second party can be developed. Some believe New Right views can surface as the dominant force in the Republican party; others believe that the conservative part of the Democratic party, which is surprisingly large, can once more become dominant. I think that the only way such a new force will come about is through a coalition of the conservative parts of both political parties, allied with the special groups.

Such a coalition can eventually become the dominant party and win elections. Meanwhile, with the absence of such a coalition and with the rise in strength of the various special groups, the nation will become increasingly difficult to govern. That, I believe is unfortunate, and that is why I believe in trying to work toward a meaningful coalition that can develop a real program for change in America.

Commentaries

Stephen W. Thomas

While political action committees existed long before the Federal Election Campaign Act, their recent and rapid proliferation since the law was enacted has raised a number of questions about the role of PACs in the electoral process.

If for the moment we set aside considerations of ideology, political purpose, and sources of funding, all PACs can be said to share certain features. They represent an effort through the accumulation of economic power to influence the outcome of elections, to establish favorable relations with elected officials, or to do both.

It can easily be argued that such activity conflicts with the notion of "one man, one vote" and represents a distortion of democratic government. But that is to level criticism on the basis of an ideal that no democratic society has ever approached. Even if public elections were fully financed with public funds, economic bias would not be eliminated. It would simply be bureaucratized, with consequences that we cannot adequately foresee.

Certainly as long as private funds are used to finance public elections, the political action committee has a legitimate role to play. To the extent that PACs broaden popular participation in financing elections, they also contribute to the health of the political system. It is this consideration—the desirability of democratizing campaign finance—that makes the limits on individual contributions essential. Labor PACs have always raised their campaign funds from large numbers of people, not only because their membership is large but also because their individual members are not wealthy. This is far less true of "ideological" or self-styled "public interest" PACs, which solicit predominantly from upper-middle and middle-class contributors. It is probably least true of business PACs, which have access to a predominantly affluent constituency.

The present limit of $1,000 on an individual's contribution to a political action committee serves two purposes. It encourages committees with a primarily affluent constituency to structure their fund-

82

raising activities in order to reach a larger number of contributors than they might without the limits. The contribution limits also establish rough economic ground rules for competition between conflicting political interests.

On the grounds of both broadening popular participation and establishing a more equitable basis for competition, a strong case can be made for lowering the limits on individual contributions to $500 and possibly to $100. Such a reduction would go a long way toward equalizing the economic base from which political action committees derive their political influence.

A second provision of the law, which limits to $5,000 per election the amount that a PAC may contribute to any one candidate, is aimed at placing an overall limit on the extent of influence that any one committee may exercise on an election. Not surprisingly, individual PACs have attempted to surmount this limitation in a variety of ways. By carefully scrutinizing the actual budgetary needs of a campaign, by weighing the closeness of the race, and by contributing early, especially during a primary, a PAC can substantially increase the impact of its contribution. Some PACs have substituted in-kind contributions in the form of campaign consulting to increase their impact on a campaign.

Finally there is a natural tendency for PACs that share a common political interest to rally to the same candidate. If BIPAC contributes to a candidate, its action may well trigger, or at least encourage, contributions to the same candidate from other business PACs. Similarly, a candidate who receives support from COPE is virtually assured to some level of funding from other labor PACs.

It is the impact of PAC contributions in their aggregate that has prompted a demand that the limit on contributions by PACs be lowered from $5,000. In defense of PAC contributions is the fact that they represent a large number of people and are therefore entitled to a higher contribution limit. If this argument has validity, it only gains strength as the base of a PAC's economic support—the number of its contributing members—is broadened.

What this argument does not address is the fact that control of dispersing contributions is often left to the officers of the PAC, that through the contributions of many a very few individuals are able to accumulate major political influence. Of course, in raising funds a PAC must make a statement of its overall objectives, and if its subsequent actions are in obvious conflict with those objectives, it will rapidly lose its contributing membership. Nevertheless, in most cases a great deal of flexibility is left to PAC officials regarding which candidates to support and to what extent.

One way to resolve this dilemma is the method of fund raising that my own committee, the Council for a Livable World, has employed since it was established in 1962. It is not a method of fund raising that would be suitable for every PAC, but it is certainly a method that could be adopted to good advantage by some.

The council raises its funds through voluntary contributions from some 12,000 supporters scattered throughout the entire country. Solicitation is primarily by mail, eight to ten letters a year, and occasionally by telephone. The council supports candidates for the United States Senate only, and is normally involved in a substantial effort in six to ten Senate campaigns in any election year.

What is distinctive about our fund raising is that control of contributions to candidates rests with the individual contributor, rather than with the soliciting committee. A normal fund-raising letter will recommend two or three candidates for support and will also ask for contributions to the council to meet our own operating expenses. We provide a profile of each candidate who is recommended, a profile of the opponent, and a brief description of the race. The appeal concludes with the statement:

> Unless you have a preference to the contrary, please make your check payable to:
>
> *X for Senate Committee* if your last name begins with one of the letters A–G.
>
> *Y for Senate Committee* if your last name begins with one of the letters H–P.
>
> *Council for a Livable World* if your last name begins with one of the letters Q–Z.

Contributors send all contributions to us in a return envelope. We in turn bundle the contributions and forward them to the appropriate campaign.

The recipient of such an appeal is free to exercise personal discretion in supporting any candidate recommended. Some members simply contribute according to the recommendation, but many contribute to another candidate recommended in the letter or to the council. Some will contribute to all recommended candidates in a mailing, preferring to divide their resources.

The normal response rate to a mailing is 10 to 15 percent. While contributors often exercise a preference contrary to our recommendations, these individual decisions usually tend to cancel each other out so that the alphabetical division of the membership list is a fairly accurate basis for allocating anticipated contributions to different campaigns.

Under the Federal Election Campaign Act, the reporting requirements for such "pooled" contributions are identical with the requirements for earmarked contributions. All contributions regardless of size must be reported along with the contributor's name and address (and occupation and place of business if the contribution is in excess of $100), the ultimate beneficiary, and the dates when the contribution was received by the committee and when it was forwarded to the campaign. In turn the campaign must report the same information plus the name of the committee from which the contributions were forwarded.

Perhaps the most striking feature of this method of fund raising is the way in which it relates to the limits on PAC contributions imposed by the Federal Election Campaign Act. Individual contributions made payable directly to the campaign committee of a congressional candidate are attributed to the contributor's limits. No member or supporter of a PAC may contribute over $1,000 to a candidate in any election, but there is no limit on the aggregate of such individual contributions that a PAC may stimulate. The PAC's contribution is the cost of the mailing, or the appropriate portion of that cost, which is reported as a contribution in kind to the candidate's committee.

Thus the committee serves as a catalyst, precipitating the political participation of many others. It is entirely possible with this method of fund raising to encourage individual contributions to a political candidate that may total $10,000, $20,000, $30,000 or more, and yet keep mailing costs, which constitute the committee's contribution to the candidate's campaign, within the $5,000 limit.

Some cautionary notes are in order. I have already indicated that this method of fund raising will not be suitable for all PACs.

Perhaps the fundamental issue is that of control. If a PAC solicits by mail or telephone and the membership is in no sense obligated to the PAC officers in an economic or any other way, then the control of dispersal clearly rests with the contributor. If there is an employer-employee relationship between the PAC officials and the membership, then the picture may become clouded, particularly because the PAC is required by law to maintain records of individual contributions.

A secondary consideration is the nature of the PAC's political activity. The council limits its major support to six to ten Senate candidates in any election year. That number accommodates itself very nicely to our mailing program. A PAC, however, that solicits on behalf of ten or fifteen Senate candidates and forty to sixty House candidates faces a very different problem. Under these circumstances encouragement of individual contributions to a particular candidate becomes unmanageable through the mails. There is, of course, an offsetting factor. Such a committee is already likely to limit its contributions to individual candidates to $5,000 or less.

If the method of fund raising that I have outlined here is not suitable for all PACs, it should provide an attractive option for some. To the extent that any method of fund raising broadens popular participation in financing elections, it will also contribute to the health of the political system.

Larry Pratt

How do you regulate freedom—in this case, freedom of speech and of the political process? Theoretically, there is no obvious answer. Practically, the solution is, "However it benefits the regulator."

That is the way I think an analysis of the Federal Election Commission (FEC) has to proceed. Congress responded to the perception of public concern about morality in government in the aftermath of Watergate with the time-honored solution—"pass a law." We should not be surprised that the members of Congress did not intentionally enact a law that worked against themselves, posturings to the contrary notwithstanding.

The perception of Watergate was that people in Washington were abusing public power. Congressmen control abundant public power. The Federal Election Campaign Act (FECA) is a good example of shifting the point of the question. Instead of insisting that government officials, whether elected or in the civil service, obey existing law, Congress passed a law that mainly restricts the ability of people not in government to get into government. In other words, the principle applied was: "What's mine is mine, and what's yours is negotiable."

The traditional idea of law in the United States is that it should apply equally to all, or else it is a bad law and should be repealed, assuming it was enacted in the first place. The FEC, try as it may (or may not), has been unable to establish uniform criteria for all candidates, for all committees, or even for particular candidates and committees over a period of time. Whenever an unpredictable decision is finally handed down, an inordinate amount of time has often been allowed to go by in a campaign which by definition cannot tolerate the cumbersome, time consuming, decision-making processes of a bureaucracy.

Gun Owners of America (GOA) found this out at first hand, when it was fined $11,000 for its trouble in scrupulously seeking minute advice from the FEC, sometimes on a daily basis. This is the story: in 1976, the GOA Campaign Committee was sharing its office space and its administrative personnel with the Gun Owners of California Campaign

Committee and the GOA Legislative Action Fund. This sharing of both the overhead and the administrative expenses had been approved verbally by several FEC staff personnel.

A letter from the special counsel of the FEC to GOA had also approved a formula for the distribution of these costs. At this time, the three groups of Gun Owners attempted to estimate what share of the overhead expenses each group should pay. The initial calculation—15 percent to the GOA Legislative Action Fund, 40 percent to the Gun Owners of California Campaign Committee, and 45 percent to the GOA Campaign Committee—turned out to be incorrect. The actual calculation of the shared expenses was not determined until an independent audit in July 1977. As a result, it turned out that both the Gun Owners of California Campaign Committee and the GOA Legislative Action Fund (mostly made up of corporate funds) had overpaid the actual amount owed. Those sums were paid back by the GOA Campaign Committee.

The FEC, through the office of its general counsel, advised GOA that it did not consider the FEC bound by its own informal advice. An approved procedure thus suddenly became an alleged violation. It was then decided that rather than continue to maintain a high visibility over the issue—and thus inject irrelevant matters into campaigns GOA would be involved in—it was more convenient to pay the fines and sign conciliation agreements indicating that there were no intentional violations of FECA. Talk about a chilling effect! Who would want to win a case and lose thirty campaigns from adverse publicity?

The chilling effect of FEC procedures is pervasive. It has now reached the point that "What if?" questions can no longer be raised without reference to what a particular campaign or committee actually is contemplating. The choice, then, is either to take the risk of "telegraphing" privileged information and then to wait for many, many weeks before doing anything (except perhaps to lose an election), or to proceed on the assumption that this is really a free country, and then risk getting fined or going to jail.

As John Bolton pointed out last year,[1] the FEC has earned a reputation for producing inconsistent regulations without explanation. To rule without giving reasons, however, is to rule unaccountably.

I found David Jessup's treatise on democratizing influence to be most provocative. Political influence is sought in an inherently competitive process. Further attempts to legislate a democratization of resources are likely to take us down the already unhappy road taken by the FEC.

---

[1] John Bolton, "Government Astride the Political Process—The Federal Election Commission," *Regulation* (July/August 1978), pp. 46-55.

If the goal of our society is to be that of equality of resources rather than that of equality of treatment under the law, then we will witness an acceleration of the polarization of American politics that so many observers have mentioned. The attempt to legislate an equality of resources dramatically raises the stakes of politics. It is no wonder that as the resource-equalitarian impulse proceeds, political action committees (PACs) proliferate. The reason for the fact that multinational corporations have tended to remain aloof from the political process by not forming PACs may indeed be as Jessup suggests: that they can avoid the nuisance of meddling bureaucrats better than the smaller company forced to stand and fight. On this point, Jessup seems to underscore Budde's argument that PACs are a response to government, and not to the opportunity of the new law.

Jessup, understandably, finds it easier to spot internal divisiveness on his own side reflected in the role of the unions rather than apparent within the business community. In fact, however, business cannot play the political game as well as the unions do. The union movement is known for remembering its friends and for playing hardball politics.

To view the business community in the same light is to be off the mark. Business is often all too willing to cooperate in deepening their entanglement in the same regulatory web that they complain about at the Rotary Club.

To give but one example, a leading gun manufacturer went on record in support of gun control—only temporarily, I should add. The company only backed down in the face of the strong, vocal opposition of consumers. A look at the pattern of that company's sales reveals that it would probably end up with a near monopoly of the hand gun market if private sales were restricted, because it is so prominent in government sales. In spite of the company's rhetoric supporting gun control, it is not unfair to place more weight on their anticipation of satisfying their market appetites through the exercise of public power for their private benefit.

Mr. Jessup overplays his hand in denigrating the ability of unions to compete politically with business. It is rather misleading to emphasize difficulties in getting out the vote when so many millions of dollars are spent for that kind of nonreportable political activity—apparently with fair results in the Congress for a movement that Jessup complains represents a mere one-quarter of the workforce.

As if the regulation of political speeches in a campaign situation were not bad enough, Jessup is further proposing that all speeches directed to the subjects of public policy and of public officials be similarly registered.

I submit that the unions who joined an ad hoc lobbying effort to defeat the Alaska land seizure might never have enjoyed such an opportunity if they had had to register their lobbying effort at the grass roots, presumably with a Federal Lobbying Commission modeled after the FEC. I nevertheless agree with Jessup that unions can be a bulwark against the leftists who would eliminate the economic and recreational uses of public lands to satisfy the intellectual fancies of a class unconcerned with the need to make ends meet. Jessup, however, is also proposing measures that would work against what he himself wants. The regulation of lobbying at the grass roots would be as obnoxious in principle and as chilling in practice as is the present FEC.

I cannot agree that the financing of congressional elections by the taxpayer is anything but protectionism for incumbents. There is no public support for such a boondoggle, as a recent survey indicates.[2] The bottom line of financing by the taxpayer is represented by limits on expenditures—say $200,000 for each candidate. The incumbent, however, has two years to spend his $1,000,000 worth of public relations perks from his office, and $1,200,000 weighing in against $200,000 is not really a fair fight. The incumbent will campaign while drawing his government salary. A challenger will have to leave his job if he works for a corporation. In addition, he will have to fend for himself against an FEC that makes life difficult for independents, losers, and campaign committees unattached to incumbents—and in general for anyone who cannot vote against the FEC.

The country would be better off without an FEC and with a campaign law that required the filing of expenditures and receipts with the General Accounting Office (GAO), as previously. Filings should only be required for receipts over $1,000 in order to remove some of the possibility of intimidation by incumbents of constituents who contribute against them. If we really need to know who has contributed over the lesser sum of $100, we are saying our elected officials can be bought very cheaply indeed. Contribution limits should at least be raised, if not eliminated. The argument that free speech is for hire without limits cannot answer the real threat of tyranny by those in control of a governmental regulatory machinery that enforces controls by throwing people in jail. We can surely agree that the jailing of political opponents is more obnoxious than Clement Stone's $2,000,000 contribution to Nixon.

Walter Moore of the National Committee for an Effective Congress (NCEC) makes a noteworthy point—that the FECA has forced com-

---

[2] Civic Service, Inc., "Attitudes toward Campaign Financing—A Nationwide Public Opinion Sampling" (St. Louis, Mo.: Civic Service, Inc., March 1979).

mittees such as his own and the GOA into the expensive alternative of replacing large donors with direct mail solicitations which are usually in the $10 to $15 range. Without financial limits, or at least with substantially higher limits, issue-oriented committees could avoid a good deal of the expense of their operation. Before we come down too hard on the cost of direct mail fund raising, however, it should also be pointed out that this vehicle has involved more people in the political process than ever before.

Those who argue for the financing of congressional elections by the taxpayer are advancing a proposal that is almost guaranteed to tremendously reduce, if not to eliminate, this new participation in politics. Moore himself seems to argue against this involvement by citing the NCEC suit against the congressional campaign committees set up by various potential (and some now actual) presidential candidates. These committees will have no doubt increased identification by the public of the names of such presidential candidates. A good deal of good will for the candidate's own campaign will also have resulted from these efforts. What is wrong with this? I think it is very positive if these committees offer a legal way around the arbitrary limits imposed on campaign expenditures for presidential elections, so that a candidate has a chance to get elected in spite of the law. The NCEC should be looking for more ways to get numerous private contributions into the political process rather than try to close them off. Once private dollars are effectively shut off, the result will be pressure for funding by the taxpayer through an even bigger and even more irresponsible FEC.

Moore refers to the near impossibility of finding out what was discussed by the FEC during a compliance decision. Even other departments of the FEC do not necessarily know what transpired during such a debate. No wonder, then, that the FEC is so inconsistent in so many of its rulings. Moore goes on to point out that Congress is the only "industry" in the country to write its own regulations. Again, I think the best way out of this impasse would be to abolish the FEC and return the enforcement of actual law breaking to the Justice Department. That step would restrict most campaign violations to libels and to violations of postal regulations. We will not have really free elections until free speech is itself free of the threat of conflicting federal felony charges and convictions that await the hapless candidate or committee unable to afford enough accountants and lawyers.

Moore also points out that NCEC has refrained from a particular suit because of the expense involved. GOA considered the same problem when they were set upon by the FEC. What proportion of a committee's funds—funds raised from contributors—should be expended on legal fees, and how much should go to the elections that, were it not for the FEC, could be the sole purpose of the committee's existence?

A good idea for a partial solution is NCEC's proposal to exclude the first $5,000 of an individual's contributions to a multi-candidate committee for the purpose of defraying administrative, legal, and accounting costs.

Bernadette Budde's description of the bureaucratic nature of decision making by corporate PACs, coupled with a look at the tendency of such PACs to give more money to incumbent Democrats who are also backed by unions, should, as a practical matter, allay the fears of both Democrats and of union leaders. I have also not heard of business groups being able to compete with the justly famed professionally run phone banks of the unions. In the light of what actually happens, Jessup's support for the hamstringing of PACs, and financing of elections by the taxpayer, really is an overkill. Businessmen are on the whole a rather timid group, and, as Budde points out, the prospect of being harassed by the FEC will probably keep many of them from getting involved in politics by forming a PAC.

Paul Weyrich believes that PACs formed around single issues tend to make the country more difficult to govern, and Jessup believes that certain issues (including those about guns), but not others (those involving unions) are part of some conservative conspiracy. Both observers seem to overlook the fact that one-issue groups are not a new phenomenon in American politics. Such groups represent one of the strengths of our system, rather than being a problem for government, or some sort of sinister threat. People can in fact organize to accomplish mutual objectives through a variety of ways, including political action. Groups such as GOA are a response by thousands of people to a common felt need. The only unhealthy thing about such groups is external to them—the constant danger they face from Congress and the FEC of being put out of business. If that should ever happen, the country may well become ungovernable, and witness the emergence of some sinister conspiracy operating outside the scope of a law drawn so tightly that only incumbent office holders will possess effective political rights.

William C. Oldaker

There are few areas of federal activity as sensitive as election campaign regulation. The Federal Election Commission (FEC) operates in the area of the most fundamental First Amendment rights and must be constantly attuned to the delicacy of the issues that come before it. We

91

therefore often find ourselves walking a tightrope between conflicting political and economic forces.

In such a situation it would be naive to think we could measure success in terms of praise. Perhaps the fact that on particular issues we sometimes find ourselves criticized by both ends of the political spectrum means we are on the right course. The papers presented here provide an apt example of the dilemma in which we often find ourselves. The National Committee for an Effective Congress (NCEC) criticizes us for allegedly not having proceeded to conciliation on any of its complaints, while the respondent in one of those complaints, the Committee for the Survival of a Free Congress (CSFC), accuses us of having taken too long in investigating the complaint's allegations. As Gilbert and Sullivan put it, "A policeman's lot is not a happy one."

While on the subject of the NCEC's criticism, I would like to set the record straight. One of the NCEC complaints, filed against the political action committees of the National Right to Work Committee and the Public Service Research Council, resulted in the filing of a civil action in U.S. District Court. Although the Public Service Research Council has entered into a conciliation agreement with the Commission, the suit is still pending against the National Right to Work Committee.

In assessing the FEC's impact on the electoral process, one should bear in mind that we have been navigating in uncharted waters. Although efforts to regulate the financing of federal campaigns can be traced to the Pendleton Act in the late nineteenth century and the Tillman Act of 1907, the establishment of the Federal Election Commission in 1975 marks the first comprehensive attempt to enforce campaign disclosure and contribution limitations in a single agency. Few prosecutions had been brought under the preceding legislation, the Federal Corrupt Practices Act of 1925, and this factor, combined with numerous loopholes in the statute itself, resulted in its provisions being virtually ignored by 1972 when the Federal Election Campaign Act was enacted. The abuses in the 1972 election further demonstrated the need for more comprehensive legislation and independent supervisory authority. To answer that need the FEC was created.

It was probably inevitable that an agency such as the FEC would have a difficult infancy, but not since the early days of the New Deal has an agency had a more difficult start. Its constitutionality was immediately challenged in *Buckley* v. *Valeo,* and the Court's decision in that case rendered the commission powerless through most of the spring of 1976. Once reconstituted in May, at the height of the first election in its history, the commission faced the challenge of writing an entire body of regulations and establishing new procedures based on the revisions in the act.

Considered against this background the FEC's record has been successful, although we certainly recognized the need for changes as we gained more experience. A problem of which we became especially aware in 1978 was the increase in complaints filed close to an election. Many of these were simultaneously made public by complainants. We recognized that to be fair to both parties. We had to decide prior to the election whether there was a reason to believe a violation had occurred. During the last two weeks of the general election campaign we therefore made a special effort to expedite consideration of complaints. With no increase in manpower, we were able to make an initial decision on almost all complaints filed prior to the general election.

The Committee for the Survival of a Free Congress's paper mentions as an example of partisanship our expeditious processing of a number of complaints filed on behalf of the National Right to Work Committee (NRTWC). In fact, our expeditious dismissal of those complaints was the result of the procedures instituted for all complaints during the preelection period. Another factor enabling us to act quickly on the complaints was the similarity of the legal issues in question to those presented in a complaint filed by the NRTWC in connection with the 1976 election. At that time we considered the NRTWC's allegations and arguments at length and determined that a violation had not occurred. Nothing presented in the 1978 complaints indicated a need to reconsider our previous determination.

I might also add that in the lawsuit against us which the CSFC mentions, our decision to dismiss the complaints was upheld by the district court. Characterizing the complaints as a "shambles" that offered "not a scintilla of evidence" to support the assertions made, Judge Richey found on June 14 that the commission's action had been "eminently reasonable" and granted summary judgment to the commission.

In addition to better handling of enforcement matters, processing of advisory opinion requests has been made more efficient. During 1978, 105 advisory opinions were drafted by a staff of two attorneys and two paralegals. All but 12 of these were issued within four to eight weeks after receipt. Recently new procedures for reviewing such requests were instituted, which promise to cut the processing time even further so that during 1980 we expect to issue most advisory opinions within three to four weeks after receipt of a complete written request.

In the heat of an election campaign it is of course difficult for candidates and committees to postpone action pending a response to a request for an advisory opinion. The statute, however, prohibits us from giving an opinion of an advisory nature outside the formal process. While we make every effort to answer information inquiries in as responsive a manner as possible, this restriction means that questions of first impression may only be addressed through the procedures required for a formal advisory opinion. As more opinions are issued, however, there will be a greater store of previous interpretations on which candidates and committees may make decisions.

We are also applying the experience we have gained since 1976 to revising our entire set of regulations, incorporating new material, and clarifying existing material. Revised regulations on primary matching funds were prescribed on May 7, and revised regulations for convention financing will be transmitted to Congress shortly. In addition, the commission has made several recommendations to Congress for changes that would simplify the requirements of the act. Many of these have been included in amendment bills to the Federal Election Commission Act recently reported in the House and Senate.

One of the greatest challenges facing the commission is maintaining impartiality. There is no more partisan activity than an election campaign and therefore it is all the more important that the commission scrupulously avoid even the appearance of partisan decision making. Being composed of three Democrats and three Republicans, the commission, of course, reflects varying political philosophies. It should be remembered, however, that any action by the commission requires an affirmative vote of at least four members. It is therefore impossible for one party to dominate decision making. Also, few questions the commission faces are really black-and-white partisan issues. Even if the immediate impact of a decision is on a particular political or economic interest, the precedential effect of the decision is likely to cross party or economic lines.

The commission will soon be concluding its fifth year in operation. When one compares the election climate of today with that prior to the FEC's creation, the difference is striking. Today there is full and reliable disclosure of campaign contributions and expenditures. A wealth of reliable information is provided to voters that was virtually non-existent in the past. Instead of campaign laws being ignored or evaded through loopholes, an extraordinary level of voluntary compliance has been achieved due in great part to a serious nonpartisan enforcement effort.

As we gain more experience, and as candidates and committees become more familiar with the law, a substantial body of administrative interpretations and case law is being amassed that will make compliance with the act easier for all concerned. While we are the first to acknowledge some difficulties in the past, our record of continual improvement and refinement makes us confident that the next five years will be a period of maturation in election law, of which we will be justly proud.

Authors' Replies

Walter K. Moore

I would like to respond to Mr. Oldaker's paper. I would applaud the improvement in the FEC over the last five years. A lot of complaints were voiced about the FEC after the experience of 1976, but fewer were heard after the experience of 1978. But one constant complaint of the people who give candidates and political committees information through the Information Office is that the Information Office does not generally have access to the discussions of the executive session of the FEC. My experience at the commission suggests that real, substantive decisions were more often made at executive sessions than through the advisory opinion process. Unfortunately, that means many candidates cannot be privy to the state of the law as it stands. These factors could change the outcome of elections. There are good reasons for the executive session at the commission, but at some time we will have to deal with how the law is being determined by decisions made after discussions in the executive sessions. The public needs to be informed of how those decisions are arrived at.

Aside from this, my only reservations concern our FEC complaint, which Mr. Pratt and I can go over.

Paul M. Weyrich

I would be remiss if I didn't comment on Mr. Jessup's contention that the New Right and the business PACs have a close relationship with each other because the New Right goes out early and then the business PACs come in later. It may work out that way on paper, and it is easy when you are not part of an overall ideological grouping to make judgments from outside about how it operates. I did the same thing when I analyzed the symbiotic relationship between certain labor unions and left-wing groups, and found later, when I became acquainted with the people involved, that my judgments were quite wrong.

Next to Mr. Jessup's organization, I would put many of the business PACs on the top of my list of enemies when it comes to practical political operation. The extent to which we have made any contribution in helping to elect people is the extent to which we have opposed business PACs especially in primary elections. In the case of Orrin Hatch, in the case of Gordon Humphrey, in the case of Roger Jepsen, in the case of dozens of members of the House, where we supported the tough conservative, the business PAC was always for the establishment, or for the moderate candidate, or it didn't want to be involved in the election at all, saying, "Well, either one of these candidates is acceptable to us." And so it was up to ideological PACs such as ours to help these harder-line candidates win the primary elections, many times fighting the business community all the way. Some of the most heated arguments I have had in the political process have not been with opposition groups, but with business groups that have a foggy view of the electoral process.

David Jessup

I question the democratic procedures in corporate PACs: Many allow contributors to earmark their contributions to candidates, but that really proves the point I made, that the corporate PAC is just another vehicle by which wealthy executives and businessmen influence the political process. Businessmen can contribute as individuals to a campaign. Then they can turn around, earmark a contribution to the corporate PAC, and have it go to the same candidate. In this way they exceed their contribution limits.

The other point is that the stockholders, who are theoretically the real owners of corporations, and whose money is being spent on the administrative costs of corporate PACs, have no democratic say in how the corporate PAC is run. Stockholders do not hold conventions as labor does. They have no COPE endorsing conventions in which the shareholders come together and, on the basis of representatives elected by one man–one vote, have a say in who is endorsed by these PACs. This situation is ridiculous, and it can well be questioned why corporate PACs should be able to solicit employees at all. A speaker here made the point that the FEC created a caste system that allows corporate PACs to solicit some employees and not others. I agree that is a caste system, and it ought to be done away with. PACs should not be able to solicit any employee because of the inherently coercive nature of the employer-employee relationship. Let the PACs solicit the stockholders. The stockholders are the owners of the corporation.

Bernadette A. Budde

I hate to come across like Alice in Wonderland, but I am continually amazed at our search for the bogeyman when we talk about PACs and dollars and politics. Different groups identify different bogeymen, and all are probably equally erroneous in their search. This should teach us something about the political process and what we are trying to regulate, who the regulators are, and what their definitions are of what is corrupt or potentially corrupt.

The FEC has been identified as the bogeyman here. Some of us are not willing to blame the FEC. We are more willing to blame a lack of understanding of what went into the initial laws. Others are willing to blame the bogeyman who is the right wing or Richard Viguerie, and perhaps that is not fair either. Others are willing to identify labor as the bogeyman, and we have heard that corporate people don't understand much about how labor operates. Finally, the bogeyman who always gets blamed for everything is the way that business operates in the political process.

Again, I don't wish to sound like Alice in Wonderland, but I just don't understand it. I am puzzled by our misunderstanding of one another. Fundamentally, we all have to get back to some basic definitions before we can talk about writing a new law or even evaluating the current one. Forums such as this are so valuable because most of us run around and make assumptions about how others behave, and we truly don't understand. Perhaps misunderstanding among members of the press and of the academic world who are studying PACs perpetuates the myth that there has to be a bogeyman somewhere. I happen to believe there is no bogeyman. For the reasons presented today, we have to do a lot of evaluating before we think about fiddling with the political process, because we are very often wrong in our initial target and very often wrong in presenting a solution to that target.

Discussion

MARY MEEHAN, Committee for a Constitutional Presidency: I would like to ask Mr. Oldaker how he could possibly speak of voluntary compliance when the law provides such heavy civil fines and criminal fines along with the possibility of jail terms.

MR. OLDAKER: The law does, in fact, talk in those terms, but I think the commission has constantly, through its pronouncements and through its actions, looked toward voluntary compliance and has always taken this into consideration whenever it has had a compliance matter. Further, the commission has referred only one case to the Department of Justice for criminal prosecution, and that involved the Shapp for President campaign, which was an egregious violation of the act. So, in most instances, the commission looks at the civil side and has great compassion for people who honestly do not understand the act.

BONNIE WHYTE, National Association of Manufacturers: Currently there is an Obey-Railsback bill pending in Congress that would limit PAC contributions, limit the amount candidates can accept from PACs, and limit the credit limitations for candidates. What are the various opinions on how these amendments would affect the FEC law and your own operations?

MR. MOORE: I am speaking for the staff and not for our board so far, because we really don't know much about Obey-Railsback. We are generally against a lowering of the PAC limit. I am not completely familiar with the bill, but I believe the credit extension is only for candidates. I am not certain if it is for PACs as well, but as I remember, it is $1,000 over a month. The normal course of business with some of the direct mail firms we work with would put us well over that sum, so I think that it should be raised. The $5,000 limit also has a lot of problems, but we would support the $50,000 limit on total PAC contributions.

98

MR. WEYRICH: We are opposed to the entire amendment and would caution anybody who supports the $50,000 limitations that we are in a period of extreme inflation. I see no end to that. What may seem reasonable today, $50,000, is well within the limit of a lot of campaigns, but it may seem very unreasonable five or six years from now. The amount of PAC money received by candidates who defeated incumbents despite the enormous perks of office was far in excess of $50,000 in most cases. I would submit that contributions of this magnitude will be necessary if we are to have a chance of defeating incumbents. So, if you love the present Congress, you will love Obey-Railsback.

MS. BUDDE: I don't like the whole concept of the $50,000 limitation. It inhibits challengers and candidates for open seats where there are no incumbents. Even incumbents who are seriously challenged will need more money than that.

It is surprising how many of the cosponsors of the Obey-Railsback bill are still conducting business as usual. They fear the general influence of PACs in the process. Yet they are going ahead with Washington fund-raisers, some more than doubling the amount of money that they had requested in previous years. If it was $100 last year, it is $250 this year.

If we are looking for bogeymen, are the corporate or other PACs providing a corruptive influence in the process, or are the incumbents, who are continuing their fund raising in Washington, somehow contributing to the misconception that PACs have a corrupting influence? I am a very puzzled person because Obey-Railsback and the continuation of fund-raisers in Washington just do not fit together.

MR. JESSUP: We support the Obey-Railsback bill on the grounds that at least within the PAC category, it might help to equalize resources a bit. But we do not cherish the illusion that no other ways will be found to finance campaigns. Business money has lots of channels open to it. Individual contributions in large amounts are no less organizationally tied than those that come through the PAC mechanism.

Incumbents tend to win, not because of campaign money, but because of Congressional perks and because of Congressional district boundaries. Where a truly marginal district exists, there seems to be plenty of money around to fund challengers. If there is a chance of winning a race, people on all sides will get into the race and put up plenty of money in order to win. I don't see that as a problem.

MR. THOMAS: I can only speak for myself since the Council for a Livable World does not have a position on Obey-Railsback at this time. I would not favor a $50,000 limit, and I would not favor a reduction in the $5,000 limit, but I would favor a reduction in the amount an individual could contribute to a PAC, as I indicated earlier.

MR. PRATT: I tried to make fairly clear in my presentation what I think about such a proposal. I am against it. It is an incumbent's protection bill.

MR. MALBIN: Mr. Oldaker, I suppose you would not feel free to comment on whether such a bill should pass, but has the FEC analyzed the administrative implications of the $50,000 limit?

MR. OLDAKER: We have not. We have not been asked to do so. We would if asked. It would increase the burden, and that would be a question which we would deal with at that time.

VALERIE EARLE, Georgetown University: I want to commend Ms. Budde on her comment that the search for bogeyman seems quite useless and time-consuming—really a waste of time.

The questions the discussion should focus on—and perhaps this afternoon and tomorrow they will—are these: Was the law enacted to secure reforms? Are these reforms helpful to the democracy? Madison observed there will always be interest groups and they should be active in the political life of the country. What, then, is the point in looking for bogeymen? Are all these interest groups bogeymen?

Another question that needs to be focused on is this: Can the FEC, admittedly a young commission facing a difficult task, possibly perform better than it has? That executive committee meetings are more informative than the Information Office, of course, is not surprising, but it is still quite dismaying. Have these reforms been worth seeking? Did those responsible for electoral reforms foresee their consequences? Were the reforms intended to add to the health of the democracy, or did the incumbents have very much in mind their own health when they enacted the law? Finally, can something be done about the FEC?

MR. MALBIN: I want to thank you for asking these questions. I know that some of your observations will be echoed in future sessions here. Unfortunately, we are near the end of this panel and cannot begin to do justice to your questions now. Does anybody on the panel want to say anything, or should we leave it as it stands, promise to return to it, and get to another question now?

NEIL STAEBLER, former commissioner, FEC: As a former member of the Federal Election Commission, I attempted to respond to these questions, but it took some forty pages. So, I shall not attempt a response now, but if you will leave me your name, I will happily send you the forty pages. That goes for everybody else.

Ms. BUDDE: I think the response to the question whether the Congress understood what it did when it reformed the law is probably no. Members of Congress who have to ask advisory opinions of the FEC act as puzzled as I do at the responses they receive.

An obstacle in making the FEC more responsive may lie in the makeup of the membership of the commission. For a while it was top-heavy with former Congressmen, people who had been candidates. No member of the Federal Election Commission comes out of a current PAC background. Mr. Harris comes from a labor background, but no other group which operates in the political process has anyone on that commission with direct experience of a PAC. The questions that are now asked of the FEC concern the political behavior of interest groups and the guidelines for dealing with them. It might help in this regard if the representation were broader.

JOHN GREEN, Cornell University: It seems to me that the issue underlying everything we are talking about is the influence of money on Congress, and I should like to hear if the various groups here feel that the value of the dollar they contribute to campaigns has been affected one way or the other by these regulations.

MR. MOORE: Affected by the regulations, certainly. First of all, the new law forced everyone operating a PAC to spend probably—I don't know the exact figures—in the neighborhood of 5 to 10 percent, just to keep up with the administrative burden the law gave us.

I frankly think that was a positive aspect of the law. Congress really foresaw it when it imposed the $1,000 limitation, forcing us to go further in democratizing the process, and in disclosing our finances as well.

MR. MALBIN: May I ask, do you want to know whether or not a limit on contributions affects what you buy with your contribution? Is that what you are asking?

MR. GREEN: Effectively, yes.

MR. MOORE: It affects us all in the same way. The situation forces us into in-kind contributions.

101

MR. WEYRICH: I am still not clear about the import of your question. Are you saying that because we can contribute less, do we have less effect on how members of Congress vote? Is that what you are asking?

MR. GREEN: Yes, I was wondering if that was the case.

MR. WEYRICH: I don't find we have any effect on how they vote. I have been upset with certain members in whom I had confidence and whom I helped elect. When they get a million dollars worth of perks after they are elected, they can turn on us in a flash. So I find that, in many cases, it doesn't matter what we have contributed to them. They go their own way once they have been elected.

MS. BUDDE: The impact has been that we have fewer dollars to give away than we used to. It's costing us more money to raise money because of the quirks of the law. When we are involved in a campaign, our contribution does highlight that campaign. In that sense, our dollars have been magnified even though there may be fewer dollars for individual candidates. We do no lobbying, so we have no way of measuring whether or not our involvement in the campaign has paid off.

MR. JESSUP: I don't think the limits have hurt our contributions all that much. We haven't changed that drastically. Unfortunately, the contributions haven't gone up, as some people seem to think. We have obviously had to absorb some administrative costs in trying to work out the legal reporting requirements, but it has not been an excessive burden.

An interesting question we have to ask ourselves—and maybe all the groups must ask themselves—concerns not just these reforms, but other reforms of party and seniority rights in Congress. Have incumbent officeholders somehow succeeded in making themselves independent of all groups to a certain extent so as to operate on their own? Is this in the best interests of democracy? I believe it is not.

MR. THOMAS: The $5,000 limit has restricted the ability of a committee to influence the outcome of a campaign. But the limit has no effect on the behavior of the officeholder once he is elected. To suggest a precise equation between the amount of campaign contributions and one's influence on the officeholder is simplistic. My own experience and what I have heard so far of other groups confirm this. We tend to look for somebody who has a record of which we approve, or who has a position on issues with which we are concerned, and then help that person.

JOHN MANGONI, United Auto Workers: I have heard all the speakers at the front table either discuss or allude to democratizing the process and say that their organizations are all contributing to participatory democracy.

It seems to me one of the ways to minimize the effect of corporate PACs would be to open up the electoral process to the people. Nevertheless I see the conservative groups in opposition whenever legislation is proposed to liberalize registration. It seems to me that if everyone from labor, industry, or trade association PACs would join hands we could get a bill passed that would liberalize registration.

Ms. BUDDE: I mentioned the problem of the caste system within corporations. It is now very difficult for corporations to conduct programs of voter registration because of their inability to communicate with everybody.

Opening up the process is not necessarily related to that. Every group here might agree with liberalizing the tax deduction for political contributions to candidates. This is a powerful incentive to bring small contributions into the political process. It will be effective if candidates have the seed dollars they need from organized groups to be able to reach those small contributors.

MR. WEYRICH: It is a myth that if the requirements for voting are lowered, participation is increased. In fact, every time that requirements for voting have been lessened, people regard voting as less important, and therefore vote in progressively fewer numbers.

A good test of union support of the instant voter registration legislation took place in Ohio, where the voters repudiated that effort by a substantial margin. I would certainly regard Ohio as a state with a fair union representation.

MR. JESSUP: Business organizations do not spend a lot of money on registration to get out the vote because their constituency already registers and votes at a very high level. It is a more affluent constituency, and it is something of a disadvantage that we have to spend a lot of money and resources to get our constituency to register and vote at a level that, even at its highest, remains several points below the Republican business constituency.

As to the other point, it is simply not true that registration reform laws have not helped participation; they have. We did the study of this, comparing the 1976 election with the 1974 election and comparing states which had changed their laws with those which had not. We found a significant increase in participation especially in states that went all the way to have election-day registration.

I agree with the point that was made from the floor, that if we want to democratize political influence, we ought to figure out a way to remove the barriers that prevent people from voting, especially the psychological barrier. We ought to be making it easier for these people. Election-day registration has done this in a number of states, including Minnesota, which has one of the highest participation rates of any state in the country.

MR. PRATT: These arguments were not persuasive in Congress or in Ohio because when even election officials from Chicago say that such a proposal is open to fraud, people are going to back away from the arguments. Secondarily, but not to be overlooked, is the administrative cumbersomeness of such a proposal. If people really want to vote, registration thirty days prior, as we have in Virginia, seems to be perfectly adequate. We never have long lines.

Registration in a rural area is probably unnecessary. States like North Dakota do not have registration. It works fine. But in an urban area, with turnover, with lots of vacant lots and abandoned gas stations and things like that, it is needed.

MR. MOORE: Election fraud was brought up, and several studies have concluded that election fraud is not perpetrated by people going in large numbers to the polls. It is corruption of election officials themselves. Study after study, when the FEC was looking at this problem, confirmed this.

MR. MALBIN: I am glad we are ending on this question precisely because it is not about campaign finance. The way the question was asked points out there are many different legal approaches to some of the campaign finance law's objectives while the campaign finance law itself is dealing with many different purposes at the same time. This business of sorting out objectives and means is something we need to do more of as we proceed.

Part Two

Interest Groups and the Law: Two Overviews

Business and Labor under the
Federal Election Campaign Act of 1971

Edwin M. Epstein

The manner in which congressional elections are currently financed is a national disgrace. Special interests view campaign contributions as a way to buy into the office of a present or future Member of Congress. . . . A major source of this distrust comes from the changing way in which our campaigns are being financed. More and more political action committees, known as PACs, are being created and are involving themselves in congressional elections. Their patterns of contributions, largely to incumbents, is what causes public cynicism. . . . It is becoming a system of purchasing access and the expectation of legislative favors, and it is time for a change.

REPRESENTATIVE JOHN B. ANDERSON [1]

My personal impression is that political action committees have given the great influx of new participants in our political system that we've seen in my political lifetime. Thousands of people contribute through their associations and neighborhood groups, companies, unions, et cetera. They have had a piece of the political action that they have never had the chance for before because they haven't been solicited by candidates. And I see you guys trying to value their influence.

REPRESENTATIVE BILL FRENZEL [2]

We believe that the growing power and resources of the political action committees, which all but negate the importance of the small contributor,

This paper was prepared under a grant from the Russell Sage Foundation, New York, N.Y., administered by the Institute of Governmental Studies, University of California, Berkeley. Support services were rendered by the Institute of Industrial Relations, University of California, Berkeley. The views expressed here are not necessarily those of the three above-named institutions. Yolanda Lopez, Richard Glass, and Robert Pease provided valuable assistance on this project. They are not, however, responsible for any errors of omission or commission herein.

[1] Prepared statement of Representative John B. Anderson (R-Ill.), U.S. Congress, House of Representatives, House Administration Committee, *Hearings on H.R. 1 and Related Legislation,* 96th Congress, 1st session, March 1979, p. 216.

[2] Statement of Representative Bill Frenzel (R-Minn.), *Hearings on H.R. 1 and Related Legislation,* p. 227.

call for a public system of financing Senate and House elections. . . .
Public financing would all but eliminate a clearly corrupting system in
which national legislators owe too much to the special interests and too
little to their constituents.

LOS ANGELES TIMES[3]

While business is by no means as single-minded as labor about where it
stands and what it wants from the rest of the polity, the trend of corporate
behavior through PACs suggests a sharpening of political consciousness
in the business community. The vitality of the private sector of the
economy is a major guarantor of that political diversity on which the
advantages of American life depend. That business is developing a
heightened sense of itself as part of the political process should, at least,
clarify the dialogue with its critics.

THE WASHINGTON STAR [4]

Throughout the congressional hearings in the spring of 1979 regarding
proposed amendments (H.R. 1 and S. 623) to the Federal Election
Campaign Act of 1971 (FECA), which would have provided for partial
public financing of congressional general election campaigns,[5] no subject
generated more heated debate than the rapid growth of political action
committees (PACs). The federal regulatory framework that evolved
during the 1970s explicitly legitimated certain labor and business electoral practices, which, if not patently illegal hitherto, were under a cloud
of legal uncertainty. Moreover, the FECA limited greatly the ability of
individuals and political parties to make campaign contributions to
federal candidates. These regulatory developments have increased substantially the formal role of corporations, of other business-related
groups, and, to a lesser extent, of labor unions in federal elections, and
they have institutionalized the political action committee as the primary
vehicle for organizational participation in electoral politics.[6] Unless
there are significant changes in federal law governing elections, the
approximate electoral balance between business and labor that exists at
present will unquestionably tip in favor of business, particularly in the
area of raising and contributing money to federal candidates through the
use of PACs.

---

[3] "A Clearly Corrupting System," *Los Angeles Times,* May 30, 1979, part 2, p. 6.
[4] "Business in Politics," *The Washington Star,* March 5, 1979.
[5] This paper will not cover the activity of so-called "ideological" or "single-issue"
PACs that have flowered during the 1970s.
[6] H.R. 1, House of Representatives, 96th Congress, 1st session, and S. 623, Senate,
96th Congress, 1st session (1979) to amend 2 U.S.C. 431–455 and 26 U.S.C.
9001–9042 (1976).

The emerging advantage of business vis-à-vis organized labor in the area of campaign financing is not a result of astute political behavior on the part of the business community. It is, to the contrary, an unintended consequence of labor pursuing its own short-run political objectives during the three rounds of FECA legislation in the 1970s. Although FECA of 1971 as amended in 1974 and 1976 has legitimated and facilitated the establishment of political action committees by both business and labor, ironically it has eroded labor's position in the electoral process and has strengthened that of business-related groups. The irony is that during all three legislative rounds organized labor was instrumental in drafting and securing passage of the key provisions relating to PACs in an attempt to improve its own electoral position. In the absence of major legislative changes relating to elections—such as total public financing of all House and Senate races, or a reversal of present congressional policy concerning political action committees—PACs affiliated with business are likely to expand in numbers and strength during the next several years and to play an increasingly important role in federal elections. A final irony is that the legislative changes of the 1970s occurred in a setting of political reform, which was seeking to reduce the impact of wealthy persons and other "special-interest" groups and to enhance the influence of the average, unaffiliated citizen in the electoral process. As with all social phenomena, some consequences of comprehensive federal regulation of elections were intended by proponents of electoral reform, while others were undesired, unanticipated, and, indeed, opposed by both citizen reformers and their legislative allies.[7]

In this paper, I examine (1) the consequences of federal regulation of electoral politics during the 1970s relative to labor and business, and (2) the implications of these developments for the American political process.

Background

Federal Regulations of Corporate and Labor Electoral Activity Prior to 1971. As James Madison recognized nearly two hundred years ago in *The Federalist, no. 10,* the efforts of economic interests to influence government are a staple of American politics. Electoral involvement first of business corporations and subsequently of labor unions evoked, not surprisingly, a strong reaction among those elements of American society that considered themselves to be severely disadvantaged by the

---

[7] Common Cause, for example, in 1974 vigorously opposed the successful effort by the AFL–CIO to amend 18 U.S.C. §611 (1974) of the U.S. Criminal Code to permit corporations and labor unions that are government contractors to establish political action committees.

ability of these organizations to muster for political purposes financial and organizational resources not available to ordinary citizens. Corporations and labor unions since 1907 and 1943, respectively, have been forbidden to contribute their treasury funds to federal election campaigns. Between 1947 and 1972, the basic provision, 18 U.S.C. section 610, prohibited both corporate and union contributions and expenditures in federal primaries, in general elections, and in nominating conventions.[8] The two policy reasons underlying this prohibition were: (1) the perceived need to prevent large economic interests from subverting the integrity of the political process by dominating the selection of public officials; and (2) the desire to protect corporate shareholders and union members from having their invested or contributed money used to finance candidates and causes to which they had not assented.[9]

Business and Labor Electoral Activity Prior to the 1970s. Although organized labor's political behavior has not changed significantly in the past decade, the growing electoral involvement of business—particularly through the PACs—is clearly an outgrowth of the regulations covering federal elections that developed during the 1970s. Union experience with PACs dates to the mid-1930s, when John L. Lewis established labor's Non-Partisan Political League. Then, in 1955, the merger of the American Federation of Labor and Congress of Industrial Organizations was accompanied by the creation of the Committee on Political Education (COPE), which became the model for virtually all political action committees. From the outset, national, state, and local units of COPE have not only raised and distributed funds, but have also served as the mechanism for organized and widespread union activity in the electoral process, for example, in voter registration, political education, and get-out-the-vote drives. By the time the FECA went into effect on April 7, 1972, organized labor had over thirty years of experience with the political action committee.[10]

Business, however, had little experience with PACs before 1972. At no time during that era did the number of business-related committees

---

[8] 18 U.S.C. §610 (1951).

[9] See United States v. CIO, 335 U.S. 106 (1948), pp. 115, 134–135, and United States v. International Union UAW, 352 U.S. 567 (1957), p. 570.

[10] The information about COPE is drawn from Alexander Heard, *The Costs of Democracy* (Chapel Hill: University of North Carolina Press, 1960), pp. 178–208; Fred Greenstone, *Labor in American Politics* (New York: Alfred A. Knopf, 1969), pp. 39–80; J. Cottin and C. Culhane, "Committee on Political Education," in *Political Brokers: Money, Organization, Power and People,* ed. G. Smith (New York: Liveright/National Journal, 1972); and Harry M. Scoble, "Organized Labor in Electoral Politics," *Western Political Quarterly,* vol. 16, no. 3 (September 1963), pp. 666–685.

much exceed fifty, the great majority of which were industry- rather than company-based. Indeed, until the campaign financing laws were reformed in the 1970s to impose strict limitations on individual donations and to provide for effective public disclosure of the sources of funds, there was little need for business PACs; money from business-related sources could legally enter the electoral arena, almost undetected, in almost unlimited amounts in the form of individual contributions by wealthy persons affiliated with corporations and other business organizations. Thus, for example, the Business-Industry Political Action Committee (BIPAC), which had been formed by affiliates of the National Association of Manufacturers during the early 1960s and became the prototype business-related PAC, was a pale shadow of COPE.

Prior to 1971 there existed an important distinction between the electoral activities of business and labor—a distinction that, although still pertinent today, is rapidly becoming less viable. From the outset, organized labor based its electoral strategy on the mobilization of union members and their families into mass political participation. Campaign contributions to candidates and parties, while surely important, were but one facet of union activity. Conversely, electoral efforts of business focused almost exclusively upon stimulating financial contributions among the elite population, for example, senior executives and directors of corporations and trade associations and major shareholders, all of whom could be reached most effectively through quiet, informal, and direct solicitation.[11]

The Legal Framework: The FECA of 1971 and Amendments. Since I have written elsewhere at considerable length about the pertinent legal developments during the 1970s that have determined the present position of business and labor in federal electoral politics,[12] I shall but highlight briefly the critical legislative, judicial, and administrative decisions of this decade.

---

[11] Business electoral involvement prior to 1971 is discussed in Heard, *The Costs of Democracy*, pp. 98–135; Herbert E. Alexander, *Money in Politics* (Washington, D.C.: Public Affairs Press, 1972), pp. 137–182; and Edwin M. Epstein, *Corporations, Contributions, and Political Campaigns: Federal Regulation in Perspective* (Berkeley, Calif.: The Institute of Governmental Studies, 1968).

[12] See Edwin M. Epstein, "Corporations and Labor Unions in Electoral Politics," *Annals of the American Academy of Political and Social Science,* vol. 425 (May 1976), pp. 33–58; Edwin M. Epstein, "Labor and Federal Elections: The New Legal Framework," *Industrial Relations,* vol. 15, no. 3 (October 1976), pp. 257–274 and Edwin M. Epstein, "The Emergence of Political Action Committees," in *Political Finance,* Sage Electoral Studies Yearbook, vol. 5, ed. Herbert E. Alexander (Beverly Hills, Calif.: Sage Publications, 1979), pp. 159–197.

The Federal Election Campaign Act of 1971 is the root of the growth of business electoral activity, particularly the tremendous expansion of PACs, during the 1970s. That act allowed corporations and labor unions (1) to communicate on any subject (including partisan politics) with stockholders and members, respectively, and their families; (2) to conduct nonpartisan registration and get-out-the-vote drives directed at these same constituencies; and (3) to spend company and union funds on the establishment and administration of a "separate segregated fund" to be used for political purposes—that is, for setting up political action committees.[13]

The provision authorizing PACs was added to the bill on the House floor through an amendment drafted by the AFL–CIO. In this amendment, organized labor was seeking insurance against the possibility that the Supreme Court, in a case pending, would uphold a court of appeals' ruling that a PAC organized by a pipefitters' local in St. Louis was compulsory and union-financed rather than voluntary and member-financed, and was therefore illegal.[14] Not surprisingly, the thus far unsuccessful course of the *Pipefitters* litigation had caused considerable alarm in labor circles. Unions were, according to AFL–CIO officials who helped draft the amendment authorizing PACs, taking a calculated risk, for political necessity required that corporations and unions receive identical rights in any new legislation. Since previous corporate electoral activity had been aimed at upper-level management rather than at shareholders and had focused primarily on fund-raising activities rather than on nonfinancial endeavors, few labor leaders thought business firms would establish PACs. Union political strategists calculated, therefore, that the benefits from removing the threat to union political action committees posed by the *Pipefitters* case would exceed the risks of giving business a virtual *carte blanche* to create PACs. Although the new 1971 law provided the basis for the Supreme Court's reversal of the court of appeals in *Pipefitters* (1972),[15] it nonetheless turned out to be a strategic (if, perhaps, unavoidable) error for labor in the longer term. Business, ironically, played no substantive role in shaping the legislation.

Corporate PACs played a relatively small role in the 1972 election. Some ninety corporate PACs operated in 1972, the great majority of which were established after the 1971 act went into effect. The entrepreneurship of the Finance Committee to Re-Elect the Presi-

---

13 P.L. 92–225, 86 Stat. 3 (1972), §205, Codified as 18 U.S.C. §610 (1972).

14 Pipefitters Local Union No. 562 v. United States, 434 F. 2d 1127 (CCA 8th, 1970).

15 407 U.S. 385 (1972). For additional discussion of the *Pipefitters* decision see Edwin M. Epstein, "Corporations and Labor Unions in Electoral Politics."

dent in making solicitations (it raised substantial sums from business sources) was another reason for the minor role of corporate PACs in the 1972 elections. Still another reason was that many companies having government contracts were fearful of establishing political action committees after Common Cause, in a lawsuit against TRW, Inc., questioned whether the authorization of corporate PACs was compatible with another section of the 1971 Act (18 U.S.C. §611, 1972) that prohibited campaign contributions by government contractors.[16]

The post-Watergate disclosures provided new impetus to campaign reform. The 1974 FECA[17] was intended to alter fundamentally the character of campaign financing by reducing the influence of large individual and "special-interest" contributions.

Labor was also concerned about the Common Cause suit, because a number of unions were government contractors by reason of their federal manpower training and development contracts. Thus, in the debate of the 1974 FECA amendments, labor led the successful campaign for a provision specifying that corporations and labor unions having government contracts were not prohibited from establishing PACs.[18] But, as in 1971, the effort backfired—in this instance because the overwhelming majority of government contractors are corporations. Thus business, not labor, once again became the major beneficiary of labor's effort to secure its electoral position.

In late 1975 the newly created Federal Election Commission (FEC) issued its ruling in SUN-PAC,[19] easily the most momentous advisory opinion in its four-and-a-half year history. In a controversial 4–2 decision, the FEC held that Sun Oil Company could (1) use general treasury funds to establish, administer, and solicit contributions to SUN-PAC, its political action committee; (2) solicit contributions to SUN-PAC from both stockholders and employees; and (3) establish multiple PACs, each having separate contribution and expenditure limits, as long as the money came solely from voluntary contributions. Members of the FEC who dissented argued that the legislative history of the 1971 FECA and 1974 amendments indicated clearly that corporations could solicit PAC contributions from stockholders and their families. To hold otherwise, they argued, would destroy the political balance that Congress had sought to establish between corporations and unions since

---

16 Common Cause v. TRW, Inc., C.A. 980–72 (D.D.C. 1972).

17 P.L. 93-433, 88 Stat. 1263 (1974).

18 18 U.S.C. §611 (1974).

19 Federal Election Commission, Advisory-Opinion 1975–23, *Federal Register,* vol. 40, no. 233 (December 3, 1975), pp. 56584–56588.

a company PAC would have many more potential contributors than a union PAC, which could solicit funds only from its members and their families. While the 1971 FECA and 1974 amendments provided the legal authority for business PACs, SUN-PAC provided the spark for the explosion in their size and numbers.

In the six months following the FEC's decision, over 150 corporations established PACs, bringing the number in existence to nearly 300. Not surprisingly, labor groups vigorously denounced the SUN-PAC ruling and turned again to the Congress when, in early 1976, the Supreme Court issued its decision in *Buckley* v. *Valeo*,[20] holding unconstitutional a number of key provisions of the 1971 FECA, as amended in 1974. The hub of the subsequent compromise worked out by Congress within the 1976 FECA[21] was a provision that limited corporate PACs to soliciting contributions from stockholders and "executive or administrative personnel" and their families, while, as before, labor unions were limited to soliciting contributions from union members and their families. Union and corporate PACs could, however, make use of "crossover" rights twice a year—that is, they could solicit the other's constituency by mail, using an independent third-party conduit. Organized labor achieved a key objective when it was allowed to use payroll deduction plans ("check-offs") to collect contributions from its members if the company PAC used that method with its stockholders or executive/administrative personnel. Finally, a "nonproliferation" provision was included: while a corporation could set up an unlimited number of PACs, all such affiliated committees were restricted to a contribution limit of $5,000 per candidate per election. This provision was designed to eliminate the multiple PACs established by corporations seeking to take advantage of the SUN-PAC ruling. Labor's triumph was only partial, however, since union and union-affiliated PACs were limited in the same way. Moreover, membership organizations, trade associations, cooperatives, and corporations without capital stock—the great majority of which are clearly business-related—were explicitly authorized to establish PACs.

In summary while the 1976 amendments restored part of what organized labor had lost as a result of SUN-PAC, they gave the business community far greater running room in the electoral process than heretofore. Ironically, as a consequence of three rounds of election legislation during the 1970s, both labor and especially business are in a position to exert a much more direct and stronger impact upon federal electoral

---

[20] 424 U.S. 1 (1976).
[21] P.L. 94–283, 90 Stat. 475 (1976).

politics than they could at the beginning of the decade, a development neither anticipated nor desired (and, indeed, vigorously opposed) by reformers who have sought to free the electoral process from undue influence by "special interests."

The PAC Era: The Data

The tremendous growth in the number of political action committees, particularly business-related PACs, is well documented. FEC data make it possible to trace precisely the growth of such "nonparty" committees over the past five years and to develop an increasingly accurate picture of the demography, characteristics, and electoral behavior of PACs. Accordingly, observers of campaign financing disagree little on the *figures* arising from what I have termed elsewhere the "PAC Phenomenon." [22] These same observers are likely to disagree on the *meaning of* these figures and their *implications* for the electoral process. The quotations at the beginning of this paper indicate the diversity of opinion on what effect the flowering of PACs during the 1970s has had on American electoral politics, as well as what this development portends.

PAC Growth. Analysis of Federal Election Commission statistics for the 1975–1976 and 1977–1978 election biennia strikingly reveal the rapid expansion—in numbers and level of activity—of PACs in general and business-related PACs in particular. From the beginning of 1975 to the end of 1978, the number of PACs rose from 608 to 1,633 (1,938 PACs were registered at some point during the 1977–1978 campaign cycle) and total spending by these committees rose from an estimated $36.9 million in 1975–1976 to $77.8 million in 1977–1978. In 1977–1978, PAC contributions totaling $35.1 million to congressional candidates represented 18 percent of the $199 million that the candidates received from all sources, while in 1975–1976, nonparty committees contributed an estimated $20.5 million, some 20 percent, of the nearly $104.8 million received by congressional candidates.[23] By comparison, Common Cause estimates that in the campaign of 1974, "interest group" donations to congressional candidates totaled $12.5 million.[24]

Focusing specifically on business-related and labor PACs, the data presented in Tables 1 and 2 document clearly the expansion in numbers and vigor, particularly of the business PACs.

---

[22] Edwin M. Epstein, "The Business PAC Phenomenon: An Irony of Electoral Reform," *Regulation,* vol. 3, no. 3 (May/June 1979), pp. 35–41.

[23] See sources cited in Table 2.

[24] Common Cause, *1976 Federal Campaign Finances, Vol. 1, Interest Group and Political Party Contributions to Congressional Candidates* (Washington D.C.: Common Cause, 1977), pp. vi–viii.

TABLE 1

Growth of Nonparty Political Action Committees, 1974–1978

	Dec. 1974		Nov. 1975		May 1976		Dec. 1976		Dec. 1977		Mar. 1978		Aug. 1978		Dec. 1978	
	No.	%	No.	%	No.	%	No.	%	No.	%	No.	%	No.	%	No.	%
Corporate	89	14	139	19	294	30	433	38	538	40	595	40	694	40	784	48
Labor	201	33	226	31	246	25	224	20	216	16	242	16	266	15	218	13
Other[a]	318	52	357	49	452	46	489	43	601	44	655	44	790	45	631	39
Total[b]	608	99	722	99	992	101	1,146	101	1,355	100	1,492	100	1,750	100	1,633	100
Total business-related[c]	248	41	318	44	520	52	678	59	839	62	923	62	1,089	62	1,100	67

NOTE: N = number of committees registered with the Federal Election Commission.

[a] Composed of all PACs classified by the FEC as No-Connected, Trade/Membership/Health, Cooperatives, and Corporations without Capital Stock.

[b] All percentages do not add to 100 because of rounding.

[c] Includes figures for corporate PACs plus the half of the "other" PACs that are assumed to be business-related.

SOURCE: Federal Election Commission data drawn periodically from FEC "B Index," Federal Election Commission, FEC *Annual Reports* from 1975 to 1978 and periodic press releases issued by the FEC.

TABLE 2
NONPARTY PAC FINANCIAL DATA: CONGRESSIONAL CAMPAIGNS 1976 AND 1978
(in millions of dollars)

	Number[a]		Adjusted Receipts		Adjusted Disbursements		Contributions to Candidates	
	1976	1978	1976	1978	1976	1978	1976	1978
Corporate	450 (390)	821 (697)	6.8	17.7	5.8	15.3	4.3	9.8
Labor	303 (265)	281 (211)	18.6	19.8	17.5	18.9	8.2	10.3
Other[b]	489 n.a.	836 (551)	n.a.	43.0	13.6[d] (est.)	43.6	—	15.0
Total business-related (est.)[c]	695	1,239 (973)	n.a.	39.2	12.6[d] (est.)	37.1	7.1[e] (est.)	17.3
Total	1,242	1,938	n.a.	80.5	36.9[d] (est.)	77.8	20.5 (est.)	35.1

[a] Includes all PACs that engaged in activity any time during the two-year election cycle, rather than year-end figures as in Table 1. The numbers in parentheses represent PACs actually making contributions to federal candidates.
[b] Composed of all PACs classified by the FEC as No-Connected, Trade/Membership/Health Cooperatives, and Corporations without Stock.
[c] Includes figures for corporate PACs plus the half of "other" PACs that are assumed to be business-related.
[d] Figures for 1976 total expenditures (36.9), business-related expenditures (12.6), and contributions (7.1) are estimated from data that appeared in Fortune (March 27, 1978), together with FEC data relating to labor and corporate financial activity during 1976.
[e] This estimate is drawn from Common Cause data on Campaign 1976, which distinguishes business from agriculture, health, lawyers, ideological, and "miscellaneous" groups in its compilation of Interest Group Contributions. Hence, the data base differs from that used for estimating aggregate business activity in 1978 (See note c).

Until the time of the FEC's SUN-PAC decision (November 1975), there were more labor than corporate PACs in existence (226–139). As of December 31, 1978, however, the number of corporate PACs had far surpassed the number of labor PACs (784–218) (Table 1). While labor PACs outraised, outspent, and outcontributed their corporate counterparts in the election campaigns of both 1976 and 1978, the labor margins for each category were cut drastically for the latter campaign (Table 2).

In 1976, labor PACs outraised corporate PACs by $11.8 million, $18.6 million to $6.8 million. By 1978, the margin had been reduced to $2.1 million, $19.8 million to $17.7 million. In 1976, labor committees gave $8.2 million to congressional candidates compared with $4.3 million contributed by corporate PACs; by 1978, the margin was reduced to $400,000, $10.2 million to $9.8 million. Simple comparisons of this type, however, understate significantly the extent of business's electoral role during both 1976 and 1978. This is so because the FEC's classification scheme separates groups that are not explicitly corporate or labor into four categories: no-connected organizations (for example, Business-Industry Political Action Committee), trade membership/health organizations (for example, National Association of Realtors), cooperatives (for example, Associated Milk Producers, Inc.), and corporations without stock (for example, California Almond Growers Exchange). As Table 2 shows, in 1978 these four categories accounted for 836 PACs having receipts of $43.1 million, disbursements of $43.6 million, and direct contributions to candidates of $15.0 million. If we assume that only half the amounts raised, spent, and contributed to congressional candidates by the noncorporate, nonlabor PACs emanate from business-related committees—a very conservative estimate, indeed —the receipts and disbursements attributable to business rise by over $21.5 million and contributions to congressional candidates rise by $7.5 million. Thus, the estimated totals for aggregate corporate and business-related PAC activity are: receipts, $39.3 million; disbursements, $37.1 million; and contributions to congressional candidates, $17.3 million. These estimates indicate that business and business-related groups outraised and outdisbursed labor groups by almost two to one in 1978 and outcontributed them by almost 70 percent. Indeed several of the largest noncorporate business-related PACs, such as those of the National Association of Realtors and the National Automobile Dealers Association, outraised, outspent, and outcontributed (or matched) the two biggest labor committees, AFL–CIO COPE and UAW-V-CAP. These noncorporate business-related PACs, moreover, outstripped even the largest company committees—those of Standard Oil of Indiana, Amer-

TABLE 3
LARGEST CORPORATE, LABOR, AND OTHER BUSINESS-RELATED PACs,
1976 AND 1978
(in thousands of dollars)

Category	Receipts		Disbursements		Contributions	
	1976	1978	1976	1978	1976	1978
Corporate						
Standard Oil of Indiana	59.8	266	32	266	34[a]	155
American Family Corp.	98	261	77	260	66[a]	114
Int'l Paper Corp.	80	225	63	240	42[a]	173
Winn-Dixie Stores	21	232	7	124	—	113
LTV/Vought Corp.	105	221	87	209	47	94
Labor						
AFL–CIO COPE	1800	1440	1200	1340	936	921
United Auto Workers: V-CAP	1500	1430	1200	1160	895	964
United Trans-Union	758	873	754	946	450	558
Int'l Assn. Machinists	694	790	732	673	525	537
United Steelworkers	631	674	649	811	465	595
Noncorporate Business-Related						
Nat'l Assn. of Realtors		1850	894[b]	1810	570[a]	1120
Nat'l Assn. of Automobile Dealers		1460	557[b]	1540	369[a]	976
Assoc. Milk Producers, Inc.		917		1020	563[a]	446
Nat'l Assn. of Life Underwriters		643	325[b]	595	234[a]	381
Dairyman Inc.		598		449	191[a]	226

[a] These figures are drawn from Common Cause data for 1976. All other figures derive from FEC data.

[b] *Fortune*, March 23, 1978, p. 56.

SOURCES: *FEC Report on Financial Activity, 1977–1978,* Interim Report no. 4, vol. 4 (May 1979); *FEC Disclosure Series, No. 8* (1977) and *10* (1978); Common Cause, *1976 Federal Campaign Finances,* vol. 50 (1977); and Walter W. Guzzardi, Jr., "Business Is Learning How to Win in Washington," *Fortune,* March 27, 1978, pp. 52–58.

ican Family Corporation, and the International Paper Company—by a factor of six to one.

Several aspects of the growth of business PACs are of particular interest. Whereas labor PACs that were most active politically in 1976 (in terms of receipts, disbursements, and contributions) remained so in 1978, there was a substantial turnover in corporate ranks between the two elections. In 1976, the nine largest corporate PACs (ranked on the basis of receipts or disbursements exceeding $100,000) were affiliated with Chicago and Northwestern Transportation, General Electric, United Technologies, Coca-Cola, General Telephone and Electronics, Hughes Aircraft, LTV/Vought, Union Oil and Pacific Lighting.[25] In 1978, only General Electric, LTV/Vought, and Chicago and Northwestern Transportation still ranked among the top ten firms in either receipts or expenditures. They were joined by PACs established by Standard Oil of Indiana, American Family Corporation, Winn-Dixie Stores, International Paper, General Motors, Dart Industries, Grumman, Boeing and General Dynamics. While United Technologies was not among the top ten PACs in receipts or disbursements in 1978, it placed tenth in terms of total contributions to congressional candidates (in 1976, it ranked second in this category to General Electric, which was sixth in 1978).[26]

Perhaps even more important than the change in the most politically active corporations was the escalation in the order of magnitude of corporate PAC activities. Whereas in 1976 only nine company PACs had receipts and expenditures exceeding $100,000, by 1978 twenty-eight companies were in this category and six had receipts or expenditures exceeding $200,000 (two companies, Standard Oil of Indiana and American Family Corporation, exceeded $260,000 in each category). In 1976, only General Electric ($109,000) contributed above $100,000 to congressional candidates. By 1978, ten companies exceeded or were within a hair's breadth of that amount and the two leaders, International Paper and Standard Oil of Indiana, both contributed more than $150,000 to candidates. As Table 4 indicates, union-related committees also expanded in the 1978 campaign. In 1976, forty-two union committees had receipts in excess of $100,000; by 1978, the number had increased to forty-seven. The number of unions receiving $30,000–99,999 decreased from forty-seven to thirty-nine. Unlike the corporate situation, however, there was little change from 1976 to 1978 in the unions

---

[25] Federal Election Commission, *FEC Disclosure Series No. 8: Corporate-Related Political Committees' Receipts and Expenditures, 1976 Campaign* (Washington, D.C.: Federal Election Commission, 1977), p. 12.

[26] Ibid. Federal Election Commission, press release, May 10, 1979, p. 7.

TABLE 4
GROWTH IN CORPORATE AND LABOR POLITICAL ACTION COMMITTEES,
BY RECEIPTS, 1976 AND 1978

	Corporate PACs		Labor PACs	
	1976	1978	1976	1978
$100,000 and above	9	28	42	47
$30,000–99,999	49	143	47	39
$10,000–29,999	134	266	55	61
$1–9,999	193	323	121	95
$0	65	61	38	38
Total	450	821	303	281

SOURCES: *FEC Disclosure Series, No. 8* (1977) and *10* (1978), and *FEC Report on Financial Activity, 1977–1978*, Interim Report no. 4, vol. 4 (May 1979).

having the largest PACs. Of the ten leading labor PAC contributors to federal candidates in 1976, nine remained in the top ten in 1978; the ninth-ranked union in 1976 was replaced in 1978 by a union that had been thirteenth during the earlier election.

Business-related associations also expanded between 1976 and 1978. As Table 3 indicates, during this period PACs affiliated with the National Association of Realtors and the National Automobile Dealers Association increased their expenditures from $894,000 to $1.81 million and $557,000 to $1.54 million respectively. BIPAC went from $410,000 to $555,000. Although it is classified as a "health" organization, the American Medical Association's AMPAC, has been associated politically with business-related groups, particularly those in the health services. In 1978, AMPAC led all PACs in contributions to congressional candidates with $1.64 million—up from $1.1 million in 1976—with receipts of $1.66 million and expenditures of $1.88 million. Only three conservatively oriented "ideological" committees (Citizens for the Republic, National Conservative Political Action, and the Committee for the Survival of a Free Congress) exceeded AMPAC in both adjusted receipts and expenditures. The single largest PAC, Citizens for the Republic, reported receipts of $3.1 million, disbursements of $4.5 million, and contributions of $433,000. Thus between 1976 and 1978 corporate contributions to congressional candidates more than doubled, while labor's contributions rose by 24 percent. It is impossible, however, to calculate precisely the aggregate contributions by business-related PACs in 1976. The $7.1 million figure (for all races) used by Common Cause unquestionably underestimates the amount. A figure of $10 million plus is probably closer to the mark. By 1978, aggregate business contributions had risen to an estimated $17.3 million. Whatever the measure, business-related PACs (both corporate and noncorporate) obviously played a far more important role in 1978 than they had in any previous election.

PAC Contribution Patterns. Although in both 1976 and 1978 labor and business-related PACs demonstrated a clear propensity to be what management scientists term "risk averters," we can detect some differences in the contribution patterns within each group during the two biennia. Both business and labor gave predominantly to incumbents rather than to challengers or candidates in open races. In 1976, labor gave $4.7 million (67 percent) to incumbents, $1.6 million (22 percent) to challengers, and spent $1.2 million (11 percent) in open races. Almost all of labor's money (97 percent) went to Democrats. In 1978, labor gave $6.1 million (59 percent) to incumbents, $2.2 million (21 percent) to challengers, and $2.0 million (19 percent) to candidates in open races. Democrats received 94 percent of the money. The reduction in support for incumbents (a sizable number of Democratic congressional incumbents did not seek reelection in 1978) was matched by an increase in level of support for candidates in open races.

More difficult to compare directly are the contribution patterns of business-related PACs. The most reliable source of 1976 data, Common Cause's study, *1976 Federal Campaign Finances,* vol. 1,[27] lumps together all business-related committees without designating their affiliation—corporate, trade association, cooperative, or whatever. While differentiating between corporate and other PACs, the 1978 FEC figures, as we have seen, do not distinguish between business-related PACs and nonbusiness PACs listed in the other FEC reporting categories (for example, no-connected organizations and trade/membership/health groups). Notwithstanding these difficulties, some comparison of business contributions in 1976 and 1978 is possible. Common Cause figures for 1976 indicate that of the $6.7 million given by business-related PACs to congressional candidates who ran in the general election, $4.8 million (71 percent) went to incumbents, $1.2 million (18 percent) to challengers, and $765,000 (11 percent) was spent in open races. Business groups gave $3.8 million (57 percent) to Republicans and $2.9 million (43 percent) to Democrats. In 1978, the pattern of corporate contributions was almost identical to labor's in favoring incumbents ($5.8 million or 59 percent) over challengers ($2.0 million or 20 percent) and candi-

---

[27] Common Cause, *Federal Campaign Finances,* vol. 1.

dates in open races, ($2.0 million or 20 percent). Republicans received $6.1 million (63 percent) and Democrats $3.6 million (37 percent), an increase of 6 percent from 1976 for Republicans. An analysis by the *National Journal* of preliminary FEC data for 1978 indicates an interesting aspect of corporate contribution patterns for that campaign.[28] Through September 30, 1978, although corporations divided their contributions between Republicans ($2.5 million or 53 percent) and Democrats ($2.2 million or 47 percent), they heavily favored incumbents ($3.4 million or 72 percent) over nonincumbents and open race candidates together ($1.3 million or 28 percent). In the last month of the campaign, however, corporate PACs contributed heavily to Republicans ($2.9 million or 71 percent) over Democrats ($1.2 million or 29 percent) and slightly favored nonincumbents and candidates in open races ($2.1 million or 51 percent) over incumbents ($2.0 million or 49 percent) as the viability of Republican challengers and the identity of the close open races became more apparent. The ten largest corporate PACs (in terms of 1978 contributions, FEC preliminary figures), which gave $1.2 million to congressional candidates, favored Republicans (68 percent) over Democrats (32 percent), and incumbents (54 percent) over nonincumbents (46 percent).[29] To summarize, controversial wisdom that corporate-related dollars were automatically Republican dollars was heartily disproved in 1976 and 1978. While both elections indicated an overall corporate PAC preference for incumbents over challengers and open-seat candidates, in 1978 corporate PAC managers appeared to be targeting increasing amounts to nonincumbents, who were mainly Republicans. Given the short tenure of many members of Congress (over half the members of the House have served three terms or less), the apparently rising inclination on the part of senior congressmen not to seek reelection, and the diminishing power and perquisites associated with congressional seniority, particularly in the House, it seems reasonable to expect corporate PACs to devote even more resources to challengers and candidates in open races than was the case in 1978 and to play a more active role in primary races. In short, more corporate PACs than before are likely to become "risk takers," a move that will favor Republican nonincumbents.[30]

---

[28] Maxwell Glen, "At the Wire, Corporate PAC's Come Through for the GOP," *National Journal,* February 3, 1979, pp. 174–177, Table, p. 176.

[29] Ibid., p. 177.

[30] Business organizations and conservative groups have been vigorously urging corporate PACs to increase their support for business-oriented candidates, typically, Republican challengers and candidates in open races, over incumbents, who are usually Democrats. See for example, memorandum to Washington Representatives by Clark McGregor for the National Chamber Alliance for Politics (October 17,

During the 1978 campaign, the contribution activity of trade, membership, and health groups was similar to corporate PACs. Of the $11.5 million donated by PACs in this category 59 percent went to Republicans, and 41 percent to Democrats. Incumbents received 58 percent of the total, challengers 20 percent, and open-seat candidates 22 percent. No-connected organizations, which in addition to various ideological groups includes a number of business-related PACs, including BIPAC, overwhelmingly favored Republicans ($1.9 million or 73 percent) over Democrats ($700,000 or 27 percent), and preferred challengers (44 percent) over open-seat candidates (28 percent) and incumbents (28 percent). Only cooperatives (75 percent) and corporations without stock (71 percent) heavily supported Democrats. PACs in both of these categories (whose combined contributions to federal candidates totaled only $1.0 million) strongly favored incumbents over challengers but gave approximately 25 percent of their money to open races.[31] In 1978, then, these noncorporate, nonlabor PACs gave in aggregate $6.4 million (43 percent) to Democrats and $8.6 million (57 percent) to Republicans and favored incumbents ($8 million or 54 percent) over challengers ($3.5 million or 23 percent) and candidates in open races ($3.4 million or 23 percent).

Other Electoral Activities. Several further points should be noted before we leave the subject of business and labor behavior during the 1976 and 1978 campaigns. First, in addition to establishing PACs, corporations, unions, and other groups may advocate (in communications to their stockholders, managerial personnel, and members) the support or defeat of particular candidates as long as they report to the FEC expenditures of $2,000 or more in this connection. In 1976, sixty-six labor organizations reported spending slightly more than $2 million in internal communications, while only four corporations reported spending a total of $31,000.[32] No data have been released yet by the FEC for 1977–1978. The vast majority of companies surveyed in spring 1978 by the Washington-based Public Affairs Council indicated that they did not intend to communicate on partisan matters with employees or stockholders.[33]

1978), accompanying letter by Donald M. Kendall, Chairman of Pepsico (October 17, 1978), and *The New Right Report* (Viguerie Communications Corporation), vol. 8, no. 11 (July 31, 1979), "Corporate PACs: Some Improvements, But Still Disgraceful," pp. 1–4 and attachment.

31 FEC press release, May 19, 1979, p. 3.

32 Federal Election Commission, *FEC Disclosure Series No. 5: Index of Communication Costs by Corporations, Labor Organizations, Marketing Organizations and Trade Associations, 1976 Campaign* (Washington, D.C.: Federal Election Commission, 1979), pp. 1–7.

33 Public Affairs Council, "Results of the Public Affairs Council's 1978 Political Action Committee Survey," June 29, 1978, unpublished.

Second, the above figures do not include labor union spending for registration, get-out-the-vote drives, logistical support for candidates, and general political education—activities that benefit labor-endorsed candidates and are considered by many political observers to be more important to a candidate's campaign than direct financial contributions. Michael J. Malbin estimates that in 1976 organized labor at all levels spent almost two-thirds as much on these nonreportable items (and overhead) as it did in reported expenditures of $17.5 million.[34]

Stipulations filed by three large unions in conjunction with the Republican National Committee's suit against the Federal Election Commission[35] give some indication of the nature and extent of labor activities in 1976. The International Association of Machinists reports that in 1976 aggregate outlays by all constituent units of the IAM (international, state, district, and local) were $151,000 for election support of the Carter/Mondale campaign (primarily internal communications to members) and $200,000 for voter registration and get-out-the-vote activities, a total of $351,000.[36] The United Autoworkers stipulation indicates that for the period July 15, 1976, to November 2, 1976, aggregate expenditures for internal communications by the UAW and all its constituent units were $466,000 for Carter/Mondale election support and $1.14 million for voter-related activity, including voter registration and get-out-the-vote activities, a total of $1.6 million.[37] AFL–CIO-COPE indicates that state COPE expenditures post–July 15, 1976, were: membership identification, $263,000; registration, $460,000; get-out-the-vote, $867,000; presidential endorsement and publicity, $146,000; and overhead, $168,000—a total of $1.9 million. National COPE expenditures post–July 15, 1976 were: membership identification, $276,000; registration, $177,000; get-out-the-vote, $153,000; presidential endorsement and publicity, $444,000; and overhead, $26,000—a total of $1.08 million, making the aggregate COPE figure nearly $3 million.[38] All told, labor probably spent nearly $20 million for these items in 1978.

While, thus far, some national business groups (such as BIPAC and the Chamber of Commerce of the United States) and occasionally a corporation have undertaken serious political education efforts, business in general has participated very little in voter registration, get-out-the-

[34] Michael J. Malbin, "Labor, Business and Money—A Post Election Analysis," *National Journal,* March 19, 1977, pp. 412–417.
[35] Republican National Committee, et al. v. Federal Election Commission, 78 Civ. 2783 (LPG) (S.D.N.Y.).
[36] Ibid., IAM Stipulation, 13.
[37] Republican National Committee, et al. v. Federal Election Commission, 78 Civ. 2783 (LPG) (USDC) (S.D.N.Y.), UAW Stipulation, p. 5.
[38] Republican National Committee, et al. v. Federal Election Commission, 78 Civ. 2783 (LPG) (S.D.N.Y.), AFL–CIO Stipulation, Appendix A.

vote activities, internal political communications not related to candidates, or "in-kind" support of political candidates. To date, in these endeavors, labor's expertise and comparative advantage in terms of experience and human and other organizational resources surpass those of business. My discussions with managers of corporate and other business-related PACs indicate that they will explore such involvements for 1980 but do not anticipate extensive business activity in these areas before 1982 or 1984, by which time their more mature PAC solicitation and contribution programs will have developed, thereby permitting greater resources and opportunities for experimenting with new forms of electoral involvement. Indeed, one major business group, the U.S. Chamber of Commerce, has directed the activities of its PAC, the National Chamber Alliance for Politics, to specialize in "in-kind" contributions and other forms of logistical assistance to candidates—for example, consulting services, communications counseling, and transportation—rather than to direct contributions to candidates.

Third, political action committees and individuals can make "independent expenditures" advocating the election or defeat of a candidate so long as such expenditures are not made with the "cooperation" or "prior consent" or "in consultation with or at the request or suggestion" of a candidate or his agent.[39] Such expenditures can be used to buy media time or space and to promote or oppose a clearly identified candidate. The independent expenditures of associational PACs affiliated with the American Medical Association and the National Rifle Association of America were approximately $48,000 and $60,000, respectively, in 1978 primarily for magazine advertisements.[40] To date, however, most corporate and business-related PACs have eschewed this use of independent expenditures. Many candidates, leery of heavy business-sponsored advertising on their behalf (the content and timing of which they cannot control legally), actively discourage independent expenditures. Moreover, most PACs have not had sufficient resources to make such expenditures in preference to direct campaign contributions. As funds become available, however, business-related PACs are quite likely to make more independent expenditures than they have in the past, although the amounts will not be great unless new and severe restrictions are placed on permissible PAC contribution activities or unless comprehensive public financing eliminates the need of candidates for direct donations.

---

[39] Federal Election Commission *Regulations* §109.1 (a), 11 F.R.C. §109.1 (a) (1977).

[40] Maxwell Glen, "How to Get Around the Campaign Spending Limits," *National Journal,* June 23, 1979, pp. 1044–1046.

A Closer Look at PACs

We have seen that the great increase in total business PAC activity between 1974 and 1979, particularly since 1976, is largely due to the sharp rise in number of corporate PACs. While labor PACs increased some 35 percent and those affiliated with other interests doubled their number, the number of corporate PACs expanded more than sevenfold (see Table 1). Let us look more closely at the demography of business PACs, particularly those of corporations.

According to FEC records, 821 corporate PACs operated during the 1978 election (Table 5). Using the most recent compilations by *Fortune* of the top 1,000 industrials and 300 leading nonindustrials (1,300 firms in all), we find those companies having PACs were distributed as follows: 202 were affiliated with the top 500 industrials; 42 with the second 500; 124 with the leading nonindustrials—a total of 368 companies ranked by *Fortune*—and the remaining 453 were associated with companies not ranked by *Fortune*. Thus, contrary to popular belief that the corporate PAC phenomenon reflects a wholesale adoption of the PAC mechanism by American big business, 55 percent of all committees have been formed by firms not ranked by *Fortune* (substantial though these enterprises might actually be) and 72 percent of the companies listed by *Fortune* had not established a PAC. Impressive as the growth in corporate PACs has been, even more significant is the small number of PACs, given the total population of potential corporate PACs.

The 821 corporate PACs active in the 1978 elections (assuming for the moment they all fell into the $100 million or more category) represented only 22 percent of the 3,755 U.S. corporations with reported assets of $100 million or more (1974) and a meager 3.4 percent of the 23,834 corporations with reported assets of $10 million or more.[41] In short, the potential for PAC formations is virtually untapped, even if we consider only the very largest business firms.

Company Size. Focusing exclusively on the *Fortune*-ranked companies, we note a direct correlation between size of the company and its propensity to form a PAC (see Table 5). Whereas 149 (60 percent) of the top 250 industrials (including 70 percent of the leading 100) formed PACs, only 53 (21 percent) of the next 250, and 42 (8 percent) of the second 500 firms followed suit. A similar tendency is evident among nonindustrial corporations. The higher its position on the *Fortune* list of top 50 companies, the more likely the firm is to have a PAC. Moreover, the size of a PAC is related to size of the firm. Of the 14 corporations

---

[41] U.S. Department of Commerce, Bureau of the Census, *Statistical Abstract of the United States* (Washington, D.C.: U.S. Government Printing Office, 1977) p. 561.

TABLE 5

PACs of Fortune-Listed Corporations (Ranked by Firm Size)
Active in 1978 Election Campaign

Size Category (based on 1978 revenues)	PACs No.	PACs Percentage
Fortune's top 1,000 industrials		
First 500 firms with PACs		
1st 50	33	66
2nd 50	37	74
3rd 50	31	62
4th 50	31	62
5th 50	17	34
6th 50	13	26
7th 50	11	22
8th 50	12	24
9th 50	9	18
10th 50	8	16
Subtotal	202	40
Second 500 firms with PACs		
1st 100	23	23
2nd 100	8	8
3rd 100	5	5
4th 100	0	0
5th 100	6	6
Subtotal	42	8
Total, *Fortune's* 1,000 industrials	244	24
Fortune's leading 300 nonindustrials (50 firms in each category)		
Commercial banking	25	50
Diversified financials	19	38
Life insurance	5	10
Retailing	15	30
Transportation	29	58
Utilities	31	62
Subtotal	124	41
Total, *Fortune's* 1,300 firms	368	28

NOTE: Some companies have more than one PAC. For example, American Telephone and Telegraph, the top-ranked utility, has twenty PACs registered in the name of its separate operating companies.

SOURCES: *FEC Report on Financial Activity, 1977–1978,* Interim Report no. 4, vol. 4 (May 1979) and *Fortune* Directories, May 7, 1979, June 18, 1979, and July 16, 1979.

TABLE 6

PAC BEHAVIOR IN 1978 ELECTION OF FIRMS AMONG
FORTUNE-RANKED INDUSTRIALS
(in thousands of dollars)

	Fortune Ranking				
	1–14	101–112	256–294	438–501	682–980
Total adjusted receipts	1,100	267	223	85	45
Total adjusted expenditures	1,100	227	139	66	31
Total contributions	701	210	124	56	19

NOTE: Figures are totals for ten companies in each category.

listed by the FEC as having the top ten PACs in terms of adjusted receipts, adjusted disbursements, and contributions to candidates, 13 were ranked by *Fortune*: 6 were in the top 50 industrials, 2 in the second 50, 3 in the second 100, 1 in the 200–250 group, and 1 was the eleventh-ranked retailer.[42] Only one firm, American Family Corporation, an insurance and financial services company, did not appear in any of the *Fortune* lists. As a further test of the relationship between size of firm and level of PAC activity, I have examined the receipts, expenditures, and contributions of five groups of ten PACs active in 1978, stratified by size of firm as ranked by *Fortune* (Table 6).

As Table 6 indicates, the larger the firm, the more vigorous its level of PAC operations. This difference is most pronounced when the largest companies (those at the top of the *Fortune* industrial lists) are compared with firms in the middle (between 438 and 501) and bottom (682–980) of the rankings. The available evidence indicates that for the nation's largest industrials, company size correlates positively with both the existence of a PAC and the level of activity that the PAC maintains. A similar pattern is evident among nonindustrial firms, although there is considerable variation among industry categories (see Table 7).

Overall, companies within the top 20 of each of the six non-industrial categories listed by *Fortune* (120 out of the total of 300 companies, or 40 percent) formed 63 of the 132 PACs (48 percent) created

---

[42] FEC Press Release, May 10, 1978, p. 7; and *Fortune* Directories, May 7, 1979, June 18, 1979, and July 16, 1979.

TABLE 7

PAC Behavior of Fortune-Listed Nonindustrials (300), 1978 Campaign

Category	No. of PACs	Percentage with PACs	Receipts ($000)	Top 20 as % of Top 50	Expenditures ($000)	Top 20 as % of Top 50	Contributions ($000)	Top 20 as % of Top 50
Commercial Banking								
Top 20	13	65	282	54	235	53	70	60
Top 50	25	50	523		447		117	
Diversified Financial								
Top 20	8	40	215	56	178	49	96	46
Top 50	19	38	387		367		210	
Life Insurance								
Top 20	1	5	16	27	13	27	9	28
Top 50	5	10	59		49		32	
Retail								
Top 20	11	55	529	84	358	81	294	80
Top 50	15	30	631		442		366	

Transportation							
Top 20	17	85	728		642		442	
Top 50	29	58	1,100	66	984	65	639	69
Utilities								
Top 20	13	65	1,100		885		339	
Top 50	31	62	1,300	85	1,100	80	528	64
Totals								
Top 20	63	53	2,900		2,300		1,300	
Top 50	124	41	4,000	73	3,400	68	1,900	68

SOURCES: Federal Election Commission, *FEC Reports on Financial Activity, 1977–1978*, Interim Report no. 4, vol. 4 (Washington, D.C.: Federal Election Commission, May 1979); Federal Election Commission, *FEC Disclosure Series No. 8: Corporate Related Political Committees' Receipts and Expenditures, 1976 Campaign* (Washington, D.C.: Federal Election Commission, 1977); Federal Election Commission, *FEC Disclosure Series No. 10: Labor-Related Political Committees' Receipts and Expenditures, 1976 Campaign* (Washington, D.C.: Federal Election Commission, 1978); Walter W. Guzzardi, Jr., "Business Is Learning How to Win in Washington," *Fortune*, March 27, 1978, pp. 52–58; and Common Cause, *1976 Federal Campaign Finances: Vol. 1, Interest Group and Political Party Contributions to Congressional Candidates* (Washington, D.C.: Common Cause, 1977).

by the 300 *Fortune*-ranked companies. PACs were formed among the top 120 companies at a rate of 53 percent, while for all 300 firms the rate was 44 percent. The 63 PACs affiliated with the leading 120 non-industrials (top 20 in each of six categories) had 73 percent of the adjusted receipts ($2.9 million out of $4.0 million) of the top 300 *Fortune* nonindustrials (top 50 in each of six categories). Similarly, 68 percent of the contributions ($1.3 million out of $1.9 million) came from the leading 120 nonindustrials.

As Table 7 indicates, six categories differed considerably with regard to the role played in 1978 by PACs affiliated with the top 20 companies. PACs associated with the largest firms were most active among transportation companies, utilities, and particularly retailers. They were somewhat less active, though still of considerable importance among commercial banks and diversified financial companies. The number of PACs among life insurance companies is too small (only 5 of the top 50 firms created PACs) to be of analytical interest. The higher incidence of PAC formation among *Fortune*-listed nonindustrials when compared with industrial companies (see Table 6) is not surprising. Since only 50 firms are ranked in each category, the 300 nonindustrials tend as a cohort to be larger than their industrial counterparts. In other words, if the nonindustrials were interspersed with the industrials, the group would occupy the higher levels of a combined *Fortune* 1,300 listing. I recognize that, in a sense, this is comparing apples with oranges, since *Fortune* ranks industrials on the basis of sales whereas it ranks non-industrials on criteria that differ for the various categories (assets for commercial banks, life insurance companies, diversified financial firms, and utilities; sales for retailers; and operating revenues for transportation companies). However, the industrial and nonindustrial lists all contain asset figures as well as some revenue data that permit at least rough comparisons. Since PAC formation appears to be related to size of firm, the vigor of PAC activity among the nonindustrials is understandable. The low rate of PAC formation among life insurance companies may be associated with a decision by some life insurance companies to channel contribution activities through regional trade-association PACs. For example, the Hartford-based life insurance companies centralized their contributions through the Insurance Association of Connecticut (Connecticut Insurance Political Action Committee, CIPAC).

Another factor in the case of life insurance companies, however, may partly explain why *Fortune*-ranked nonindustrials have tended to form more federal PACs than have industrial companies, that is, the greater impact of the decisions of the federal government on the operations of a firm, in contrast to those of state governments. Because tradi-

132

tionally the life insurance industry has been regulated by the states, the activities of the state legislatures have been of greater interest to these companies than the decisions of Congress. Although this regulatory primacy of the states is eroding rapidly—as federal regulations continue to encompass life insurance firms and the decisions of Congress and the executive branch increasingly affect every aspect of insurance company activity—a shift in the political focus of the industry toward Washington has been relatively slow in coming about. Even so, in the next few years large life insurance companies will no doubt follow the lead of other industrial firms and create PACs.

More generally, the formation of PACs in the business community appears to depend on the extent to which federal decisions bear on the operations of any given industry or firm. In the nonindustrial category, commercial banks, diversified financial companies (a substantial number of which have savings and loan associations, consumer finance companies, mortgage banks, and security brokerages as important parts of their operations), utilities, and transportation companies are all highly regulated by the federal government or otherwise greatly affected by governmental decisions pertaining explicitly to their companies. Retailing companies, which might be considered an anomaly in this group since historically they were not "regulated" by the federal government, have been primary targets of federal consumer legislation in the past decade and a half. Overall, the categories of nonindustrials ranked by *Fortune* are probably more keenly influenced by industry-specific federal policies than are many industrial firms. The leading nonindustrial firms' greater size and the importance to them of decisions from Washington help to explain the higher incidence of PACs when compared with *Fortune* industrials.

Industry Groupings. Further information concerning firm size and the importance of federal governmental decisions relative to the creation of company PACs appears in Table 8, which summarizes PAC activity of firms in twenty-one industrial categories during the 1976 and 1978 campaigns. In each instance, *Standard and Poor's* classification of firms is used as it appeared in *Business Week*'s "Corporate Scoreboard" of March 19, 1979.[43] Except for aerospace, beverages, and railroads, where fifteen firms are listed by *Business Week*, and tobacco, where only six companies appear, each category consists of the twenty leading companies in the industry selected on the basis of sales.

In addition to documenting the growth in number and size of PACs among the leading firms in each category of industry between 1976 and

---

[43] *"Business Week*'s Corporate Scoreboard: How 1,200 Companies Performed in 1978," *Business Week,* March 19, 1979, pp. 60-104.

TABLE 8

PAC ACTIVITY AMONG FIRMS IN SELECTED NONFINANCIAL INDUSTRIES, 1976 AND 1978

| Category ($000) | PACs among Top 20 Firms in Industry[a] | | | | Adjusted Receipts | | Adjusted Expenditures | | Contributions |
| | 1976 | | 1978[c] | | 1976 | 1978 | 1976 | 1978 | 1978[b] |
	No.	%	No.	%	($000)	($000)	($000)	($000)	($000)
Aerospace[c]	6	40	9	60	269	735	225	671	372
Airlines	5	25	18	90	126	471	77	354	253
Automotive	6	30	12	60	163	627	152	573	395
Beverages[c]	8	53	9	60	221	268	204	255	185
Building Materials	3	15	5	25	44	79	39	84	50
Chemicals	10	50	14	70	307	525	214	502	378
Conglomerates	3	15	11	55	221	570	157	465	296
Drugs	5	25	12	60	70	354	61	314	249

Electrical, Electronics	6	30	11	55	291	536	288	463	335
Food Processing	2	10	9	45	28	277	25	206	111
General Machinery	3	15	7	35	16	108	11	72	56
Metals & Mining	10	50	12	60	201	374	160	320	278
Misc. Manufacturing	5	25	10	50	33	311	30	323	168
Natural Resources	12	60	15	75	478	999	422	942	755
Office Equipment, Computers	0	0	3	15	0	77	0	67	43
Paper & Forest	9	45	14	70	406	735	372	717	595
Railroads[c]	7	47	9	60	455	493	433	538	338
Steel	6	30	10	50	171	398	142	364	255
Tire & Rubber[b]	0	0	3	23	0	16	0	8	8
Tobacco[c]	0	0	3	50	0	73	0	34	29

[a] Ranked on basis of sales.

[b] 1976 corporate contribution figures not available in *FEC 1976 Disclosure Series No. 8*.

[c] Fifteen rather than 20 firms in category for Aerospace, Beverages, and Railroads, 13 for tire and rubber, and 6 for tobacco.

SOURCE: *FEC 1976 Disclosure Series No. 8*, FEC 1978 Interim Report no. 4, and *Business Week*, March 19, 1979, pp. 60-104.

135

1978, Table 8 discloses other interesting facts. When only the largest firms in each category are considered, the incidence of PACs (55 percent) is close to that of the top nonindustrials (53 percent). Except for building materials, office equipment, tire and rubber, and general machinery, over half (58 percent) of the leading firms in each industry had established a PAC by 1978, up from 35 percent in 1976. In ten industries, 60 percent or more of the companies had created political action committees by 1978. Between 1976 and 1978 more PACs were formed in the following industries: airline (from five to eighteen of the twenty leading firms), drug (five to twelve), and automotive (six to twelve) industries and among firms classified as conglomerates (three to eleven).

Natural resource companies—consisting of crude, integrated domestic, and international oil, and coal companies—have been from the outset particularly vigorous in PAC formation and financial activity. These companies far surpassed all other industry groupings in 1978 in terms of PAC receipts, expenditures, and contributions (led by Standard Oil of Indiana). In 1976, they were first in adjusted receipts and second only to railroads in adjusted expenditures. In all likelihood, PAC formation here has been influenced by the ongoing debate within Congress and the White House regarding this nation's energy policies. Similarly, PAC formation and activity among airlines increased during a time when an airline-related issue—deregulation—was on the congressional agenda. Further, paper and forest product companies are vitally affected by federal environmental decisions and the allocation of timberlands. So, too, drug firms, automobile manufacturers, aerospace companies, railroads, beverage producers, steel and nonferrous metal processors, chemical corporations, electronic companies, and conglomerates are influenced by a wide range of industry-specific and general federal and administrative decisions. Not surprising, therefore, are both the adoption of the PAC mechanism by the largest firms in these industries and the substantial growth in PAC activity within nearly all of these groupings between 1976 and 1978. Finally, Table 9—which details PAC formation by trade/membership/health organizations categorized by industry—indicates to what extent persons and companies associated with these industries have increased their electoral activities. We find little correlation between the frequency of PAC formation by companies in an industry and the creation of associational PACs.

This may be seen by comparing the PACs affiliated with various industries that appear in Tables 7 and 8 (nonindustrials and nonfinancial industrials) and the eighteen industries marked with an asterisk in Table 9, omitting any consideration of professional (for example, lawyers,

TABLE 9

PAC FORMATION BY TRADE/MEMBERSHIP/HEALTH ASSOCIATION,
CATEGORIZED BY INDUSTRY, THROUGH JUNE 30, 1979

	Number of PACs	Percentage
Agriculture	37	6.7
*Aerospace	1	0.2
*Airlines	4	0.7
Architects, Engineers	2	0.4
*Automotive	13	2.4
*Beverages	3	0.5
*Building Materials, Construction	58	10.6
Business	9	1.6
*Chemicals	1	0.2
*Commercial Banking	58	10.6
Conservation	6	1.0
Dental	30	5.5
*Drugs	2	0.4
*Electrical	16	2.9
*General Machinery	8	1.5
Hotels, Restaurants, Clubs	5	0.9
Ideological	21	3.8
*Insurance	8	1.5
Lawyers, Legal	28	5.1
Medical	89	16.2
*Metals, Mining	6	1.0
Miscellaneous	43	7.8
*Misc. Manufacturing	18	3.3
*Natural Resources	14	2.5
Non-Bank Financial	7	1.3
*Paper, Forest Products	5	0.9
Realtors	7	1.3
*Retail	19	3.4
*Transportation	9	1.6
*Utilities	13	2.4
Unknown	9	1.6
Total	549	100.0

* Industries that are analyzed in Tables 7 and 8.
SOURCE: *FEC Report on Financial Activity,* Interim Report no. 4, vol. 4.

architects, and engineers), health (for example, medical and dental),
ideological, agricultural, and miscellaneous industry groups. Among
commercial banks, 52 percent of the top fifty firms formed company

PACs, and fifty-eight associational PACs (10.6 percent of all trade/ membership/health PACs) were created. On the other hand, top firms in the building materials industry had a low incidence of corporate PACs (25 percent), but fifty-eight associational PACs (10.6 percent) were registered in the trade/membership/health category. Whereas the aerospace, airlines, beverage, chemical, metals and mining, drug, paper, and forest product industries had few associational PACs, the automotive, electrical, and natural resource industries had considerably more. Life insurance, transportation, and utilities—life insurance having a modest rate of PAC formation among its largest firms (10 percent in 1978), and the latter two having high rates of PAC creation among their leaders (62 percent and 68 percent respectively)—demonstrated almost the same incidence of associational PACs (1.5 percent–1.6 percent). An explanation of any significance that these industry variations may have will have to await further examination of the activities of company-formed and association-affiliated PACs within each industry. For the moment, however, it is of interest to note the variations in industry behavior.

The above data regarding business-related (primarily corporate) PAC activity during 1976 and 1978 have shed some light on the patterns of electoral activity among corporations of differing size and industrial classifications. The analysis, however, must still be considered preliminary for it requires both amplification and refinement as additional data are made available from the Federal Election Commission, and as there is greater opportunity to subject these data to systematic and comprehensive computer analysis in the months ahead.

The PAC Phenomenon: Three Assessments

What can we learn from the data presented here? What should we make of the very discordant perceptions of PACs reflected in the quotations at the beginning of this paper and in other public pronouncements?

Tables 1–9 reveal impressive growth in both numbers and financial activity of PACs, particularly those related to business. The figures suggest that whereas growth opportunities are limited on the labor side, the potential for corporate and other business PAC formation and expansion is virtually unlimited. The data also indicate that among both unions and corporations the size of organization correlates with the incidence of PACs and the level of PAC activity in terms of receipts, expenditures, and contributions. The larger the corporation or union, the more likely it is to have a vigorous PAC. In addition to organizational size in the case of corporations and other business-related groups, a second key factor influencing PAC formation and activity appears to be the importance of federal government decisions to the well-being of a firm or industry. Business and labor PACs have generally supported incumbents, although less so in 1978 than in 1976. While labor PACs have overwhelmingly (95 percent) favored Democratic candidates, corporate and other business-related PACs have been more bipartisan (preferring Republicans to Democrats by approximately a 6:4 ratio). Figures for 1978 also indicate that ideological groups, particularly those with conservative orientation, have surpassed both business and labor in raising money. Finally, the data suggest that PACs in general, and business-related and labor committees in particular, contribute a relatively small amount of funds to congressional candidates. In the campaign of 1978, for example, the $35.1 million contributed by all PACs amounted to less than 18 percent of the nearly $200 million raised by all candidates, while combined business and labor donations probably provided less than 14 percent of the congressional total. The $10.2 million from labor accounted for slightly over 5 percent of congressional receipts while business-related groups contributed another $17.3 million (8.7 percent), of which $9.8 million (4.9 percent) came from corporations and an estimated $7.5 million (3.8 percent) from other business-related groups.

The significance of these figures is not entirely clear, however. Several other recent assessments have disagreed on the impact of PACs, especially those associated with business and labor. The most negative assessment is that of a bipartisan coalition of some 150 House members, headed by Representatives David R. Obey (D-Wis.) and Tom Railsback (R-Ill.), which introduced the Campaign Contribution Reform Act of 1979 (H.R. 4970). This proposal would reduce the amount that a PAC could contribute to a House election from $5,000 to $2,500 (primary, runoff, and general elections are treated separately)—a total of $7,500 per election cycle—and would prohibit House candidates from receiving more than $50,000 from all PACs per election cycle. The bill also seeks to limit to $1,000 the credit extended by professional fund raisers and campaign consultants (such as Richard A. Viguerie) to their candidate-clients for media advertising or direct mail fund-raising services. According to a statement released by Representative Obey, chairman of the Democratic Study Group, the bill was catalyzed by the sharp rise in the number of House candidates receiving more than $50,000 in PAC money, from 57 in 1976 to 176 in 1978, including 45 of 77 freshman members of the House. While acknowledging that "special-interest" groups have a legitimate role to play in the electoral process, Obey states that "their role must be kept in place to protect the integrity of the congressional process and the rights of all Americans."[44] Calling PAC activity "giving with a purpose," Obey at the same time expresses concern about the relationship between PAC contributions and the subsequent lobbying of the groups involved, particularly where the interests of a variety of groups coincide, as when unions and companies in a given industry have a common position on a given issue.

> When that occurs, when a large number of groups which have made substantial contributions to members are all lobbying on the same side of an issue, the pressure generated from those aggregate contributions is enormous and warps the process. It is as if they had made a single, extremely large contribution.[45]

Obey urges prompt passage of the bill "because the longer we wait, the harder it will be to kick the PAC habit," and states that unless PACs are restrained now, "they may become too influential to curb in a few years."[46]

A different assessment, particularly of PACs associated with business groups, appears in two recent articles by the convenor of this conference, Michael J. Malbin, a perceptive observer of the PAC scene. Calling the business PAC phenomenon "neither a mountain nor a molehill,"[47] Malbin notes that aggregate PAC contributions as a percentage of total congressional receipts did not grow from 1976 to 1978. He questions, moreover, whether the overall electoral involvement of business actually has risen in the aftermath of the campaign reforms of the 1970s and suggests that much of the PAC money may be simply "old wine in new bottles" (my language not his), that is, money that was given previously in the form of personal campaign contributions by executives and corporations through both legal and illegal means. Malbin also points out that the new PACs have been less supportive of incumbents than the older committees associated with trade groups. He concludes that "as fast as the funds from business PACs have poured in, fund raisers have been able to find other ways to raise money, and thus keep the PACs proportionately in their place."[48] In a recently published

---

[44] Statement of Representative David R. Obey on the "Campaign Contribution Reform Act of 1979," July 26, 1979, press release issued by the Democratic Study Group, p. 2.

[45] Ibid.

[46] Obey statement, p. 3.

[47] Michael J. Malbin, "The Business PAC Phenomenon: Neither a Mountain nor a Molehill," *Regulation,* vol. 3, no. 3 (May/June 1979), pp. 41–43.

[48] Ibid., p. 43.

EDWIN M. EPSTEIN

companion piece, "Campaign Financing and the 'Special Interests,' "[49] Malbin further develops this thesis, arguing that "PACs, and the connection between their gifts and congressional policy, are a good deal less significant than we have been led to believe."[50] He asserts further that:

> *In light of the record, it is hard to justify the notion that campaign gifts, particularly ones from the more broadly based labor, corporate or ideological PACs, are a special-interest group's downpayment for future special benefits. Some associations may think that way, but associations have become a decreasingly important part of business giving as corporate PACs have grown.* [Emphasis in the original][51]

Rather than focusing on PACs, Malbin argues, reformers should concentrate on outgrowths of the electoral laws such as the increased importance of direct mail specialists who typically appeal to narrowly based extremists at the ends of the political spectrum and raise money for both electoral candidates and issue lobbies in a manner that further polarizes the political process.

An intermediate position between the "kick the PAC habit" view expressed in the Obey statement and what may perhaps be characterized as the "much ado about nothing" thesis advanced by Malbin is taken by the Campaign Finance Study Group associated with Harvard University's Institute of Politics in its recent Report to the Committee on House Administration.[52] This report focuses on three problems arising from the FECA, as amended: (1) individual contribution limits that are too low result in the underfinancing of political campaigns and in a weakening of the political parties that have become increasingly divorced from the process of providing support to candidates; (2) overregulation of the political process places a great burden on all actors in the political system; and (3) money channeled through political action committees has grown.[53] Decrying the fact that present limitations on individual contributions have made candidates increasingly reliant on personal resources (a boon to wealthy individuals) and political action committees, the study group report notes:

[49] Michael J. Malbin, "Campaign Financing and the 'Special Interests'," *The Public Interest,* no. 56 (Summer 1979), pp. 21–42.

[50] Ibid., p. 21.

[51] Ibid., p. 36.

[52] The Institute of Politics, John F. Kennedy School of Government, Harvard University, *An Analysis of the Impact of the Federal Election Campaign Act, 1972–78: A Report by the Campaign Finance Study Group to the Committee on House Administration of the U.S. House of Representatives,* May 1979. Most of the study group's useful critique of PACs is the product of Xandra Kayden.

[53] *Study Group Report,* Summary, p. 1.

If one purpose of the campaign reforms of the 1970s was to reduce the influence of interest groups by restricting their financial importance to candidates for Congress, that aspect of the policy has failed. The growth of PAC funding has generally favored incumbents and Republicans.[54]

The tone of the report reflects considerable concern about PACs—for example, "An increasing torrent of money has been channeled through the political action committees [PACs]"; "understanding the role of political action committees is especially troublesome"[55]—and points to their increasing role in financing congressional candidates. The report notes that PAC money is "interested money"—that is, it is linked to a legislative lobbying agenda; that reliance on PAC funds had led to a nationalization of the sources of money available to candidates, bringing in funds from outside a candidate's state or district (particularly Washington); and that the growing role of PACs has resulted in political money becoming bureaucratically organized—that is, detached from their source and aggregated in a fashion which renders them unaccountable.[56] Notwithstanding these concerns, the study group eschews recommending the imposition of additional limitations on PAC activity. Noting the virtual impossibility of legislatively rolling back the clocks to 1974 to make PACs simply disappear, the study group considers that the most probable result of reducing the amount that PACs can contribute to candidates would be to

> merely divert, but not stem, the flow of money. Proliferation of political action committees, perfectly legal cooperation among PACs, and a rapid expansion in independent expenditures by PACs are the clearly predictable consequences. Considering the combined reasoning which governed the *Buckley* and *Bellotti* decisions, there does not appear to be a legislative remedy for this development that will pass constitutional muster.[57]

Rather, the study group proposes to resolve (at least in part) the problem of burgeoning PAC contributions by indirect rather than direct action, urging Congress to raise the individual contribution limit to $3,000 (or, better still, $5,000), thereby making congressional candidates less dependent on money derived from PACs.

---

[54] *Study Group Report,* pp. 2–39.
[55] *Study Group Report,* pp. 1–6 and 1–7.
[56] Ibid., pp. 1–8.
[57] Ibid., pp. 1–9.

A Fourth Public Policy Perspective on the Role of PACs

The three assessments presented in the preceding section offer different perspectives on the present impact of business-related and labor PACs; they also imply very different future roles for these nonparty committees in the American electoral process. Although my own view of the present status and public policy implications of business and labor electoral activities has certain elements in common with these accounts, I perceive PAC growth and activity in yet a fourth way.

PAC operations in 1976 and 1978 reveal only the tip of a possible iceberg—clearly for corporations and other business-related groups, but to some extent even in the case of labor. Let us look briefly at the union PAC potential.

The number of union PACs will *not* increase much beyond the 303 that functioned during 1976. Indeed, as we have seen, the number of labor PACs active during the 1977–1978 election declined to 281. Most unions that are politically active have been operating PACs for years. Moreover, union PAC activity tends to be highly concentrated. In 1978, the 10 largest union PACs contributed slightly over half of all money that labor gave to congressional candidates. Eight of the 10 PACs were affiliated with top 25 unions ranked on the basis of size; 1 (the Seafarers International) was the forty-fifth ranking union, and only 1 (the Marine Engineers) had fewer than 100,000 members.[58] Of the 303 labor committees active in 1976, 42 committees having receipts or expenditures of over $100,000 raised and spent 82 percent of labor's funds. If another 21 union PACs having receipts or expenditures of $50,000–100,000 are added in, we have nearly 90 percent of the union total. The remaining PACs represent either small unions or affiliates of large international unions and, as such, were subject to the single contribution limit. It is pointless, therefore, to look for growth in the number of labor committees.

Labor's pool of voluntary political dollars could probably benefit from more productive fund-raising techniques. Very few unions, whether AFL–CIO-affiliated or independent, have average contributions of a dollar per worker per year. If even that small amount were collected from each unionist, organized labor would raise some $19.4 million annually—or nearly $39.0 million biennially—from its U.S. members; this would be almost double the amount generated by labor for campaign 1978 ($19.8 million) and would enable unions to contribute some

58 U.S., Department of Labor, Bureau of Labor Statistics, *Directory of National Unions and Employees Associations, 1975* (Washington, D.C.: U.S. Government Printing Office, 1978), pp. 17–46.

$20.0 million directly to congressional candidates. Some unions are beginning to use payroll deductions (checkoffs) to increase their per-member annual yield where this method is available through either reciprocal rights or collective bargaining. Others are considering direct mail campaigns among their members—a technique used to good advantage by conservative groups and by the National Republican Congressional Campaign Committee. It is assumed that labor will maintain unabated its political research and education, voter registration, and get-out-the-vote activities (financed largely out of treasury funds) that constitute its political forte. Notwithstanding its declining membership and some evidence of organizational malaise, organized labor's constituency and resources remain sufficiently large, and its political expertise runs sufficiently deep to give the union movement a viable political base, at least in the short run.

The most interesting view of the PAC iceberg is from the corporate side. We have already traced the rapid growth in numbers and vigor of corporate PAC activity in the less than five years since the 1974 FECA amendments became operative, and we have noted that there is considerable room among companies for further formation of PACs, even if only the very largest firms are considered to be PAC prospects. A recent "Memo from COPE" reports that more than a hundred corporations have formed political action committees since the beginning of 1979.[59] Moreover, most corporate PACs that are already functioning have ample opportunity to increase the size and scope of their operations. Given the trends and the potential, company committees show great promise for continuing to increase their numbers and the magnitude of their funds. In the campaign of 1980, there could be over a thousand corporate PACs operating with aggregate receipts of $25–30 million and contributions of $15–18 million. By 1982, the number of corporate PACs could reach 1,250 with receipts of $40–50 million and contributions of $25–30 million to congressional candidates (assuming that the present ratio of disbursement to contribution does not change drastically). My research suggests, moreover, that at least some companies will begin to undertake new forms of electoral involvement such as automatic payroll deduction, nonpartisan registration, get-out-the-vote drives, and internal political communication among managerial level employees and shareholders. I consider these projections of future corporate PAC operations to be conservative estimates and not reckless speculations. Similarly, business-related (but noncorporate) associations are likely to increase both the size and the activity of their PAC

---

[59] Committee on Political Education, AFL–CIO, "Memo From COPE," August 6, 1979, p. 1. FEC sources place the number closer to 50.

operations and to explore more vigorously independent expenditures and "in-kind" contributions. If a provision currently in the Senate version of the FECA amendments of 1979 becomes law, trade associations and other groups will find it easier to solicit members and employees of constituent organizations. The pool of potential PAC registrants among associations is large. For example, of approximately 5,100 trade and professional associations across the nation, an estimated 1,500 currently have headquarters in Washington, D.C., alone. The number of noncorporate, nonlabor PACs could increase to 1,000 for the 1980 campaign.

Social scientists have long noted that political phenomena frequently have unintended and even paradoxical effects. Labor's efforts during the 1970s to legitimize the PAC mechanism and to liberalize the legal constraints surrounding PAC electoral activities provide a case in point of such unintended consequences. During the 1970s labor clearly fought for and won the legislative mandate to establish political action committees and to engage in other forms of partisan and nonpartisan political activity. Labor's legislative successes had, however, a direct and beneficial effect upon business. This rapid success of PACs in the business community was not anticipated by organized labor's political leadership. Nor did the leadership foresee that the growth of business PACs would erode labor's electoral influence *position* by providing alternative sources of funding for both congressional incumbents and challengers (particularly Democrats) who in the past depended heavily on union money for their campaigns. Although labor's overall electoral effectiveness vis-à-vis business has not yet been seriously impaired, it unquestionably has been weakened. The irony of all this is that organized labor unwittingly sowed the seeds that have borne the very fruit it sought to prevent— enhanced business electoral effectiveness—through business use of labor's favorite mechanism, the political action committee.

A critical aspect of the aggregate effect of three rounds of FECA legislation during the past decade has not, I believe, been appreciated fully by either those who see business electoral behavior during the 1970s as so much *déjà vu*, or those who fear that business hegemony is rapidly developing (if it has not already developed) within the American electoral process. As Malbin and others have argued, campaign funds coming from business may not have really increased in either an absolute or a relative sense, and PAC money may in fact constitute primary funds that business had previously channeled into campaigns either directly or sub rosa through company or associational officials, or through various in-kind or otherwise masked contributions, some of which were patently illegal. The essential point, however, is that even if these sums remained constant, the *process* by which corporations and other business-related groups raise and expend campaign monies has changed fundamentally.

While in the past the raising and spending of funds were largely ad hoc, informal, and unsystematic activities, today such efforts have become institutionalized within companies and are in the hands of staff professionals (usually in public affairs positions) who serve on an on-going basis as the organizational focal point for electoral activities. PACs are therefore visible to office holders, prospective candidates, and party officials—as well as to each other—and have become ports of call for office seekers and fund raisers, as well as mechanisms for more effective coordination of business groups. In summary, PACs allow corporations and business-related associations to organize and *institutionalize* their electoral activities in a highly efficient way. For most companies, however, PAC efforts are still at a rudimentary stage, having been devoted primarily to raising funds from upper-level management employees, for contributions to individual campaigns. Currently these efforts are being expanded to lower levels of administrative and executive personnel and, in the case of some companies, to shareholders. As labor has so well demonstrated for years, PACs provide an ideal way of coordinating within a company a wide range of grass-roots political activities that make use of human and other organizational resources found in a corporation and that are therefore so valuable in an election campaign. In the 1980s we are likely to find much greater corporate efforts to increase political participation by employees, shareholders, and even retirees. The result could be a more comprehensive and extensive electoral involvement by members of the business community than we have seen in the past.

In addition to institutionalizing electoral activity within the corporate entity through the political action committee, the campaign reform legislation of the 1970s has legitimated that activity both within firms and in the greater community. Electoral politics, so to speak, has come out of the corporate closet and is now recognized as a legal and appropriate activity for business. Such enhanced status, together with a defined legal mechanism for such activity—the PAC—makes it possible for companies (1) to encourage political participation among corporate personnel (who might otherwise be reluctant); (2) to encourage other firms to increase their electoral involvement by establishing PACs, thereby "keeping up with the Joneses"; and (3) in general, to undertake political activity with a heightened sense of rectitude and purpose. Political legitimacy coupled with the institutionalization of politics within the organizational framework no doubt will lead to increased and more effective corporate political action. In short, I am suggesting that even if to date there has been little change in the degree of business electoral involvement, when measured in terms of dollars infused into political campaigns, there has been a fundamental in-kind change in that involvement.

Whether this institutionalization and legitimization of business electoral activity and its consequences is considered as beneficial or deleterious to the electoral process depends upons one's normative stance and, to a large degree, upon whose ox is being gored. Advocates of the Obey-Railsback bill clearly believe that the current rate of activity by "special interest" PACs is excessive and wish to curtail it. Organized labor wisely supports these efforts to limit individual and aggregate PAC activity. In the last Congress, the same labor representatives who were most instrumental in shaping the PAC provisions in the earlier campaign acts urged that PAC contribution limits be reduced from $5,000 to $2,500 and that partial public financing of House general election races be instituted. Arguably, the effect of the proposed halving of PAC contributions might be more cosmetic than real, since the great bulk of both labor and business contributions come in amounts of less than $2,500; yet it is noteworthy that union PACs gave more contributions of $2,500 and above in 1976 than did business. Labor apparently is willing to forgo the short-run advantage of maintaining a higher limit in exchange for the long-run benefit of forestalling large corporate contributions that could come once company PACs have assembled truly substantial funds. For similar reasons, during the spring of 1979 organized labor strongly backed the two public financing bills (H.R. 1 and S.623) considered and shelved by Congress. Many labor officials would like to have unions, corporations, and other interest groups prohibited from making direct money contributions through their PACs to political candidates and party committees. Because they foresee business contributions eventually outstripping direct labor donations, labor officials would prefer to restrict business and labor involvement to activities in which labor has the greatest comparative advantage—voter registration, political research and education, and get-out-the-vote drives.

Some thoughtful persons, such as Malbin, do not concede that business and labor electoral involvement has become a problem. While recognizing the potential influence of business-related and particularly ideological PACs on electoral politics, they believe that more serious possibilities are the erosion of the parties and the successful appeal to extremist positions by the "new breed" of direct mail political fund raisers and the candidates they support. Although disagreeing with Malbin on the political importance of PACs formed by economic and other "special-interest" groups, the Harvard Study Group agrees that the redress of present imbalances in our system of financing elections lies more in raising contribution limits for individuals and enhancing the role of the parties than in restricting PACs. While, I share this general view, my own position is that reducing the amount that a single PAC can give to a candidate during a single election to $2,500 ($7,500 overall) will not in any case prevent a candidate from raising necessary campaign funds nor prevent PACs from supporting their favorites. Arguably, such a limitation might help a particularly wealthy PAC avoid the temptation to throw its financial weight around. Two other factors should be noted, however: (1) contributions of over $2,500, while hardly unknown among labor or business PACs, are not the norm in the corporate community; and (2) given the rapid rise in inflation, even if there is no lowering of the limits, within a few years inflation will have greatly reduced the significance of the current $5,000 limit.

Nonetheless, I consider this limit proposed by the Obey-Railsback bill to merit serious consideration, with the caveat that it be reviewed periodically to permit upward and downward revision to reflect significant changes in the cost of living and the consequent value of the dollar. I have considerable reservations, however, concerning the imposition of limits on the aggregate amount that a candidate can accept from PACs, particularly the ceiling of $50,000 established in the pending Campaign Contribution Reform Act. Recent studies by Gary C. Jacobson demonstrate convincingly that limiting the amounts that candidates can spend in an election favors incumbents over challengers. Says Jacobson

> In general, any increase in spending by both candidates will help the challenger (by bringing him to the attention of the voters). Public subsidies—or any other policy which gets more money into the hands of challengers—should therefore make House selections more competitive. . . . On the other hand, any reform measure which decreases spending by the candidates will favor incumbents. This includes limits on campaign contributions and groups, as well as ceilings on total spending by candidates.[60]

If PACs do in fact become increasingly less incumbent-oriented—a large "if" indeed—limiting the amount challengers can accept from a PAC to $50,000 will place a challenger of modest means under a very

---

[60] Gary C. Jacobson, "The Effects of Campaign Spending in Congressional Elections," *American Political Science Review*, vol. 72, no. 3 (June 1978), pp. 469–491 at 489. Also, Gary C. Jacobson, "Public Funds for Congressional Campaigns: Who Would Benefit?" in *Political Finance*, Sage Electoral Studies Yearbook, vol. 5, ed. Herbert E. Alexander (Beverly Hills, California: Sage Publications, 1979), pp. 99–127.

severe constraint, particularly if there is no public financing of congressional elections and if excessively low contributions limits for individuals are maintained. Far better, in my opinion, to provide partial public subsidization of congressional candidates and to raise the ceiling on individual contributions to a more realistic figure ($3,000–5,000) than to attempt to impose burdensome—and possibly, unconstitutional—constraints on candidates by restricting the amount they can receive from PACs.

There is yet another anomaly arising out of the FECA that pertains to unions, corporations, and other business groups that should be addressed by Congress. The reforms of the 1970s have given both business and labor a distinct advantage over social interests that have neither the legal right to use organization funds for PAC start-up and administrative costs, nor the requisite financial or organizational resources to emulate labor or business PACs. Correction of this imbalance seems called for, perhaps by permitting PACs unaffiliated with any sponsoring organization to collect additional money (above what contributors may currently give them) to meet the committee's administrative costs. A proposal to rectify this situation was recently omitted from the draft of FECA amendments for 1979 prepared by the Senate Rules and Administration Committee.[61]

Conclusion

PACs have played a useful role in the American electoral process during the 1970s by encouraging and facilitating collective political participation by persons associated with a wide variety of economic, professional, ideological, and other social interest groups. "Special interests," including business and labor, have a legitimate place in electoral policies.[62] Difficulties can arise, however, from their participation. It is important to note that although business and labor are usually said to be electoral competitors, they in fact share enough political interests so that they can cooperate as well as compete. Joint business-labor geographical concerns or industrial needs, or the opposition of a common foe (for example, a militant environmental group), could encourage cooperation between these two powerful coalitions. Conceivably, one of the greatest challenges to the integrity of American electoral politics could arise from excessive harmony between powerful business and powerful labor. While

---

[61] *Campaign Practice Reports,* vol. 6, no. 16 (August 6, 1979), p. 9.

[62] I have developed this position with regard to corporations in Edwin M. Epstein, *The Corporation in American Politics* (Englewood Cliffs, New Jersey: Prentice-Hall, Inc., 1969), pp. 304–314.

such a coalition has not yet come about, it could do so in the future and any signs of such a development bear watching.

A second factor requiring scrutiny is the effect of the PAC phenomenon on corporate employees and shareholders, and on union members. Throughout this century, in addition to preserving the integrity of the electoral process and protecting those chosen by it from subversion by economic interests, public regulation of corporate and labor involvement has been motivated by a desire to protect individual union members and shareholders from political pressure by their organizations. Under the FECA reforms, the union member or corporate employee is probably no worse off and possibly somewhat better off now than before. The anti-reprisal provisions in the present federal legislation are likely to be prophylactic for the average union member or middle-level corporate manager who does not wish to participate in the political activities of the organization. The higher one's position in a firm or union, however, the less useful are these statutory safeguards. Upper-level business and labor officials still undoubtedly face subtle peer pressures and psychological arm-twisting. An additional pressure on potential $100+ PAC contributors arises from FECA disclosure requirements. Despite assurances of good faith by organizations that all contributions activity will be kept from the eyes of organizational superiors, corporate managers and union officials are aware that a record of their contributions (or noncontributions) is available for all to see in the FEC's open records; thus, the FEC safeguards are hardly fail-safe in protecting their intended beneficiaries. To date there have been no formal allegations of patently illegal activity. There have been occasional anecdotal reports of PAC fund-raising activities which strain the spirit if not the letter of the law. Such cases appear to be sufficiently isolated, however, as not to constitute a serious problem at present. It is to be hoped that they will not become one in the future.

By now, I am certain, the reader has detected my rather cautious, "wait-and-see" approach to suggestions that the present regulatory framework governing the involvement of unions, corporations, and other business groups requires a drastic overhauling. In large measure, what Congress chooses to do in the future may lie directly in the hands of business organizations and labor unions that operate PACs. Undoubtedly, the most important rationale underlying public regulation of corporate and labor electoral involvement has been the desire to ensure that the power of wealth does not run roughshod over the people's will. In 1978, business and labor PACs provided 18 percent of the $199 million raised by congressional candidates. This percentage does not, in my view, amount to excessive interference in the political process or present the kind of threat to the body politic that would justify dramatic new regulations for business and labor electoral activities. But we might reach that point if business or labor badly overplays its hand by misuse or overuse of its political action committees. If PACs become "too successful"—that is, if in aggregate they become a disproportionate source of funds for congressional candidates (for my taste, in excess of 25 percent), which could be the case if business-related PACs should raise $50 million per election biennium and should contribute half that directly to federal candidates, and if labor PACs should achieve their $40 million goal—we might, indeed, reach a point where too much campaign money derives from these sources. This would be particularly the case if business and labor contributions were largely reinforcing—supporting incumbents (although different ones to some extent), doing little for challengers, and thereby perpetuating the congressional status quo. Similarly, if a substantial number of our largest corporations began to generate PACs having receipts in excess of $250,000–300,000 and contributions of $140,000–200,000, so that "Big Business" became identified in the public mind with the funding of political campaigns or otherwise became too widely involved with the electoral process, the limits of public tolerance would probably be exceeded. This will be the case particularly if, as I suspect, organized labor fails to keep pace financially and thereby fails to maintain a countervailing power in electoral politics. Finally, if enough business or labor PACs coordinated closely their efforts to throw large sums of money into the final stages of an election—in an attempt to tip close races or to "get" candidates appearing on an "enemies' list"—the questioning of excessive PAC power would be justified.

As long as money and other resources from business and labor continue to be *a* factor rather than *the* factor in the financing of federal candidates, these sectors of society have a legitimate role to play in that process. If, however, by their actions, business and/or labor cross that narrow line, they will become a threat rather than a benefit to the body politic—a threat which is antithetical to the conduct of a democratic society—and must be constrained through the legislative process. Given the unforeseen and rather ironic consequences of past electoral reform efforts, let us hope that reasoned self control by business and labor will prevail and that major legislative therapy directed toward them will not be necessary. For on occasion, despite the best of intentions, the prescribed congressional cure has had nearly as many problems associated with it as the diagnosed disease—a situation not conducive to the overall well-being of the American electoral system.

Of Mountains and Molehills:
PACs, Campaigns, and Public Policy

Michael J. Malbin

Political action committees (PACs) have grown substantially since the 1974 and 1976 campaign laws were adopted. Edwin Epstein has presented the numbers documenting this growth, and they need not be repeated here. Instead this paper will concentrate on the significance of those numbers. The theses to be developed are as follows:

• Taken as a whole, PACs increased in number and became more important to the electoral process between 1974 and 1976, but—despite the picture given by most analysts—they were no more important proportionately in 1978 than they were in 1976.

• The growth in PACs since 1974 has been matched by a decline in the importance of large contributions from individuals. Because corporate PACs are increasing faster than any other PACs, and because large individual contributions in the past tended to come disproportionately from business interests, the rise of one and decline of the other seem roughly to cancel each other out. Instead of saying the law has failed to achieve its purpose of curbing the power of the "special interests," we should say—at least with respect to business interests—that the law has achieved the goal of transforming the character of business participation in politics from the undisclosed and sometimes seedy form it took before 1974 to the more institutionalized and accountable form we see today.

• PACs traditionally have favored incumbents over either challengers or candidates for open seats. It has been alleged that this imbalance occurs because PACs are trying to influence legislation directly by using their contributions to buy access to legislators, instead of trying to influence legislation indirectly by affecting the outcome of elections. Data

Some material from the second half of this essay first appeared in my article, "Campaign Financing and the 'Special Interests'," *The Public Interest,* no. 56 (Summer 1979), pp. 21–42. Peter Metters, an AEI intern assigned to work with me during the summer of 1979, is responsible for the incredible amount of work that went into the tables in this paper. For both the actual job he did and for his attitude while doing it, I owe him my thanks.

152

collected for this study give some support for this view, but not much. Incumbents, especially Democratic incumbents, do receive a high percentage of their money from PACs. However, few candidates receive so much from any one PAC or any one group of related PACs as to make them dependent on a particular industry or single set of interests for their election. Our data indicate that, while many of the older trade association and corporate PACs appear to be interested in buying access to incumbents, the newer corporate PACs are playing an electorally more sophisticated game, concentrating on close races, even when that means opposing powerful Democratic incumbents.

• The leading "reforms" of the campaign laws, which have been proposed to alleviate the supposedly excessive influence of PACs, would only play to the strengths of the newly powerful single-issue and ideological PACs, weaken the political influence of organized labor, and leave business interests virtually untouched. Because these reforms have the endorsement of the AFL–CIO, they would, if adopted, be likely to become another case Professor Epstein could add to his ongoing series of instances in which organized labor has backed something that worked ultimately to its own disadvantage.

This paper examines each of these points in detail and concludes with some general reflections on the relationship between interest-group campaign contributions and public policy. It proposes some unorthodox changes in the campaign law, which would deal with the problem of the special interests by making more money available for campaigning, not less.

PACs in the Whole Picture

The first thing we need to do is dispel the myth—fostered by Common Cause, congressional sponsors of public financing, and the press—that PACs are on a growth curve wildly disproportionate to the growth in campaign costs as a whole. Table 1 presents a more accurate view of PAC growth, even though the data from different elections in this table are not strictly comparable. The first two years are based on material originally compiled by Common Cause, which did not break down contributions from individuals in the same way in 1972 and 1974. Data for 1976 and 1978 are from the Federal Election Commission (FEC) and compare directly with each other.

Despite the difficulties with the data, a few conclusions emerge readily: First, PAC contributions to House candidates went up by about three percentage points of total receipts between 1972 and 1974 (when the law was not in effect) and two percentage points between 1976 and 1978 (when it was). The growth between 1974 and 1976, the first

TABLE 1

FUNDING SOURCES FOR CANDIDATES IN U.S. HOUSE AND SENATE GENERAL ELECTIONS, 1972–1978

Year	Amount Raised ($ millions)	Indiv. contrib. $0–100	Indiv. contrib. $101–499	Indiv. contrib. $500+	Nonparty PACs	Parties	Candidate to self	Other loans	Source unknown
Percent Distribution									
House									
1972	38.9 [a]	20	\{ 39 \}		14	17	—	—	10
1974	45.7	\{ 58 \}		15	17	4	6	—	—
1976	65.7	37	12	11	23	8	9	1	—
1978	92.2	35	10	12	25	7	9	2	—

Senate									
1972	23.3ª	40 (⎫		27	12	14	0.4	—	8
1974	28.2	49 ⎭)		27	11	6	1	—	6
1976	39.1	28	13	27	15	4	12	0	—
1978	66.0	37	11	22	13	6	8	3	—

ª May not include some data before April 7, 1972, when disclosure became required. 1972 and 1974 figures do not add up to 100 percent because the sources of some contributions are not known for those years. When the figures for 1976 and 1978 do not add up, it is because of rounding.

SOURCES:

1972 and 1974: Gary C. Jacobson, "The Pattern of Campaign Contributions to Candidates for the U.S. House of Representatives, 1972–78," in *An Analysis of the Federal Election Campaign Act, 1972–78: A Report by the Campaign Finance Study Group to the Committee on House Administration, U.S. House of Representatives* (Cambridge, Mass.: The Institute of Politics, Harvard University, May 1979), pp. 2–13 (House—1972), pp. 2–9 (Senate—1972, 1974), pp. 2–14 (House—1974). Includes candidates with major party competition only.

1976: *Federal Election Commission Disclosures Series No. 6* (Senatorial Campaigns) April 1977, and *No. 9* (House of Representatives Campaigns), September 1977.

1978: *Federal Election Commission Reports on Financial Activity, 1977–1978*, Interim Report no. 5 (U.S. Senate and House Campaigns), June 1979.

election under the new law, was five percentage points. These figures are not insignificant, but neither are they as spectacular as some press releases talking about a "50 percent increase in PAC contributions between 1976 and 1978" would have us believe. PAC contributions did go up between 1976 and 1978, but at a rate that was only slightly faster than the increase in contributions from all sources. The growth between 1972 and 1976 is more significant, but it was a predictable and fully intended consequence of the 1974 and 1976 amendments to the campaign act. One major impetus behind the post-Watergate campaign finance reforms was a desire to end large contributions from corporate "fat-cats," "double-envelope" individual contributions collected and bound together in an outside envelope with a corporation's return address, and illegal in-kind corporate contributions. Legal restrictions on corporate political action committees were ended in 1974 because the PACs were seen as a more savory and more publicly accountable conduit for business to express itself politically. The goal never was to end the role of business in politics, but to transform it. That goal was achieved.

Evidence for the view that the increase in contributions from political action committees represents a transformation in kind rather than a proportional increase in business's political role can be seen in the data on individual contributions. The proportional role of large individual contributions dropped substantially between 1972 and 1978. Contributions in excess of $100 went from 39 percent to 22 percent of all House receipts over those years. Because most of the large contributions traditionally have come from business interests, this drop seems more than adequate to account for the proportionate growth of PACs.

The fastest growth in contributions came not from PACs but from two other categories: contributions by the candidates to their own campaign (which the Supreme Court said could not be limited) and individual contributions of $100 or less. The growth in these small gifts is probably attributable directly to the increased use of nationwide computerized mailing lists for fund raising by congressional candidates.

The law has had less apparent impact on funding sources for the Senate than the House. In the Senate, PAC contributions have stayed remarkably steady, large ($500+) contributions have gone down, and small contributions up to $100 have gone up. Again, national direct mail methods of fund raising seem to account for the change.

In both the Senate and the House elections, therefore, the law seems in overall terms to be achieving two of the objectives reformers had in mind. It is true that the major economic interests have not been read out of the campaign finance picture, but why, after all, should they be? More to the point, the role played by the economic interests has been made public *without* becoming proportionally more important and perhaps even becoming less so. At the same time, the small contributors —the persons so widely praised in the reform literature of only a few years ago—are indeed playing a proportionally far more significant role than they used to play. Other consequences of 1970s campaign finance reform may not have been so benign, and we shall discuss some of these later. But to cite PAC growth by itself as an unintended and harmful result of the law seriously misses the point.

PACs and Candidate Receipts

Merely knowing that special-interest contributions have not grown in proportional importance over the years for which data are available does not settle the issue whether PACs are a problem. Even if they are no *more* important than they used to be, PACs may still play too much of a role in total campaign financing. Critics say that PACs tend to favor incumbents—especially "safe" incumbents with important committee positions—because their interest lies more in protecting their access to key legislators than in influencing the results of elections. The corollaries to this view are that PACs shortchange challengers and newcomers seeking open seats and that cutting down on the role of PACs will make challengers more competitive.

PACs do tend to favor incumbents, but the picture is by no means as clear cut as we are normally led to believe. Part of the problem stems from the way the data have been presented, both by Common Cause in 1972 and 1974 and by the FEC in 1976 and 1978. We are told what percentage of PAC money goes to incumbents, challengers, and candidates for open seats, but the data are not related either to the competitiveness of the race in question or to the percentage of candidates who fit within a given category. The importance of these factors should be apparent. First, competitiveness: since most challengers have little realistic chance of winning against most House incumbents in any given year, and since most people are reluctant to "waste" money on a candidate who has no chance of winning, it distorts the picture to talk about the receipts of all incumbents versus all challengers. A much clearer picture can be obtained by controlling for both party and competitiveness. Second, percentage of candidates in a given category: it should be obvious that if safe incumbents represent about 40 percent of all House general-election candidates (as they do) and if they receive about 40 percent of all nonparty PAC contributions to general-election candidates (as they do), one cannot use the 40 percent contribution figure to claim that PACs favor safe incumbents disproportionately.

Tables 2 and 3 compare how groups of PACs distributed their funds to groups of candidates in House and Senate general elections, divided by party, incumbency, and competitiveness. In each case, the *percentages* of a group's funds given to a certain type of candidate are compared with the percentage of candidates of that type. Definitions used in compiling these two tables, as well as Tables 4–7, are as follows:

CANDIDATES—The tables, following FEC practices, only include general-election candidates with gross receipts of $10,000 or more.

INCUMBENT BIG WINNERS AND OPEN SEAT BIG WINNERS—These candidates won with 60 percent or more of the two-party vote. Definitions for the other types of candidates follow from these two definitions.

ALL RECEIPTS, REPUBLICAN PARTY, DEMOCRATIC PARTY—These figures incorporate party expenditures made on behalf of candidates. For that reason, they do not agree exactly with figures released by the FEC.

43 LABOR PACs—The information from this and other combined PAC groups was obtained from special FEC computer runs. The 43 Labor PACs grouped together include all those with 1977–1978 receipts of $50,000 or more as of June 30, 1978. The $7,724,862 contributed by these 43 committees to candidates in the 1978 House and Senate general elections represents 75 percent of the $10.3 million distributed to all federal candidates by 211 labor committees in 1977–1978.

72 BUSINESS PACs—This group includes the 44 corporate and 28 trade association PACs with receipts of $30,000 or more as of June 30, 1978. The 44 corporate PACs' contributions of $1,603,726 to House and Senate candidates represented only 16 percent of the $9.8 million that 697 corporate PACs gave to federal candidates in 1977–1978. If we assume that about half of the money in the FEC's noncorporate, nonlabor groupings comes from business associations,[1] the $3,470,115 contributed by the 28 trade associations would represent 46 percent of the $7.5 million contributed to federal candidates in 1977–1978 by groups in this category.

Corporate and trade association PACs are grouped together, despite the author's expectation that corporate and association PACs would distribute their money differently, because these particular 44 corporations and 28 associations were found to have similar giving patterns. The author doubts that this is a universal pattern.

Only large groups were considered, even though doing so excluded most of the total contributed by corporate PACs, because the purpose of this study ultimately is to say something about the influence of con-

---

[1] Edwin M. Epstein, "The Business PAC Phenomenon: An Irony of Electoral Reform," *Regulation,* May/June 1979, p. 37.

tributions on policy. If money influences policy directly, as some contend, it seems unlikely that small PACs would have much direct influence. They might, of course, have an indirect influence, especially in a close election. If scores of PACs started sending small gifts to a candidate who is clearly more pro-business than his opponent, they could influence the outcome of that election and thereby influence policy indirectly. Whatever the indirect effect, however, no one would argue that the small gifts by themselves meant much in terms of lobbying power. (Nonetheless, it would be useful for the FEC to undertake a detailed computer analysis for all corporate and labor PACs.)

15 CONSERVATIVE PACs—This group consists of the Americans for Constitutional Action, Committee for Responsible Youth Politics, Committee for the Survival of a Free Congress, National Conservative Political Action Committee, Fund for a Conservative Majority, Conservative Victory Fund, Citizens for the Republic, Public Service PAC, Business-Industry Political Action Committee (also included among the business PACs), United Congressional Appeal, Western Intermountain Network PAC, Gun Owners of America, Right to Bear Arms Political Victory Fund, National Rifle Association Political Victory Fund, and the Committee to Defeat the Union Bosses' Candidates.

7 LIBERAL PACs—This group consists of the Council for a Livable World, National Committee for an Effective Congress, League of Conservation Voters, National Abortion Rights Action League, National Organization for Women, National Women's Political Caucus, and the Women's Political Caucus of California.

DEMOCRATIC PARTY COMMITTEES—These include ones set up by individual members of the House leadership, as well as the national party committees.

REPUBLICAN PARTY COMMITTEES—These consist of only the three major national party committees.

These tables show, first and most surprisingly, that eight of the twelve groups of incumbents in the House and Senate got about the same from all nonparty PACs as they would be expected to get if PAC money were distributed randomly to all candidates. The exceptions were Democratic House incumbents who won or lost contested reelections, and Republican Senate incumbents in the same two categories. Safe incumbents from both parties received no bonus in contributions from the PACs, despite the fact that these groups contain the largest number of people in positions of power. That is not meant to suggest that these safe incumbents did not do well. What really seems to have happened is that PACs took the money they might have given to hopeless challengers and distributed it instead to people in close races.

TABLE 2
HOUSE OF REPRESENTATIVES
How Groups of PACs Distributed Their Contributions:
Percentage Distribution by Party, Incumbency, and Closeness of Race

	All Candidates			% to All Candidates	Democrats Incumbents		
	Total contri- butions	Average contri- bution	No. of candi- dates	% to All Candidates	% to big winners	% to close winners	% to losers
All candidates in category			733	100	25	7	2
All receipts [a]	$92,537,042	$126,244	733	100	19	8	3
All nonparty PACs	22,842,190	31,163	733	100	27	12	4
43 labor PACs	5,673,537	13,381	424	100	33	23	8
72 business PACs	5,073,841	8,870	572	100	25	8	2
15 conservative PACs	1,552,180	3,900	398	100	6	1	0
7 liberal PACs	197,765	1,866	106	100	10	25	15
Republican party [a]	3,780,459	13,697	276	100	—	—	—
Democratic party [a]	829,246	2,737	303	100	21	28	13

NOTE: Figures may not add to 100 percent because of rounding.
[a] Includes party expenditures on behalf of candidates.

Labor gave disproportionately to most Democrats, except hopeless challengers. Business gave as much to Democratic incumbents as would be expected from random distribution; very little to Democratic challengers or candidates for open seats; and disproportionately to most Republicans except those challenging safe incumbents (who got very little), challengers in close races with Democratic incumbents (who got about the same as in a random distribution), and easy winners of open seats (again, about the same). The ideological PACs on both left and right concentrated heavily on close races. For House Republican candidates, the distribution of gifts by ideological PACs is surprisingly parallel to that of business PACs, while in the Senate business seemed somewhat more concerned about incumbents in trouble, and the ideological PACs concentrated on the challengers who defeated the five liberal Democratic incumbents. (Conservative PACs gave 25 percent of their Senate con-

Democrats							Republicans									
Challengers			Open seat				Incumbents			Challengers			Open seat			
% to big losers	% to close losers	% to winners	% to big winners	% to close winners	% to big losers	% to close losers	% to big winners	% to close winners	% to losers	% to big losers	% to close losers	% to winners	% to big winners	% to close winners	% to big losers	% to close losers
9	3	1	2	3	1	2	14	3	1	12	7	2	1	2	2	3
3	4	1	4	6	1	3	13	5	1	4	8	4	1	5	1	5
2	2	1	3	4	0	2	14	5	2	2	6	4	1	5	1	4
6	6	3	2	9	1	6	3	1	0	0	0	0	0	0	0	0
0	0	0	3	3	0	1	20	7	3	2	7	5	1	6	1	5
0	0	0	2	1	0	0	9	7	5	2	17	10	4	11	2	14
2	13	6	1	14	0	8	1	0	0	1	0	1	1	2	0	1
4	7	3	5	2	3	14	24	9	3	8	19	8	2	10	5	12

tributions to these five challengers, while liberal PACs gave 39 percent to the five incumbents in these same races.)

These tables suggest that a pro-incumbent bias is *not* particularly noticeable when contributions are examined from the perspective of the PACs. But another picture emerges if we look at the same contribution figures as percentages of the candidates' receipts. As Tables 4 and 5 make clear, the following types of candidates got disproportionately high percentages of their funds from nonparty PACs:

1. House Democratic incumbents of any sort
2. House Republican incumbents who were defeated
3. Republicans who won open House seats by large margins
4. Senate Democratic incumbents who won close races
5. Safe Senate Republican incumbents
6. Senate Republican incumbents who lost.

TABLE 3
SENATE

HOW GROUPS OF PACS DISTRIBUTED THEIR CONTRIBUTIONS:
PERCENTAGE DISTRIBUTION BY PARTY, INCUMBENCY, AND CLOSENESS OF RACE

	All Candidates			% to All Candidates	Democrats — Incumbents		
	Total contributions	Average contribution	No. of candidates		% to big winners	% to close winners	% to losers
All candidates in category			67	100	6	3	7
All receipts [a]	$67,751,288	$1,011,213	67	100	4	2	5
All nonparty PACs	8,879,627	132,531	67	100	6	4	10
43 labor PACs	2,051,325	41,864	49	100	4	9	27
72 business PACs	2,208,821	36,814	60	100	7	3	3
15 conservative PACs	379,833	8,829	43	100	1	0	0
7 liberal PACs	107,486	6,718	16	100	0	0	39
Republican party [a]	3,060,881	98,738	31	100	—	—	—
Democratic party [a]	452,593	15,086	30	100	8	7	22

Note: Figures may not add to 100 percent because of rounding.
[a] Includes party expenditures on behalf of candidates.

Thus, incumbents seem far more likely than anyone else to get a high percentage of their funds from PACs. A closer look at the data, however, reveals some strange things. In the Senate, all but one of the candidate categories showing PAC receipts of more than 20 percent of the total receipts were ones in which the candidates spent much less than the average Senate candidate. These candidates did not get any more from the PACs, they just took in less from other sources. If one wanted to reduce the proportionate role of PACs for such candidates, therefore, one way to do it would be to make sure they had lots of money from elsewhere. The one exceptional category contained the two Republican incumbents who were defeated (Senators Brooke and Griffin). They received high percentages of PAC money and ran high-cost campaigns. Obviously, however, the PACs were not enough to save them from defeat.

| Democrats | | | | | | | Republicans | | | | | | | | | |
| Challengers | | | Open seat | | | | Incumbents | | | Challengers | | | Open seat | | | |
% to big losers	% to close losers	% to winners	% to big winners	% to close winners	% to big losers	% to close losers	% to big winners	% to close winners	% to losers	% to big losers	% to close losers	% to winners	% to big winners	% to close winners	% to big losers	% to close losers
4	9	3	6	4	4	4	4	9	3	3	3	7	4	4	6	4
0	11	3	5	5	3	4	2	28	4	0	1	7	3	8	1	4
0	5	3	3	6	1	5	5	18	6	0	1	11	6	5	1	4
1	10	9	2	15	4	8	2	3	4	0	0	1	0	1	0	0
0	2	1	4	5	0	3	6	24	6	0	2	15	9	7	0	4
0	1	0	2	0	0	0	7	18	4	0	3	25	7	6	1	25
0	19	9	0	9	0	7	2	2	13	0	0	0	0	0	0	0
							1	28	17	0	5	13	6	9	4	17
3	20	9	8	10	2	12										

Next, consider the House. Two kinds of Republican candidates had PAC contributions of more than 30 percent of total receipts: the five incumbents who lost anyway and the four who won open seats by large margins. While nine candidacies do not provide much food for generalization, we can conclude that House Republicans, like their Senate counterparts, do not seem particularly dependent on PACs.

Among Democrats, all three kinds of incumbents show PAC receipts above 30 percent. However, this bias toward Democratic incumbents has less to do with any sinister motives on the part of PACs than with the giving habits of business, labor, and the two parties. Labor gives disproportionately to almost all kinds of Democrats, while business gives contributions to Democratic incumbents in an amount proportional to the number of incumbent Democratic candidates. Joining the two

163

TABLE 4
HOUSE OF REPRESENTATIVES
WHERE GROUPS OF CANDIDATES RECEIVED THEIR CONTRIBUTIONS: PERCENTAGE FROM SELECTED PACS

	All General Election Candidates	*Democrats* Incumbents Big winners	Close winners	Losers
Average receipts — $	126,244[a]	98,169	151,176	181,288
No. of candidates	733	181	52	14
Total receipts — $	92,537,042[a]	17,768,518	7,861,154	2,538,038
Total receipts — %	100	100	100	100
All nonparty PACs — %	25	34	36	40
43 labor PACs — %	6	11	17	18
72 business PACs — %	6	7	5	4
15 conservative PACs — %	2	0	0	0
7 liberal PACs — %	0	0	1	1
Republican party — %	4[b]	—	—	—
Democratic party — %	1[c]	1	3	4

	Republicans Incumbents Big winners	Close winners	Losers
Average receipts — $	119,859	215,967	231,010
No. of candidates	101	21	5
Total receipts — $	12,105,762	4,535,297	1,155,054
Total receipts — %	100	100	100
All nonparty PACs — %	25	24	36
43 labor PACs — %	1	1	1
72 business PACs — %	8	8	12
15 conservative PACs — %	1	2	7
7 liberal PACs — %	0	0	0
Republican party — %	7	7	10
Democratic party — %	—	—	—

NOTE: Figures do not add to 100 percent reading down each column.
[a] Includes party expenditures on behalf of candidates.
[b] 9 percent of Republican candidate receipts.
[c] 2 percent of Democratic candidate receipts.

164

Democrats

	Challengers			Open seat		
Big losers	Close losers	Winners	Big winners	Close winners	Big losers	Close losers
47,918	179,811	193,825	236,072	252,246	97,954	187,551
63	21	5	16	22	7	15
3,018,891	3,778,925	969,125	3,777,155	5,549,420	587,726	2,813,259
100	100	100	100	100	100	100
14	10	22	18	18	18	19
11	9	16	4	9	9	12
0	0	0	4	3	3	2
0	0	0	1	0	0	0
1	1	1	0	0	0	1
—	—	—	—	—	—	—
1	2	3	1	0	4	4

Republicans

	Challengers			Open seat		
Big losers	Close losers	Winners	Big winners	Close winners	Big losers	Close losers
45,163	149,403	239,427	176,227	238,699	100,474	232,038
93	52	14	4	18	12	20
4,109,871	7,768,957	3,351,971	704,906	4,296,577	1,205,685	4,640,751
100	100	100	100	100	100	100
11	18	25	31	25	12	19
0	0	0	1	0	0	0
3	5	8	10	8	2	5
5	3	5	8	4	3	4
0	0	0	0	0	0	0
9	9	9	11	9	16	10
—	—	—	—	—	—	—

TABLE 5
SENATE

WHERE GROUPS OF CANDIDATES RECEIVED THEIR CONTRIBUTIONS: PERCENTAGE FROM SELECTED PACs

	All General Election Candidates	*Democrats*		
		Incumbents		
		Big winners	Close winners	Losers
Average receipts — $	1,011,213 [a]	621,554	611,605	680,518
No. of candidates	67	4	2	5
Total receipts — $	67,751,288	2,486,215	1,223,211	3,402,590
Total receipts — %	100	100	100	100
All nonparty PACs — %	13	23	30	26
43 labor PACs — %	3	4	15	16
72 business PACs — %	3	6	5	2
15 conservative PACs — %	1	0	0	0
7 liberal PACs — %	0	0	0	1
Republican party — %	5 [b]	—	—	—
Democratic party — %	1 [c]	1	3	3

	Republicans		
	Incumbents		
	Big winners	Close winners	Losers
Average receipts — $	340,679	3,217,574	1,565,940
No. of candidates	3	6	2
Total receipts — $	1,022,038	19,305,441	3,131,879
Total receipts — %	100	100	100
All nonparty PACs — %	41	8	33
43 labor PACs — %	5	0	3
72 business PACs — %	13	3	5
15 conservative PACs — %	3	0	0
7 liberal PACs — %	0	0	0
Republican party — %	4	4	17
Democratic party — %	—	—	—

NOTE: Figures do not add to 100 percent reading down each column.
[a] Includes party expenditures on behalf of candidates.
[b] 8 percent of Republican candidate receipts.
[c] 2 percent of Democratic candidate receipts.

Democrats

	Challengers			Open seat			
	Big losers	Close losers	Winners	Big winners	Close winners	Big losers	Close losers
	36,565	1,218,061	886,494	737,956	1,062,328	759,386	851,787
	3	6	2	4	3	3	3
	109,695	7,308,367	1,772,987	2,951,824	3,186,984	2,298,297	2,555,362
	100	100	100	100	100	100	100
	22	6	14	10	17	5	16
	15	3	10	2	10	4	7
	0	1	2	3	3	0	2
	0	0	0	0	0	0	0
	0	0	0	0	0	0	0
	—	—	—	—	—	—	—
	11	1	4	1	1	0	2

Republicans

	Challengers			Open seat			
	Big losers	Close losers	Winners	Big winners	Close winners	Big losers	Close losers
	81,488	394,723	1,028,644	716,437	1,734,336	255,092	927,721
	2	2	5	3	3	3	3
	162,977	789,445	5,143,218	2,149,311	5,203,007	765,277	2,783,163
	100	100	100	100	100	100	100
	5	15	19	26	8	6	12
	0	0	0	0	0	1	0
	1	6	6	9	3	1	4
	0	1	2	1	0	1	3
	0	0	0	0	0	1	0
	4	17	8	9	5	14	19
	—	—	—	—	—	—	—

together obviously boosts the Democratic incumbent percentages well above the median.

Thus, the question whether one thinks PACs exert "too much" influence seems quantitatively to come down to whether one thinks labor should stop bankrolling Democratic candidates. In fact, there is a peculiar, perhaps unintended, animus toward organized labor beneath the surface of many of the electoral reforms sponsored in recent years by liberal Democrats. (We return to this point later.) The data here support Xandra Kayden's observations, elsewhere in this volume, that labor seems to be acting as the Democratic parallel to the Republican party organization. Democrats depend on labor in much the same way Republicans depend on their party. And, despite many well-publicized labor threats to the contrary, labor gets about as little in return for its effort as any party organization would be likely to get. It may ask for *quid pro quo*s, but when they are not forthcoming, labor rarely retaliates as a narrow "special interest" should if it were behaving according to the classic conspiratorial models. Regardless of what one thinks of organized labor's role in politics, cutting back the role of PACs would have obvious partisan implications—hurting Democrats more than Republicans—until such time as the national Democratic party committees learn to match Republican fund-raising efforts.

One would be hard pressed to argue from the numbers in these tables that business contributions are all that campaign reform rhetoric makes them out to be. While business prefers Republicans to Democrats by a three-to-two ratio, no single group of Senate candidates got more than 13 percent of all its money from the seventy-two largest business PACs (the figure for low-budget safe incumbents), and no House group was above 12 percent. Even though the percentages for these and other categories would increase if smaller business PACs were included, the overwhelming conclusion seems to be that no one industry or group of related industries is really in a position to control an election with campaign contributions. Given the small size of the average corporate contribution (a measly $505 for *Fortune*'s twenty-five top companies) and given the diversity of business interests in this country, there seems little danger of excessive control by any one set of interest groups.

If business acted as a monolith, there might be more cause for concern. In Tables 6 and 7, however, we see how different are the giving patterns of a few selected business PACs. Some PACs give almost exclusively to incumbents (for example, the American Trucking Association). Others favor Democratic incumbents to a lesser but still disproportionately high degree (General Electric for the House only, Coca-Cola, Grumman, and Hughes). Others give proportionately to

Democratic incumbents, omit Democratic challengers, and give a slightly disproportionate amount to Republicans (Ford and General Motors). Two favor most kinds of Republicans (General Electric for the Senate only, and Amoco). One focuses on Republicans in close races (Corning). Finally, three concentrate on Republican challengers and open-seat candidates (Eaton, Dart, and Coors), with the last two acting almost as conservative ideological PACs. With this kind of diversity, there is little reason to believe that greatly expanding the number of PACs would drastically change the overall picture.

Getting Down to Specifics: The Banking Industry

In certain respects, the discussion so far has been too abstract to answer the most serious criticisms of special-interest campaign financing. Advocates of campaign reform constantly bombard us with figures showing that people associated with this or that economic interest gave such and such an amount to members of a committee handling legislation in its field. The implication always is that the members' committee votes are, to use Common Cause's libelous phrase, "on the auction block." What these advocates never bother to tell us is the percentage of a member's funds coming from the interest in question. Thus, Ralph Nader's *Public Citizen* recently made much of the fact that Senator John Tower, the ranking minority member of the Senate Banking, Housing, and Urban Affairs Committee, received about $93,000 in 1977–1978 from PACs and individuals in the banking industry. As Tower ran a campaign costing more than $4 million in 1978, the banking industry gave him about 2.5 percent of his money. Can anyone seriously argue that Tower's positions were influenced by his greed for that bit of money? It seems clear that a person able to raise $3.9 million *without* the banking industry's help will only take positions on banking regulation that he thinks it *politically*, not economically, advantageous to take.

The banking industry is a good one to look at as we get down to specifics, because it is an industry with at least some PACs that appear to behave as Common Cause suggests all special-interest groups do. If we combine the contributions from the eleven PACs of national banking and savings associations, the fifteen largest state–banking-association PACs, and the seventeen largest corporate PACs owned by banks, we discover that of the $568,256 these representatives of the banking industry contributed to 429 House candidates in 1977–1978, they gave $224,916 to 38 (of the 47) members of the Committee on Banking, Finance, and Urban Affairs. In other words, 40 percent of the money from these groups went to 9 percent of the House candidates receiving contributions.

TABLE 6
HOUSE OF REPRESENTATIVES

How Some Business PACs Distributed Their Contributions:
Percentage Distribution by Party, Incumbency, and Closeness of Rac

	All Candidates			*% to All Candidates*	Democrats Incumbent% to big winners	% to close winners	
	Total contributions	Average contribution	No. of candidates				
All candidates in category			733	100	25	7	
Amoco	$ 89,350	$ 591	151	100	14	3	
Coca-Cola	30,159	363	83	100	49	5	
Coors	27,600	425	65	100	7	1	
Corning Glass	16,600	638	26	100	7	12	
Dart Industries	45,950	1,094	42	100	0	1	
Eaton Corp.	65,600	1,041	63	100	4	3	
Ford Motor Co.	43,650	464	94	100	22	4	
General Electric	55,950	288	194	100	40	12	
General Motors	59,175	392	151	100	20	7	
Grumman Aircraft	52,700	1,013	52	100	36	16	
Hughes Aircraft	40,196	372	108	100	40	10	1
American Trucking Assn.	144,620	495	292	100	36	18	

Note: Figures may not add to 100 percent because of rounding.

When we break the groups down into components, however, some interesting differences emerge. Of the $74,053 the seventeen banks contributed to 151 House candidates, they gave only 16 percent to 20 members of the committee (or 13 percent of the banks' candidate pool). Of $77,475 distributed to 113 candidates by the state banking associations, 19 percent was given to 12 committee members (11 percent of their candidate pool). In contrast, of $417,622 distributed to 324 House candidates by the national associations, 47 percent was given to 38 members of the committee (or 12 percent of their pool).

The discrepancies between the national associations and other banking PACs appear even greater when we look at the large sums received

| Democrats | | | | | | | Republicans | | | | | | | | | |
| Challengers | | | Open seat | | | | Incumbents | | | Challengers | | | Open seat | | | |
% to big losers	% to close losers	% to winners	% to big winners	% to close winners	% to big losers	% to close losers	% to big winners	% to close winners	% to losers	% to big losers	% to close losers	% to winners	% to big winners	% to close winners	% to big losers	% to close losers
9	3	1	2	3	1	2	14	3	1	12	7	2	1	2	2	3
0	0	0	6	2	1	0	24	8	2	2	10	5	1	13	1	6
1	0	0	1	1	0	6	16	6	1	0	2	3	0	6	0	1
0	0	0	1	1	0	0	4	5	0	7	22	14	6	13	3	16
0	0	0	6	4	0	0	22	0	8	0	6	9	0	26	0	0
0	0	0	13	3	1	0	3	9	0	5	22	12	2	5	0	22
0	0	0	2	1	0	0	9	5	13	2	21	20	1	12	0	8
0	0	0	2	2	0	1	23	8	6	0	6	7	1	10	1	5
0	0	0	2	1	1	1	18	7	3	0	1	0	1	5	0	3
0	0	0	0	0	1	0	27	8	8	3	6	2	2	10	0	4
2	2	0	0	0	0	2	18	10	2	2	4	0	0	5	0	0
0	0	0	2	1	0	0	15	10	3	0	1	1	1	2	0	1
0	0	0	1	3	0	1	20	6	3	0	0	1	0	4	0	1

by individuals from banking PACs. Henry Reuss, chairman of the full committee, received all but $100 of his $10,650 from the national associations. Fernand St Germain, chairman of the Subcommittee on Financial Institutions, received all of his $14,650 from the national associations. John Rousselot, the subcommittee's ranking Republican, got all but $200 of $5,950 from the national associations. Stephen Neal, chairman of the Subcommittee on International Trade and Economic Policy, received all but $100 of $3,300 from the same sources, and Les AuCoin, the ranking subcommittee Democrat behind Neal, received $10,000 of $13,125 from the national associations. (These figures are the reasons this author believes the political differences between trade

171

TABLE 7
SENATE

How Some Business PACs Distributed Their Contributions:
Percentage Distribution by Party, Incumbency, and Closeness of Rac

	All Candidates — Total contributions	All Candidates — Average contribution	All Candidates — No. of candidates	% to All Candidates	Democrats Incumbents — % to big winners	Democrats Incumbents — % to close winners	% to losers
All candidates in category			67	100	6	3	
Amoco	$71,500	$2,648	27	100	6	0	
Coca-Cola	26,910	897	30	100	20	5	
Coors	10,150	846	12	100	0	0	
Corning Glass	3,100	775	4	100	0	3	
Dart Industries	72,950	3,316	22	100	0	0	
Eaton Corp.	26,650	1,403	19	100	0	0	
Ford Motor Co.	15,170	843	18	100	3	0	
General Electric	52,135	1,086	48	100	7	4	8
General Motors	44,300	1,266	35	100	7	5	
Grumman Aircraft	25,500	3,643	7	100	20	0	
Hughes Aircraft	13,075	467	28	100	27	17	3
American Trucking Assn.	66,695	1,667	40	100	10	13	11

Note: Figures may not add to 100 percent because of rounding.

associations and corporations would be worth exploring in further research, even though the tables presented above did not reveal significant differences between the forty-four largest corporate and twenty-eight largest trade association PACs taken together.)

Table 8 expresses the contributions of committee members who got $4,000 or more from the national associations as a percentage of the member's adjusted gross receipts from all sources for 1977–1978. Paul Tsongas, another member of the House committee, was left off of this table, even though he received $11,250, all from the national associations. This sum represented 1.5 percent of the $772,513 he received in his successful race against Senator Edward Brooke (R-Mass.). Brooke, the ranking Republican on the Senate Committee on Banking, Housing,

Democrats							Republicans									
Challengers			Open seat				Incumbents			Challengers			Open seat			
% to big losers	% to close losers	% to winners	% to big winners	% to close winners	% to big losers	% to close losers	% to big winners	% to close winners	% to losers	% to big losers	% to close losers	% to winners	% to big winners	% to close winners	% to big losers	% to close losers
4	9	3	6	4	4	4	4	9	3	3	3	7	4	4	6	4
0	2	0	0	0	0	1	4	15	4	0	3	22	11	8	0	22
0	6	0	4	7	2	2	2	27	3	0	0	8	9	3	0	2
0	0	0	0	0	0	0	0	0	0	0	5	40	10	5	8	32
0	0	0	0	0	0	0	0	32	0	0	0	65	0	0	0	0
0	3	0	0	0	0	0	1	16	7	0	6	27	13	12	0	15
0	0	0	2	0	0	0	0	10	23	0	9	23	13	8	0	11
0	3	0	0	0	0	0	3	11	34	0	7	18	11	10	0	0
0	1	2	4	6	0	6	7	20	9	1	2	10	8	5	1	2
0	3	0	1	1	0	2	7	17	25	0	2	13	8	3	1	5
0	8	0	0	0	0	0	0	59	0	0	0	4	0	10	0	0
0	1	0	0	1	0	5	5	25	5	0	0	3	2	7	0	0
0	0	1	4	7	3	9	6	12	3	0	0	6	10	3	0	0

and Urban Affairs, received $11,150 (or 1.2 percent of his $957,252 total) from the national associations and another $1,150 from the other large banking PACs. This was one of the few instances in which the same PACs played both sides in a general election (as opposed to the more common situation in which a PAC supports a successful candidate in a primary and then supports the opposition party's candidate in the general election).

The table shows that most of the people receiving $4,000 or more from the national banking associations do not depend on them for particularly high proportions of their total campaign receipts and, except for St Germain, the people with the highest percentages also have safe seats and low-to-moderate budget campaigns. Indeed, we may well ask

TABLE 8

HOUSE BANKING COMMITTEE MEMBER RECEIPTS OF $4,000
OR MORE FROM THE ELEVEN LARGEST NATIONAL BANKING
AND SAVINGS ASSOCIATIONS

	Banking Association Receipts	Adjusted Receipts, All Sources	Bank Association Receipts as a Percentage of Total
Ashley, Thomas L. (D-Ohio)	$ 8,500	$117,228	7
AuCoin, Les (D-Oreg.)	10,100	252,847	4
Barnard, D. Douglas, Jr. (D-Ga.)	8,200	65,168	13
Brown, Garry (R-Mich.)	9,400	226,170	4
Derrick, Butler (D-S.C.)	11,250	90,904	12
Evans, David (D-Ind.)	7,200	213,048	3
Fauntroy, Walter (D-D.C.)	4,900	10,950	45
Hanley, James (D-N.Y.)	4,700	122,833	4
Hannaford, Mark (D-Calif.)	8,350	326,710	3
Hubbard, Carroll (D-Ky.)	9,100	120,811	8
LaFalce, John (D-N.Y.)	5,400	114,208	5
Moorhead, William (D-Pa.)	10,400	117,448	9
Patterson, Jerry (D-Calif.)	12,150	136,668	9
Pattison, Edward (D-N.Y.)	4,850	164,874	3
Reuss, Henry (D-Wis.)	10,550	77,597	14
Rousselot, John (R-Calif.)	5,750	115,864	5
Spellman, Gladys (D-Md.)	4,750	114,816	4

TABLE 8—continued

	Banking Association Receipts	Adjusted Receipts, All Sources	Bank Association Receipts as a Percentage of Total
St Germain, Fernand (D-R.I.)	14,650	135,357	11
Steers, Newton (R-Md.)	4,400	165,669	3
Wylie, Chalmers (R-Ohio)	4,000	95,113	4

for all five whose percentages are in double digits (Reuss, St Germain, Derrick, Barnard, and Fauntroy) : Who was pressuring whom with these campaign contributions? Experience seems to suggest that most interest-group money flowing to powerful committee members with safe seats comes when the candidate specifically asks the group to attend a fund-raiser. Far from pressing the money on the member, the group is put in a position where it *must* respond favorably. Because these same groups would undoubtedly gain access to these members without campaign contributions—just ask yourself whether the American Banking Association could get an appointment with the chairman of the banking committee in a world in which no group could give campaign contributions—the gifts in many cases are payments made to a demanding candidate to avoid losing access that the group would get on other grounds anyway.[2]

But even if we assumed by hypothesis that $10,000 did buy some access for the banking industry, what would that mean for policy? The national banking and savings and loan associations represent organizations whose interests are opposed to each other on many and perhaps even most issues the committee considers. To the extent that the groups are buying anything, therefore, they seem to be canceling each other out.

There are some issues on which the associations agree, of course. They agree with the rest of the business world, for example, in supporting

[2] Fred Wertheimer, executive vice president of Common Cause, in 1979 testimony before the House Administration Committee gave examples of business officials who believe their contributions buy access. But these beliefs are not dispositive; what counts are the beliefs of the members. A $500 gift may well mean more to a giver than a well-financed recipient. U.S. Congress, House of Representatives, Committee on House Administration, *Hearings on Public Financing of Congressional Elections,* 96th Congress, 1st session, 1979, pp. 295–296.

175

capital-gains tax reductions. But it seems almost ludicrous to say that a person becomes sympathetic to the needs of business, broadly defined, *because* he receives business campaign contributions. As one member of the House Democratic leadership has said: money follows a candidate's positions and not the other way around. A person's attitudes about business, labor, and the role of government are such basic parts of his political makeup as to be almost beyond his ability to offer them for sale if he wanted to. Anyone who tried to change his basic approach to policy in response to campaign contributions would open himself to losing more politically than the campaign funds could possibly buy back.

More Specifics: Railway and Maritime Labor

Some people concerned with the role of PACs in campaigns say that the real problem does not come on major questions testing one's basic political opinions or on issues dividing the active labor and business interest groups. The problem, they say, comes from those many issues specific to one industry in which narrow business and labor interests join force. Two examples frequently cited are the railroad and maritime industries.

Railway labor unions made contributions to every Democratic member of the House Commerce Committee—which has jurisdiction over railroad regulation—except two representatives from Southern right-to-work states. Railroad companies also concentrated on the Commerce Committee, giving something to almost every member of the committee, but saving the big gifts for committee Democrats. On the face of it, therefore, the railway industry and union groups seemed to be engaged in straightforward special-interest activity. Yet their resources were hardly sufficient to "buy" votes on legislation, if the votes indeed were there to be bought. The biggest recipient by far of railway PAC gifts was Fred Rooney, the chairman of the Transportation Subcommittee. Yet Rooney's $8,000 from railroads and $5,700 from railway groups together made up only slightly more than 10 percent of the total money he raised in a race he ended up losing to the underfinanced Don Ritter.

The maritime unions gave heavily to some members of the House Merchant Marine Committee favoring, for obvious reasons, those who supported a cargo preference bill that was at the top of these unions' legislative priority list. The fourteen largest maritime labor PACs distributed $148,108 to 28 members of the committee. However, this represents only 12 percent of the funds distributed by these unions, and the 28 committee members were 9 percent of the 313 candidates getting contributions. The 7 committee members receiving a total of $8,000 or more from the fourteen committees were as follows:

- Gene Snyder (R-Ky.) : $8,000 (5 percent of his total receipts)
- Joshua Eilberg (D-Pa.) : $8,400 (6 percent)
- Thomas L. Ashley (D-Ohio) : $8,500 (7 percent)
- Don Young (R-Alas.) : $11,900 (5 percent)
- Les AuCoin (D-Oreg.) : $12,000 (5 percent)
- Leo Zeferetti (D-N.Y.) : $19,233 (22 percent)
- John Murphy (D-N.Y.) : $25,500 (12 percent)

Again, we see that these gifts do not make up especially large percentages of the candidate's total receipts, except for Murphy, the committee's chairman, and Zeferetti. However, because both of them come from districts in which much of New York City's port activity is located, neither can credibly be said to have developed their pro-maritime bias because of these kinds of contributions. As with rural Mississippians who favor sugar subsidies or Louisianans and Texans who favor the oil industry, these members' districts clearly would require them to take the positions they do even if no private-interest group gave money to any federal candidate. The most a locally powerful interest can be said to be "buying" in this situation is a member's continued interest in a subject. That is of no small importance, of course. A member's decision to focus his committee work on some of the diverse interests within his district more than others can have an important impact on policy. Still, if that is what the maritime unions hoped to get out of Zeferetti, they failed. Zeferetti left the Merchant Marine Committee in 1979 to go on the Rules Committee, where he is in a position to help his former committee on occasion, but where maritime issues no longer dominate his work.

Contributions and Public Policy

We have seen that few members of Congress are really beholden to any one PAC or group of related PACs for a significant portion of their campaign funds. Interestingly, the converse of this is also true. Just as members do not depend on any one set of groups for significant portions of their campaign funds, neither do the most successful groups rely on contributions as the basis of anything more than a small part of their overall lobbying strategies.

Campaign gifts must be examined from the two different perspectives of congressional life: that of Washington and that of the home district. Members are concerned about their reputations in both places, but to maintain and enhance their reputations they must do very different

177

things in each. In Washington, a member gains respect and networks of deferential supplicants because of the role he plays on specialized subjects of national scope. He tends to enjoy being liked and respected for this special role. The gifts he attracts from Washington-based organizations are accepted as his due, and the amount of the gift is often less important than the ambiance of which it is a part. The member expects groups he has supported to support him, but the relationship is not a mercenary one. Members appreciate $100 gifts, or other forms of political support, from groups that can do no more, but think little of $250 contributions from groups that normally give out $1,000 checks or even $1,000 checks from labor unions that fail to produce their promised volunteer assistance.

This is not meant to deny that Washington-based interest groups affect congressional policy in important ways, but rather to downplay the importance of campaign contributions within the Washington community. If campaign contributions from Washington-based organizations were prohibited, the rest of what the Washington "issue networks" do would remain untouched. Relieved of the need to attend command-performance fund-raisers, the networks would roll on as before, with more resources to put to other uses.

The second perspective is that of the congressional district. Here too, campaign gifts are only of indirect importance. The member's ultimate electoral objective in the district is to win votes. Campaign contributions help buy some of the things that can be used to win votes, but votes—not dollars—are what the politician finally is after. Gifts that produce bad publicity, for example, are a political loss. So, too, organizations with volunteer networks in the district are far more important than ones from outside that can supply nothing but money. National organizations (such as the National Committee for an Effective Congress on the Left, and any of three or four ideological organizations on the Right) that provide candidates with technical services also tend to be more valuable to the candidate than those that only offer a direct money gift. Finally, organizations such as Environmental Action, with its "Dirty Dozen" list, and the right-to-life groups, with their imitative "Deadly Dozen," can generate reams of front-page publicity in the district that may be worth as much as a candidate's entire public-relations budget. In light of this, it is absurd to focus on any group of related PACs that give a candidate 5 percent or so of his campaign funds as though the PACs somehow had the power to make or break the member in his district and thereby determine his vote in Washington.

As with the Washington perspective, however, this observation is meant only to downplay the importance of special-interest campaign money, and not the much larger lobbying strategies of which the contributions are a small part. Two defeats suffered by organized labor in the last Congress ought to put this in perspective. Labor clearly outspent business in the 1976 congressional elections and overwhelmed business in the presidential election.[3] Yet, labor lost its two most important institutional votes in the 95th Congress: common-situs picketing and labor-law revision.

House Speaker Thomas P. (Tip) O'Neill, speaking to a representative of the Massachusetts Federation of Labor, offered this explanation of what happened on common situs: "You lost it in the district." Said the labor representative: "I know." Construction associations had persuaded contractors from districts with uncommitted members to write and even come to Washington to urge their members that a bill allowing any one union striking a subcontractor to shut down a whole construction site could have disastrous economic consequences. Labor, relying on its Washington lobbyists, never countered this argument effectively. More to the point, the absence of grass-roots labor pressure confirmed an impression shared by many young Democrats that, except for its money, labor cannot deliver in the district, where it counts.

The same thing, magnified many times, happened in the Senate on labor-law revision. There, a Senate filibuster was supported by a grass-roots business-lobbying campaign estimated by people on both sides to have cost around $5 million. That was $5 million on one bill—compared with $9 million for contributions from all corporate PACs for the year.[4] Moreover, the money was spent in a highly sophisticated way. Conservative ideological organizations used their mailing lists, as they had on the Panama Canal debate, to stimulate a massive letter-writing campaign. This was coordinated with a business-lobbying effort that had Senate corridors flooded with executives, many from small businesses, who were flown in specifically to lobby against the bill. The executives and letter writers argued that the law would mean a loss of jobs in the senators'

---

[3] An article of mine in the March 19, 1977, *National Journal* estimated that labor spent approximately $11 million in the 1976 general election to aid President Carter, most of which was not disclosed. (Direct contributions to candidates were prohibited in this publicly financed campaign, of course.) The money was spent on communications with union members and their families and on supposedly nonpartisan registration and get-out-the-vote drives that in fact were coordinated with the Carter-Mondale campaign. Business spent a mere $28,000 in the 1976 general election campaign on behalf of President Ford.

[4] *The New York Times,* August 9, 1979, p. D14:2 contained another example showing just how trivial campaign contributions are as a part of the total lobbying picture. In "Capital's Diverse Oil Lobbyists: Much Criticized, Often Effective," Richard Halloran said that it "seems safe to say" that the cost of oil lobbying "runs into hundreds of millions of dollars" per year.

home states. Labor was unable to counter business's *political* message. It failed to demonstrate that constituents "back home" were much concerned about labor laws. The key, once again, was grass-roots lobbying that had a credible connection with the voters.

What's Really Wrong with the Campaign Laws

The evidence about lobbying shows that Washington issue networks and single-issue grass-roots lobbying campaigns are more important to the contemporary lobbyist than campaign contributions. The problem with the "reformed" campaign laws is that they work to reinforce these phenomena, whereas the law could act as a counterweight if it were less structured or structured differently.

The primary reinforcement comes from the $1,000 limit on contributions from individuals. Contribution limits were enacted for understandable reasons. People became uncomfortable with the importance of contributors like Clement Stone, Robert Abplanalp, Stewart Mott, and Max Palevsky. But as understandable as the discomfort with large contributors may have been, the limits appear to be exacerbating a more serious disease than the one they were meant to cure. National candidates used to be able to raise large sums of money on quick trips to New York and California. Local and statewide candidates usually could do proportionally as well in selected areas within their districts. Now a candidate who is not wealthy and wants to raise a lot of money has only three ways to do it: by tapping the Washington issue networks; by spending huge blocks of time—much more than ever used to be spent at fund raising—at upper-middle-class cocktail parties; or by delegating work to professional fund-raising specialists, many of whom rely on direct mail techniques.

Every one of these fund-raising methods has serious drawbacks. The Washington networks may not depend on campaign gifts for their power, but it seems unwise to structure the campaign laws in a way that forces candidates to go to them. Spending time with upper-middle-class voters is not in itself bad, but a candidate who spends too much time with any single class of voters is likely to end up with a distorted view of what the voters as a whole are thinking. Finally, anything that makes nationwide direct mail fund raising look tempting to a candidate must have harmful long-range effects on our politics, for it encourages those willing to play on the polarizing emotions that make direct mail work best. These effects make the evils of the old system, such as the alleged "sales" of ambassadorships, seem mild by comparison.

Richard A. Viguerie is the wizard of direct mail fund raising on the right. In an interview several years ago, Viguerie told me that direct mail fund raising favors the politics of polarization. "People who take strong identifiable positions," Viguerie said, "have greater success because their people are committed and are willing to put up money. But somebody who tries to straddle the fence maybe doesn't offend too many people, but he doesn't turn any on." Viguerie turns people on to his candidates. He does more than that. He retains ownership of his mailing lists and continues turning people on with his publications, his appeals on behalf of issue groups, and his campaigns to stimulate grass-roots lobbying. What is usually thought of as a device to help candidates is turning into a year-round public-policy pressure machine.

The lesson of Viguerie's success has not been lost on others. Stanley Sheinbaum, frustrated by the contribution limits from underwriting liberal Democratic candidates, has been trying to help Richard Parker become the Viguerie of the Left. Parker is the thirty-two-year-old former publisher of *Mother Jones*, a radical-chic San Francisco–based periodical that used direct mail to build up a circulation of more than 200,000. Parker, in a recent interview with this author, said that he explicitly intends to model himself after Viguerie. He said he is "worried" about the implications of his own activity for politics but does not "see any alternative" to it.

If we want the politics of the future to be dominated by a series of direct mail specialists, each with his own cluster of polarizing issues, there is nothing more we need to do: that is where the campaign laws are leading us. If, on the other hand, we do not want this, then we had better make sure that candidates have other ways of getting the resources they need.

The simplest way to counter the power of direct mail specialists would be to do away with the contribution limits. Doing away with private financing would *not* work. The direct mail people and other highly organized groups would then be in an even stronger position because they would be among the few able to spend money to influence an election directly, using the "independent expenditures" protected by the Supreme Court in *Buckley* v. *Valeo*. Moreover, these constitutionally protected expenditures can occur in amounts that, like the lobbying expenses mentioned earlier, trivialize the concern being shown for direct campaign contributions. The National Conservation Political Action Committee (NCPAC) recently has said it has budgeted more than $700,000 for an independent advertising campaign opposing the reelection of five liberal Democratic senators.[5] Anything that would limit the flow of money to candidates directly would simply enhance the power

---

[5] See Charles W. Hucker, "Five Senate Incumbents Face Negative Campaign," *Congressional Quarterly,* July 28, 1979, p. 1540.

of groups, such as NCPAC, that have the organizational base and sophisticated media skills to go their independent and legally illimitable ways.

If doing away with the contribution limits seems too radical a step, then at least they could be raised. There is no justification for using the same limits for all levels of office. If a $1,000 limit makes sense for representatives, then a $5,000 limit for senators and $50,000 for the president would carry the same proportional weight. (Also, these limits should be indexed for inflation; they are not now.)

It would also be worth bearing in mind that candidates who are not wealthy are most susceptible to the appeal of a direct mail specialist at the start of a campaign, when the specialist can lend little-known candidates enough to get their direct mail started. Given the importance of seed money to little-known candidates, it seems worse than counter-productive to make them raise their first dollars under the same limits that apply throughout a campaign. Even if a plan to raise all contribution limits cannot be agreed upon, it should not be too difficult to devise a scale of sliding limits that would allow candidates to get started with a few large gifts and then require them to raise the rest of their money in smaller amounts.

The Obey-Railsback Bill

Limiting the influence of the upper-middle-class ideological PACs by increasing the diversity of campaign-fund sources seems the furthest thing from the mind of those campaign reformers who want us to recoil in horror at the present role of the special interests. Instead, they propose limiting campaign funds even further than they have been limited so far. Their first effort was through a congressional public-financing bill that the House Administration Committee soundly defeated on May 24, 1979. When that failed, 151 members of the House led by David Obey (D-Wis.), president of the Democratic Study Group (DSG), and Thomas Railsback (R-Ill.) proposed a set of amendments drafted by the DSG's staff that would limit PACs to contributions of $5,000 (instead of $10,000) in a two-year election cycle and limit candidates to accepting a total of $50,000 from all PACs.

While these proposals are superficially appealing, their adoption would have a highly partisan impact. Table 9 lists the number of occasions on which the ten largest PACs in each of the Federal Election Commission's six groupings of nonparty committees gave more than $5,000 to a congressional candidate. As the table makes clear, almost the only groups that would be affected by the $5,000 limit would be unions, realtors, and the American Medical Association. But realtors and

TABLE 9
NUMBER OF TIMES PACs CONTRIBUTED MORE THAN
$5,000 TO A CANDIDATE, 1977–1978

	Senate	House
10 Largest Labor PACs	83	123
10 Largest Association/Membership/Health	55	129
(Above without National Association of		
Realtors and American Medical Association)	(19)	(20)
10 Largest Corporate PACs	7	4
10 Largest Coops	5	13
10 Largest "No Connected Organization"	16	30
10 Largest Corporations without Stock	0	0

the AMA could easily shift to independent expenditures while urging their members—as the Council for a Livable World now does—to give directly to favored candidates. Organized labor cannot do this. Its money comes from people who are not likely to give directly to candidates. In addition, labor's organizational support is at least as important to a candidate as its direct contributions. Furthermore, once labor works with a candidate, it cannot legally shift to independent expenditures. A cynic might ask why the Democratic sponsors of this proposal are out to hurt organized labor. It almost looks like another round in the post-1972 labor–new-politics battles within the Democratic party disguised in a rhetorical antibusiness cloak.

Of course, the proposals are not being pushed against labor's will. The AFL–CIO supports them out of fear of the possible future role of corporate PACs. With the typical corporate PAC now giving an average of less than $500 per candidate, that future seems far away indeed. And, in the unlikely event that corporate PACs ever should bump up against the $5,000 limit, their response would be predictable: large individual contributions from business executives would simply start upwards again.

In contrast with the $5,000 limit on contributions, the $50,000 limit on candidate receipts would not be likely to have a discernible partisan impact. But it would require campaign managers in hotly contested races to become financial contortionists in a campaign's closing days. It also would tend to stifle "come-from-behind" campaigns by candidates whose opponents were able to seize the early momentum.

The Deeper Issues

Before Congress embarks on yet another round of campaign finance reform, it should do some serious thinking about the basic purpose of campaign laws. Ultimately, this should have something to do with the purpose of campaigns and in fact with the purpose of representation—of empowering some people to govern in the name of all, while leaving citizens satisfied with the process, even when their candidates lose.

Laws that favor a polarizing, negative politics run counter to these goals. The politics of the direct mail specialists and the single-issue extremists must be allowed their freedom—they surely do add worthwhile material to the political debate. But it is suicidal to "reform" politics in a manner that systematically favors their tactics.

A well-designed set of campaign laws could help counterbalance these groups in a number of ways, such as by encouraging the parties to play a greater role in financing campaigns and by assuring candidates a variety of possible sources for their all-important "seed money." The data in this paper suggest very strongly that *increasing* the amount of money in politics decreases the power of individual interest groups, while restricting money would be likely to increase the power of those groups organizationally able to take advantage of the situation. Thus, paradoxically, the way to decrease the power of the special interests may well be to let them flower. If this sounds a bit like *Federalist No. 10*, the similarity is intentional. And if unabashed pluralism leaves some people less equal than others, that problem should be addressed by increasing their resources through vouchers, public aid for the parties, or other means. Cutting down on the ability of private groups to contribute money to campaigns would *not* help the disenfranchised. It would only give more power to groups that do not rely on direct contributions.

We should remember as we debate this subject that specific proposals may be less important than the framework within which they are placed. Campaign-reform issues cannot be discussed intelligently unless they are seen in the context of the more general difficulties facing our representative institutions and processes. These difficulties, and not the shallow and essentially diversionary issues of the growth of political action committees or campaign costs, ought to be at the center of public deliberation.

Commentaries

Richard P. Conlon

Neither Michael Malbin nor Edwin Epstein see any reason for concern over the growing role of political action committees (PACs) in the political process or the increasing dependence of congressional candidates on such special interests to finance their campaigns. Epstein, who does concede the possibility of "difficulties" in the future, bases his judgment on a single statistic—that in 1978, PACs provided 18 percent of the $199 million raised by all candidates for Congress. The percentage, he says, does not amount to a sufficient "interference" in the political process to justify legislation such as Obey-Railsback. But should aggregate support from PACs exceed 25 percent, Epstein adds, that would be a "disproportionate" amount for congressional candidates to receive from such sources. If that is to be the threshold for action, then it has already been reached in the House of Representatives.

Misleading Statistics

I would like to focus first on Epstein's 18 percent figure because it was widely used by opponents of public financing and is now being used by opponents of Obey-Railsback. The figure is accurate, but misleading because it is an overall statistic based on aggregate receipts and aggregate contributions by PACs to candidates for both the House and the Senate, as well as candidates in primary elections and those representing fringe and minor parties. Thus, the statistic is distorted, first, by including primary, fringe, and minor party candidates, the vast majority of whom never see a penny in PAC funds. They do raise campaign money, however, and their inclusion therefore inflates total receipts. (Malbin, on the other hand, uses data pertaining to general election candidates only, thereby cutting out primary losers and fringe and minor party candidates.) Second, the figure is distorted by combining House and Senate data. In terms of the amounts of money raised and spent and the level of PAC activity, there is almost as wide a gulf between House and

Senate elections as there is between Senate and presidential elections. H.R. 4970, the Obey-Railsback bill, applies *only* to candidates for the House of Representatives. Thus, *only* House data is relevant; the measure must be judged on the basis of data pertaining to the House alone, not the House and Senate combined.

What then is the picture in the House? In 1978, nonpartisan PACs provided House candidates with 25 percent of their campaign funds ($23 million out of $92.2 million). More important, however, is the fact that incumbents received 32 percent of their campaign funds from PACs ($14.7 million of $45.7 million) compared with 17 percent for their nonincumbent opponents ($4.3 million out of $25.2 million) and 20 percent for open-seat contenders ($4.2 million out of $21.3 million). Because the majority of incumbents are reelected to the House of Representatives, most members have already exceeded Epstein's 25 percent threshold—in fact, they exceeded it in 1976, when incumbents received 28 percent of their campaign funds from PACs.

Malbin bases his judgment that the PAC problem has been exaggerated on a greater number of platforms, but they are just as rickety. For example, he states that PACs "were no more important proportionately in 1978 than they were in 1976." That statement can be justified only by mixing House and Senate data together as Epstein has done. But when data for House and Senate candidates are examined separately, a different picture emerges. The proportion of Senate campaign funds contributed by PACs declined slightly from 15 percent of total receipts in 1976 to 13 percent in 1978. In the House, on the other hand, the PAC share of total receipts increased from 22 percent in 1976 to 25 percent in 1978.

PAC Growth—Myth or Reality?

The first thing we need to do, according to Malbin, is dispel the myth that PACs are on some sort of steady growth curve disproportionate to the growth in campaign costs as a whole. However, Malbin's own data shows that this is precisely what is happening in the House. The percentage of total House campaign funds supplied by special-interest PACs has increased from 14 percent in 1972, to 17 percent in 1974, to 22 percent in 1976, and to 25 percent in 1978.[1] That's not even a curve; it's a straight line of growth. The Senate's percentages of funding by PACs, on the other hand, have fluctuated from election to election.

With respect to Malbin's contention that the increase in PAC contributions is nothing more than a switch on the part of business interests

---

[1] Malbin shows 1976 PAC receipts as 23 percent of total receipts. FEC reports, however, show 1976 receipts for House candidates totaling $65.7 million and PAC contributions totaling $14.7 million, or 22 percent.

from contributing via individuals to contributing via PACs, all one can say is that it is an interesting theory but totally unsubstantiated. The relatively modest increase in individual contributions in excess of $100 as compared with total receipts during the period 1972–1978 is hardly more than a coincidence which may well be due to other factors. For example, there has been a sharp decline in large contributions from non-business liberal contributors in recent years as a result of an uncertain stock market, the economy, and disillusionment with government and politics in general.

The role of political action committees *is* significant. It has been growing steadily for the past several years, and it will continue to increase in the years ahead unless there is some restraint imposed. As Epstein notes, "the market for potential PAC formations is virtually untapped."

Do PACs Favor Incumbents?

Malbin argues that there is only an element of truth to the assertion that PACs favor incumbents, and that it is distorting to talk about the receipts of all incumbents versus all challengers. Instead, one should consider the competitiveness of the election and the percentage of candidates in a given category. He cites the fact that safe incumbents constitute about 40 percent of all candidates in House general elections and that they receive about the same percentage of all nonpartisan PAC contributions to general election candidates to dispute the claim that PACs favor safe incumbents disproportionately. That is certainly a nice round formulation, but it does not disprove the fact that most PAC money goes to incumbents (63 percent in the last election, compared with 17 percent to challengers and 20 percent to open-seat contenders).

Nor do I find much relevance to the issue of the bias of PACs toward incumbents in Malbin's contention that, although many of the older trade associations and corporate PACs appear to be interested in buying access to incumbents, the newer corporate PACs are playing a more sophisticated game, concentrating on close races, even when that means opposing powerful Democratic incumbents. That sophisticated game is called "Shoot the Sick." Here is how it's played: A business PAC behaves normally by buying access to a Democratic incumbent as long as the incumbent is likely to continue holding office. If there is a good chance the member can or will be defeated, then the business PACs switch over to help the Republican challenger. This tactic was used last year, apparently with some success as eight of the fourteen losing Democrats were defeated by challengers who received more PAC money than the incumbent. Nonetheless, PACs give most of their contributions to incumbents because incumbents decide legislation and because 96 percent of them get reelected every two years.

Before turning to the Obey-Railsback bill, I feel duty-bound to at least record wonderment with the following comments in the Malbin paper:

- That $93,000 from a single industry would not influence a particular Senator because it represented only 2.5 percent of his money
- That volunteer help and free technical services are more important than money to a candidate.

Obey-Railsback Bill

The Obey-Railsback bill is really a rather modest proposal. It contains three provisions:

- Reduce the amount a PAC may give a *House* candidate from $10,000 ($5,000 primary and $5,000 general) to $5,000 overall per election cycle
- Limit the aggregate amount a House candidate may receive from all interest-group PACs to $50,000 per election cycle
- Prohibit PACs, political consultants, and other campaign service vendors from extending credit in excess of $1,000 for more than thirty days for media advertising or direct mail.

The bill is not intended to force sharp cutbacks in present PAC operations. Instead, it is designed to prevent aggregate PAC influence from getting out of hand *in the future* and to curb the growing dependency of House candidates on such sources for campaign funds. House incumbents received almost a third of their campaign funds from PACs in 1978 and nearly that amount in 1976. Another indication of this dependency is that 112 members received over half of their campaign money from PACs in 1978 compared with only 66 in 1976. That is an increase of 70 percent. Also, the number of House candidates receiving more than $50,000 from special-interest PACs increased from 57 in 1976 to 176 in 1978.

Some observers downplay the significance of these figures because there also was a substantial increase in total receipts. Thus, while the amount of PAC money in House elections increased 56 percent over 1976, the share of PAC contributions to total receipts only increased from 22 percent to 25 percent. Percentages are useful analytic tools; they help us make comparisons among confusing data. But they can also mislead. Who, for example, is more dependent on PACs: Candidate A, who has a $25,000 campaign and receives $20,000, or 80 percent, of his money from PACs, or Candidate B, who needs $500,000 and receives $100,000, or 20 percent, from PACs? I submit that the actual dollar amount makes a significant difference regardless of the percentage.

With respect to the impact of H.R. 4970, Malbin and Epstein express concern that we Democrats and labor may be about to shoot ourselves in the foot by passing legislation that will play into the hands of business PACs and conservative ideological groups. We appreciate their concern. However, one has to ask, if it is so obviously going to hurt Democrats and labor, why are the Chamber of Commerce and other conservative groups gearing up to fight the bill? Are they as oblivious to their own self interest as Epstein and Malbin would have us believe labor is?

The impact of H.R. 4970 would, in fact, be balanced. For example, the law would have had the following results, had it been in effect in 1978:

- The $5,000 limit on contributions from a single PAC would have reduced the amounts received by 100 Democrats (58 incumbents and 42 nonincumbents) and 107 Republicans (46 incumbents and 61 nonincumbents).
- The $50,000 aggregate limit on PAC contributions would have reduced the amounts received by 96 Democrats (74 incumbents and 22 nonincumbents) and 80 Republicans (32 incumbents and 48 nonincumbents).

The Direct Mail Threat

Nonetheless, Malbin and Epstein contend that placing restraints on PAC money will promote independent expenditures and more reliance on demagogic direct mail solicitations. Where is there any evidence that direct mail fund raising has a harmful effect on our politics? Granted, some foul solicitations have been placed in the mail—mostly, I might note, on the far Right. However, Malbin's assertion that direct mail techniques tend to be "polarizing" connotes massive and wrenching political and social divisions such as we experienced with issues like the Vietnam War and abortion. Certainly that overstates the case. A direct mail solicitation will attempt to "milk" contributions from those on one side or the other of a divisive issue, but direct mail does not polarize society or even the political community. Even the most massive mailings go to only a fraction of the population, and most recipients throw it out unopened.

The idea that multitudes of House candidates will rush into nationwide direct mail fund raising is ridiculous. Most House candidates cannot make money with a mailing in their own district, much less at the national or the state level. There is simply too much competition.

Moreover, simply because the Far Right has been successful with extremist, demagogic mailings does not mean everyone can do the same. Those techniques may work with right-wing conservatives and social shut-ins, but they will not work with political liberals, moderates, and other segments of society. To benefit from direct mail, a candidate must be well-known to those who receive the mailing and must provide a substantive rationale for recipients to make contributions. Thus, candidates who can raise money by direct mail are doing so already, and nothing will change for those who cannot use it now.

There is one problem area with respect to direct mail which is addressed by H.R. 4970. Some mailers have developed a system whereby they will do a mailing for a candidate and collect their fee over time from the proceeds of the mailing. In effect, the mailer is making a large contribution to the candidate under the guise of credit, thereby circumventing the contribution limits. H.R. 4970 would prohibit this practice.

Independent Expenditures

The threat of independent expenditures has been the boogeyman of American politics since the Supreme Court enunciated the concept in 1976. However, the easy assumption that PACs will automatically plunge into independent expenditures if further restraints are placed on their contributions does not prove viable. This assumption seems to be based on the notion that PACs have a pot of money ready to be spent. To the extent that this is the case, there are other options a PAC might want to exercise before getting into the thicket of independent expenditures. For example, a PAC may decide to contribute to House candidates not on its initial list of recipients or to give additional help to favorite Senate candidates.

Furthermore, there are many drawbacks to independent expenditures that will certainly inhibit many PACs that might otherwise be inclined to follow that route. For example, it is one thing to make a contribution to a candidate; it is quite another to go to all of the trouble and expense of making independent expenditures for or against a particular candidate. Independent expenditures are much more visible than contributions, and if the wrong candidate wins, the group could find itself with an implacable enemy in office.

Another drawback is the requirement that the expenditure be made without consultation or discussion with the candidate or his staff. Proving that there was no such contact in the case of an incumbent could be a problem for an organization that is also dealing with the member on legislative matters. Also, in the absence of consultation on the expenditure—a newspaper ad, for example—there is always the risk that it could for some reason hurt rather than help the intended candidate beneficiary. Finally, there is the fact that independent expenditures require more staff expertise than simply writing a check. Someone has to figure out what to do, how best to do it, and when to do it—all without talking to the candidate or his staff. Most PACs do not have such campaign expertise at present, and it is questionable that they will find it useful to acquire such expertise in the future. It is clearly an option available only to larger PACs with substantial resources.

Individual Contribution Limits

The proposal to remove or increase the $1,000 limit on contributions from individuals is fascinating. It has impressive support from people like Malbin and Epstein, from Harvard's prestigious Institute of Politics, from astute national political reporters, and from various campaign experts. They contend that removing or increasing the individual limit would:

- greatly increase the amount of money candidates could raise from individuals
- limit the potential influence of PACs
- contain the direct mail threat
- encourage candidates to concentrate more on local fund sources and less on Washington sources
- permit candidates to spend less time fund raising and more time campaigning.

I submit it would not do any of those things insofar as House candidates are concerned because it would not produce the river of big contributions its backers say it would. I wonder, who are these people who will double, triple, or quadruple their contributions if only the limit were raised or removed? Presumably, they are already giving the maximum if the limit is a barrier to more.

Precise data on the number of $1,000 contributors to House candidates in 1978 are not yet available, but one can get a good idea of the situation from FEC data on contributions in excess of $750. These data show that there were 6,259 "big givers" to House candidates in 1978, and that they contributed a total of $6.1 million or an average of $975 each. Since the individual limit is actually $2,000 ($1,000 for the primary and $1,000 for the general election), an average cumulative contribution of $975 does not indicate that a multitude of "fat cats" is being restrained from giving more. Given a base of 6,200 major contributors, most of whom gave well below the limit in 1978, it is improba-

191

ble that increasing or even removing the limit would produce more than a 33 percent gain over 1978 contributions. That would be an additional $2 million in contributions to House candidates. Hardly the bonanza supporters envision.

An even more serious drawback to this proposal, however, is the fact that it moves in the wrong direction. Instead of widening the base of support for congressional elections, increasing or removing the individual limits would give a tiny fraction of the electorate who can already contribute up to $2,000 ($4,000 in the case of a couple) even more political leverage than they presently possess. Our objective should be to stimulate greater participation by the average citizen through public financing, through a voucher system, or through tax credits.

Fred Wertheimer

Half a decade ago, Congress, responding to the Watergate scandals, enacted a major campaign finance law: the Federal Election Campaign Act (FECA) Amendments of 1974. That law established two different systems for financing our federal elections. Beginning in 1976, presidential campaigns were to be financed primarily by public funds from the dollar checkoff box on income tax returns. Congressional campaigns were to continue to be financed entirely by private funds.

During the 1974 congressional elections, political action committees (PACs) gave $12.5 million to candidates for Congress. In 1976, PACs gave $22.5 million to congressional candidates, while contributing only $1 million to presidential candidates.[1] In 1980, if no changes in the law occur, and this dual system continues, PACs are likely to contribute over $55 million to congressional candidates while giving some $2 million to $3 million to presidential candidates.

In examining the growth of PACs, and the significance of that growth, it should be noted at the outset that this discussion focuses on congressional elections. As a result of the public financing of presidential

---

These remarks have been revised and extended since the conference. The author wishes to acknowledge the outstanding assistance provided by Kathryn Kavanagh-Baran of Common Cause's Issue Development staff and the excellent research contributed by Bruce Yannett. Bruce Adams, director of Issue Development for Common Cause, has also provided very helpful suggestions.

[1] Sources for 1974 and 1976 data: Common Cause, *Federal Campaign Finances* (Washington, D.C., 1974 and 1976). Sources for 1977-1978 data: Federal Election Commission, *Reports on Financial Activity, 1977-1978,* Interim Report no. 4, *Party and Non-Party Committees* (Washington, D.C., May 1979), and Interim Report no. 5, *House and Senate Candidates* (Washington, D.C., June 1979). (Unless otherwise noted.)

campaigns, PAC contributions play a very minor role today in the financing of presidential candidates.

Since 1970, Common Cause has played an active role in the campaign financing area, preparing detailed studies, lobbying for reforms, and supporting legislation in the courts. From our analysis of PACs during these nine years, four major points stand out.

- PAC contributions are generally contributions with a legislative purpose, made by interest groups which have specific legislative goals and which conduct organized lobbying programs in Washington.
- PAC money has a major and negative impact on the legislative process.
- There has been an explosive growth in the number of PACs and in the amount of giving by PACs since the enactment of the 1974 campaign finance law.
- The PAC movement must be contained before PACs have the power to veto any legislative efforts designed to bring their activities under control.

I will expand on these four points with particular reference to the papers prepared for this conference by Michael Malbin and Edwin Epstein.

Contributions with a Legislative Purpose

Contributions by PACs have a special quality—they are generally given by groups which are also regularly engaged in organized lobbying efforts in Washington. They are contributions with a legislative purpose. This qualitative characteristic of PAC money is recognized in the recent study by the Campaign Finance Study Group of Harvard University which found that ". . . PAC money is *interested* money."[2]

The relationship between PACs and the desire to influence government policy is also recognized in the papers presented at this conference by Bernadette Budde, political education director of the Business-Industry Political Action Committee, and by Edwin Epstein. Budde finds that industries that are more regulated and more obvious as congressional targets are more likely to have political action committees.

---

[2] *An Analysis of the Federal Election Campaign Act, 1972-78: A Report by the Campaign Finance Study Group to the Committee on House Administration, U.S. House of Representatives* (Cambridge, Mass.: Harvard University, The Institute of Politics, May 1979), p. 1-8. Emphasis in original.

Fred Radewagen, serving as political participation director for the U.S. Chamber of Commerce, said, "The prevailing attitude is that PAC money should be used to facilitate access to incumbents."[3]

Justin Dart, chairman of Dart Industries, which had the third largest corporate PAC in 1978, has spoken quite clearly about his intentions. He has said that dialogue with politicians "is a fine thing but with a little money they hear you better."[4]

Michael Malbin states in response to such comments that the beliefs of business officials who feel their contributions buy access are not dispositive; what counts are the beliefs of the members of the House and Senate.

No member, however, understands the congressional system and how it works better than Senator Russell Long, chairman of the Senate Finance Committee and a thirty-year veteran of Capitol Hill. He has said that campaign contributions "can often be viewed as monetary bread cast upon the water to be returned a thousand fold."[5]

The investment nature of giving by PACs is clearly evident in their strong backing for incumbents over their challengers, regardless of party. In 1978, for example, PACs gave $3.3 to House incumbents for every $1 they gave to their challengers.

Why do PACs favor incumbents over challengers at such a high rate? The Washington bureau chief of the *Wall Street Journal* put it well: "The bulk of special interest contributions represents a sort of investment in the careers of incumbent Congressmen and Senators with the aim of enhancing the influence of the financing groups. Obviously this money is given to buy influence."[6]

During the 1974 elections, for example, the PACs of the American Medical Association (AMA) gave contributions totaling $151,165 to twenty-nine of the thirty-seven California incumbents facing reelection. This total included seventeen incumbent Republicans and twelve incumbent Democrats ranging in the ideological spectrum from conservative Republicans such as John Rousselot and Barry Goldwater, Jr., to liberal Democrats such as Ron Dellums and John Burton, Jr. Only two chal-

---

[3] As quoted in Charles W. Hucker, "Explosive Growth: Corporate PACs Are Less Oriented to Republicans than Expected," *Congressional Quarterly*, April 8, 1978, p. 850.

[4] As quoted in Neil Ulman, "Companies Organize Employees and Holders into a Political Force," *Wall Street Journal*, August 15, 1978, p. 1.

[5] Common Cause, *How Money Talks in Congress: A Common Cause Study of the Impact of Money on Congressional Decision-Making* (Washington, D.C., October 1978), p. 2.

[6] Norman C. Miller, "Congressmen Begin to Push for Campaign Kitties," *Wall Street Journal*, March 21, 1977, p. 18.

lengers to California incumbents received AMA contributions. In each case their incumbent opponents received larger contributions.

Michael Malbin argues that comparing all incumbents with all challengers is a distortion, since most people are reluctant to "waste" money on a candidate who has no chance of winning. If his point were correct, however, then the distribution of individual contributions between incumbents and challengers should be the same as the distribution of the money from PACs. It is not. In 1978, for example, individual contributions went to House incumbents in preference to their challengers by a ratio of 2 to 1 compared with the higher 3.3 to 1 ratio for money from PACs.

Malbin also attempts to challenge the view that PACs are using campaign contributions to invest in legislative decisions by arguing that safe incumbents received no "bonus" of contributions from PACs. He finds that safe incumbents represent about 40 percent of all House candidates in a general election and that they receive about 40 percent of all contributions by PACs to general election candidates.[7]

The money that goes to safe incumbents, however, is not needed for campaigning. It therefore represents an even more obvious investment than contributions from PACs to more "competitive" incumbents.

Why, for example, did Representative Daniel Rostenkowski (D-Ill.), a member of the Democratic leadership and a ranking member of the powerful Ways and Means Committee, who was as safe last year as any Democrat in the House, still receive more than $112,000 in contributions from PACs during 1977–1978?

Gifts from PACs to safe incumbents, with both the donors and recipients aware that the funds are not necessary for immediate reelection purposes, can only be considered a "bonus" and of an investment nature.

Malbin finds "an element of truth" in the proposition that PACs favor incumbents, but there is a lot more than just "an element" involved. In supporting incumbents over challengers by a wide margin—3.3 to 1 in the House, about 3 to 1 overall—PACs substantially add to the non-

---

[7] The data base used by Malbin for his analysis of corporate PACs cannot be relied on for general conclusions about activities by corporate PACs in the 1978 elections. Malbin analyzed only forty-four corporate PACs on the basis that these PACs had each raised $30,000 or more by June 30, 1978. He notes that the decision to include only these groups left out 84 percent of the $9.8 million distributed by corporations in 1978 but argues that this is not a problem because small PACs are unlikely to have much direct influence on policy outcomes.

Notwithstanding the failure to recognize any cumulative impact from aggregate corporate giving to candidates during the 1978 elections, there were 171 corporations (not 44) that wound up raising $30,000 or more during the election year. Malbin thus omitted the bulk of the corporations who, by his own definition, are the larger corporate PACs which needed to be analyzed.

competitive nature of congressional elections. This is especially so in the House where incumbents who run for reelection are returned to office at roughly a 95 percent rate.

It is clear that individual contributions can and have been tied to achieving legislative aims. That is the basis for the limits placed by the 1974 law on individual contributions: $1,000 per candidate per election and $25,000 overall for all candidates. It is important to recognize, however, that there is a *qualitative* difference in our political system between individual contributions which may or may not be tied to organized lobbying efforts and money from PACs—which almost always is.

Legislative Impact of Money from PACs

The issue of whether campaign contributions provide access and influence and affect government decisions is not a new one. The Supreme Court, in upholding the constitutionality of contribution limits, found that "To the extent that large contributions are given to secure political quid pro quos from current and potential office holders, the integrity of our system of representative democracy is undermined."[8] Unlike Malbin, who takes no note of the public view regarding campaign contributions, the Supreme Court specifically recognized in this case that we are dealing not only with the actuality of abuse by public officials but with the appearance as well.

The interrelationship between organized lobbying and contributions by PACs is clear to the participants. The process is subtle. Articulated quid pro quos are rarely involved. The process nevertheless provides access and influence, and it affects decisions.

Incumbents and potential members of Congress both receive important contributions from groups that they know have legislative interests pending in Congress—interests that often have enormous economic implications. In accepting the contributions, candidates understand that givers from PACs will be lobbying them for assistance. Donors know that the money is being accepted by candidates who are aware of their legislative interests and their desires for support. As a *New York Times* editorial has questioned "How often can even scrupulous legislators be expected to forget their dependence on PACs?"[9] Common Cause has conducted various studies that show how money from PACs

---

[8] *Buckley* v. *Valeo* 424 US 1, at 26 (1976).
[9] "How to Stop Ducking the PAC Problem," *New York Times,* July 25, 1979, p. A22.

affects legislative decisions, including our 1978 study, *How Money Talks in Congress.*[10]

Whether PACs are seeking out incumbents to support, or incumbents are pressuring PACs for donations—and a fair share of both activities occur—there is little solace in the result. Either way, political money is lubricating the connection between lobbying activities and congressional actions.

Malbin argues that contributions from PACs are generally too small, when viewed as a percentage of total receipts, to function in a role whereby they influence decisions. He cites numerous examples of contributions from interest groups "only" representing 5 or 10 percent of a candidate's total receipts and concludes that few members of Congress receive enough to be affected.

In arguing this position, Malbin incorrectly discounts the actual size of contributions, incorrectly portrays these percentages as too small to be important to candidates, and incorrectly ignores the cumulative impact of PAC contributions.

He has, for example, invented a new standard in campaign giving— the $93,000 small contribution. He describes the $93,000 received by Senator John Tower (R-Tex.) from PACs and individuals in the banking industry as an insignificant "bit of money" because it only represented 2.5 percent of Tower's total contributions. On that theory, Clement Stone's $2 million contribution to Richard Nixon in 1972 was also a small contribution, because it only represented 3 percent of his total receipts.

There are no magic formulas under the present rules that allow congressional candidates to conclude that they have raised enough money so that a further 2.5, 5, or 10 percent of it would no longer be needed. Even if there were, 2.5, 5, or 10 percent of a campaign fund is often a large, not a small, amount. The larger the actual sums involved, furthermore, the harder it will be to replace them, regardless of the percentage of total receipts involved.

Given the present system, there are no easy alternatives for replacing funds from PACs: in fact, just the opposite is true. For most incumbents, money from PACs is not only the cheapest to raise but also the most accessible.

Malbin also gives no weight to the potential cumulative impact of contributions from PACs. There is no recognition of the potential dependency and obligation that emerges from a system where PACs provide significant sums to a member every two years, campaign after

---

[10] See Common Cause, *How Money Talks in Congress.*

campaign. There is, further, a lack of recognition of the cumulative impact that comes from the receipt by 433 House candidates of an average of $3,718 from the AMA in 1978, or the fact that 369 candidates received an average of $2,612 from the National Automobile Dealers Association, or that 431 candidates received an average of $2,620 from the National Association of Realtors.

Contrary to Malbin's assertion, contributions often play a major role in overall lobbying strategies. In the celebrated words of Jesse Unruh, campaign contributions are the mother's milk of American politics. Political money is an essential ingredient in this context, and both the donors and the recipients of PAC money understand this: its capacity for influence is clearly understood.

One of Washington's premier lobbyists, Thomas Boggs, Jr., has written in the American Trial Lawyers' journal that: "It is important that professionals volunteer their time and exert their influence in the political process. Yet the most valuable contribution they can give is a periodic financial transfusion. Dollars, after all, are the lifeblood of political action committees."[11]

One example of the process involved can be seen by looking at the campaign contributions of the American Trial Lawyers' Association. During the 1976 Senate elections, there were five candidates, including four incumbents, who each received a $5,000 contribution from the Trial Lawyers' PAC, and then went on to lose their general election races. Following the defeat in November of these five candidates, the Trial Lawyers turned around and made substantial contributions to each of the five candidates who had defeated them. Not one of the winning candidates had received any contributions from the Trial Lawyers during their campaign.[12]

Malbin also argues that money follows a candidate's positions and not the other way around. The enormous imbalance in the distribution of money from PACs between incumbents and challengers surely demonstrates that political money is not simply following the views of candidates. It is much more aggressive than that.

Even when money from PACs is given in response to previous positions taken, donors are usually interested in the future as well. Again, both donor and recipient understand this: the contribution is there to

---

[11] Thomas Hale Boggs, Jr., "PACs: Business' Political Renaissance," *Trial* 14 (January 1978), p. 7.
[12] See "Trial Lawyers Group Contributes Almost Quarter of a Million Dollars to 1976 Congressional Candidates, According to Common Cause; No-Fault Legislation Pending in Congress," Common Cause press release, February 28, 1978.

have its impact down the road. The public perception is still going to be one that relates campaign contributions to legislative decisions.

The PACs stand out as one of the major causes of the growing fragmentation of our political system and also of the increasing difficulty we experience in our attempts to reach national consensus. They are a key factor in the growth in America of the special-interest state.

It should be recognized that PACs are today serving substantially to weaken further an already anemic political party system. They present a major and an ongoing challenge to party responsibility and to party responsiveness in Congress.

Malbin has suggested that perhaps the solution to our present problems of campaign finance is a return to the old system wherein there were no contribution limits. Let the special interests flower, he says, and thereby decrease their power. The model of special interests competing with each other in Congress in order to evolve appropriate public policy is not a realistic one.

In certain conflicts between business and labor, notably those involving labor law reform, common-situs picketing, and the Davis-Bacon Act, we still see classical examples of competition between interest groups. In certain major confrontations, the national focus of public attention adds a competitive factor to this environment.

More and more, however, we are witnessing in Congress struggles between the particular interest of an organized segment of our society and the more generalized interest of those who are not organized and who are less directly involved. In this kind of political equation, campaign contributions, generally representing only the organized interest, take on an even greater importance.

What organized interests, for example, compete on an ongoing basis with the dairy interests on agriculture policy, with the realtors on housing policy, with the maritime unions on maritime policy, and with the truckers and teamsters on transportation policy?

We are also seeing more and more cases of special-interest groups exercising their increasing power to veto policies that affect their own interests. It is easier to block legislation in the congressional process than to pass it. With the existence of greater limitations on government resources, the veto power takes on even more significance. The result is a growing paralysis in government.

Ironically, the most traditional model in the classical approach— the struggle between business and labor—has been rapidly breaking down. In recent years we find cases of business and labor lobbying together on such issues as defense spending, environmental regulation,

199

maritime legislation, trucking legislation, and nuclear power. We can expect this to be a growing phenomenon.

Epstein argues that a serious challenge to the integrity of American electoral politics could arise from excessive harmony between powerful business and powerful labor. He concludes that this has not been a serious problem to date, but could become one in the future. We are already experiencing, however, a far more serious development than Epstein recognizes.

Explosive Growth of the Role of PACs

The remarkable growth in the number of PACs from 1975 through 1978 is not disputed. Corporate PACs led the way, increasing nearly tenfold (from 89 to 821), while the overall number of PACs registered approximately tripled (from 608 to 1,938). Total contributions from PACs to congressional candidates almost tripled during this period, from $12.5 million in 1974 to $35.1 million in 1978.

In 1974, there were only 12 energy-related PACs: four years later, there were 110 such PACs. Epstein finds that PACs from oil and coal companies far outdistanced all other industry groupings in 1978 in terms of their receipts, expenditures, and contributions. Some observers (including Epstein) have incorrectly labeled the explosive growth in the number of PACs and the increase in contributions by PACs as the unintended consequences of election reform.

Two key actions taken by Congress in its consideration of the 1974 campaign finance law set the stage for what has occurred. The first involved the defeat of a fundamental reform. The second involved the passage of a nonreform.

In 1974, public financing was considered by Common Cause and others to be the key reform for changing the system of financing Congressional races, just as it was for presidential elections. The 1974 law, however, as has been noted, established a dual system of public financing for the presidency and private financing for Congress. While the 1974 law also established the first limits on contributions by individuals and by PACs to congressional candidates, it nevertheless literally invited the influx of contributions by PACs into Congress that subsequently occurred.

Even with the defeat of public financing of congressional campaigns, we would not have experienced the growth of PACs that has since occurred if it had not been for a second key action taken by Congress in 1974, an action specifically designed to benefit PACs.

A provision authorizing government contractors to establish PACs was adopted in the 1974 law. The provision amended a thirty-four-year statute[13] prohibiting government contractors from making either direct or indirect campaign contributions to federal candidates to exempt PACs from the prohibition.

Labor organizations were concerned that, without this change, their training contracts in the areas of government manpower would make their existing PACs illegal. Business also saw the provision as an opportunity to eliminate a major roadblock for corporations desiring to establish new PACs.

This legislative effort has been cited as an example of election reform leading to unanticipated consequences—in this case the enormous growth in business-related PACs that has occurred since 1974. The provision involved, however, never was a reform and its potential consequences were not unanticipated.

Common Cause strongly opposed the provision at the time Congress considered it precisely because its potential consequences were so obvious. Senators William Proxmire (D-Wis.) and Robert Stafford (R-Vt.) led an effort to defeat the provision in the Senate which failed by thirty-six votes to fifty-one. As *Congressional Quarterly* reported at the time, conservative Republicans with business ties and liberal Democrats loyal to labor teamed up to protect their constituencies among special-interest groups.[14]

In discussing the issue of the growth of PACs, Malbin argues that what we need to do is dispel the "myth"—which he asserts is fostered by Common Cause, congressional sponsors of public financing, and the press—that PACs are on some sort of a growth curve wildly disproportionate to the growth in campaign costs as a whole. The data he cites, however, contain basically the same information that has led the Harvard Study Group to read the opposite conclusion. The study group found that "the percentage of funds coming to congressional candidates from PACs has been steadily increasing over the past four elections."[15] They concluded that "PAC contributions have grown significantly in both total amounts and as a proportion of all contributions."[16]

To make his point, Malbin focuses on the narrow time frame from 1976 to 1978 and argues that the relatively limited proportional growth during this period disproves any claim of explosive growth in the proportional importance of special interests. Malbin's own figures show that, between 1974 and 1978, giving by PACs to House candidates went

---

[13] The Hatch Act of 1940, 54 Stat. 772.

[14] *Congressional Quarterly Almanac* 29, 1973, p. 747.

[15] Campaign Finance Study Group, p. 1-7.

[16] Ibid., p. 2-37.

up from 17 percent to 25 percent of total receipts, a 47 percent increase.[17] An examination of House incumbents alone reveals the same substantial increase, but at even higher levels. Contributions by PACs to House incumbents, as a percentage of total receipts, increased from 21 percent in 1974 to 32 percent in 1978.

If we look behind the percentages, we find substantial increases in the number of House members dependent on very large amounts of giving by PACs. In 1975, 78 members of the House had received 40 percent or more of their total contributions from PACs during the 1974 elections. In 1979, the number of House members receiving similar amounts in the 1978 election rose to 136, while PACs accounted for 56 percent of the funds spent by House committee chairmen up for reelection in that campaign. In his paper Epstein concludes that, by any measure, the business-related PACs (both corporate and noncorporate) played a far more important role in 1978 than they had in any previous election.

A real irony of the movement linked to PACs is that while it has experienced explosive growth during the past four years, in many other ways it is still in the incubation stage. During the period from 1974 to 1978, contributions from the National Automobile Dealers Association's PAC grew 6,000 percent, from $14,000 to almost $1 million. Over the same period, contributions from the National Association of Realtors increased from $261,000 to $1.1 million, with their PAC director being quoted as saying that this potential was just starting.[18]

Dozens of the new PACs formed since 1974 have the capacity to achieve similar growth. Thirteen of the fifteen largest corporations in America now have their own PACs. None gave more than $160,000 in 1978. There is no doubt, however, that General Motors, AT&T, Ford Motor Co., Mobil Oil, Texaco, Standard Oil of California, IBM, General Electric, Chrysler, Standard of Indiana, Atlantic Richfield, Shell, and U.S. Steel all have the capacity to generate million dollar PACs over the next few years.

Malbin refers to the "measly" $505 average corporate contribution for the top twenty-five *Fortune* companies. Many of the new PACs are small today because they are just getting started, not because they have a track record of being small. Many are just learning the ways to raise money. The average contribution for the National Automobile Dealers Association grew from $263 in 1974 to $2,612 in 1978. The National Association of Realtors gave an average of $1,034 in 1974 and $2,620

---

[17] Common Cause figures show giving by PACs in 1974 as 18 percent of total receipts. This results in a 41 percent increase over the four years between 1974 and 1978.

[18] Don McCloud, "Special Interest Politics," *Associated Press*, March 12, 1979.

in 1978. We can expect similar developments on a much wider scale in the years ahead.

While Malbin shows no interest in, and takes no notice of, the potential for future growth in PACs, Epstein finds that, "PAC operations in 1976 and 1978 reveal only the tip of a possible iceberg—clearly for corporations and other business-related groups, but to some extent even for labor." He subsequently concludes that the market for potential formation of company PACs is virtually untapped, and that company PACs give every promise of continuing to increase both in numbers and in the magnitude of their funds.

Malbin, having first argued that there has not been a steady growth of giving by PACs as a percentage of total receipts, then goes on to state that the growth in PACs basically reflects a transfer of that money which in the past was given directly by individuals with business interests. He concludes that the role played by economic interests has been made public without becoming more important, and perhaps even becoming less so.

He offers as proof of his assertion evidence of a proportional drop in contributions of $100 or more to House candidates, from 39 percent of all receipts in 1972 to 22 percent in 1978. In making this argument, Malbin departs from the thesis that money from PACs has remained relatively constant on a proportional basis and appears to embrace the position that the amount *has* increased, but only as larger individual contributions have decreased.

Malbin's position is disputed by a number of those engaged in the business PAC movement. In her paper for the conference, for example, Bernadette Budde claims that corporate PACs have brought thousands of individuals who had never made contributions before into the process.

More importantly, Malbin's discussion of relative percentages overlooks one basic point—that the entire pie has been increasing. During the period of the last three elections (1974–1978), total contributions from individuals have grown by 55 percent, significantly faster than the rate of inflation.[19] The total of contributions from those individuals giving $500 or more has grown by 61 percent, and that has occurred even though contributions were limited to $1,000 per election after the 1974 elections.

Contributions from individuals (in particular business-related individuals, according to the Malbin view) have not decreased, but increased. They have been augmented, however, by business-related money from

[19] Based on figures provided by Gary Jacobson, "The Pattern of Campaign Contributions to Candidates for the U.S. House of Representatives 1972-78," Campaign Finance Study Group, p. 2-8.

PACs which has been increasing at a faster rate. The fact that such money has been increasing in significance does not make individual business-related contributions insignificant. Candidates cannot and do not look at campaign contributions simply in relative terms. They need to look at them in terms of total needs.

Malbin's claim that the role played by economic interests has not become more important, and perhaps has become less so, simply has no credence. This is especially so given the real growth of larger individual contributions and the relatively greater growth of business-related contributions from PACs. Even if Malbin were correct, furthermore, and we were only dealing with a direct transfer, the impact of the funds would be qualitatively changing, as indeed Epstein has recognized in his paper.

Acting before the Power to Act Is Gone

The most significant development in the financing of congressional campaigns since 1974 has been the growth of PACs. There is every reason to believe that what has happened to date will be dwarfed by future expansion, unless changes are made in the campaign finance laws.

Though Malbin describes the growth of PACs as a "shallow and diversionary issue," Epstein treats it more seriously. As has been noted, he talks of such developments to date as the "tip of a possible iceberg" and finds that "the potential for corporate and other business PAC formation and expansion is virtually unlimited."

Epstein concludes that we might reach the point where too much campaign money for congressional candidates comes from PACs. He defines this point as being more than 25 percent of total receipts in donations from PACs. We have, however, already reached Epstein's danger point in the House of Representatives. The 1978 record shows that the 968 candidates who ran in the House general election received 25 percent of their total receipts in money from PACs (with House incumbents receiving 32 percent).

Epstein supports partial public financing for congressional campaigns as one remedy, while Malbin basically ignores it. The Harvard Study Group in its recommendations also ignores public financing as a solution, but for a different reason.[20]

---

[20] The Harvard study was commissioned and paid for by the House Administration Committee, a majority of whose members have led the fight against congressional public financing since 1973. In receiving the contract to do the study, the Harvard Study Group was explicitly told it could not propose public financing of congressional races. After the release of the study, the head of the Harvard Study Group stated publicly that a majority of the study group favored some form of congressional public financing.

Public financing is the fundamental reform needed for congressional elections. The immediate focus of attention in Congress now is on another important piece of legislation, designed to deal directly with PACs. Introduced by Representatives David Obey (D-Wisc.) and Tom Railsback (R-Ill.) and sponsored by more than 130 members, the bill would reduce individual contributions by PACs from a maximum total of $10,000 to $5,000 per candidate, and place an overall limit of $50,000 on the amount that a candidate can get from all PACs.

Despite Malbin's view that the legislation would weaken organized labor and leave business virtually untouched, and the Chamber of Commerce's opposite view that the bill would weaken business and benefit labor, the legislation provides no clear advantages or guarantees for anyone. It is designed to cap the impact of all giving by PACs, and it would do so on an across-the-board basis.

The Obey-Railsback bill is designed to deal with the problem of contributions by PACs which are providing an inappropriate influence in our political system. It does not deal with the need for substantial additional funds for challengers in order to make congressional races more competitive—public financing is required for that.

Malbin's proposal to return to the pre-Watergate days by eliminating contribution limits would open up the campaign financing system to enormous potential abuse in terms of influencing public policy. There is simply no case to be made for this approach.

The act of substantially increasing the individual limits would also be inappropriate. It would supply some (but not a lot of) additional funds to challengers, but it would also supply far greater funds to incumbents. It would do nothing to broaden the base of givers, but rather would allow a select few larger givers to contribute more.

While it can be stated as a general proposition that money from PACs has a greater capacity to be tied to lobbying efforts, this capacity also exists for large individual contributions, particularly if they come from a few individuals with the same interest. The higher the limit, furthermore, the greater the capacity.

Conclusion

The growth in PACs presents a clear and present danger. It is a direct threat today to the legitimacy of congressional decision making and is likely to become an even greater threat in the future without changes in the campaign finance laws.

We are at a critical stage. If PACs are not brought under control shortly, their powers may prevent us from ever bringing them under control.

Any system of financing political campaigns is going to have rough edges. Perfect laws with a completely predictable impact simply are not going to be devised. One of the consequences we should anticipate for any law or system of laws is that there are always going to be some unanticipated consequences: that, however, should never be an argument for failing to deal with fundamental problems.

Our campaign finance laws must ultimately protect the integrity of our political process and allow our system of democracy to function competitively. Neither of those goals are being met today at the congressional level. It is time to bring the fundamental task of reforming our campaign finance laws to a successful conclusion.

Clark MacGregor

During the course of the discussion, we have heard some interesting concepts. The first is that a vigorous and creative exercise of First Amendment rights is misguided at best, evil at worst. The second is that political contributions, a vital First Amendment right, should be made with no purpose whatever. The third is that no incumbent seeking reelection is worthy of support.

You may think I react a little too strongly to the last point, but I must confess that, having sought reelection four times as an incumbent in the House of Representatives, I do think that there are incumbents worthy of support—a great many of them in both political parties. And yet, the fact that PACs have given up to 60 or 70 or 80 percent of their campaign funds has been treated as if that were alarming, when 95 percent seeking reelection get reelected. I think the figures indicate a lot of sophistication on the part of PACs and a lot of risk taking—not a lot of buying access, but a lot of risk taking. Otherwise you would see a much higher percentage of total contributions going to incumbents.

"Contributions should be made with no purpose." It was not asserted that way. It was asserted that a contribution with a purpose behind it is evil. Imagine, if you can visualize them with me, a couple who have had a pretty good year and have $300 to put aside to support candidates of their choice. This is a fundamental First Amendment right, but to support the candidates of their choice would be to act with a purpose in mind. We are told they shouldn't do that. So, they get an old roulette wheel. They put in three balls. They spin the wheel. One turns up Ron Dellums, another turns up George McGovern, and the third Elizabeth Holtzman. Now, it happens that these two people are conservative in their views. Nevertheless, contributing with a purpose is evil, so they make the contributions entirely at random, with a sovereign disdain for purpose, regardless of political philosophy. Hogwash.

Now, let me come to the vigorous and creative exercise of First Amendment rights, and that is what PACs are, and why they are authorized by the Congress, specifically sanctioned by a decision of the Supreme Court (in *Buckley* v. *Valeo,* January 30, 1976), and very well regulated by the Federal Election Commission.

We have not heard in any of this discussion that contributions are voluntary. I know of no major lawsuit nor any major citation by the FEC—and I will stand corrected if one can be called to my attention—that demonstrates, by any standard of proof, the exercise of coercion in the making of a voluntary contribution. The practices of PACs with which I am familiar, and indeed they are business PACs, indicate that chairmen, chief executive officers, and boards of directors go overboard in making absolutely sure that there is no coercion.

On the subject of coercion, let me give you an example of a letter sent to all employees by a major corporation at the institution of that corporation's PAC. After describing the decision of the board of directors to go forward with the establishment of a political action committee, these words appear in the chairman's letter:

I hope you will decide to take part in this program, but there is absolutely no pressure on you to do so. Whether or not you take part is up to you and will have no bearing on your present position or future with our company. There will be neither rewards nor reprisals whatever your decision. Should anyone even imply anything to the contrary, I ask that you immediately bring this to my personal attention.

I find, in one way or another, that that message, reemphasized each year of solicitation, is characteristic of the operation of the business PACs in this country. We are talking about voluntary contributions. We are not talking about windfall profits realized by some insensitive corporation trying to purchase influence with the government of the United States. We are talking about individuals who contribute voluntarily.

Let us look at the average amount of contributions made to PACs of business corporations. Definitive figures are not available, but I did obtain a cross section of the statistics from business corporations that I respect. I have seen a figure during the 1978–1979 biennium of about $10 million, or a little less, for corporate PAC contributions to candidates. If the average contribution was $100, about 100,000 citizens voluntarily contributed to that business PAC effort. Actually, the number of contributions to a business PAC below $100 outnumber those above

$100 by a rough ratio of 2 to 1. Consequently, in this biennium, the figures would suggest that roughly 150,000 individual citizens made voluntary contributions to corporate PACs. Not only is this sort of activity sanctioned by the First Amendment, but I hope it will always be encouraged.

A suggestion was made that the largest companies have the largest PACs. Of course they do. They have the most employees. But there are exceptions like Winn-Dixie Stores which is not a massive company. For the most part, firms whose PACs appear on the FEC's listing of the ten largest corporate PACs are there because they have the most employees, including the most employees in the so-called executive, managerial, or administrative level of the corporation. No wonder that they raise more money than smaller corporations. They have more people, and it is the individual voluntary contributions from the individual citizen we are talking about here.

An assertion was made about the proverbial iceberg, that we have only seen the tip of the iceberg. I suspect that those who made that assertion, both in writing and orally, have never been chairmen of corporate PACs and have never tried to raise voluntary contributions in the face of the repeated assurances of the chairman of the corporation that no one has to participate and that no arm twisting will be tolerated.

I think 50 percent of the corporate iceberg is already above water in PACs. I seriously question whether the future will witness anything like the rapid growth in corporate PACs of the last three or four years, since the SUNPAC (Sun Oil Co. Political Action Committee) decision and since *Buckley* v. *Valeo*. From now on additional corporate PACs will be few and far between in contrast to their rapid proliferation since 1976. I cannot prove this, but I have a strong feeling it will be this way. I would bet that the next five years will not see—inflation discounted— a doubling of the aggregate amount contributed voluntarily by individuals to their corporations' PACs.

I listened to Mr. Conlon with great interest, and I have been talking to some of the sponsors of Obey-Railsback. To them I said, "If you are concerned about inordinate influence exercised by the PACs in our political process, why do you have the $50,000 limit on every House candidate regardless of the population of his district?" I am talking about voting population; we all know that districts are roughly equal in population, but don't tell that to Clair Burgener, who has over 900,000. When they are established as a result of the decennial census, the districts are roughly equal in population, but they are not equal in votes. We all know that. In some of the southern states, fewer than 100,000 people vote in a congressional election. In some of our more spirited areas, where the contests are heated and the competition is open, almost 300,000 votes are cast. Why limit to $50,000 every candidate for the House? If we are sincerely interested in reducing the possible impact of PACs, why not limit their contribution to a percentage of total amount raised by a given candidate, say, 50 percent?

In that way, we would account for and equalize the campaign funding for both challenger and incumbent, and would provide for the districts where an incumbent has to spend only $50,000 to be reelected— and there are many of them. In such a district the candidate could, under the Obey-Railsback bill, raise his entire funding exclusively from PACs, whereas in a district where $300,000 is required for reelection, the incumbent can realize from PAC contributions only 16¢ out of every dollar he needs. It seems to me that there is a gap between the argument advanced for the $50,000 ceiling and the practical effects of the $50,000 ceiling.

Now, finally, I should like to make just of couple of comments about the concern that if one backs a loser, he will make an enemy of the winner, who in turn will take revenge by his votes in Congress. Sure, there are some revenge-minded people around, but I suggest to you there are more around with the spirit of Hubert Humphrey. When he soundly defeated me in 1970 for the United States Senate, he said, "Clark, you would have beaten me if I hadn't made all the effort over the years to go to those big business tycoons who supported the Republican candidate, after the election, and said, 'No hard feelings. How can I help General Mills? What can I do to be of interest to Minneapolis Honeywell? How does 3M see its problems, and let's talk about them.' " For every revenge-minded winner, there are more who follow the politics of the late Hubert Humphrey and who are smart enough to realize the best way to get reelected is to conciliate the forces that were arrayed against them and in favor of their opponents in the last election.

There will be more risk taking now because there is more sophistication. This is a healthy process, not an unhealthy process. But something really ought to be done along the lines suggested by Mr. Malbin, about who is pressuring whom. I had the delightful experience, while I was testifying before a congressional committee, of having a congressman come into the hearing room and say to me, "Clark, before you leave, I would like to have you come up to my office and talk to me about your PAC making a contribution to my campaign." I said, "I will pretend you didn't say that because we are in the Longworth House Office Building, and I believe what you have done is a violation of federal law." He said, "I didn't solicit a contribution; I just suggested we have a conversation."

There ought to be resistance to pressure from those in the business PAC field. And there ought to be resistance on the part of elected office-holders to contributors who say, "Okay. Now, you deliver with your votes."

Indeed, I take a much more optimistic view about the operation of our system than many speakers who have preceded me.

Authors' Replies

Michael J. Malbin

Fred Wertheimer and Richard Conlon are perhaps the two most important people inside and outside Congress who have worked behind the scenes for the campaign finance reforms of 1974 and 1976, for public financing of congressional elections, and for legislation to limit the role of political action committees (PACs). Their criticisms, fully expected, are welcomed for the way they sharpen the issue. Some of the criticisms, however, particularly those of Wertheimer, are based on misreadings or misstatements of my argument. As such, they confuse the issue. In these remarks, I shall first try to set the record straight on a few points and then present what I believe to be the underlying differences of principle between us.

Setting the Record Straight

There are four specific points at issue, and I will deal with each of them in turn.

First, Wertheimer and Conlon both wonder why the Chamber of Commerce and other business groups oppose the limitations of the Obey-Railsback bill on contributions by PACs if labor would be the big loser. I do not know the answer to that question and suggest it be directed to the chamber. As Epstein's paper showed, the history of campaign finance "reform" is riddled with examples of organizations supporting amendments that work to their own long-term disadvantage. I do believe, however, that the chamber is more upset about the overall ceilings for candidates than the limits on contributions by individual PACs, while I argued that the limits on individual PACs were what would hurt labor.

Incidentally, my comments were directed primarily at the uneven impact of the Obey-Railsback bill. I do not particularly oppose some

This reply has been revised and extended since the conference.

cutting of the contribution limits for individual PACs, provided that such a change is linked to others that would produce a net increase in campaign funds. These would be: to increase the individual limits at least as high as the limit for PACs, to enact one-for-one tax credits with a low cutoff point to help low-income voters, and to omit the ceilings on cumulative limits on PACs. In other words, I believe that some of the specific provisions in Obey-Railsback may be helpful. My quarrel is with the basic *direction* in which the policy would move us, because I believe we need more money in politics, not less.

Connected with this issue is a second one—Wertheimer's assertion that I "basically ignore" public financing. I happen to support some forms of public financing and said so briefly at the end of my paper. Specifically, I think that a voucher system, one-for-one tax credits, and in-kind grants to candidates and parties would do much to democratize influence in the electoral process. I do oppose spending limits, but I believe these raise different conceptual issues from those of public financing—although they normally are treated together. Public financing was mentioned only briefly in my paper because I believe it has little to do with the basic sources of interest-group power in this country.

Thirdly, Wertheimer and Conlon both take me to task on the question of contributions by PACs to incumbents. Conlon at least tries to respond to my argument, Wertheimer ignores it; but both essentially rest their positions on the well-known fact that incumbents get more money than challengers. I agree. Incumbents as a whole clearly do better than challengers as a whole. Challengers in competitive districts, however, do about as well as incumbents, so incumbency cannot by itself be the issue. When we look at individual PACs or groups of PACs, moreover, we discover that business PACs do not invest disproportionately in safe incumbents.[1] The purpose of looking at this from the perspective of the PACs as well as from that of the candidates is to find out whether the data indicate that they are simply trying to buy legislative

---

[1] One comment about Wertheimer's criticism of my data base. I share his wish that I could have included all corporate PACs with year-end (instead of June 30) receipts of more than $30,000 or, better yet, all corporate PACs. Unfortunately, the FEC's Interim Report on PACs containing year-end data was not available until the research for this paper was completed, when redoing the job by hand would have been impossible. More importantly, the fact that I am dealing with only a sample of corporate PACs—which is acknowledged in my paper—does *not* bias my argument about the ability of PACs to influence legislation. The *cumulative* impact of all business PACs taken together becomes important only on major economic issues and I argue elsewhere that these issues are too important politically for members to let themselves be swayed by contributions. For all smaller issues, what we are interested in seeing is the possible influence of single PACs or related groups of PACs.

influence. I believe that they are not, and that they would concentrate much more heavily on safe incumbents if they were.

Finally, Wertheimer repeatedly misstates my position on what has been happening to the role of special-interest money in politics. Although one would never know it from his or Conlon's comments, my paper acknowledged that there has been a substantial increase in the percentage of campaign money coming from PACs and in the absolute amount coming from large contributors. What I said, and what they never dealt with, is that the *proportional* increase in the importance of PACs since 1972 has been matched by a *proportional* decrease in the importance of large contributions, leaving large "special-interest" contributions in roughly the same place *proportionally* as before.

Differences of Principle

The basic issues running through these and other specific criticisms of my argument relate to two themes: the extent to which contributions and policy are linked and the best mechanism for controlling special-interest-group power.

With respect to the linkage between contributions and policy, the $93,000 in banking money received by Senator Tower in 1978 is as good a place to start as any, since Wertheimer and Conlon both seem preoccupied with this example. I asserted that candidates would not dare to shift their positions on *basic* issues of political economy—such as the need for private capital formation or wage-price controls—because of campaign contributions. These issues form too much a part of a candidate's history and political appeal to be changed without political costs far higher than those that a contribution could make up. The question of influence, therefore, resolves itself into whether a candidate would do things for a *specific* industry *because* that industry gave a candidate 2 or 5 or even 10 percent of his funds. (No one doubts, incidentally, that office holders often push proposals to benefit specific industries in their district; the question is whether they do so *because* of campaign contributions.) My own position is that candidates who try to help industries in their districts would continue to do so even if private campaign contributions were barred entirely, while candidates who even appear to respond to contributions on specific and demonstrable items in our post–disclosure law world will find the resulting publicity politically damaging. When contributions and votes are in accord in today's world, it usually is because the candidate has a *political* reason to believe the vote can withstand and perhaps even benefit from the light of publicity— hence the assertion that money follows positions, and not the other way around. If people could be bought as easily as Common Cause suggests, we would have a hard time explaining the many legislative victories won in recent years by Common Cause and other "public interest" lobbies.

But what about the more difficult case of a person dealing with a technical subject likely to result in little publicity? Is it not likely that someone like Senator Tower would use his position on the Banking Committee to show his gratitude to his contributors? The problem with this argument is that open committee meetings and disclosure have made it very risky to count on avoiding publicity. And even if he would like to "pay off" his contributors with a public policy "gift," he would soon discover it to be impossible to please all of his contributors at once. The issues that do not make headlines tend, by and large, to be issues that divide the banking industry: however Tower votes on these issues, he will please some supporters while displeasing others. Whatever he does, he will find groups to support him. About the only thing a member cannot afford is unpredictable inconsistency. He is free to define his constituency as he sees politically fit, but he has to recognize that constituents have memories, and that they like to be remembered. These forces produce incentives for special-interest logrolling with dynamics that go much deeper than any explanation based primarily on campaign finance can begin to comprehend.

Wertheimer and Conlon both suggest that the picture I am painting of competition between interest groups is of declining relevance in today's legislative world. To make their point, they (and Epstein) note the number of issues on which labor and business are on the same side. Why should we assume, however, that competition must take the form of labor versus business? A far more normal situation is that in which labor and business in one industry join to oppose labor and business in another. Wertheimer thus asks: Who opposes truckers and the teamsters on transportation policy? The answer: railroads and railway labor. Who opposes the dairy industry? The answer: major food producers, soybean farmers, and others with an economic stake in margarine and other dairy substitutes. Who opposes the cotton industry? The answer: major chemical corporations. The list could go on endlessly, without even beginning to get to the issues on which media-oriented "public interest" groups provide effective political competition for industry lobbyists.

Interest Groups and *The Federalist*

This brings us to the fundamental issue dividing me from our discussants: How best to control interest-group power? (At this point, I ought to add that I never called the role of interest groups a shallow or diversionary issue—only the growth of PACs.) Clark MacGregor was more frank than most people when he said that "of course" campaign contributions are contributions made with a purpose. Indeed they are, as were most of the large undisclosed contributions, legal and illegal, of the pre-Watergate years. Wertheimer's unhappiness with this leads one to suspect that his aim goes beyond that of opening up and cleaning up politics, to creating a world in which people do not try to use politics to achieve private ends—or, at least, not private economic ends. Such a world, alas, is not to be. "If men were angels, no government would be necessary," James Madison reminded us in *Federalist, no. 51.*

Madison was no stranger to the idea of "special interests." His *Federalist, no. 10* discusses that very subject. In that paper, the most important, and most brilliant, document ever written explaining the fundamental principles underlying the United States Constitution, Madison asked his readers to think about the basic purpose of the Constitution —the preservation of liberty. He wrote that there were two ways liberty could be threatened: by a minority and by a majority. Fighting tyranny by a minority is, in principle, fairly easy in a democracy although in practice it is not always so easy. The way to do it is to make sure that the people have the final power to decide who will, and who will not, represent them. In terms of the debate over campaign finance, this means that the people have to know who is giving what to whom. In other words, it means disclosure. Once disclosure is attained, the people are then free to decide for themselves what they want. (Incidentally, I should like to add that my position also leads me to support lobbying disclosure if, and this is a big if, a way can be found to gain disclosure without harassing politically marginal fringe groups.)

Madison, however, was not worried *primarily* about tyranny by a minority. He was much more worried about what he called the peculiar danger of democracy: a majority faction that might join together under a single all-consuming passion to deprive the minority of its liberty. We do not need to be reminded that this is a real danger that can never be eliminated entirely in a democracy. At least it can be minimized, however, and that is what our Constitution is all about.

How can the dangers of tyranny by a majority faction be minimized? Madison suggested there were two ways. The first would be to prohibit people from forming factions in the first place. Madison, quite rightly, called this a cure that would be worse than the disease: destroy liberty for the sake of preventing tyranny. No one today wants to do away with factions and interest groups entirely. I submit, nevertheless, that the so-called public-interest groups would move us in this direction in their zeal to prevent decisions by a minority, to decrease the role of private interests in politics, and to limit or do away with political action committees.

Madison's second alternative, the way of our Constitution, was to create a set of conditions in which factions would flourish and multiply. The more factions flourished, the less likely would be the chance that any of them could get its own way without compromising and taking the interests of others into account. How, then, do you make factions flourish? This would be done by downplaying the importance to voters and citizens of issues that might produce religious or ideological warfare, and upgrading the importance of commerce. The way to avoid tyranny by the majority, in other words, was to create a modern, commercial society in which diverse economic interests would flourish and compete with each other. As all competed, each would have an interest in preventing any one of the others from dominating the picture.

Nothing is as important in our constitutional scheme of things as the preservation of a system in which a multiplicity of factions flourishes. If any of these factions should manage to impose its will on the majority —by slipping a special-interest amendment through a committee, for example—then let us deal with that democratically, through disclosure, through publicity, and through the mobilization of countervailing force. If we, the consumers and taxpayers in the majority, lose some of these battles—as we do every day—let us not react in frustration by killing off the system that is the basis of our political liberty.

I agree with Wertheimer and Conlon that we do not live in a perfectly competitive open-market world. We would probably also agree that the public good does not equal merely the sum of private interests. (That is why I support some forms of partial public financing.)

If we truly want to decrease the influence of particular interests, however, we should listen to Madison and let them be fruitful, multiply, and compete. Increase everyone's resources, and the resources of any one become less important. Limiting the PACs will do nothing to help the disenfranchised, and will favor those groups that use other, less accountable, methods to press their political point of view, such as constitutionally protected independent expenditures, "soft-money" spent on registration or on getting out the vote, or influence over the media.[2] I find it hard to believe that Fred Wertheimer, of all people, or Common Cause, of all organizations, would want us to go back to a pre-Watergate world in which the advantage returns to people whose power is not disclosed and is not publicly accountable.

---

[2] It is worth reiterating the point made in both Epstein's paper and in mine that the 1976 presidential election, which Wertheimer characterized as being free from the influence of the special interests, involved $11 million of unreported, legal expenditures in the general election by organized labor on behalf of President Carter.

Edwin M. Epstein

I reviewed my own paper and was reminded again of the importance of *The Federalist*. What *The Federalist* contains is very helpful in interpreting what has happened over the last decade or so.

All of you know the aphorism, "Everyone is crazy but me and thee, and at times I wonder about thee." I guess the same can be said about special interests. Everyone has a special interest but me and thee, and at times I wonder about thee. And everyone is very concerned about the impact that other group will have on the political process.

To me, the real question of concern about PACs is, How much is too much? I have adopted a consistent position over the past dozen years. It is this: both business and labor have a legitimate role within the electoral process, and that role includes being able to make donations through PACs. My position antedates the legislation of the 1970s.

The question is, How much should emanate from these sources? If contributions go beyond a certain threshold, is the openness of our political process adversely affected?

I am concerned about the business iceberg, to which I have alluded, and about which Clark MacGregor commented. I think it is fine that corporations have formed PACs. I would be uneasy, however, if I began to see a really substantial number of corporate PACs with kitties in the half-million to million dollar range contributing hundreds of thousands of dollars each. Similarly I would be very much concerned if labor so substantially increased its contributions that they amounted to two or three times their present size. If that happened, there would be so much money emanating from economic interest groups that those groups might play a disproportionate role in a society that sees itself as democratic, pluralistic, and tolerant of open dialogue by all groups on its political stage. That does concern me.

In my paper I discussed the Obey-Railsback bill. I bought half of it, but not all. I bought the notion of a $2,500 limitation for each election campaign—that is, the primary, the general election, and a possible runoff. This limit could be adjusted for cost of living. Most groups can do quite well with a $2,500 limitation. In fact, very few contributions presently exceed $2,500.

In talking with business, labor, and ideological group committees over the last half-dozen years, I found that, with few exceptions, most feel no need to contribute more than that to support candidates sympathetic to their positions.

I am quite concerned, however, for the reasons specified in the Harvard study and in the work by Gary Jacobson, about limiting to

217

$50,000 the aggregate amount a candidate can accept from PACs. This limit has a potentially severely adverse effect on challengers who generally have greater need for money than incumbents. To forbid them to accept more than $50,000 from PACs, though those PACs may have widely divergent political interests, makes very little sense.

Discussion

MR. WERTHEIMER: I'd like to make a few quick comments on Clark MacGregor's comments. He cited Hubert Humphrey. Hubert Humphrey, I think, eloquently described the private system of raising money as "demeaning, degrading, and disgusting"; it was not exactly his favorite pastime.

MR. MACGREGOR: He described everything eloquently.

MR. WERTHEIMER: Clark MacGregor gave a nice example of a PAC being pressured by a member. Although it is fair to say that it happens on both sides, Mr. MacGregor is not the best one to raise this example.

I think I am correct in saying that in 1976 Mr. MacGregor circulated a memo among business PACs, exhorting and urging them to provide more business money for candidates—

MR. MACGREGOR: 1978, that was.

MR. WERTHEIMER:—1978—more business money for candidates. He circulated information about their support for labor positions and basically argued that businesses were supporting pro-labor candidates, but they had better turn around their money and start giving it to pro-business candidates. Now, that goes a little bit against his earlier theory about all the fine incumbents from both parties who are entitled to get their money.

MR. MACGREGOR: Absolutely. Contributions given with no purpose are ridiculous and contrary to our system.

MR. WERTHEIMER: On this point Mr. MacGregor again cited the theoretical approach: Everyone should be free to support those people in whom he believes. But he was less enthusiastic when he found businesses supporting candidates with high COPE ratings.

219

Finally, about the Supreme Court decision. That decision upheld the limits on individual contributions. I would just like to read from it:

It is unnecessary to look beyond the Act's primary purpose to limit the actuality and appearance of corruption resulting from large, individual financial contributions in order to find a constitutionally sufficient justification for the $1,000 contribution limit. To the extent that large contributions are given to secure political quid pro quos from current and potential office holders, the integrity of our system of representative democracy is undermined.

That was the basis of the Court's decision.

MR. MACGREGOR: I am sure you wouldn't want these people to believe that that decision did not also say the following:

Section 610 permits corporations and labor unions to establish segregated funds to solicit voluntary contributions to be utilized for political purposes. Corporate and union resources, without limitation, may be employed to administer these funds and to solicit contributions from employees, stockholders, and union members.

MR. WERTHEIMER: No, I wouldn't want them to miss that at all, but I do want to repeat that the purpose of these provisions is to limit the role of contributions. The Court based its decision on contribution limits.

STEVE WALKER, Public Affairs Council: I would like to comment briefly on several issues not touched on today. One is the issue of celebrity status and its effect on fund raising. For example, Senator Kennedy, or Henry Kissinger, or Jane Fonda, or Pat Boone can lend their names to innumerable fund-raising events—one a week, if they wish. Their mere presence will ensure a good turnout and therefore raise more money. In contrast, I am limited to a thousand dollars for a candidate for a federal office. As someone without celebrity status, I am competing against celebrities in a disadvantageous way.

I should also like to comment on something we saw in California: the initiative issue, Proposition 6, the Briggs Amendment. That issue seemed to me hysterical. If that initiative had been operating under campaign limitation, the opponents of Proposition 6 would have never raised the necessary money to defeat it.

NELSON W. POLSBY, Chairman: That referendum proposed to keep homosexuals from teaching in public schools, is that it?

220

MR. WALKER: That's right.

MR. POLSBY: Yes. That would have no impact on the celebrities, though.

MR. WALKER: No, but seriously, I am looking ahead twenty years, when everybody in this room might be faced with an hysterical issue that, under campaign contribution limitations, they would be unable to counter.
May I ask for comments on these two issues?

MR. MACGREGOR: I think Jack Kennedy was the author of a statement, oft repeated by the current occupant of 1600 Pennsylvania Avenue. I am referring to your first point, not the second. Life is unfair, and Jane Fonda does have more clout than you or I. It bothers me, too. But to be serious for a moment, you cannot constitutionally limit voluntary activity.

MR. WALKER: What I am asking is why we do not remove the limit on what you and I can do by writing checks? What is wrong with Stewart Mott's giving $740,000 to George McGovern? What is wrong with that?

MR. WERTHEIMER: What is wrong with it is that these laws were passed by Congress and upheld by the Supreme Court. Unlimited contributions provide the opportunity within the political process for enormous abuse in affecting legislative decisions. Our concern is not about the reality of that impact, but about the appearance of that impact. The Court also stressed this point in its decision, so I think such contributions are a very serious problem. They basically undermine the integrity of the political process.

As regards initiatives, the Supreme Court's *Belloti* decision means that there will never be any limits. According to *Belloti*, limits in initiatives are unconstitutional. Not just limits on total spending, not just limits on individual and group spending, but all restrictions on how corporations, or labor unions, or anyone else uses his money are unconstitutional.

So, you have the system that you desire for initiatives. But its consequences have to be faced up to in terms of the disproportionate ability of some to put resources into those campaigns.

MR. WALKER: Now, suppose that decision were applied to races between candidates.

MR. WERTHEIMER: If the Supreme Court's *Belloti* decision were extended to campaigns, and General Motors, or AT&T, or the AFL–CIO were free to spend $20 million, or $30 million, or $100 million on a presidential election, we wouldn't have to bother with this discussion, because we would have a totally different system, a system that would wipe out the impact not just of the 1970 law, but of all the laws that deal with campaign finances over the last seven years.

MR. MALBIN: The question of celebrity status illustrates the fact that there are many ways in which money can be raised and many types of influence that can be used to raise money. To the extent that one or another source is limited, the importance of the others is disproportionately increased. Power is not thereby granted to the disenfranchised. Certain groups that already have power are being cut down to size, leaving the rest of them in place.

On the question of large contributors, the Supreme Court agreed with Common Cause's brief that Congress may address not just the reality, but the appearance of a conflict of interest. Despite that agreement, I find this a very odd justification for a law if the appearance cannot be shown to reflect reality fairly. The appearance in fact is created by organizations with access to the media that constantly keep the appearance before the public eye. In this case, Common Cause used its access to create an impression that the public's cynicism about government resulted from campaign finance abuses. I believe that cynicism stemmed more from such things as stagflation, Vietnam, and the Watergate cover-up. And if the cynicism did contain a component relating to campaign finance, that component was not sufficiently related to post–disclosure law realities to be an explanation of the precise path taken in 1974. Yes, some candidates do find fund raising demeaning, but that cannot justify what was done either: a candidate's feelings are a small price to pay for adequately financed, competitive politics.

Next, consider Mr. Wertheimer's claim that we would have a totally different system if corporations or labor unions could spend $20 million or $30 million on electoral politics. They are able to do that now, and they in fact do it, but not with direct contributions. They use independent expenditures; they use get-out-the-vote drives; they use trade magazines, and so forth. There are many ways in which money is spent to shape political opinions and to shape elections. Campaign contributions are a very small part of the total picture, but they are the only part that has been regulated. They are the only part that constitutionally can be regulated.

THOMAS McCOY, political consultant: I am troubled by the Obey-Railsback bill. I assume the Court can decide it is legal to limit individual contributions to $1,000. I assume it can rule that PAC contributions can be limited to $2,500. But the $50,000 limit on overall contributions from PACs seems to me so exclusionary that the Court can not possibly rule that it is constitutional. If it did, I and many others would be awfully offended.

Consider the example of a political candidate who took $50,000 in PAC money at the beginning of a House race from ten corporate PACs. If in early October the candidate began to make statements attractive to labor people, and they suggested that he go on television to get those views across, the candidate could not take any money from the labor people, and the labor people would consequently be excluded from that process. I cannot believe that is what the Constitution guarantees.

DAVID W. ADAMANY: While the issue has not been litigated, there is at least one state that has a similar limitation which applies not only to PACs but to all groups, including parties. When he was asked his opinion of this limitation, the state attorney general said, probably correctly, that its legality depends on whether the limit is described as a "contribution limit" or as an "expenditure limit." This area is extremely unclear, since the distinction between contributions and expenditures, in itself, is an artifact of contemporary campaign financing laws, but the critical issue probably centers on whether limitations exclude people from participating in the political process and, therefore, prevent them from exercising freedom of speech.

Since the PACs and other groups, including political parties, can engage in independent expenditure, they have an alternative for having their opinions aired. A limit on total group and party contributions probably could be sustained on the theory that public officeholders should be subjected neither to the reality nor the appearance of being unduly indebted to groups which may be thought by many Americans as threatening to the integrity of the political process. This argument appeared in the brief giving the opinion of a pretty sophisticated state attorney general. From a constitutional standpoint, whatever we might think about the usefulness of the limitations, a substantial constitutional case could be made.

MR. WERTHEIMER: Let me just add that Obey-Railsback is described as a "contribution," not an "expenditure" limit.

MR. POLSBY: Do you want to disclose the name of the state?

MR. ADAMANY: Wisconsin.

MR. McCOY: Apart from the legal question, I had always assumed that politics, in addition to being a means of selecting a candidate, was also an educational process. We ought not be looking for ways of limiting the amounts of money spent in educating the public on either side. I find it awfully difficult to find liberals—of whom I happen to consider myself one—arguing for further encroachments and limitations on personal rights with regard to election practices.

MR. EPSTEIN: One of the unanswered questions regarding limitations on corporations, unions, and other interest groups is whether they can be constitutionally prohibited from spending money to express political views. I am not talking about independent expenditures out of their PACs; I am talking about a union or a corporation using its money to make an independent political statement about a candidate. The language in the *Buckley* decision suggests that limiting expenditures, even of treasury money, is of very doubtful constitutionality.

MARY MEEHAN, Committee for a Constitutional Presidency: Mr. Wertheimer, are you saying, in effect, that special-interest groups have far greater influence now than they did in the early 1970s when Common Cause first rode forth to do battle with them? And if this is the case, shouldn't you quit now before it gets even worse?

MR. WERTHEIMER: I don't think we are going to quit. The special interests do not have greater influence in the publicly financed presidential elections. But, as regards congressional elections, the defeat of public financing in 1974 and in the following years, combined with the successful election efforts of labor and business, indicate to me that organized groups, particularly because of the growth of PACs, do have more influence. But I think I will hang in there for a while, anyway.

GEORGE E. AGREE: I have a question for Mr. Wertheimer from my son, who is a merchant seaman. Since he became a seaman, he has developed a passionate interest in cargo preference legislation. He asked me to put to you the question of why, when you listed the maritime interest contributions to members of Congress who supported such legislation, you did not at the same time list the oil company contributions, or the contributions of companies that own or otherwise control "flag of convenience" ships, and whether you would do that in the future, should such an issue arise again?

DISCUSSION

MR. WERTHEIMER: We have done a number of studies on the potential impact of campaign money on votes, on committee votes and on floor votes. Our studies have focused on the group particularly interested in an issue, and not on the groups only marginally involved. We tried to identify priority interests as in the case of the maritime unions and the National Association of Realtors. It is fair to say that if one group has a paramount interest in a particular vote, a review of that group's campaign contributions and the voting record of the recipient gives a sense of the potential impact of the contributions.

MR. AGREE: I would suggest that although the oil companies have more important interests than cargo preference, they have a substantial interest in that issue as well. If their presence in the arena of political contribution is as large as I have heard it is—and I would like to be informed about this—then oil companies' influence on maritime legislation may well be no less and possibly even more than the influence of a very small industry like the maritime industry for which that legislation is of paramount interest.

MR. WERTHEIMER: That might be, but I think it has not been the case. There is a fair basis for reaching the conclusion we did, although I should point out that energy companies—oil, gas, and coal—have increased the number of their PACs in the last four years from 12 in 1974 to 110 today. Mr. Epstein points out that they were probably the most active industry grouping in 1978.

MR. POLSBY: Mr. Agree, did you get an answer to your son's question?

MR. AGREE: I did not.

MR. POLSBY: Do you want to give an answer to the question, Mr. Wertheimer?

MR. WERTHEIMER: Yes. My answer was that we did not look at oil company money in that case, and we felt it was appropriate not to do so.

MR. AGREE: Now I have my answer.

MR. MALBIN: I just want to use this example to reiterate a point I made once before. Earlier, Mr. Wertheimer was talking about drawing a distinction between one's basic positions, which I think do not change before or after a contribution, and low-publicity issues, where he said campaign contributions make a difference.

225

I believe that on most of those issues, members of Congress could make PACs or private individuals beholden to them no matter how they vote. Except for the broad economic issues, or what David Jessup called "class issues," the issues of a specific industry generally involve an opposition industry as well. Of course, the person who champions the maritime industry will get more money from maritime PACs, while those opposed to the cargo preference bill will be favored by the oil industry. How he votes does not hurt the member of Congress, unless his district happens to be overwhelmingly oil or maritime. He will get the contribution from one source or the other.

GREG MANIER, International Association of Machinists: I wanted to ask Mr. MacGregor about his statistics on small contributions to corporate PACs. We conducted a study of the leading corporate PACs and found that the average contribution was about $200. The Public Affairs Council, which surveyed a much broader spectrum of PACs, arrived at an average figure of about $124.

We also found, in regard to your contention that the contributions are completely free and voluntary, disturbing reports, as in the article in the *Wall Street Journal* during August 1978 in which Justin Dart was quoted as saying, "I would use the PACs' records, and those people who don't give, they get a phone call from me, and they are asked why they don't give."

Everyone recognizes the potential for coercion in employer-employee relationships. Employers are completely dependent upon employees for PAC contributions. Stockholders, who cannot be coerced and in whose interest the corporation is formed, do not participate at all in PACs.

MR. MACGREGOR: Oh, yes, they do. We have had voluntary contributions from shareholders, even though we have not solicited them.

MR. MANIER: If the amount of money received from shareholders and from employees were compared, I am sure that the shareholder part would be minimal.

MR. MACGREGOR: I think you probably want us to solicit some of our shareholders. We are in the process of doing that, and I think we will get an excellent response, probably 10 or 15 percent, as we get from our executive group.

MR. MANIER: And the first question, How do you come up with the smaller number for average contributions?

MR. MacGREGOR: I gave the answer in my presentation. I said I didn't presume to say that it was accurate, and I do not know that you can get an accurate account. But I did canvass a number from, as I said, a representative group of political action committees, whose performance I have come to respect. That is the number I got.

MR. WALKER: Our survey comprised 168 corporate PACs, most of them large corporate PACs and members of the council. I would conclude from that survey that the overall average for all corporate PACs was considerably less than $125.

ANDREW MOLLISON, Cox Newspapers: I know that every discussion has to be limited, and this discussion is limited to PACs, but I would like to suggest something that I can only infer from spot checks of the files. It is that contributions from business have been increasing less rapidly through PACs than through individual contributions. Naturally, every contributor tends to have some occupation or another, because otherwise he has no money to give. Nevertheless, when a spot check on a particular day shows that fifty-five people from the same company each gave $100 or $125, or, in the cases I don't see, fifty people from a company gave $50 apiece, this too can be seen as the moral equivalent of a PAC contribution. I am not so much objecting to that as saying it is an area that I, as an individual reporter, do not conceivably have the resources to investigate, but I hope that a subsequent discussion will address the issue of the occupations of contributors, which I think have changed over the last six years.

It is my judgment, from instinct and from spot checks, that small businessmen gave a smaller percentage of the individual contributions in 1978 than they did when the first set of records came out. This is a pattern which may change some of these percentages. With sophisticated methodology, some distinction could be made between the individual who happens to have an occupation and gives to a candidate, and an individual who gives strictly because he is a member of a particular occupational group.

MR. EPSTEIN: Your point is very well taken. Despite the charts and the tables we have generated, the data is still incomplete, and in virtually all instances, it has been analyzed manually without being subjected to really sophisticated computer analysis. How does categorizing individual contributions by employees, officers, directors of unions, of trade associations, of corporations correlate, or does it correlate at all, with what a

PAC does? Do we find de facto PACs, which have not registered? We do not know, except for spot checks of the type you mention.

If I might make a pitch here, there is hope that improvement, sophistication, and practical accessibility of FEC data will be achieved in the years ahead, and then contribution issues can be properly dealt with through accessible data.

MR. MALBIN: We cannot do that now because the FEC does not let people use their computer tapes. They are afraid of people using the tapes for solicitation. For any scholar to be able to do what you are talking about, the FEC has to figure out a way of letting him examine the tapes, perhaps with dummy names, so that if he used the tapes for solicitation, he would be exposed.

I looked at individual business contributions for only one person, John Murphy, the chairman of the House Merchant Marine Committee. His record seemed to bear out your point. The amount of money he received from individuals associated with the maritime industry was at least as significant as the amount he got from maritime PACs, labor and corporate. I believe that probably holds true in a lot of cases. It led me to the conclusion that a limit on PACs would not do all that much, because the money would simply filter back through individuals.

MR. WERTHEIMER: I want to comment on that point, because I want to share the views expressed about the need for availability of that information. I think the commission has done good work on the information it has made available in this last campaign. It has provided comprehensive summary information, but I think it is not doing its job, and the public is not being served because of its refusal to make available, particularly to scholars, but also to newspaper reporters and others, the information they need for analysis. If the commission itself will not do the analysis, it has the responsibility to make the information available for others who would. So far the commission has refused. This is wrong.

MR. ADAMANY: I wish to address my question to Mr. Conlon. I do not know him; he does not know me. I testified before the congressional committee in favor of limits. I have written in favor of them, sometimes at least. I helped to write state statutes which include limits and have helped to administer those statutes while I served on a state election board.

The problem is that we have had to tighten the limits increasingly in order to make them workable. I think we are coming increasingly close to trenching on some constitutional values. Whether or not the limits trench on the constitutional visions of this Supreme Court seems less important than whether they are getting at some core values to which those of us who consider ourselves liberals have at least traditionally adhered. Moreover, there seems no end to the screwing down that we need to do.

The problem used to be big contributors; it is now the proliferation of PACs. At the next turn, it's celebrities, and afterwards it will be back to the system which a number of us know from the 1950s, in which solicitors went through the offices of corporate management, picked up a bunch of checks, and delivered them en masse to candidates, so that there was no doubt in anybody's mind, though they were all legal, small contributions, just what their source was. And there will be no end to that. We will have to rewrite Obey-Railsback to deal with those problems in due course.

Moreover, the evidence is now becoming clear that the marginal effect of every dollar for the challenger is much greater than the marginal effect of every dollar for the incumbent, unless we are talking about amounts that are so great that the marginal increase gets to be almost zero. As a long-time supporter of the Democratic Study Group and all its works, I must ask whether the group is not asking us to go too far when the alternative of genuinely generous public financing exists to ensure a competitive system in which opposition to every congressman is available. Public financing would solve most of the problems that we are trying to solve with limits. It would expose the activities of special-interest groups, hold congressmen up to scrutiny, and make them all nervous. I just don't know how much longer we can all go along with limits.

MR. CONLON: I am not sure; What is the alternative?

MR. ADAMANY: Some genuinely generous form of public financing.

MR. CONLON: I am all for it. We worked our heads off trying to pass the bill. In fact, we specifically kept out of that bill any limitation on PACs. Even though a principal reason for the bill was to provide an alternative source of money to PAC funding, we felt it should be voluntary. We would provide the alternative and members could take their choice, and disclosure would do its job with the electorate. We paid a price for that, because we were characterized as simply pushing a bill that was dipping into the public till.

MR. MALBIN: Congress never has been offered an uncluttered vote on public financing. The bills proposed so far have mixed different concepts and objectives. They have contained spending limits, which would favor incumbents, and public financing which would favor challengers and would limit dependence on special interests. If we are genuinely interested in limiting the role of special interests and in encouraging competition, we should support public financing without spending limits.

Part Three

Campaign Finance and Campaign Strategy

Presidential Campaign Strategy under the Law

Robert J. Keefe

Politicians have noted for many years that money is the mother's milk of politics. The campaign finance law coming into play for the first time in the last presidential election changed the flow of mother's milk, and thereby altered the strategies employed in a presidential nominating campaign. And campaigns, like everything else in modern life, are now more expensive. The reforms we Democrats forced on American politics following our 1968 campaign squabbles have doubled the number of presidential primary elections and have thus drastically increased the cost of a presidential campaign.

Money has always been a controlling factor in the presidential nominations. The rich candidate normally does better than the poor candidate. In fact, it is difficult to think of a nominee who was, in fact, the poor man's candidate. But before the new reforms, we did not have the kind of expenses today's presidential candidates will face in running in several primaries a week, week after week, in a total of thirty-five states. And those states that do not have a primary have something worse called a caucus, where it is possible to spend as much or more to attract the delegates to those little precinct meetings all over the state. Undeniably, the addition of the primaries and the change of the caucus system have greatly increased the cost of running for president.

In the old days, money was somewhat easier to come by. I am not saying that fund raising was easy, but a candidate able to attract funds could do so faster and more easily because he could do it in bigger chunks: he could sit down with a half dozen people—or a single person—and come up with a large chunk of money in a very quick period. Today, he can get a half dozen people together, and they may give *checks,* not cash, totaling $12,000 if they are all married and have joint accounts and can prove their spouses control a large enough *percent* of the bank account to make a contribution in their names, too. That means two things: big money from single individuals is gone, and more time and organizational skills are needed to raise money. Couple that with the fact that Hugh Scott made credit less available by his little

233

amendment of a few years back, and the result is a substantial cash flow problem.

Of course, "in-kind" contributions have always augmented cash contributions to a presidential campaign. In-kind contributions were, in many cases, corporate contributions, but we did not seem to notice them in those days. No laws were changed making corporation contributions of "in-kind" service illegal—they already were—but the realization that they were illegal, and the public scrutiny of campaigns, came at about the same time as the new act and can really be included in the overall reforms of which the Federal Election Campaign Act was a part.

Finally, before the reforms, there was no campaign-spending limit. Did that mean that the elections could be bought in those days and not today? Not really. A lot of money could be invested in a given place then, but a lot of money can be invested in a given place today. There just is not as much of it around today.

The campaign spending limits of the new act may not be as controlling as the contributions limitations. There is only one state where the campaign spending limit has any impact—New Hampshire. It is a state with high impact but low population, thus low spending limits. It is the only state that I know where any candidate worries about his spending limits. But the spending limits also impose requirements for centralized control to prevent overexpenditures and to keep track of reported income. That means it is more difficult for a campaign to live off the land. If General Washington had to fight the Revolutionary War by the standards of the Campaign Finance Act, we would still have a king and would not have to worry about the campaigns.

Let me illustrate what I mean by living off the land. The ordinary way to run a state campaign in the old days was to have local people raise money, secure "in-kind" services locally, and do what the campaign manager who was sent in from headquarters told them to do, if they accepted his ideas. The national campaign disbursed additional funds and handled the media and a few other things if the state was, in fact, important enough to warrant concern. A lot of the things that were required in day-to-day campaign work never showed up as expenditures in the national campaign, and the money that paid for them never showed up in the income columns. It just happened on the local level. It was reasonably efficient, and there was not much attention paid to it.

Now, because most treasurers of campaigns are criminally liable for correct and true reporting of all contributions, be they "in kind," in cash, in check, or in money order, this living off the land cannot be accomplished as easily. It is burdensome—ask the Udall campaign. They tried it, and despite the genuine good efforts of all their people, it was a nightmare to them to get all their reports audited to the satisfaction of the FEC.

The demise of living off the land has also had the effect of inserting the national campaign a little more deeply into the local happenings. Of course there were always wastes when local people decided what to do, but frankly, a lot of campaigns do much better when they are in the hands of the locals rather than the headquarters types. The regulations have removed a lot of local initiative from the campaign.

The only way a campaign can be assured flexibility in its strategy and freedom from monetary restrictions is to follow the example of Jesse Helms's Senate campaign: raise three or four times the amount needed, do it early, and then stop worrying about how it is spent. No presidential campaign as yet has been able to do that, although there are a couple on the Republican side this time that may fall into that category.

Money is important, but more important still is cash flow, that is, having money at the right time to implement well-laid strategy. Furthermore, cash flow becomes ever more critical as the campaign grinds along, because the campaign law slows down the ingress of money to a campaign by requiring it be raised by organizational effort. In the early states—like Iowa and New Hampshire—everybody can be a big spender. Then the grind starts. Campaigns can spend money relatively quickly in those next few weeks, and it is difficult to replenish it as fast as the campaign spends it. By the end of a month or six weeks, the campaign's resources may be drained. Then come the really tough decisions—where to spend what little remains and how to cut corners in campaign planning. Thus, cash flow really dictates strategy.

Most business activities can solve cash flow problems by creating debt; campaigns cannot. The principal debtors in most campaigns turn out to be the employees or principals of the campaign. Vendors for the most part no longer extend credit, and the really expensive items are media and telephones—they want money up front. In fact, the phone company takes Senator Scott's amendment so strictly to heart, that their deposit criteria have really become a little ridiculous.

Let's look at some of the implications of the new act on campaign strategy.

1. Money is more important, not less, in today's campaign. Money is momentum. Recent editorial commentaries on the Carter campaign have created a host of serious questions about the viability of the president's campaign, all based on the public record of his financial contributions.

2. Spending limits are not really important. The state-by-state limitations add up to three or four times the overall ceiling. They are critical only in the very important, small states—really only in one state,

New Hampshire. Next year a candidate will be able to spend up to $318,000 in New Hampshire. All candidates will have the money to spend there, because campaign funds will not yet have been depleted, and all candidates will want to spend money there, because the outcome is likely to influence other primaries. So they will be worried about campaign spending limitations. Fortunately for the candidates, they can buy media time in Boston which will be televised in New Hampshire and charge only 18.64 percent to their New Hampshire campaign budget.

One advantage of the spending limitation is the creativity it develops in campaign staffs because every campaign believes it is going to raise and spend the total limit—few have, but they all think they will. So the staffs devise campaign events which have direct vote impact but which look like fund-raising events or programs. That way they can be charged against the 20 percent allowance of the campaign spending that applies to fund raising. Aside from that, the state by-state spending limitations are really meaningless outside of New Hampshire, and on the Democratic side of things, the overall spending limits are well beyond the capability of the poor people's party to develop campaign war chests for its candidates. I know both Ford's and Reagan's 1976 campaigns hit the limit about convention time, but we Democrats just haven't experienced that kind of problem yet.

3. The impact of cash flow is momentous. Having money at the right time is tougher to get, and credit is unavailable, so the ability to have the right amount of cash at the right moment becomes terribly important to a campaign. In 1976, it was the Carter campaign's ability to handle cash flow and to use debt creatively that enabled it to implement its strategies. Other campaigns were less creative, less well-managed when it came to money, and thus less successful.

4. Campaigns are less free-wheeling. The strictness in reporting demands tighter control over all income and expenditures. This spoils a lot of grass-roots effort and creativity that was probably good for campaigns. Hundreds of times during my experience in Senator Jackson's campaign, I would recognize a good idea and have to think first, How do I do it under the act.

5. The treasurer's office, the comptroller's office, and the accountants have become indispensable to the campaign, and their creativity can lead to a campaign victory. In 1976, Jimmy Carter was a terrific candidate; Ham Jordan laid out a terrific strategy; Tim Kraft and a bunch of other guys put together a fine organization; Jody Powell fed it through the media in grand style; and Gerald Rafshoon's advertising helped. They were out front and got the credit. However, the boys in the shop back in Atlanta who kept the money available deserved hero badges, too. They turned a campaign plan into a positive cash flow

program by borrowing against accounts receivable from the media. They used many vendors, allowing them to carry more commercial debt than they could with only a few. [Editor's note: The law limits the amount an individual vendor may lend a candidate, but not a candidate's total debt.] They did a lot of little things in the campaign, all legal and all very creative, that I think gave them the wherewithal to have a free-wheeling strategy that did the rest of us in.

6. Knowledge of the law and how its interpretations can be used most advantageously is tremendously important. Political strategy often needs to be made without caution about the cost of things, but money controls because it enables campaigns to implement strategies, undertake projects, and buy materials. Many times the key effort does not require massive expenditures—not the ability to spend $50,000 or $100,000—maybe just $2,000 or $3,000 for an extra phone bank somewhere. Knowledge of the law and the regulations and understanding how to work creatively within that law in managing money can give a campaign a little more flexibility and make the difference in those little expenditures. That's what wins elections.

Have the changes that have come over our political system under the Federal Election Campaign Act been for the good? I do not claim that they have substantially improved our quality of life or government, but they have squarely addressed and helped solve a lot of legitimate problems. The administration of the act has become a bit of a nightmare, however. The Federal Election Commission does not decide key issues and does not know how to ask the right questions on which to base a decision. And the independent expenditure loophole is probably big enough to drive a president through.

The Democratic party's own reforms created mass confusion, what with the thirty-five primaries and grass-roots reflections of presidential preference in caucuses, at a time when the structure of campaign financing was changing. These concurrent happenings created a very different world for politicians. I think I am pretty much in agreement with the political implications of a bumper sticker I spotted out in Ohio a couple of years ago, when there was a state-wide referendum on bingo. The bumper sticker said, "Vote Yes—Let's put gambling back in the churches where it belongs." I think I am ready to "Vote Yes—Put politics back into the hands of the politicians where it belongs."

The Law's Impact on Presidential and Congressional Election Campaigns

Richard B. Cheney

I will divide my comments into two sections, the first dealing with presidential campaigns and the second with congressional races. I think the distinction is important because the law treats the contests differently, providing public financing for presidential races but not congressional contests, limiting spending only for presidential campaigns, and limiting the size of contributions from individuals and political action committees for both.

Presidential Campaigns

In assessing the impact of the campaign finance laws on presidential campaign strategy, the foremost question to be asked is whether the statutes force a fundamental change in a candidate's strategy—a change which would not occur in the absence of the statutes. I believe this has indeed occurred.

The statutes have led to a reallocation of resources so that some activities now receive more time, attention, and money than was previously the case, while others which were historically important in presidential campaigns are now virtually ignored and even actively discouraged. An artificial set of constraints has now been imposed, which can significantly alter the outcome of the nominating and electing process. The allocation of resources among the various primaries is now a much more complex problem, and numerous other phases of presidential campaign activity are affected as well. Finally, constraints on both fund raising and spending have limited the ability of a campaign organization to meet legitimate costs, just as other political reforms and changes have significantly increased the costs of campaigning.

In the discussion that follows, I want to emphasize my recognition that questions of campaign financing have been key to the conduct of any presidential campaign in modern times. Certainly, the first candidate to suffer from lack of funds had to close down his campaign long before anyone thought of limiting candidates' fund-raising abilities by placing limits on contributions. Nonetheless, I think a candidate's in-

238

ability to finance his campaign adequately is a more serious matter when it stems directly from constraints imposed by federal law.

New Activities Required by Campaign Finance Laws. No discussion of the subject can begin without first pointing out the obvious—that the requirements of the law have added significantly to the administrative and regulatory costs of campaigning. A significant portion of the funds available to a candidate have to go for accountants, lawyers, and report filing. One recent news account estimated that the costs of compliance—accountants to keep records, copiers to copy records, and lawyers to interpret regulations and sometimes to get around them—will run at least $1.5 million for each campaign that makes it to the 1980 nominating conventions. That is roughly five times what each candidate will be allowed to spend in New Hampshire, the first and traditionally the most important primary.

A recent news story on the impact of the laws on the 1980 campaign contained the following examples of how the financing laws have added to administrative overhead:

All told, some sixty people are currently employed in seven campaigns performing compliance chores, according to campaign officials. These efforts are needed not only to provide the voluminous reports and records required by the FEC, but also to plan campaign strategy in light of the rules and regulations.

By the time the FEC comes in to audit us, . . . we will have audited ourselves three times. There will be a manual check before it goes into the computer, and another check when it comes out.

The need to get out accurate and immediate budget reports on a daily basis has become critical. Take a state with a spending limit of $260,000, for example. If you feel you've spent $200,000, and when the real figures come in you've spent $275,000, you may have a problem.

As a result, the accountants are likely to have expanded roles in campaign planning. We can expect them to be a part of every strategy session.

At George Bush for President headquarters in Houston, a 225-page manual of FEC rules and regulations is called "the bible." Furthermore, the Bush operation is segregated by floors to make compliance easier. The fund-raising operation is segregated on the fifth floor because fund-raising expenses, including the rent, are to be aggregated for FEC reporting. The operation devoted to winning Texas delegates to the 1980 GOP convention is confined to the third floor because the state-by-state expenditures must be carefully controlled to avoid exceeding FEC limitations. And the national political operation of the Bush campaign is handled separately on the second floor to avoid commingling it with other segregated expenditures. (*The Washington Post,* June 14, 1979)

Many of these obligations were present in the 1976 campaign but are likely to be even more onerous in 1980 because the requirements will cover the total preparation and conduct of the campaign. In 1976, the Ford campaign expended considerable resources on these administrative and regulatory requirements in order to comply with the letter and the spirit of the law. From all indications, even more will be required of a conscientious candidate in 1980.

Discouraged Activities. One of the major results of the spending limitations has been to encourage the development of highly centralized campaign organizations with elaborate controls over spending. Unless a campaign develops such an organization, there is virtually no possibility that it can account for all of the funds expended or adequately comply with federal regulations. While this makes for a more efficient campaign operation, it has had the effect of choking off the kind of grass-roots activity that historically has been a part of American presidential campaigns.

The experience of the Ford campaign in 1976 showed conclusively that it was easier to discourage grass-roots activity than to try to control and report it. In previous campaigns, it was possible to tell a local campaign or party official to go ahead with a project as long as he could raise the money to finance it. Now, federal law places a premium on actively discouraging such activity because of the danger that it could well lead to a violation of contribution or spending limits in the primary. Furthermore, in the general election, because no contributions are permitted once federal funds become available, it is even more important to discourage such activity.

Such considerations lead to shifts in spending priorities and, therefore, campaign strategies. State-by-state primary spending limitations, the overall limitation on prenomination spending, and the requirement that none of the money raised before the convention be used to promote the general election effort (which has to be totally financed with federal funds), all serve to discourage organizational activities. We found it much easier during the 1976 Ford campaign, for example, to spend money on identifiable goods and services, such as electronic media and production costs, in the general election campaign than to spend it intelligently on local and state organizational efforts. This was especially true because we had discouraged organizational activity that was not directly under our control during the primaries. The case of the Florida primary, held in March 1976, is illustrative of the difficulties posed by the new law. The Ford campaign poured significant resources into the Florida effort and won our second major victory over Governor Reagan. Within days of the election, the entire Florida operation had to be totally shut down because of the various limitations we faced. As a result, there were no resources available to keep even a symbolic operation going through the summer in preparation for the fall campaign—no headquarters facility, no phones, no paper clips, and no staff.

The same thing happened in virtually every state where we contested a primary in 1976. It was hardly surprising, then, that with only a little more than two months for the general election campaign, we found it difficult to spend money on organizational efforts at the state and local level when we had dismantled the nucleus of our organization at the end of each primary campaign. It made a lot more sense to spend it on media.

I firmly believe that the effect of the campaign finance laws in this area has been to discourage grass-roots political activity, to discourage participation, and to place a premium on strategies that rely on activities that are easily controlled and reported. Given a choice between local spontaneity and enthusiastic participation, on one hand, and control over spending, on the other, the cautious campaign manager has little choice but to opt for activities that are "controllable."

Impact of Spending Limitations. A candidate's ability to raise money has always been a factor limiting his campaign strategy, but only recently have limits been imposed by statute on a candidate's ability to *spend* money. These limits have made his strategic problems infinitely more difficult.

Clearly, the selection of primaries to enter and the allocation of resources among primary states are among the most important decisions any candidate can make. These strategic decisions were very important in 1976. The Ford campaign's decision to downplay the North Carolina primary kept Governor Reagan's candidacy alive and nearly cost Ford the nomination. Some analysts have argued persuasively that the Reagan camp's decision not to go all-out in Ohio and New Jersey may have cost the governor the nomination.

As we move into the 1980 primary season, decisions about resource allocation among primary states are uppermost in the campaign manager's mind. Should he go for broke in the early primaries, or hold back funds in the expectation that resources will be needed for the long haul? Is his candidate more likely to be able to achieve a significant victory in

New Hampshire or Illinois? If he does not do well in New Hampshire, can he survive until Illinois? Will an early victory generate sufficient financial support to sustain the effort in the later primaries?

Such questions have been asked by all modern campaign managers, but two new developments make them more difficult to answer than ever before. The first development is the rapid expansion in the number of states holding presidential primaries. When John F. Kennedy captured the Democratic nomination in 1960, two primaries were paramount, Wisconsin and West Virginia, and most states still relied on conventions or party leaders to select their delegates to the national convention. Between 1968 and 1976, just eight years, the number of states holding primaries more than doubled to thirty. Another six or seven states will have been added to the primary roster by 1980. To some extent, this profusion of states holding primaries is the result of efforts to "open up" and "democratize" the delegate selection process. Nonetheless, it has added enormously to the cost of seeking the presidential nomination of either party.

While the number of primaries was expanding, a second development took place—the imposition of aggregate and state-by-state spending limitations on preconvention campaigning. Thus, as more and more states adopted procedures that force a would-be president to undertake a major, statewide campaign with all the expenses associated with a general election campaign, the FEC statute has sought to limit the amount a candidate can spend to capture a state's delegates.

Clearly, it is far more expensive to win delegates selected through a primary election than through a convention. Yet, the campaign finance law makes no distinction between primary and convention states in terms of the allowable spending ceiling. At the same time, the formula leads to absurd results, such as imposing the same spending limitation for the New Hampshire primary as it does for the convention held on Guam, an estimated $264,600 for 1980.

The fact that the sum of a candidate's spending ceilings for individual primaries ($28.4 million) is approximately 114 percent higher than the aggregate ceiling ($13.2 million) adds another element of complexity and ensures that no one will be able to spend the maximum allowed in every state. All candidates are forced by virtue of the law to shape their strategies accordingly. The result is that resources are often allocated not only on the basis of political considerations, but also on the basis of arbitrary criteria that have little in common with political reality.

Political reality is that New Hampshire has traditionally been the most important primary in the nation. One of Governor Reagan's 1976 campaign advisers estimated that a victory in New Hampshire is worth

15 to 18 percent of the vote in later primaries. Any candidate who seeks to challenge an incumbent president or overtake a front-runner has to assign New Hampshire top priority. In 1976, 1,500 votes in New Hampshire in February were far more important to President Ford and Governor Reagan than were a million votes in California in June.

The candidates contesting the 1980 nomination obviously understand the importance of New Hampshire, and their campaign staffs are busily engaged in finding ways to magnify the impact of their New Hampshire spending by buying Massachusetts television time, by having their candidates stay overnight in towns in bordering states, and by seeking other means of legally circumventing the limits. There was even speculation in the press that the Connally campaign may refuse any matching funds until after the New Hampshire primary in order to be able to exceed the FEC ceiling in that primary. Of course, the FEC has responded by suggesting that it may impose a new regulation designed to deny matching funds to any candidate who exploits this new-found loophole. This simply proves once again that there is no limit to the creative genius of campaign managers, to the regulation-writing authority of a federal agency, or to the capacity of the Congress to pass laws that have unanticipated consequences. Overall limitations are proving to be as important as state-by-state limitations in their impact on strategic campaign planning. The campaign finance laws have eliminated the impact in recent years of the traditional ability of the GOP to raise funds. Historically, Republican presidential candidates have been able to offset the numerical advantage of Democrats among registered voters by raising and spending more. The advent of public financing and the imposition of spending limits have ended all that. Democratic campaign advisers, in discussions after the 1976 election, made clear that they were well aware that President Ford would have to spend the same amount as Jimmy Carter in the general election. Furthermore, the Ford campaign plan, prepared before the Kansas City convention in 1976, pointed out that the GOP would no longer be able to fall back on a better financial campaign as an offset to the Democrats' greater numbers among the electorate.

Certain prohibitions in the act or in regulations designed to implement the act create strange situations which affect the development and implementation of a campaign plan. In 1976, the Ford plan for the general election had to be completed before the Kansas City convention, but because the law prohibited the use of primary funds to promote a candidacy in the general election, planning had to be done on a "volunteer" basis. Stu Spencer, political director for the Ford campaign, took several days off and went home to California to write his portion of the plan to avoid a situation in which we could be charged with misusing preconvention funds.

When a decision was made to produce a biographical film to be shown in conjunction with President Ford's acceptance speech at the convention, financing problems arose. Production had to begin well before the convention, but since the film would actually be shown *after* the nomination, it could not be paid for out of prenomination funds. At the same time, since the nomination was yet to be decided, there was no guarantee that general election funds would go to the Ford campaign to pay for the film. In the end, the film was produced only after President Ford signed a personal note to obtain the necessary funding.

As with most other items, the costs of campaigning have increased significantly in recent years. Taking into account the increased number of primaries, the total amount of money required to run a successful presidential campaign has gone up more rapidly than the rate of inflation. Limitations on the amount any individual can contribute have served to make it more difficult for the candidate to raise the necessary funds, and these limitations have not been increased despite inflation. This, in turn, may have stimulated early declarations of candidacy and longer campaigns. It simply takes a great deal more effort to raise $10–15 million, if it only comes in amounts of $1,000 or less, than it does if there are no upper limits on the amount an individual can contribute. Time spent on fund-raising activities, even if the costs are not counted against the allowable spending ceilings, detracts from the basic purpose of the campaign—persuading a majority of the voters to support a particular candidate.

In the future, I would expect the operation of the campaign finance laws to affect the timing of the parties' national conventions. In 1976, convening the GOP convention in August probably aided the Democratic cause. The lateness of the convention had a major impact financially, aside from reducing the time available for Ford to whittle down the lead enjoyed by Carter. The Ford campaign was forced to lay off a large number of people from its national campaign staff early in the summer because no more money could be spent until after the convention. Because the Democratic convention was held in July, the Carter campaign received its allotment of federal dollars for the fall campaign a month before the GOP convention was held. In years to come, I anticipate that a premium will be placed on holding conventions as early as possible in July to take maximum advantage of the receipt of federal funds and to allow for adequate planning of the fall campaign.

I suspect, although I cannot prove, that the availability of federal matching funds has led some individuals to become candidates who might otherwise stay out of the race. These long-shot candidates jump into the race in the hope they can score an upset early on, thereby generating sufficient private and public financial support to sustain a serious campaign. They probably also believe that the limitation removes any advantage previously enjoyed by the candidate who could generate large contributions. They probably underestimate the costs of campaigning and choose to ignore, at their own peril, the fact that there is no limitation on what it costs to campaign for president, only on how you pay for it. One might ask whether Jimmy Carter was such a candidate, one who could never have obtained the necessary financial backing on his own, but one whom circumstance and the operation of the new campaign financing law served to put in the White House.

Congressional Campaigns

The impact of the campaign finance laws on congressional races has been somewhat different from original expectations, which is frequently the case with reform legislation. The absence of a spending limit for congressional candidates has helped their campaigns keep pace with rising costs. At the same time, the limitations on presidential spending and the provision of federal funds for the presidential campaign have probably made more money available to certain House and Senate candidates.

Clearly, the most restrictive provision applying to congressional races is the limitation on individual contributions. The $1,000 limit makes it very difficult for a newcomer to raise sufficient funds to get his campaign off the ground. The result is that a would-be candidate finds it necessary to finance his beginning efforts himself because no one else will, especially if he is running against an incumbent or in a primary.

My own experience in 1978 is illustrative. Because of my background, I could raise campaign funds more easily than most of my freshman colleagues in the House. Yet, I had to come up with $50,000 out of my own pocket to finance the primary effort. I had to risk everything I had to make the race. So did my opponents. Because I won, I was able to recover my original investment. My primary opponents, who made similar commitments, sunk virtually everything they had in a losing cause. In the general election, my Democratic opponent, whose net worth was in excess of $1 million, spent some $80,000 of his own funds in a losing effort. The proper conclusion, I believe, is that the limitation on contributions has placed a higher premium than ever before on candidates who are able and willing to invest their personal wealth in a race. A person who has no assets simply cannot afford to participate.

Now, I know some will say, But what about the PACs? Haven't they taken up the slack? Hasn't the rapid expansion in the number of political action committees made more funds available? The answer is, yes, more money is available, but usually not until it is clear who the winner is going to be. From the perspective of the candidate looking for financial support, the PACs are relatively slow and often timid.

Again, referring to my own experience in 1978, there were very few PACs willing to get involved in a primary race. There were a few notable exceptions, but for the most part the people who run PACs are not gamblers. They like to have some degree of confidence that a candidate can win before they commit their resources. I raised approximately $22,000 for my congressional campaign. During the last ten days of the race, some $83,000 came in, much of it from political action committees. By then it was pretty clear to everyone that I was going to win. I will venture the guess that an analysis of the timing of PAC contributions across the country would show that PAC money is late money; that a relatively small amount is available to candidates early enough to have much impact in hotly contested races; and that the alleged "influence" PACs derive from these contributions is substantially overrated.

Any consideration of the effect of the campaign financing requirements has to address the question whether campaign spending makes any difference. Does it really matter how much a candidate has to spend? I believe the answer has to be an unequivocal yes, at least where nonincumbents are concerned.

I like to think that I was elected solely on merit to represent the people of Wyoming in the U.S. House of Representatives, but I am also enough of a realist to know that my election was due in part to the fact that I was a better fund raiser than any of my opponents. In the final analysis, the Cheney for Congress Campaign Committee was successful because it was able to make known to the voters the qualities of the candidate. This was possible because sufficient funds were obtained to carry out an effective campaign strategy.

A good deal of research suggests that financing does, indeed, make a difference. One of the best articles I have seen on the subject was by Gary Jacobson in the *American Political Science Review,* June 1978. Jacobson found that "spending by challengers has a substantial impact on election outcomes, whereas spending by incumbents has relatively little effect; the evidence is particularly strong for House elections."

No one could say it better than the report by the Institute of Politics and the Campaign Finance Study Group to the Committee on House Administration:

> Adequate campaign funds are essential to competitive Congressional elections. The essence of an election campaign is to provide voters with a choice among alternative candidates. That process requires the communication to voters of some minimum quantity of information about the contestants. In contemporary America, providing that information to the voters costs substantial amounts of money.

Every study based on the information available since 1972 has shown that *most campaigns have too little, not too much money.*

The study also points out that the major difficulty is the fact that "the individual contribution limits are too low."

Conclusions

At the presidential level, I believe the operation of the campaign finance law has had significant unanticipated consequences on the conduct of campaigns.

• The administrative burden of complying with the federal statute and with the FEC requirements and regulations has effectively bureaucratized the political process. Success increasingly goes to those who can hire the best accountant and the most creative lawyer.

• To the extent that the election campaign provides a testing ground for candidates, those who succeed may be better equipped to serve as director of the Office of Management and Budget than as president, because the campaign increasingly involves complying with federal statutes and avoiding red tape, while spending federal dollars.

• The restrictions on spending, both at the aggregate and state levels, place unnecessary burdens on a campaign and provide insufficient funds in light of the very large number of states now holding primaries.

• Even the disclosure requirements have not worked as expected. They place an unnecessary burden on the campaigns and produce far more paper than the FEC can usefully process. The delays encountered in completing the audits of the 1976 race, coupled with the filing of over 5,000 pages of amended reports by the Carter campaign less than one week after the 1976 election, raise serious questions about how the disclosure requirements are being administered.

At the congressional level, the act has served to enhance the advantage of those wealthy enough to finance their own campaigns and has made it difficult for those who do not have substantial personal assets to obtain adequate funding. The contribution limits have not made sufficient funds available to finance the kind of campaigns that will stimulate competition and encourage higher levels of participation.

In the months ahead, Congress is going to have to choose between two basic approaches to campaign financing. The first is represented by the Campaign Contribution Reform Act of 1979, H.R. 4970, introduced by Reps. David Obey of Wisconsin and Tom Railsback of Illinois. That act would cut in half the amount a candidate could accept from a political action committee, place a ceiling of $50,000 on the total amount that can be contributed by PACs to a candidate in any one election cycle, and limit the ability of campaign service firms to extend credit to candidates. H.R. 4970 is based on the same faulty assumption that got us into difficulty in the first place. It embodies the notion that money and politics do not mix, that somehow money is an inherently evil force in American politics. The clear implication of the bill is that congressmen can be bought for a $5,000 contribution from a PAC, but not for a mere $2,500. I hope we will reject this approach.

The second approach, far more honest and effective, recognizes that adequate campaign financing is an important part of enabling the voting public to make enlightened election decisions. Underfinanced campaigns and unnecessarily restrictive and burdensome regulations lead to less voter awareness, lower rates of participation, and less competition. I would enthusiastically endorse the recommendations of the Institute of Politics, not as the ideal solution, but as a far better alternative than that offered by Obey-Railsback.

Discussion

ALLEN CLUTTER, executive director, Ethical Practices Board of the State of Minnesota: We have a public financing program for both constitutional and legislative candidates. Practically, can a federal candidate for the presidency not accept public financing, and politically, can he accept—if he chooses not to accept public financing—the political heat of an opponent accusing him of raising large sums of money for his campaigning?

REP. CHENEY: It is not really practical to talk seriously about a candidate not accepting federal funds once he is in the race. Given the limitations on how much any individual can contribute, which are unaffected, all that a candidate avoids if he declines federal funds is the limitation on spending. If he turned them down, he still would be restricted in terms of how much anybody could give to his campaign. Realistically, he has no choice but to accept federal funding because he could not raise enough money without it in the time available.

MR. NEIL STAEBLER, former commissioner, FEC: What changes do you recommend at the congressional level and what corrections at the presidential level?

REP. CHENEY: Let me begin by saying that I have a fundamental hang-up with the notion of public financing of even presidential campaigns. I try to be a realist, however, and recognize that that system is probably here to stay. We do need to allow larger individual contributions at the presidential level—perhaps larger there than we allow at the congressional level—and we need to raise the total amount that can be expended in a campaign. We might want to put a limit on the subsidy that is made available through public funding, but there should not be a limit on the total amount of money that is expended by a candidate, if he can raise it. Especially the state-by-state limitations and the formula that is used to set limits now—sixteen cents per eligible voter make no sense at all. We have to take the rules and regulations and the statute out of the business of deciding who wins those elections: in effect, they do this now.

With respect to congressional races, I support the recommendations of the Harvard group that I mentioned earlier. Specifically, the amount that an individual can contribute to a candidate should be raised significantly. They recommend $3,000, but that should be a minimum; perhaps an individual should be allowed to contribute as much as $5,000.

The operations of PACs should be left alone. The extent to which people are frightened by the development and role of political action committees is not justified. If you want to reduce the total influence of PACs, then give a candidate an alternative source of financing. Let him go to private individuals and be able to get $4,000 or $5,000 from an individual contributor, rather than being restricted to $1,000.

The Harvard group also suggests a reduction in the reporting requirements. That would be wise because an enormous amount of time, energy, and money is spent in reporting and filling out forms. Perhaps we could raise the minimum level of the contributions that need to be reported to $500 or $1,000. No one reads those reports in the way that was originally intended. Aside from the FEC having to pore over them, and having to do postaudits, their disclosure, as it is currently practiced, does not help the public to make wise decisions from knowledge of who is contributing to whose race. Even the press finds it difficult to wade through the vast amount of paper that candidates generate every year. The reporting requirements should therefore be reduced.

The suggestion that a one-for-one tax credit be allowed for contributions to campaigns at some specified level is an excellent idea.

We should look for ways to increase the funding that is available to candidates who want to run for office, and that means reducing the restrictions that have made inadequate sums available in order to have the first-rate competitive situation that we would all like to see.

MR. JESSUP: This seems to contradict your opening statement that more money was raised and spent than ever before in the congressional elections.

REP. CHENEY: I don't believe I said that.

MR. JESSUP: Well, it is true, nevertheless. More money was raised and spent than ever before in the congressional elections, and yet there seems to be this myth that there is not enough money in congressional elections. There seems to be a contradiction there.

In the marginal races and open seats a good deal of money is attracted. Where there is a real chance of a competitive race, money is attracted from many sources: ideological groups, special-interest groups, wealthy individuals, and so forth. There is no dearth of money in a competitive race. If seed money is a problem in some cases, why would you turn to wealthy businessmen for that seed money, since that is what raising the individual contribution limit really means? Only those people are able to put in that amount of money as individuals. If I am given a choice between a wealthy individual who is self-financed and an average individual who has to depend on an outside group of wealthy businessmen for his seed money, I think I would rather have the former.

REP. CHENEY: How many of your COPE members can afford to plunk down $50,000 or $60,000 to begin a campaign?

MR. JESSUP: None.

REP. CHENEY: That's right. A paradox has indeed developed: there is more money available than ever before, but there is also a shortage of funds to get campaigns started. I tried to cover that in the question of timing. My experience—and probably that of many candidates who run successful races—is that we do spend more money than ever before in those races. The costs go up every year, and part of this increase is simply a reflection of the inflated cost of campaigning.

However, the money available through new mechanisms such as the political action committees is late money. It comes in after the outcome has already been determined. I do not mean to discourage my friends in PACs, labor or otherwise, from contributing; it is nice to have that money at the end of the campaign. However, when the candidate is right down to the wire in August or September, and he has a primary and only $10,000 left in the bank—which was for his children's college education or whatever—he has to make that final decision perhaps to buy a last week of television time. A poll at that late stage is too costly and it would only scare the pants off him. He has to decide whether or not to risk all on a roll of the dice. In those dog days in August before the primary, there aren't very many people around who really want to contribute. He has already tapped out friends and relations and everybody else willing to support a nonincumbent involved in a primary contest for an open seat. That is when a candidate needs help, and it is never available then. So he may be forced to take a second mortgage on the house to finance that campaign.

After he gets over that hump and the word is given out through the network back here in Washington—that everyone in the country is plugged into politically—that he may win, then he can raise money.

251

CAMPAIGN FINANCE AND STRATEGY

That is to say, much of the money that is said to be available for campaigns really does not appear until after the race has already been decided. A creative political scientist probably could analyze the timing of PAC contributions and perhaps prove or disprove my theory. Nonetheless I do believe we are faced with this paradox of new money being available while the candidates who are actively seeking office are finding it difficult to raise money.

ANDREW MOLLISON, Cox Newspapers: Your North Carolina example seems limp. Ford dumped campaign manager Bo Calloway, a southerner, in the middle of the North Carolina primaries, and Reagan supporters decided independently to use the Florida film. It could be that substantive campaigning had more to do with the result of that primary than the budget decision that you have mentioned.

REP. CHENEY: Yes. I did not intend to link the North Carolina result specifically to the allowable spending limit in North Carolina. The fact is we made a political judgment, as opposed to a financial judgment, to lay back in North Carolina, and it was wrong. This is just an example of the type of strategic decisions made in a campaign.

MR. MOLLISON: When it came to encouraging grass-roots activity, why, during the last presidential election for example, didn't the parties encourage local party activists to spend whatever they raised and count it against their state and national spending limits?

REP. CHENEY: It is extremely risky to tell someone in a campaign to spend whatever he can raise on a particular project when all those reporting requirements have to be met. We had bills from New Hampshire coming in six months after the fact in the Ford campaign, even though our bookkeeping was one of the tightest, most efficient operations around. A former comptroller of the Defense Department, probably our most valuable person, kept the books. When the audit was completed, it was only about $2,800 off; partly because of three shipments of apples that we hadn't reported properly.

Perhaps in 1980 people will be more accustomed to living with the law than they were in 1976. The Ford campaign of 1976, probably influenced by the memory of the Committee to Re-Elect the President of 1972, did not want to do anything that would raise the least question about not complying with the spirit and letter of the law. As a result, whether we were dealing with party people or our local campaign organization, we did not encourage anyone to do anything unless he had signed

252

on the dotted line, filled out all of the appropriate forms, had reported in, had the right person sign the check, and so forth. This procedure became standard in everything we did. Consequently, when someone said he had a great idea, we asked: Has it been signed off on? Is it part of the plan? Is it in the budget? Where are you going to get the money? These were all important considerations.

Part Four

Parties and Campaign Finance Laws

The Nationalizing of the Party System

Xandra Kayden

It is generally accepted that American parties have tended to be "labels rather than organizations," and that even as labels they are of declining influence and interest to both the American electorate and candidates for elective office.[1] One reason for the lack of organizational strength has been the effect of political reform on the parties throughout this century. This reform, directed at a variety of abuses of power, was focused first on local machines and later on the process itself in an effort to increase participation in the selection of candidates. One effect of reform has been to weaken whatever strength the parties as organizations may once have had; a partial consequence of that dilution has been a decline in party identification on the part of American voters.

The focus of this paper is not on the electorate or the party system, but rather on party structure—the organizational strength of the two major parties. As in the past, recent changes in party organization are the result both of political reform (in this case the Federal Election Campaign Act of 1971, as amended) and changes in other areas—principally campaign technology—which were not directed toward the parties but are, nonetheless, having unintended consequences on party structure.

Whether or not the American party system is in the midst of a realignment,[2] it seems likely that there is a restructuring of party organization, starting at the top. This restructuring will change the national

This paper is based on interviews conducted either in person or by telephone with national party leaders by myself and Andrew McKey as part of a study by the Campaign Finance Study Group (Institute of Politics, Harvard University), for the House Administration Committee on the impact of federal campaign election law. We also spoke to two-thirds of the state party leaders by telephone. I owe a debt in the development of this paper to Stephen Hess, Seymour Martin Lipset, James March, David Mayhew, Samuel Popkin, Leonard Ross, Giovanni Sartori, William Schneider, and Susan Shirk.

[1] James Q. Wilson, *Political Organizations* (New York: Basic Books, 1973), p. 95.
[2] See Everett Carll Ladd, Jr., and Charles D. Hadley, *Transformations of the American Party System* (New York: W. W. Norton and Co., 1978); and Walter Dean Burnham, *Critical Elections and the Mainsprings of American Politics* (New York: W. W. Norton and Co., 1970).

parties from passive institutions dominated by state and local interests to highly professional organizations, with limited mass participation, whose primary function is to provide campaign consulting services to candidates. The national parties may begin to intervene in campaigns and party committees at the state and local levels, as well as to participate in elections of federal officials, thereby reversing the traditional flow of party influence. Although it is unclear whether this new structure will be controlled by professionals interested in winning office, or by activists interested in advancing issue positions, the future of the political system may be profoundly affected by the outcome of this struggle for control. This paper will consider evidence pointing in each direction.

The following discussion will trace the influence of both federal law and changes in technology which appear to be transforming national party organization. It will begin with a discussion of expectations about party reform and end with some thoughts about the nature of organizational change and the two-party system.

Expectations of Party Reform

Around the turn of the century progressive reformers, representing a new urban middle class, sought to break the control of city machines which neither represented their interests nor maintained their values. Among the results of these efforts were nonpartisan city elections and a decline of what one contemporary political scientist referred to as the "tyrannical" control by parties over elected officials.[3] Most of those interested in the parties since that time have been less hostile toward them, although there are serious differences in normative expectations. Among political analysts, two views appear to have dominated in the latter half of our century. The first group are advocates of *issue-oriented* parties responsive to voter concerns and responsible for government policy. This view, which is often expressed when comparisons are made to European parliamentary parties, was strongly held by political scientists several decades ago, and has hardly disappeared.[4] A second perspective among political observers focuses on the dependency of parties on other phenomena in the political system and might be described as a market view. To these observers, the party is less important in developed societies which support well-educated, middle-class citizens with access

---

[3] M. Ostrogorski, *Democracy and the Organization of Political Parties* (London: Macmillan, 1902).

[4] Most notably led by E. E. Schattschneider and the Committee on Political Parties of the American Political Science Association in a report entitled "Toward a More Responsible Two-Party System," 1950.

to other vehicles for learning about candidates and issues and other vehicles for political expression. The relevance of the party to the political setting depends upon the issues and is used accordingly by candidates and political strategists.[5]

Among political activists, two views also seem to be represented. One group espouses open, *participatory* parties which place emphasis on the democratic nature of the political process. A second group consists of *traditionalists*. This group, who might be termed "regressive reformers," would prefer to undo the impact of past party reform and return several functions to the party, especially control of nomination. The objective of the traditionalists is a responsible party system which exercises control over office holders and which in turn is held accountable for its choice by the electorate.[6]

There are a number of typologies which have been developed to demonstrate alternatives among different sorts of parties and party systems. Since the focus of this discussion is on current beliefs and expectations about the American two-party system, it should be sufficient to say that within the context of a universe dominated by one or the other party (and the assumption that they will alternate in office), there appear to be only two variables of significance for explaining behavior. These are (1) organizational structure, which determines how parties operate, and (2) the objectives of the parties. A recent study by Robert Nakamura and Denis Sullivan offers an interesting illustration of these dimensions.

Since those who see parties as passive participants in the political system cannot properly be said to have described an organizational structure, their views are not represented in the matrix. Instead, Nakamura and Sullivan have added a fourth structure—the "party as firm"—which reflects a market interpretation of democratic processes and which may well come to represent the national party of the future.[7] Indeed, it may already be seen in the national Republican party.

---

[5] Jean Blondel suggests, for instance, that right-wing parties try to ride out storms of political upheaval and left-wing parties seek out such storms as a way of expanding their influence. See *Political Parties: A Genuine Case for Discontent?* (London: Wildwood House, 1979), pp. 157–158. Either approach suggests a passive influence of parties on the process, at least as initiators of change or action. See also Leon Epstein's essay "Political Parties," in *Handbook of Political Science*, Fred I. Greenstein and Nelson W. Polsby, eds., vol. 4 (Reading, Pa.: Addison Wesley Publishing Co., 1975), for a typology based on conceptions of the party as a dependent, independent, or intervening variable.

[6] See James Q. Wilson, *The Amateur Democrat* (Chicago: University of Chicago Press, 1962).

[7] It is based on Anthony Downs, *Economic Theory of Democracy* (New York: Harper & Row, 1957).

FIGURE 1
MODELS OF DEMOCRATIC CONTROL

Organizational Dimension

		Centralized, hierarchical party organization	Decentralized, nonhierarchical party organization
Motivational Dimension	*Issues as primary*	Responsible party model	Participatory model
	Winning as primary	Party as firm	Pluralist-organizational model

SOURCE: Robert T. Nakamura and Dennis G. Sullivan, "Party Democracy and Democratic Control," *American Politics and Public Policy,* Walter Dean Burnham and Martha Wagner Weinberg, eds. (Cambridge: MIT Press, 1979), p. 27.

The Federal Law

Many of the efforts toward party reform are the result of historical developments such as the progressive movement, already mentioned; frustration of antiwar activists during the Vietnam period; and certainly, the impact of Watergate. Most party law is state law, although there have been federal laws on the books since the early years of the century. There are also internal party reform efforts, reflected in charter commissions which arise from time to time to revise the rules. This study is based on an analysis of the last round of federal legislation, the Federal Election Campaign Act of 1971, which was amended in 1974 and 1976 and is likely to be further amended in the next several years. This round of legislation is the first serious federal intervention in party operations since 1925 when the Corrupt Practices Act was passed.

Direct Impacts. Although most of the recent federal legislation is directed toward campaigns and campaign contributors, there were efforts made to strengthen the political parties, albeit a generally held view that the impact of the law on the parties can only be considered "adverse or perverse." Such general effects notwithstanding, there are four principal features of the law which support parties.

Increased contribution limits. The new law allows higher contribution limits for parties than for campaigns or other nonparty, multicandidate committees (known as political action committees or PACs).[8]

Higher expenditures for parties. Parties are also now entitled to make higher expenditures than other nonparty committees; in the last several elections expenditures were set at 2 cents per voter in presidential and Senate races, and $20,000 in House races. PACs, in contrast, can contribute a maximum of $5,000 per election to a candidate, although both PACs and individuals can make independent expenditures of any amount on behalf of a candidate as long as the spending is truly independent of the campaign and the candidate.[9]

Additional funding during campaigns. During presidential election campaigns, the public financing extended to the candidates is also extended to the two major parties; the Federal Election Commission (FEC) pays for the nominating conventions.[10]

Lower postage. A recent provision on behalf of the parties allows them to use two-cent postage. This brings the cost of direct mail solicitations equal to that of special-interest groups, which can often qualify for the lower postage rate on the ground of being either a nonprofit or an educational organization. Although the provision was not signed into law until after the 1978 election, it will, presumably, have a positive impact on party finances in future elections.

Indirect Impacts. The preceding features of the law were designed specifically to affect the parties. In addition, other aspects of the federal law have also had an impact on them and may, in the long run, become even more significant in terms of the relationship between parties and campaigns. One of the most important is the limitation on corporate contributions to federal candidates and to the parties. PAC contributions are acceptable because they come from individual contributors, but direct grants from corporations are not. The difficulty, however, is that many

[8] There is a $1,000 contribution limit to candidates, $5,000 to PACs, and a $20,000 contribution limit for the parties.
[9] Independent expenditures were not originally written into the law but came as a result of the Supreme Court ruling in *Buckley* v. *Valeo.* The Court held that limiting an individual's, or a group's, expenditure was contrary to the First Amendment.
[10] Minor parties are also eligible for public financing retrospectively, provided that they can demonstrate enough of a base in the electorate after the election.

states allow such contributions, and the result is a separation of funds within state parties designated for their federal, state, and local candidates.

A second provision calls for separate accounting, regardless of the use of corporate funds, and often means a centralization of party activity within the state. Disclosure requirements for funds to the parties, as well as to the campaigns, similarly cause many state parties to centralize their activities. Both the separate accounts and the disclosure requirements encourage a reliance on legal and accounting advice, which, if not available on a voluntary basis locally, has tended to force state party committees to rely on the national headquarters.

The complexity of the law and its varying interpretations by the Federal Election Commission has, at the very least, encouraged hesitation. Prohibitions, such as contribution limits and disclosure requirements, are more obvious than the allowable activities. One of the most confusing has to do with the relationship between party committees. The law allows parties to transfer funds between committees at the various levels (national, state, and local). The FEC has accepted the notion of "independent" party committees, which enables some local committees to avoid falling under the aggregate spending limit for the party.

In an advisory brief known as the *Iowa Opinion,* the FEC came to terms with the fact that the law does not specifically address party committees below the state level. In Iowa, as in many other states, all levels of party committees are established by state law and are legally independent of each other in the sense that elections to office are held without regard of one to the other. County committees do send funds to the state committee, which may or may not forward this money to a federal account, but the state rarely sends funds back to the counties. There are, in other words, few if any sanctions that can be imposed on counties from the state or national level, and therefore the county committees may be considered independent party committees.

Although the FEC intended this opinion to strengthen the position of parties in federal elections, it raises questions about the nature of state party structure and the capacity of state parties to exert a strong role in elections. The more independent the relationship between state and county party units, the less the likelihood of united efforts on behalf of a party's candidates.

Given the nature of the entire party structure, with its tendency toward the accumulation of resources at the top, the impact of the federal law will probably be toward a further centralizing or nationalizing of the parties because of forces coming from both the top and the bottom of the structure.

XANDRA KAYDEN

Effect on the Republican Party

Impact on Party Organization. The following discussion is based on observations and interviews with staff personnel in the Republican party, which appears to be representative of the party system of the future.

Centralization at the top. The national Republican party devoted much of its fund raising to direct mail solicitations in the wake of Watergate, partly to demonstrate that the party is *not* just the party of big business and does, in fact, have a constituency of small donors; and partly because small donations are convenient for reporting and matching funds, should public financing someday extend to the parties. It is also true that the party out of power is in a better position to benefit from the negative appeals most typical of direct mail approaches. In any case, the net result in 1978 was the accumulation of a considerable amount of money and the growth of the national Republican party.

With the added resources accumulated through direct mail solicitations, the national party was in a good position to provide a number of services to state and local parties. Among these were technical advice (particularly on accounting and legal issues); computer programs made available to both state parties and federal candidates to help in accounting, fund raising, research, and polling activities; and lists for direct mail campaigns conducted either at the state level or by campaign organizations.[11] In addition, the national party provided staff positions to the states and regions and made plans to open regional offices. Whereas the typical Democratic state committee consisted in 1978 of two or three full-time positions, the state Republican committees generally were staffed by five or six full-time professionals, with additional staff assigned to a two- or three-state area. One or two of these positions were either completely or partially funded by the National Republican Committee.

Although Republican candidates have historically relied more on their party for campaign support than have Democratic candidates, it was nonetheless true in 1978 that the National Republican Committee took a moderately active role in providing both funds and services to their candidates for both federal and state elections. This intervention by the party in local state legislative races, while something of a departure for the national party, reflected its concern about the apportionment likely to follow the 1980 census, and hence is pertinent to federal elections. It also reflects the belief of the current national party chairman

---

[11] The maintenance of lists are particularly difficult for campaign organizations because of their temporary nature. Temporariness also makes it difficult for campaigns to develop and sustain the standard operating procedures necessary to support some of the federal law's requirements in filing reports.

that the party must be built from the bottom up; however, as will become clear, the gulf between candidates for state and federal office may become wider rather than narrower. In any case, the intervention in primary campaigns (albeit on the same basis as any multicandidate PAC, which is to say with stricter limits and without the benefit of the special provisions for parties made in the law) was intended to assure the party the strongest possible candidate during the general election.

Centralization from the bottom. At the same time that the national party has begun intervening in what has historically been the purview of state and local party activities, other factors at the local level are encouraging federal candidates, particularly, to rely more heavily on the national party committees and less on their state and local organizations.[12]

Perhaps the most important provision of the federal law encouraging a greater dependence on national party committees is that which calls for separate accounts between federal and state candidates. A good deal of a state party's normal activity concerns state and local elections. To many of a party's contributors, federal elections are too distant and abstract to warrant support. Insurance companies, for instance, which are regulated by state law, are more likely to contribute to state races and state parties than to the national party or its candidates. But separate accounting and filing procedures, along with specific campaign contribution limits and party expenditures on behalf of federal candidates, have meant that many state parties have begun to separate not only the accounts but also the activities on behalf of federal candidates from those for local candidates. In the past, for example, a congressional or Senate candidate might typically be the lead attraction at a county pancake breakfast or fish fry. Such events are often held not only to raise money, but also to gear up the local volunteers for voter registration and get-out-the-vote efforts on election day.

Reporting requirements and the complex task of allocating a fair share to each candidate has meant that fewer and fewer federal candidates and their parties cared to risk breaking the law in 1978; consequently, local party events tended to focus more and more on local candidates to the exclusion of federal candidate interests. Even though the law has made special provision to encourage such activity on the

---

12 Federal elections usually mean support for candidates from at least two out of three committees in Washington: the national party committee, and the congressional and Senate campaign committees each party maintains. In addition, there can also be separate committees such as those sponsored by the majority and minority leaders, or liberal, conservative, or special-interest caucuses. The year 1978 also saw the emergence of financial support by legislators seeking leadership, such as the campaign committee of California Democrat Henry Waxman which contributed to a number of his colleagues' campaigns.

part of federal candidates—such as allowing "slate cards" in which a party lists all its candidates—it appears that the number and scope of combined activities will decline. The effect is a peculiar separation of federal from state and local candidates, with an uncertain impact on future elections or on the American party system in general.

All this is not to suggest that combined events cannot occur, but rather that party leaders and party workers have demonstrated a hesitancy to become involved and take risks which might lead to a federal investigation by either the FEC or the Justice Department. Although the argument was occasionally made that taking such risks might lead to victory at the polls in November and, at worst, would result in a fine the following April, when those involved were long gone, most party officials said that the complexity of the law and the distaste for federal regulation had a chilling effect on local party activity. The various committees of the national Republican party actively discouraged local committees from participating in federal elections.

For Democrats, who have traditionally relied on labor to provide the organizational backbone necessary for registration and get-out-the-vote drives, to say nothing of door-to-door canvassing on behalf of its candidates, the decline of party activity at the local level was probably minimal. But for Republicans, who have always relied more on their party for such organizational support, the active discouragement may have been more serious in 1978, and will certainly continue to be a problem unless a way around it is found.[13] The incentives to overcome the problems raised, however, may not be very great if it is true that most local efforts are made on behalf of local and state candidates from whom party workers expect a return in one form or another.

Impact of Technology. The most significant technological development to have an impact on structural party strength is the computer. Not only does it assist in coping with the millions of pieces of information necessary for filing reports, it also has become an essential element in the maintenance of lists of potential donors.

The use of direct mail solicitation campaigns has become a fact-of-life in politics, beginning with the 1964 Goldwater campaign, and especially since the 1972 McGovern presidential campaign.[14] Although the

---

[13] There are provisions in the law exempting some local party activity in an effort to overcome just these problems, but the message was not widely disseminated in 1978.

[14] Although 1978 was not a presidential campaign year, the tendency among lower-echelon campaigns is to copy presidential campaign techniques developed in previous elections. See discussion of this in Xandra Kayden, *Campaign Organization* (Lexington, Mass.: D.C. Heath, 1978), pp. 136–137.

technology has existed for some time, its impact has grown substantially in recent years. One reason, already noted, is the law itself which provides for matching public funds for presidential candidates—a procedure that may be extended to other federal candidates and the parties. For the Republicans, there was, as well, the aftermath of Watergate. Perhaps even more significant has been the emergence of Richard Viguerie as a dominant figure in conservative fund raising. Although the interests of Viguerie and of the Republican party are hardly synonymous, he did demonstrate the efficacy of appealing for small donations to large numbers of people who might be considered Republican sympathizers. It is also true that some of the staff people currently working for the party were formerly with Viguerie and brought with them their experience and approach to fund raising.

Whatever the reasons, the income for the Republican party has increased substantially in the last few years, and the great bulk of that increase is due to direct mail solicitations. Although direct mail advocates argue that such appeals dramatically increase the number of people participating in politics, the nature of such appeals—usually on single issues which are divisive in nature—may have other consequences for the party system that are not quite so beneficent.

Although the past may not necessarily predict the future, it is a generally held belief among direct mail fund raisers that the most successful letters are those which appeal to strongly-felt, often hostile, views. It was possible, for instance, to raise money to oppose such issues as the Panama Canal Treaty or SALT, but not to support them. The motivation, presumably, is that one will give a small amount of money to support those issues one feels strongly enough about to forgo any reward but personal satisfaction. In the days before campaign contribution limits, large donors gave to candidates in return for access. Small donors, on the other hand, are unlikely to receive any attention beyond another letter from the same group, or from another organization which bought the mailing list from the first group. It may be that this strategy is not the only way to raise money from small contributors, but as long as the dominant view holds, the very nature of the appeal will force the party, and any other organization or individual making such appeals, into taking divisive stands.

Another factor in Republican party fund raising is the impact of direct mail appeals made by single-issue PACs. It may not be the party alone that is educating donors about issues; their opinions may be shaped instead by single-issue groups which then encourage potential donors to support only those who accept their views.

Historically, Republicans rely on conservative donors, and Democrats raise money from liberals. According to Republican fund raisers, moderate or liberal Republicans do not give to their party, nor do conservative Democrats give to theirs. The reason is obvious: in the minds of most Americans, the parties represent somewhat opposing ideologies, and those who wish to change their party's views would not do so by supporting the established groups within the party.[15] Since Republican party fund raisers expect to raise money from the right, and since direct mail strategies are based on hostilities, the net effect is to move the party further and further to the right, at least as far as its contributor base is concerned.

The benefit the Republican party gained in 1978 from its direct mail campaigns was due in large measure to the fact that the Democrats were in the White House. As the party out of power, they were in the best position to benefit from negative issues. This is, however, likely to be a short-term benefit. When the Republicans regain the executive, the issues will fall to the Democrats, who presumably will take much the same advantage. One might envision this as something of a pendulum swinging further and further out with each change of administration. The net effect will be to lead both parties to greater dependence on divisive ideological issues in order to gain contributors, and hence to force both parties into the issue-oriented position political purists have advocated for some time.

Differential Impact on Republicans and Democrats

The greatest impact of the federal law has been, naturally enough, at the national and state levels. It is at these levels that resources are collected and full-time professional staffs run the organization. Below the state party level, both parties are generally run by volunteers and there is often very little difference between Republicans and Democrats in terms of their organizational structure or strength. The differences between the two major parties, however, are important when it comes to interpreting the impact of the law and the technological changes which have taken place.

Republicans. Since its reorganization by Mark Hanna at the end of the nineteenth century, the Republican party has been a much more struc-

---

15 According to a yet-to-be-published study undertaken by Warren Miller, 80 percent of the politically active respond to labels of liberal and conservative, and with the exception of conservative Democrats, there is general agreement about what those labels mean when translated into issues and the role of the parties. Paper delivered by Miller at Stanford University, June 1979.

tured organization than its Democratic counterpart. Some have assumed that the reason comes from the greater business orientation of the Republican party, which has led to an adaptation of business procedures within the organization. Another factor may be the minority status of the Republican party, which has forced it to focus its resources and require greater solidarity in Congress. A related explanation is that the party has been forced to recruit candidates as one of its major functions, and has offered the benefits of organizational strength as an inducement.

Being "number two" may also have forced the Republican organization to "try harder" by hiring a more professional staff, by experimenting with new techniques, and by evaluating the results more carefully. The younger staff has made the organization more open to different ways of doing things, more at home with the latest technology, and perhaps more eager to seek advances.

The Republicans, for reasons having nothing to do with their size, have also had to cope with more than their Democratic opponents. The rise of right-wing organizations in the last few decades has put tremendous pressure on the Republican party, a pressure made even stronger as Richard Viguerie began amassing resources and supporting candidates with instructions to bypass the party if it was not sufficiently supportive.[16] It is too soon to discern the impact of this pressure, but two directions seem at least possible: the party will move to the right in order to avoid losing its constituency; and/or the party will form a tighter organization to delineate itself clearly, in contrast to other groups.

Democrats. It is almost proverbial in Washington for political observers to note that Republicans always have the money and Democrats always have the votes.[17] The differences, however, are more apparent than real. Athough it is unquestionaby true that thus far the Repubican national party has outraised and outspent its Democratic opponent, the measure is not entirely accurate. Democratic candidates outspend Republican candidates (1978 was a rare exception), and Democratic campaigns are usually quite sophisticated, employing and developing the latest technological adaptations to winning elections.

Whereas P.epublicans put their organizational energy into the party, the Democrats have always put their energy into the campaign. Since the emergence of the Democratic coalition of the New Deal, Democrats have been able to rely on labor to provide the backbone of their organizations,

---

16 Christopher Buchanan, "New Right: Many Times More Effective Now," *Congressional Quarterly,* December 24, 1977, pp. 2649–2653.

17 See for example, Charles W. Hucker, "Political Party Finance: It's *David* vs. *Goliath," Congressional Quarterly,* June 24, 1978, pp. 1607–1613.

in terms of workers and financial support. Typically, a Democratic candidate outside the South could expect to receive more than half of his group contributions from labor.[18] Although more money tends to be contributed in the latter stages of campaigning by all forms of PACs, labor money is likely to be more relatively evenly distributed throughout the course of the campaign period; at least 20 percent in 1978 could be counted upon to arrive early, with all the benefits that entailed for the campaign organization.[19] Although organized labor threatened to withhold support from Democratic candidates who had not supported labor views in Congress before the 1978 election, the historical alliance between the two groups has been of tremendous advantage to Democratic candidates and has operated efficiently enough to enable the central Democratic party structure to remain in what might be called "arrested development."

Labor's membership in the Democratic coalition is only part of the reason, however, for the amorphous structure of the Democratic party. Another factor has to do with the nature of coalition politics: being made up of clearly identifiable groups, most Democratic campaign organizations are easily assembled by employing representatives from each group whose task is to mobilize their constituencies.[20] Certainly any group as large as the Democratic party can expect factions—great divergences of views from region to region and even within regions as the heirs of various historical strains take up the name of Democrat. The advantage of the Republican minority status is a relatively closely knit organization. It is one of the goods coming from the "ill winds" of being number two.[21]

Another reason for weak Democratic party structure at the national level is a function of winning. As long as a Democratic president sits in the White House, or Democrats control the leadership in Congress, there is little incentive to build or maintain a third major vehicle for party expression in Washington. While the Republican party has devoted so much of its resources in the last few years to developing its direct mail

---

[18] William Schneider and Gregory Schell, "The New Democrats," *Public Opinion,* November/December 1978, p. 10.

[19] From a survey of 1978 campaign managers in "An Analysis of the Impact of the Federal Election Campaign Act, 1972–78: A Report by the Campaign Finance Study Group to the Committee on House Administration of the U.S. House of Representatives," Institute of Politics, Harvard University, to be published by Congressional Quarterly Press.

[20] Kayden, *Campaign Organization,* pp. 90–91.

[21] See V. O. Key, Jr., *Southern Politics* (New York: Alfred A. Knopf, 1949), chap. 14, "Nature and Consequence of One Party Factionalism," pp. 298–311; and Austin Ranney, *Curing the Mischiefs of Faction* (Berkeley: University of California Press, 1975).

solicitation strategy, the Democrats have had little incentive to follow suit because it is still cost-effective to hold a large fund-raising dinner, with the President, members of his family, cabinet officials, and so on in attendance as keynote speakers. It was also clear in the summer and fall of 1978 that the Democratic National Committee did not have the staff capability to embark upon such a complex task as a direct mail campaign.[22]

There is a mild irony in the focus of the Democratic party on large donors in contrast to the small donations likely to come from direct mail campaigns. Since the New Deal, most Americans have identified the Democratic party as the party of the "common man." Since the presidency of John F. Kennedy, however, the focus has been on large contributors—easier targets when one has control of the executive and the Congress.

Even if all of these factors are true, the Democratic party may be in the process of a dramatic reorganization, mostly because of the impact of the Federal Campaign Finance Act and the regulations established by the Federal Election Commission.

The most important factor in Democratic party reorganization has to do with the relationship between organized labor and the party proper. As Edwin M. Epstein has pointed out, the effect of labor-supported reform has often backfired.[23] There is little doubt that the tremendous growth of corporate PACs has significantly altered the fund-raising strategies of Democratic candidates and lessened labor's role in the Democratic party.When Congress failed to pass legislation the AFL-CIO believed important in 1977, the Committee on Political Education (COPE), the political arm of the top labor coalition, made it clear that it would not blindly support Democratic candidates who were not loyal to labor. As one leader noted, "We are willing to give up the seats of Democratic summer soldiers who desert us when there is a real fight."[24]

The problem for organized labor is fairly complex. Not supporting Democratic incumbents, and thus contributing to their loss of office, would not necessarily lead to the election of a candidate more kindly

---

[22] Actually, they did in a sporadic fashion and have been building toward a more comprehensive direct mail campaign. The national party has been hampered by (1) not having the issues—the first such letter was a call to contribute to counteract the fund raising of conservative organizations—and (2) not having the staff capability because of turnover of personnel, among other things.

[23] Edwin M. Epstein, "Labor and Federal Elections: The New Legal Framework," in *Industrial Relations,* vol. 15, no. 3 (October 1976), pp. 257–294.

[24] Alexander Barkan, director of COPE, cited by Philip Shabecoff, *New York Times,* October 25, 1978. Other articles citing labor's views appeared in the *Congressional Quarterly* early in 1978; for example, Charles W. Hucker, "Organized Labor Takes a Hard Look at Whom It Will Support This Fall," January 28, 1978, pp. 193–98.

disposed to labor's interests. And if the Democratic incumbent is able to compensate for the loss of labor money and retain his or her seat, the probability is quite high that the compensation will come from business interests, thereby reinforcing a probusiness bias. As one political observer noted, labor is not

> really going after people they don't like because they don't work that way. . . . The only other way is to punish your friends if you can't beat your enemies. And the friends' only alternative source of money will, in the long run, influence the way they think. Getting business money has to temper their feelings, or they would feel like ingrates, and that exacerbates labor's difficulty all the more.[25]

And then, of course, there is the diversity within the labor movement itself, which had a major impact on the legislative process in the Ninety-Fifth Congress. According to one labor leader:

> In the last few years, some of the unions that were never active with COPE have become active—building trades, a number of white collar unions, and the maritime trades as well. There has been a recognition on the part of union leadership of the need to work together, but the question remains of how much of that sifts down to the rank and file. A lot of blue collar workers will support candidates who will direct their campaigns to them alone and not to the rest of the labor movement. The building trades make more money and only look to their interest. And that's true of other unions as well. When these groups feel they have been affected, they will go out and do a job, but it very often has to affect them directly. Other unions are more socially oriented and the low-wage unions have done a better job educating their people—they have more reason to. They understand needing government on their side—the people on the borderline.[26]

As unions representing different segments of the work force begin to establish their interests, the apparent solidarity declines and legislators become the target of a tremendous variety of interest group pressures. There have been many arguments to explain the voting pattern of Democrats during the Ninety-Fifth Congress,[27] but the relevant question for this discussion is what will happen to Democratic candidates and the Democratic party if labor withdraws support.

---

[25] Cited in "Impact of the Federal Election Campaign Act," Campaign Finance Study Group.
[26] Ibid.
[27] Schneider and Schell, "The New Democrats."

During the course of our interviewing, several Washington-based political activists spoke of labor's (particularly COPE's) strategy of withdrawing support from unresponsive incumbents. The view was taken that labor would continue to support those candidates who came from marginal districts and who, consequently, would be likely both to appreciate labor's loyalty and to have been forced by local district considerations to temper their voting records. A truly marginal district would be the most likely to return an antilabor candidate under these circumstances. The group of incumbents one step away from marginal, however—the people identified by labor as "quasi-marginals" as of the summer, who might have supported labor and chose not to—were thought by labor to be another matter. It was this group, more than any other, that labor wanted to impress.

Given COPE's strategy, the question was what would happen during the 1978 election. Would these quasi-marginals compensate for labor's loss by appealing to business? Would they find another source such as the party? Or would they do without and win or lose with less money? It was uncertain whether a quasi-marginal position in the summer would translate into marginal status as the election drew near in November (many of them did), but the greatest uncertainty was and remains to be what long-term impact labor's behavior would have for the Democratic party.

The following table shows labor contributions to the twenty congressmen and women who seemed likely candidates for quasi-marginal status. The table is organized chronologically, displaying first the total 1976 contribution these candidates received from labor. The next two columns show the total labor contribution as of August 1978, and that figure as a percentage of the 1976 total. Since we do not have the timing of the 1976 donations, the 29 percent figure may or may not suggest that labor was carrying out its threat to withhold funds, but evidence from interviews suggests negotiations were going on between the candidates and COPE during the election period. The fourth column represents total labor contributions as of early January 1979, exclusive of post-general election donations; and the fifth column shows the total election period donations as a percentage of the 1976 total. The last two columns represent the total committee contributions received in 1978 and the labor contributions as a percentage of that total.

Not only did labor contributions to these incumbents decline in relation to their 1976 total by a significant 25 percent, but they also declined in proportion to total committee contributions. The 1978 quasi-marginal incumbents received only 44 percent of their committee support from labor, a figure considerably lower than the average labor contribution

TABLE 1

Labor Contributions to Democratic "Quasi-Marginal" Incumbents in the 1978 House Elections

	1976 Labor Total	August 1978 Labor Total	% of 1976 Labor Total	1978 Labor Total as of Jan. 1979[a]	% of 1976 Labor Total	1978 Party and Nonparty Committee Total	Labor Percentage of Committee Total
Leon Panetta (Calif.)	$45,451	$ 6,845	15%	$16,445	36%	$47,520	35%
Jim Lloyd (Calif.)	51,417	25,850	50	34,200	67	62,450	55
Pat Schroeder (Colo.)	53,388	7,600	14	32,450	61	45,047	72
Timothy Wirth (Colo.)	49,504	12,650	26	50,475	102	86,945	58
Abner Mikva (Ill.)	40,867	19,600	48	43,300	106	74,776	58
Floyd Fithian (Ind.)	51,789	11,750	22	31,750	61	68,895	46
David Evans (Ind.)	35,686	7,900	22	30,550	86	94,060	32
David Cornwall (Ind.)	16,646	9,000	51	26,800	161	50,117	53
Martha Keyes (Kans.)	42,484	1,540	04	11,940	28	44,262	27
David Glickman (Kans.)	13,936	3,100	22	4,400	32	24,157	18
Robert Carr (Mich.)	48,204	17,850	39	42,200	88	65,501	64
David Bonior (Mich.)	32,833	8,840	27	36,140	110	48,900	74
Helen Meyner (N.J.)	26,029	7,375	26	20,835	80	43,891	47
Jerome Ambro (N.Y.)	29,447	6,450	21	15,650	53	37,050	42
Edward Pattison (N.Y.)	16,547	150	09	7,650	46	32,517	24
Theodore Risenhoover (Okla.)	33,678	15,300	45	23,500	70	54,300	43
Thomas Larkin (Ohio)	38,140	19,020	50	34,220	90	88,542	39

Table continued on next page.

TABLE 1 (continued)

	1976 Labor Total	August 1978 Labor Total	% of 1976 Labor Total	1978 Labor Total as of Jan. 1979[a]	% of 1976 Labor Total	1978 Party and Nonparty Committee Total	Labor Percentage of Committee Total
Robert Edgar (Pa.)	31,960	8,600	27	27,650	87	59,069	47
Allen Ertel (Pa.)	12,909	4,300	33	13,600	105	53,672	25
James Mattox (Tex.)	66,250	19,850	30	15,200	23	75,633	20
Average:	36,858	10,679	29	25,948	75	57,865	44

[a] Not including postelection contributions.

SOURCE: The Federal Election Commission, August 20, 1978; January 4, 1979.

TABLE 2
PARTY CONTRIBUTIONS TO DEMOCRATIC "QUASI-MARGINAL"
INCUMBENTS IN THE 1978 HOUSE ELECTIONS

Leon Panetta (Calif.)	$12,500
Jim Lloyd (Calif.)	6,000
Pat Schroeder (Colo.)	8,500
Timothy Wirth (Colo.)	7,805
Abner Mikva (Ill.)	11,500
Floyd Fithian (Ind.)	4,500
David Evans (Ind.)	12,000
David Cornwall (Ind.)	6,267
Martha Keyes (Kans.)	8,500
David Glickman (Kans.)	2,000
Robert Carr (Mich.)	5,500
David Bonior (Mich.)	6,000
Helen Meyner (N.J.)	7,500
Jerome Ambro (N.Y.)	7,500
Edward Pattison (N.Y.)	6,500
Thomas Larkin (Ohio)	6,000
Robert Edgar (Pa.)	8,500
Allen Ertel (Pa.)	5,050
James Mattox (Tex.)	2,500

NOTE: Average contribution $7,085, compared with $2,600 average contribution of Democratic party to House incumbents. Theodore Risenhoover did not receive any party money.
SOURCE: The Federal Election Commission, January 1979.

Democratic incumbents would have expected from the 1976 showing of 57 percent.[28]

Clearly, these incumbents were able to compensate to some degree, though a further look at the committee contributions turned up another factor. Whereas the average national Democratic party contribution to incumbents was $2,600 for members of the House in 1978, the quasi-marginals received an average party contribution of over $7,000.[29] This figure is based on the sum of congressional campaign committees and Democratic National Committee contributions, and is not in itself a sure sign of great strength in the national party. The party did *not* make up for all the labor money these candidates lost. On the other hand, it is suggestive and does seem to indicate the possibility for a shift of candidates' reliance on labor to the party.

28 Ibid.
29 Report published by the Federal Election Commission.

In itself this would not necessarily mean that labor's place in the Democratic coalition is an insignificant factor in Democratic victories. Labor provides far more than money to the candidates it supports, as already noted. But the problems faced by labor now in its relation to the party are not easily resolved.[30] And the problems for labor may well lead to a change in Democratic party organization.

This possible trend of reliance on the party raises the last issue likely to have a long-range impact on national party politics. As V. O. Key noted in a seminal study of factional politics, "Organization begets counter-organization."[31] If one party is highly structured, the other party is apt to follow suit (Michigan, Indiana, and Minnesota come particularly to mind). If one party so dominates a state that it breaks into factions, the opposing party is likely to be only slightly better organized than one of the factions. If the Republicans have a highly developed structure, the Democrats are likely to do the same.

During the course of our interviews with state party chairpersons, several commented on the growing tendency for Democratic candidates to ask their state parties to provide the services their opponents received from their party: help with polling, fund raising, and so on. And certainly the national Democratic party intends to devote more of its resources to direct mail fund raising, even though dinners are momentarily more cost-effective. Time and the loss of the White House or control of one of the houses of Congress will, of course, tell.

Conclusion

It is the thesis of this paper that the decentralization and weak organizational structure characteristic of American parties at the national level are changing, and will continue to change until the parties have reached the stage of organizational development characteristic of other organizations. That is to say that they will become national bureaucracies with hierarchies, divisions of labor, and so on. It is the complexity of the law and technological developments which account for this change for two

---

[30] Despite the tremendous growth of corporate PACs in the past few years (from 150 in 1975 to over 775 in 1978), Democrats still come out ahead in PAC contributions partly because both corporate and trade association PACs show a marked preference for giving to incumbents as the most likely victors. This is the case despite the fact that business (combined corporate and trade association PACs) outspent labor $10.9 million to $6.0 million. Business-oriented PACs contributed $5.3 million to Democrats and $5.6 million to Republicans. But since more than 90 percent of labor money went to Democrats, the combined business/labor contribution was $10.9 million to Democrats and $6.0 million to Republicans. See "Impact of the Federal Election Campaign Act," Campaign Finance Study Group.
[31] Key, *Southern Politics*, p. 309.

reasons: they allow the organizations to acquire sufficient resources to hire professional staffs; and politics—at least at the national and state levels—is becoming more and more complex, requiring specialization in the performance of tasks.

James Q. Wilson has suggested that a reason American parties have remained decentralized, in contrast to almost every other kind of organization, has to do with the rewards they can offer. The material benefits sought in politics are usually available only at the local level; the solidary benefits cited by several students of politics as critical to the maintenance of party organization can be thwarted by controversy, so the parties are encouraged to find positions likely to appeal to as many people as possible; and last, given the antipolitical tradition in America, a well-educated middle class is more likely to produce individuals preferring "civic work" to "playing politics."[32] According to Wilson, "This leaves purpose, principle, and ideology as a major source of incentives for party organizations," though he believes such incentives to be only episodic.[33]

It seems obvious that a professional organization at the national level will not be dependent on the rewards typically offered at the lower levels of the party. It is possible they will not need local organizations at all, given the opportunities the mass media and direct mail solicitations provide for communicating with the electorate. How that declining dependence will affect local party committees, however, remains to be seen. Such committees may disappear, or they may divert their efforts solely to local politics and further the separation of federal and local candidates.

The question remains as to what impact issue-dependence might have on electoral behavior. Will it lead, in time, to a greater ideological orientation in American politics, or is there, as some suggest, a negative correlation between issue politics and ideological politics?[34] And what impact will issues and/or ideologies have on polarization and stability? Although American politics has demonstrated a historical resistance to ideological dependence—and American political scientists have consequently remained somewhat vague on the subject—it seems that at least in terms of this discussion, attempts should be made to define the salient aspects of the terms ideology, issue, and professional.

The classic analysis of American political perceptions, *The American Voter,* defines ideology as a "particularly elaborate, close-woven, and far-ranging structure of attitudes. By origin and usage its connotations

---

32 Wilson, *Political Organizations,* p. 96; see also, Samuel J. Eldersveld, *Political Parties* (Chicago: Rand McNally, 1964); and Richard Hofstadter, *The American Political Tradition* (New York: Alfred A. Knopf, Inc., 1948).

33 Wilson, *Political Organizations,* p. 96.

34 Giacomo Sani and Giovanni Sartori, "Polarization, Fragmentation and Competition in Western Democracies," unpublished draft, October 1978, p. 4.

are primarily political, although the scope of the structure is such that we expect an ideology to encompass content outside the political order as narrowly defined by social and economic relationships, and even matters of religion, education, and the like."[35] The authors go on to speak of ideology as a "high order of abstraction" capable of subsuming particular issues. In Europe, mass parties either have formed around ideologies, or have developed ideological foci to fit into existing political structures. The American experience, in contrast, has extended only to what *The American Voter* authors describe as "attitude structures," which exist "when two or more beliefs or opinions held by an individual are in some way or another functionally related."[36]

The distinctions are rarely closely drawn in American political analysis because our party system preceded modern ideologies and we have relatively little experience with strict ideological politics. Tendencies to lean to the right or the left, to conservative and liberal, have usually been moderated by specific issues; at the most they have led to the creation of attitude structures.

Professionals—in my use of the term—refer to those political activists who are primarily concerned with winning office, with being part of the political process. Issues to these persons are vehicles for participation in the political market: evaluated and played upon accordingly. The salient distinction for this discussion is that professionals, who may in time become party bureaucrats, would not put issue purity above policy development; ideologues, or issue-intensive moralists, would.

With these definitions and limitations in mind, it is appropriate to turn to discussion of the impact of organizational structure. According to V. O. Key, "organization both elevates and restrains leaders; disorganization provides no institutional brake on capriciousness when the will in that direction is present."[37] A professional organization, it may be argued, will be inclined to seek and maintain a working relationship with the opposition, especially if one accepts the maxim that the primary objective of all organizations is to maintain themselves. The degree to which professionalism outweighs ideological or issue orientation is the degree to which the two-party system will remain an effective balance in American politics.

On the other hand, it is possible that the constraints of organizational structure will not be sufficient to overcome ideological pressures. If issue positions are founded on the support of an angry citizenry—a

---

[35] Angus Campbell, Philip E. Converse, Warren E. Miller, and Donald Stokes, *The American Voter,* abridged (New York: John Wiley and Sons, 1964), p. 111.
[36] Ibid., p. 110.
[37] Key, *Southern Politics,* p. 305.

position currently fostered by direct mail strategies—how compromising can the party afford to be, particularly when the nature of direct mail appeals is to "educate" and focus their recipients on the negative sides of issues? It seems likely that those persons charged with developing issue positions will, at least to some extent, come to believe in them. If such people—issue-oriented activists—dominate the organizational structure, it is possible that they will hire only like-minded people, decreasing the "braking" capacity of the organization to veer in extreme directions. The campaign consulting business currently offers grounds for concern over such a possibility: liberal professionals invariably work only for liberal candidates; conservative professionals for conservative candidates.

According to Giovanni Sartori, in two-party systems, "Parties *must* be aggregative agencies that maintain their competitive near-evenness by amalgamating as many groups, interests, and demands as possible."[38] Although Sartori makes the point that homogeneity and consensus on fundamentals is not a precondition for two-party systems, he suggests that under the most favorable conditions for their existence the parties "nurture" such attitudes in order to function more smoothly. He goes on to say that "The greater the ideological distance, the more a two party format is dysfunctional," and that such systems work best, and perhaps only, when there is a minimum of ideological distance.[39]

Seymour Martin Lipset makes the same point in another context:

> The ability of the two-party system to provide for generalized leadership is closely linked to the fact that one party always represents the government and actually rules the country, so that the party in power *temporarily* becomes identical with the State. Both parties are organized to be able to take full responsibility, at home and abroad, for the conduct of the nation's affairs. . . . Since the legitimacy of a party rests ultimately upon its actual or potential effectiveness as a *national* government, there is a strong pressure on both parties in a two-party system to reduce or eliminate ideology as a basis for political decision.[40]

The "catch-all" party operates by including within its ranks all those who oppose the party in power. This makes it possible to "throw the rascals out" even if one party normally dominates the political scene by having elected more officials to office and by amassing a larger body of

---

[38] Giovanni Sartori, *Parties and Party Systems: A Framework for Analysis,* vol. 1 (New York: Cambridge University Press, 1976), p. 192.
[39] Ibid.
[40] Seymour Martin Lipset, *The First New Nation* (London: Heinemann, 1963), p. 311.

party identifiers. It is this aspect of two-party politics which has enabled the Republicans to sustain themselves over the past several decades in the face of large Democratic majorities. If, however, it is no longer possible to gather all the discontented under the umbrella of the party out of power—because that party has itself become so dominated by issue-oriented activists whose positions appeal only to specific segments of the population (and small segments at that), it appears that the system would no longer operate at optimal levels. In the past this has led to the emergence of a new party system.

Key's defense of organizational structure as the safeguard against extremism is sufficient if ideologues are controlled by professionals. But which of the latter groups will dominate a centralized bureaucracy, and what role will other elements in the system—government, state and local parties, special-interest groups, and the electorate—have in the struggle?

As has been noted, it is not in the interest of either the executive or the legislative branch to have strong national parties; it would mean interference neither is willing to accept. On the other hand, there may be no option if campaigns for federal office are dependent on the services provided by the national parties. Public financing of congressional campaigns would alleviate some of the financial dependence, but cash contributions are only a part of what the national parties have to offer. And, of course, the more legislation and regulation there is, the greater the need for technical advice and assistance.

Although state and local politics have historically dominated the national parties, they seem now to be at a serious disadvantage to stem the trend toward centralization, partly because of the greater complexity of both the law and the technology, and partly because of the voluntary nature of many of these local activities. Since only part of the reason for the centralizing of activity has to do with state and local parties, they are a weak brake.

An even weaker brake on the nationalizing trend are the special interest groups (including corporate, labor, and trade association PACs). They do not act in consort, and they cannot offer the kinds of services the national parties can. Labor is in a particularly difficult situation now, given the increase in business money to candidates which weakens its influence on Democrats. None of the interest groups have the strength or the legitimacy of the parties, despite the greater vigor they appear to possess.

The most important group is the electorate, and here a certain paradox appears in relation to the new strength of the national parties: what gets money loses votes. Although there are certainly enough people willing to respond to appeals for funds on expressive moral issues, in all likelihood such appeals will not be very far-reaching. If they were, there would be little need for the intensity of emotion they generate. On the other hand, if the direct mail solicitations by the parties and the special-interest groups succeed in "educating" American citizens, the proportion of issue-intensive persons in the electorate may increase. And if the nation seriously loses confidence in its institutions and in the ability of individuals to succeed, the moderate, consensus-oriented focus most typical of the electorate may erode to the point of instability. At that point, a two-party system dependent on issue appeals will not work to the restoration of stability. It will accentuate the instability.

The changes in the national party structure suggested in these pages have come about because of minor manipulations of the electoral process, and because of relatively minor changes in organizational processes. For all the energy devoted over the years to party reform, the most profound reform may well be due to incidental, unintended occurrences. This phenomenon is not uncommon in organizations, and it may be significant for the party system as a whole.

A professional, centralized national party system may be a very positive step forward in overcoming the fragmentation, frustration, and alienation which appear to be plaguing the country, assuming that party influence in candidate selection would lead to stronger candidates for office. Such an organizational structure would play to the strengths of a two-party system by providing the electorate with realistic and reasonable choices.

Whether America can sustain such a party system depends on a variety of external factors, including the size and homogeneity of the nation, the federal system, and the constitutional separation of powers. A highly centralized national party, even one controlled by ideologues, would have to be able to take into account local diversity and allow candidates for public office at the federal level to represent constituency interests, even if those positions contradicted national goals.

The separation of powers is an even more important element in the decentralized nature of American parties. National party platforms are written at party presidential nominating conventions by people elected at the local level. Even if a presidential nominee accepts the platform over which he or she has rather limited control and wins office, neither the candidate nor the electorate can be sure of enactment of the party's programs because that would require the cooperation of at least one other branch of government. Despite aspirations to emulate parliamentary parties, a nonparliamentary system makes it impossible for issue-oriented parties to be truly responsible.

Lipset suggests there may be an even more basic motivation for decentralization in some of our most important institutions: the Protestant value of individual responsibility, and what has become our cultural antipathy (albeit sometimes latent) to strong central national government.[41] Even as our expectations rise in government's ability to solve problems, so, too, does our resentment at the intrusion it makes in our lives. A nationalized party, providing services and intervening in candidate selection at the local level, may lead to considerable resentment. On the other hand, it is also possible that this cultural trait of ours, cited fairly early by Tocqueville, is due to the vast size and heterogeneity of the population, a heterogeneity which may be declining with the growth of national media.

The dilemma between the desire for local control and individual responsibility on the one hand, and the expectation and acceptance of national action on the other, extends to more than the party system. Until recently, it has not been an issue for the national parties, but that may be changing.

---

[41] Seymour Martin Lipset, "The Paradox of American Politics," *The Public Interest,* no. 41 (Fall 1975).

State Public Financing
and the State Parties

Ruth S. Jones

The role of money in U.S. electoral politics has been at the heart of post-Watergate election reform. Many of the significant changes that have been made in rules governing federal and state campaign finance are refinements or extensions of existing regulations or traditional approaches to controlling political money. However, an important new dimension, public financing of election campaigns, has been added to U.S. electoral politics. In less than a decade of reform, public financing of election campaigns, the "ultimate tool in the election reformer's arsenal,"[1] has become established public policy in presidential elections, has been adopted by seventeen states, and is under active consideration in at least four other states.[2]

Advocates of public campaign financing argue that the infusion of public money into the state election process will enhance and strengthen the democratic character of elections.[3] They suggest that public campaign finance legislation will increase equity in access to and use of campaign funds, that it will reduce the costs of election campaigns, and that it will limit elected officials' dependence (or the appearance of dependence) on large contributors to campaign finances.

Opponents of public campaign financing challenge these conclusions and argue that present ills will not be remedied, but that new biases will be introduced into the present process. Labeling public finance as an "incumbent's protectionist act," opponents suggest that rather than making the electoral system more open for new ideas and faces, most

---

[1] Herbert E. Alexander, *Campaign Money: Reform and Reality in the States* (New York: Free Press, 1976), p. 10.

[2] The states of Iowa, Maine, Rhode Island, and Utah passed public campaign financing legislation in 1973; the 1974 amendments to the Federal Election Campaign Act provided for public financing of U.S. presidential elections. Puerto Rico has had public campaign financing since 1957, and eight Western nations have some form of campaign or party subsidies.

[3] Public campaign financing is variously referred to as public funding, public subsidies, or tax supports for elections, and these terms are used interchangeably to refer to campaign funds voluntarily contributed by citizens using a governmentally sponsored collection mechanism, the income tax return.

283

subsidy policies will work to the advantage of the status quo and may even retard the free flow of ideas by limiting how much can be spent to wage a campaign. If the opponents are correct, public campaign financing would introduce new obstacles to "sustaining candidate and party activities, maintaining the viability of opposition, and curbing the unrepresentativeness of financial constituencies in politics."[4] Clearly, the debate over public financing of elections raises questions that cut to the heart of democratic elections—questions of fairness and equity, of representation and accountability.

No complete discussion of public campaign financing can ignore these important and interrelated issues. Yet one additional area, the relationship of public campaign financing to political parties, seems of particular importance. The traditional roles of the political parties have included recruiting candidates, raising campaign funds, and mobilizing election day support for their candidates. These and other closely related functions of the party can be challenged by the introduction of public campaign financing.

The purpose of this discussion is threefold: to call attention to the fact that public financing of election campaigns is spreading across the nation at the state level; to note that state policies already in place represent creative and diverse ways of approaching the issues involved in public financing; and to explore the implications for the political party of the different ways states have chosen to answer four central questions in setting their public campaign finance policies.

Focus on the Parties and the States

We know that there are frequently sharp differences between what is intended and what is accomplished by reform legislation. For example, reforms affecting the nominating convention in presidential selection, the growth of direct primaries, and the move to nonpartisan elections all resulted in unintended or unanticipated consequences that had far-reaching implications.[5] We suspect that not all the changes brought about through various campaign finance reforms will be intentional or expected and that the political parties—generally ignored in the discus-

---

[4] David W. Adamany, *Campaign Finance in America* (North Scituate, Mass.: Duxbury Press, 1972), p. 215.

[5] See Austin Ranney, *Curing the Mischiefs of Faction: Party Reform in America* (Berkeley: University of California Press, 1975); Jeane Jordan Kirkpatrick, *Dismantling the Parties: Reflections on Party Reform and Party Decomposition* (Washington, D.C.: American Enterprise Institute for Public Policy Research, 1978); Austin Ranney, *The Federalization of Presidential Primaries* (Washington, D.C.: American Enterprise Institute for Public Policy Research, 1978).

sion of public financing policies—may be the big winners or losers depending on how the public financing game is played.

Without taking the position that political parties are essential to responsible democratic government, the fact remains that all federal and state elections in this country are organized around and legally tied to partisan organizations. Moreover, American parties traditionally have focused more on electoral and campaign activities, including providing resources for campaigns, than on any other single activity. This partisan base of elections makes it difficult, if not impossible, to consider any change in the election campaign process without relating it to political parties. Statutes that alter the traditional funding mechanisms of partisan elections will almost certainly affect the political parties.

When the problem is seen as a contest for power between political organizations and candidates, the introduction of public finance probably has the least impact on the party at the level of presidential elections. Historically the power of the national party as an independent organizational entity has always been limited, and within the party of the incumbent president it has been virtually nonexistent. Consequently, it is not surprising that the debate over public campaign finance at the presidential level has not highlighted the possible consequences for party.

The introduction of public campaign subsidies at the state level is quite a different matter. The state organization is, or can be, uniquely important in party affairs. Where it is strong it makes an impact on presidential nominations as well as on the variety of elections for state-wide and lesser offices. Variations in the actual strength of state party organizations and the importance of those variations for electoral politics—as well as in other arenas—is unmistakable.[6] It is those variations that may be affected by state public campaign finance policies.

There are also sound normative, methodological, and practical reasons for focusing our consideration of public financing on state election campaigns. The ideal of democratic elections is not confined to national elections. Concerns about the openness, equity, and choice characteristics of our electoral process are certainly as relevant to state elections as they are to national elections. Because each state has the power to regulate its own elections, states have devised unique public financing policies which address specific needs.

In the case of public campaign financing, we can view states as "laboratories of reform" in which the diverse provisions of and experi-

---

[6] V. O. Key, Jr., *Politics, Parties and Pressure Groups* (New York: Thomas Y. Crowell, 1958); Malcolm E. Jewell and David M. Olson, *American State Political Parties and Elections* (Homewood, Ill.: Dorsey Press, 1978); and Robert J. Huckshorn, *Party Leadership in the States* (Amherst, Mass.: University of Massachusetts Press, 1976).

ences with alternative forms of public campaign finance policies can be readily compared and assessed. An examination of public financing at the state level will also be of practical assistance to citizens, scholars, and policy makers in states in which public financing is part of the current legislative agenda.

Although activity with respect to other aspects of election finance reform has slowed, public subsidies are one aspect of this reform movement that continues to spread. Hawaii enacted a comprehensive public campaign finance bill during the 1979 session, and the Oklahoma legislature devised a more limited but unique subsidy program in 1979 as well; in 1978 Seattle opted for the first public finance program for municipal elections; and numerous states have created special commissions to consider public campaign finance policies. Three states had an operative public campaign finance program as early as the 1974 elections; three states only began programs with the 1978 elections (see Table 1). After the 1980 elections, one-third of the states will have conducted election campaigns supported in part or in full by public subsidies.

TABLE 1
PUBLIC CAMPAIGN FINANCE, 1977

Year Adopted	State	Allocations Made	Percent of Taxpayer Participation, 1977	Total Dollars Raised, 1977
1973	Iowa	1974–78	19.00	$222,600
1973	Maine	1974–78	0.54	3,393
1973	Rhode Island	1974–78	23.00[a]	113,066[a]
1973	Utah	1975–78	11.00[a]	82,686[b]
1974	Maryland	—	2.25	129,416
1974	Minnesota	1976, 1978	19.83	451,512
1974	New Jersey	1977	38.00[a]	1,430,000[a]
1975	Idaho	1976, 1978	11.73	62,270[a]
1975	Massachusetts	1978	4.07	93,635
1975	Montana	1976	23.25	78,380
1975	North Carolina	1977–78	8.81	261,688
1976	Kentucky	1977–78	10.40	175,387
1976	Michigan	1978	26.00[a]	248,000[a]
1977	Oregon	1978	24.48	256,095
1977	Wisconsin	1978	25.00	459,461

NOTE: Data are for the tax year of 1977; state differences in bookkeeping procedures argue against using these data for absolute comparisons between states.
[a] Figures are not official but represent informed estimates.
[b] Utah figures are for fiscal year 7/1/77 to 6/30/78.

RUTH S. JONES

A Partial Taxonomy of Statutory Provisions

One can develop an understanding of public campaign financing as theory and as policy by looking at four questions that all policy makers must answer in formulating a public campaign subsidy program. In drafting legislation to create public finance programs, state legislatures have had to decide:

- How should funds be generated?
- Who should have what responsibility for administering and enforcing the law?
- Which elections and offices should be subsidized?
- Who should receive the funds, and under what conditions?

We can achieve a feel for the present and potential diversity among state statutes and make some general observations about the juxtaposition of public campaign policies and the future of the political parties by comparing some of the ways the various public finance statutes have thus far dealt with these four questions.

How Should Public Funds Be Generated? The method of collecting funds is important because it determines how much money can be raised and how stable this source of funds is likely to be.

Money for election campaign subsidies can be raised through (1) a regular legislative appropriation which sets aside money for use in campaigns (with no special collecting mechanism used to generate additional public funds); (2) an income tax add-on system where the income tax form merely provides a vehicle for taxpayers to pay a small additional tax earmarked for election campaign support; or (3) an income tax checkoff system where taxpayers can earmark part of their normal tax liability to be set aside for use in election campaigns.

Regular legislative appropriation has received little support. Only in the case of New Jersey's first subsidized election did specific legislative appropriation activity play a role. When a New Jersey state income tax was passed in 1976, a checkoff system was added to generate campaign funding. As a consequence, New Jersey is the only state with a back-up campaign financing mechanism, but, because it has the highest participation rate of all checkoff programs, it is least likely to need a back-up system.

The add-on system is used only in Maine, Massachusetts, Maryland, and Montana; all others use some form of the checkoff system. The add-on systems not only have not gained widespread support, but also have provided very limited amounts of money for public campaign

287

funding. The experiences with checkoff systems vary considerably among states; in 1977 Michigan raised almost $2,500,000, whereas Kentucky raised only a little more than $175,000. Taxpayer participation has ranged from 9 percent in North Carolina to 38 percent in New Jersey. Within single states, however, the participation rates have been reasonably stable.

There are several possible explanations for why participation in the checkoff systems differ so among states. The political culture and context of the state is probably a significant factor. Participation in the checkoff system is lowest in North Carolina, a traditional, southern, one-party state where primary elections (not subsidized by the program) frequently are the arena of electoral choice. Participation is highest in New Jersey, a competitive, active party state but with political traditions and cultural characteristics quite different from North Carolina.

The success of public financing policies in raising money may also vary according to the efforts that officials and party leaders make to familiarize taxpayers with the program. People from state agencies and party leaders in Iowa, Utah, and Michigan, for example, feel that their efforts to educate citizens and encourage understanding and use of the checkoff systems have paid off.

There is also some evidence that the specific method of placing the checkoff system on the tax form influences the rate of participation. All states include the checkoff on the face of the tax form, and all but North Carolina placed it among the first few entries. Utah's experience, however, indicates that requiring a signature near the campaign-fund entry on the tax form depresses participation in the checkoff. Five states, all with above average rates of participation, require the taxpayer to make an expression of "no contribution," whereas the others assume the absence of a positive action means the taxpayer does not choose to participate. Officials in the "no contribution" states believe that when forced to make a "yes or no" decision, the taxpayer is more likely to think about the alternatives and ultimately decide to participate in the checkoff program. It appears that the mechanics of revenue collection, as well as the political context of the states, are related to wide variations in the rates of taxpayer participation and therefore the amount that such programs can provide for the electoral process.

Who Should Administer and Enforce? Who should administer the program and what powers of enforcement are necessary have been among the more controversial issues of state public campaign finance. Responsibility for administration and enforcement of public campaign financing has been located in established state agencies such as the Office of the

Secretary of State, as in Oregon and Utah, or in the Board of Examiners, as in Idaho. The most popular approach, however, has been to include public subsidy programs under the jurisdiction of an agency specifically created to deal with the administration and enforcement of all campaign finance laws. These agencies may be a commission of several people, as the Kentucky Registry of Election Finance, or the responsibility of a single director, as in Massachusetts.

Agency administrative tasks include routine clerical duties, conducting audits, sponsoring educational programs, arbitrating controversies during the heat of political campaigns, and litigating controversial administrative rulings. For example, the Minnesota Ethical Practices Board compiled and published extensive reports on candidate contributions and expenditures for 1976 and 1978; the New Jersey Election Law Enforcement Commission approved eighteen advisory opinions in 1977 on topics ranging from the commingling of primary and general campaign accounts to assigning costs of voter registration and get-out-the-vote drives by national and local political party organizations.[7]

The enforcement powers of these agencies or commissions range from no specifications of oversight functions or sanctions regarding public finance, as in North Carolina, to detailed powers to investigate, audit, subpoena, and refer violations to the proper law enforcement officials. In Montana, the commissioner reports violations to the appropriate county attorney, but if no action is taken in thirty days the commissioner has the power to hire attorneys to prosecute, and these attorneys have the same status as a special attorney general.

Which Elections Should Be Subsidized? Selecting the elections to receive public financing means deciding whether to go for breadth or depth (or both) in the coverage of public financing legislation. In New Jersey, for example, public financing in 1977 was available only to the gubernatorial general election candidates, whereas the Wisconsin and Minnesota statutes extended coverage to major statewide positions, as well as to state legislative races. The 1977 gubernatorial nominees of the two major New Jersey parties received a combined total of $2,070,816, but only $76,960 in public financing was available to the 1978 Wisconsin gubernatorial candidates. Almost $350,000 was, however, available to help finance state legislative races in Wisconsin, whereas New Jersey's legislative candidates had access to no public funds. The New Jersey statute gave priority to reducing the potential influence of large private

---

7 New Jersey Election Law Enforcement Commission, *Public Financing in New Jersey: The 1977 General Election for Governor* (Trenton, N.J., 1978).

contributions in the gubernatorial election process. The Wisconsin statute provided funds for legislative races where funding a campaign frequently is difficult for candidates of limited personal wealth and no ties to special interest groups. In Hawaii, Maryland, Minnesota, and Wisconsin, the priority has been given to encouraging wider candidate participation in the electoral process by providing greater equity in resources all along the election continuum.

The theoretical grounds for public financing of primaries are convincing because primary elections are frequently the place where real electoral choices are made. If a goal of finance reform is to increase alternative choice through a greater competition of candidates and ideas, then primary elections which permit a multiplicity of candidates are logical targets of campaign financing policies. Yet only three states, Hawaii, Michigan, and Massachusetts, currently provide public finance subsidies for primary campaigns because the reality of public financing at this level is one of costs—costs to the state and possibly even to the public policy of providing campaign subsidies.

The state must bear increased administrative costs when subsidies are available to a multiplicity of candidates in the primaries. In 1978 the Massachusetts commission had to keep track of public finance requests and reports from twelve candidates, while in Wisconsin, no primary candidates required time or attention from the monitoring agency vis-à-vis public funds. The administration of primary funding is also more elaborate because a procedure for differentiating legitimate from frivolous candidates is required. This is accomplished in Michigan by a requirement that candidates accept expenditure limitations and raise 5 percent ($50,000) of this ceiling in qualifying contributions of $100 or less. In Massachusetts, candidates must raise specified amounts according to the office (the governor's requirement is $75,000) in qualifying contributions of $250 or less. In Hawaii, state legislative candidates must raise $500 in private funds to qualify for $100 in public money—the maximum permitted for their office.

A serious threat to public finance as a viable public policy lies in the challenges that extended depth or breadth raise for the credibility of arguments made on behalf of public finance. When funds are spread over both the primary and general elections and over a large number of election contests, the amount of public dollars available to each campaign is diminished and the significance of public financing reduced. The narrower, more concentrated the allocation of public funds, the greater the likelihood that public finance money will be a dominant force in the election. For practical purposes, the question becomes which offices and which elections will be eligible for public subsidies.

Although Maryland was one of the first states to adopt public campaign financing, its program is so all encompassing that the add-on collecting procedure has not generated funds enough to activate the subsidy program for any election. There is a danger that when the amount of public money relative to other money is very small, public financing dollars get lost in the shuffle rather than becoming a trump card. If public funds are not sufficient to make a quantitative difference in financing the campaign, they may not be sufficient to make the qualitative difference in the election process that finance reformers seek.

Who Should Receive Public Money? Determining whether public subsidies will be given to the political parties or to the individual candidates and under what conditions this money will be allocated for what uses presents significant alternative choices to policy makers. Eight "party" states currently allocate campaign funds to political parties; eight "candidate" states give directly to candidates; and Oklahoma's new statute calls for funds raised by the checkoff system to be divided between candidates and parties.[8]

The tax forms used to collect funds vary in ways relevant to allocating money. First, all candidate states except Minnesota now collect checkoff money through a general campaign fund such as the "Fair Campaign Financing Fund" of Maryland. All party states, except Oklahoma, permit the taxpayer to designate a party preference. Five states make it possible for third or minor parties to receive designated tax funds (Idaho allocated funds to twelve different parties in 1975), and three party states permit the taxpayer to mark an "unspecified" or "general account" entry. These unspecified funds are not, as some taxpayers may assume, for nonpartisan or independent candidates. To the contrary, in North Carolina the money in this unspecified fund is divided among the political parties according to voter registration; in Idaho they are divided on the basis of party vote for governor in the last election; and in Rhode Island this money is allocated to the parties using a formula that is weighted according to electoral success for each general state office and the combined total vote in the preceding election. It is of some concern to party leaders in Rhode Island and Idaho that the money designated to the general or unspecified fund exceeds that designated

8 Montana has experimented with several variations of public campaign financing. The original 1975 bill allocated money to the political parties but specified its use for the gubernatorial campaign; in 1977 this law was amended to provide for allocations of checkoff money to campaigns "as specified by the legislature" (and then the legislature specified none); in 1979 the law was rewritten to allocate public money to candidates for governor and supreme court justices, to change to an add-on system of collections, and to eliminate expenditure ceilings.

to either of the two major parties, and the recent increase in designations for the unspecified account in North Carolina worries a few Democrats there.

In candidate states, there is always a screening mechanism (as in states where public subsidies are used in the primary) to prevent the use of money by irresponsible candidates. These procedures range from financing only certified primary election winners (Minnesota and Montana) to requiring that qualifying contributions of a specific amount be raised through small contributions as in Wisconsin and Massachusetts. The candidates may receive money through a flat grant (some percentage of the ceiling amount specified for each office), as in Oklahoma or Minnesota, or they may receive public dollars according to a matching-funds formula, as in New Jersey or Maryland. Michigan uses a matching system in the primary and a flat grant in the general election, whereas Montana divides the money in the general fund equally among all eligible candidates for the office. In party states the money is usually transferred to designated representatives of the party's state central committee. In Oregon and Utah, however, the statutes specify that the county party committees receive a certain share of the checkoff funds.

Party state statutes differ more among themselves in terms of establishing timetables for receipt of funds, internal allocation procedures, and specification of constraints attached to public funds than do the "candidate states." Utah's political parties only receive checkoff funds early in August in the even-numbered years; Rhode Island's parties get an annual appropriation in early September; and Iowa's parties receive monthly transfers from the state treasurer.

In party states, the decision as to which candidates will receive what kind of support is left to the parties. In several states the state central committees decide how to allocate funds; in Idaho, the Republican party's decision is made by a five-person committee which includes state legislative leaders. In North Carolina, the statute specifies that the state party chairman and treasurer shall serve ex officio on a committee made up of the party's nominees for all offices eligible to receive public funds; thus the nominees make the decisions on the allocation of the party's checkoff funds.

Although most state statutes prohibit the use of public funds for party organization–related nominations and elections and specify that public funds be used for "legitimate expenses," the constraints on the ways parties are permitted to use public funds differ considerably. In Idaho, the party *must* use public funds for candidate support; in Rhode Island, the parties are *prohibited* from using public campaign money for candidate support. In North Carolina, examples of legitimate campaign expenses for which public funds might be used, such as radio, television, newspaper and billboard advertising, campaign staff salaries, and candidate and staff travel expenses, are included in the statute, but Maine's statute neither prescribes nor prohibits how this money may be employed by the parties. Consequently, public money is used in a variety of ways. Table 2 provides a summary of how states differ on these statutory provisions and serves as a referent for relating public subsidy policies to political parties.

Public Campaign Financing and State Parties

The preceding discussion of provisions of state campaign financing policies identifies some of the areas in which public subsidies can be expected to influence political party organization and behavior. Public

TABLE 2
STATUTORY PROVISIONS FOR PUBLIC FINANCING OF STATE ELECTIONS

States	Check-off (C) or Add-on (A)	New Agency (N) or Established (E)	Money to Parties (P) or Candidates (C)	Uses Specified (S) or Unrestricted (U)[a]	Percent of Offices Covered
Idaho	C	E	P	S	open
Iowa	C	N	P	U	open
Hawaii[b]	C	N	C	U	83+
Kentucky	C	N	P	U	open
Maine	A	N	P	U	open
Maryland[b]	A	N	C	U	192+
Massachusetts[b]	A	N	C	U	6
Michigan[b]	C	E	C	U	1
Minnesota	C	N	C	U	207
Montana	A	N	C	U	2
New Jersey	C	N	C	S	1
North Carolina	C	E	P	U	open
Oklahoma	C	N	P/C	U	8
Oregon	C	E	P	S	open
Rhode Island	C	E	P	S	0
Utah	C	E	P	U	open
Wisconsin	C	E	C	S	139

[a] The law either excludes broad areas of traditional expenditures or narrowly limits how or by whom funds are to be used.

[b] Hawaii and Maryland laws extend to local-level elections; Massachusetts, Michigan, and Hawaii finance both primary and general elections.

financing, particularly the scope and the allocation provisions, appears likely to have the most direct and immediate influence on the internal or organizational aspects of political parties—financial independence, budgeting and planning, staffing and services, and party centralization and cohesion are all affected. The impact of public subsidies on election activities is probably more indirect, although the amount, uses, and constraints introduced by public money clearly influence the role parties play in election campaigns.

The novelty of campaign subsidies and our lack of information concerning their role in American electoral politics means that any current discussion of the impact of these subsidy programs must be tentative and incomplete. The present discussion is based on selected aggregate data from public records and on personal observations and conversations with various election officials and party leaders in public campaign finance states. It is meant to be illustrative rather than definitive concerning the relationship between state public financing and political parties, and focuses on resource availability and budgeting, organizational strength, fund raising, and electoral activities.

First, it is important to acknowledge that partisanship influences campaign finance policies; this follows because public campaign finance policies, like all state legislation, are a product of a partisan political process. In spite of the fact that supporters and opponents of public campaign finance are found in all parties and debates on subsidies for election campaigns often evoke philosophical rather than partisan themes, state legislatures are partisan bodies with specific interests to protect. The bias against third or minority parties and independent candidates that permeates many of the campaign financing statutes is a clear example. In party states the design of the collection mechanism on the tax form and the provisions for allocating "unspecified" funds work in favor of the existing party systems, if not to the benefit of the majority party. Public financing has tended to raise more money for the Democrats than for the Republicans. This differentiation in partisan impact has frequently made Republicans less supportive of public campaign subsidies than Democrats.

The most obvious feature of public campaign financing programs, in terms of party budgets, is that they represent new sources of political money. These resources are "new" in that they represent both additional amounts and additional origins for campaign funds. Clearly, how states raise campaign funds determines, in part, how sizable the increases or changes in campaign finance patterns will be. The checkoff raises more than the add-on and a $2 checkoff more than a $1 contribution. Regardless of the mechanism, however, public subsidies are a new source of funds—whether it means $3,500 in Maine or $2,500,000 in Michigan. But it appears that, as in other public subsidy programs, the recipients soon become dependent on public funds, and public campaign dollars cease to be "new" and become "necessary." One party leader admitted, "Public money is a vital link in our whole financing process; we depend on it. We couldn't get along without the checkoff money."

Public money also represents a new source of campaign funds in that it expands the base of political contributors. In every state, public subsidy programs based on the checkoff seem to elicit contributions from citizens who do not otherwise provide financial support for elections; those who regularly have supported political campaign activities apparently continue to make their private contributions as well as participate in the checkoff system. At the same time, the fact that taxpayer participation is highest in candidate states and that within party states the "unspecified" contributions are often higher than party contributions suggests that party per se may be a restraining influence on participation in public campaign finance programs.

The stability, as well as the extent, of new funding is also important. There is potential uncertainty in depending on the preferences of taxpayers; yet the record of checkoff systems indicates that taxpayers' allocations remain relatively steady within states and among parties. Indeed, these funds may be far more predictable than responses to traditional fund-raising appeals; they certainly are more cost-efficient for the parties.

Additional resources that are relatively stable permit the parties to estimate a minimum revenue base each year, and this encourages systematic budgeting and long-range planning. "We can finally plan and budget a little without having to cross our fingers," was the way one party official assessed the impact of public money. State party officials have noted that public financing also provides "early dollars," which make it possible to arrange for media time, to schedule printing, and to perform routine tasks in a systematic manner rather than in the usual, frantic if-we-get-the-money approach. One official reported that creditors (even banks) were more cooperative because they knew that the party would receive a substantial sum from the checkoff and thus could pay its bills.

But even a stable new source of campaign money affects political parties quite differently depending on how it is allocated. When money goes directly to candidates, the impact on parties appears to be mixed. If parties lose the influence they previously exercised vis-à-vis a particular campaign because their role as fund raisers has been usurped, then the parties' position is no doubt diminished. If, however, parties traditionally had shared organization resources with, for example, the gubernatorial candidate but had little or no influence on the candidate's campaign, they have been freed of a frustrating obligation by the presence of a public subsidy, and their role may actually be enhanced.

On the other hand, because all candidate financing systems require qualifying or matching funds, the candidates continue to compete with the party for funds and can use the "carrot" of pending state money to encourage contributions. Thus far, no state has devised a matching system in which parties would be able to raise funds with a similar incentive mechanism. The less a candidate has to augment public funds with private contributions, the less the party is likely to suffer, but whenever candidates continue to compete for contributions, the party qua party has a more difficult time raising campaign money.

Party organizations seldom are directly involved in financing primary campaigns, but if public funds entice numerous candidates into the primary and all candidates must raise qualifying money, sources of political money may be drained before general election fund raising even begins. In one state that experienced a crowded, intensely fought primary, the party did not even attempt a campaign fund raiser until well into the general election campaign—and thus fell far short of the fundraising goal. Certainly, party officials are more negative about direct subsidies to candidates than candidates seem to be about direct grants to parties. One leader in a candidate state said, "The party doesn't mean much anymore; they don't raise the money so they can't control the candidate. Parties that have no money have no power," while an official in a party state predicted that "if the money went to the governor, he'd be just that much more independent—the party wouldn't be needed at all."

Our initial, albeit unsystematic, inquiry provides considerable support for the conclusion that when the parties are bypassed in the funding of campaigns, the force of the party in the election campaign process is diminished. On the other hand, when money is given to the political parties, whether the use of such money is narrowly specified or not, the party appears to become a stronger political organization and a more significant force in campaigns.

In several states where public subsidies have been used for such general operating expenses as hiring staff and paying rent, public funds have apparently had a great impact. The wherewithal to hire permanent, full-time or more qualified staff is critical to state organizations for an active state party headquarters, and staff is viewed by most party leaders as the key to expanding the influence and status of the party. Party leaders make comments such as: "We couldn't operate a party headquarters without it." "No question but that the money from the checkoff is critical to the state organization. It provides 70 percent of our budget."

Parties have also used public money to finance party leadership training sessions and to recruit candidates. One party successfully recruited winning candidates by promising specific campaign assistance from the public money the party leaders knew was forthcoming. "These funds have helped to attract good candidates to run for the state legislature in both 1976 and 1978," the leaders said, adding that the checkoff "enhanced the party's role in the campaign process."[9] And one party has even gone so far as to require candidates who request funds from the party's public campaign money to provide a written outline of their campaign strategy and to specify how the public funds will be used. The state organization then uses this to encourage the use of the local or state party organization and to coordinate campaign activities as well as to evaluate the benefit derived from using "party" resources in the campaign. In Kentucky, public funds have been an important source for paying the mortgage on a new state party headquarters, and in North Carolina, checkoff funds have helped purchase a computer. In both cases, party officials viewed these expenditures as facilitating campaign coordination and efficiency.

These new resources also enable state committees to coordinate campaigns, and they have permitted the state organization to be active in more electoral areas. "Before public financing there was no way the state party could promise a dime to a state legislative race—we had to put all our efforts in congressional and statewide races. Now we can guarantee help if a candidate can make it through the primary. Often candidates then use public monies as a 'starter' and it stimulates them to go out and raise more money."[10]

Many state organizations have targeted key races and have used public money to make an all-out effort to spend (and win) in certain districts. Under these conditions, the presence of public money has meant an increase in campaign expenditures. Most party leaders agree that the more money they have, the more money they will spend for campaign purposes. This suggests that public funds, by bringing new resources into politics, merely add to the escalation of election campaign expenditures. The balancing argument, of course, is that public funds can include ceilings which retard spending. However, this argument is most meaningful when ceilings are low and funds are allocated directly to candidates rather than parties. Party leaders have many alternative

---

[9] New Jersey Election Law Enforcement Commission, *Public Financing in New Jersey.*
[10] Ibid.

ways to use public money and are unlikely to reach dollar ceilings in all the campaigns in which they have an interest. In a state like North Carolina, where there is a limit on the amount any one party can get from the public financing program, the party's "ceiling" has been raised almost annually.

In general it seems that when use of public money is restricted by law, parties frequently respond simply through restructuring their financial procedures. Accounts that formerly were used for operating budget expenses become campaign accounts and public money picks up the operating expenses, or vice versa. Clearly, there is no evidence that overall party expenditures have been decreased by the presence of a public campaign financing policy.

Fund-raising strategies, budgeting, and party electoral activities are also affected according to which offices and which elections are eligible for public funds. When the most expensive campaign in the state is largely financed with public funds, as in New Jersey or Michigan, the party's fund-raising energies may be freed to focus on other campaigns. But this also means that the parties may yield control over fund raising and expenditures to the gubernatorial candidates. This was evident in the 1977 New Jersey campaign where "neither campaign budgeted near the maximum allowable for party spending because of the desire of both candidates to maintain control over expenditures within the $1.5 million limit. To this extent local party units were denied flexibility in their own expenditures relative to the gubernatorial candidate."[11] Losing the obligation of fund raising has also meant losing an opportunity. In Michigan, the loss of the party's ability to utilize the governor fully as a drawing card for fund raising has made raising money much more difficult for the party.

When the campaigns covered by public funding are numerous as in Minnesota and the amount of money raised by the checkoff is modest relative to total campaign costs, the need to raise funds across the entire range of campaigns persists. In this case, the constraints and the record keeping associated with public financing complicate the political financing role of the party, and the funds available provide negligible relief from fund-raising tasks.

The cohesion of political parties can be challenged when public subsidies are used to finance primary campaigns. To the extent that public funding encourages competition within the party, it can serve as a vehicle for fragmentation. One Michigan party official felt there was no question but that the opportunity for public financing of primary

---

[11] Ibid., p. 25.

campaign candidates had doubled the number of Democrats who entered the gubernatorial primary; his assessment was that such a campaign "sure didn't make the party any stronger." Another party official, commenting on the multiplicity of candidates in a subsidized primary campaign, lamented, "It will take us a long, long time to recover—if we ever do."

There is also the possibility that infusion of new resources could cause disagreement within the party over how to use these new party-controlled funds. To date, there appears to be little friction associated with the internal allocation of public funds. For the most part, party activists in party states seem tolerant of, if not happy with, the subsidy policies of their state—even those parties that are in the minority feel that half-a-loaf is better than none. Party leaders in candidate states, however, are much less satisfied, and many are seeking legislative change that would channel at least part of the public campaign funds through the parties.

The activities parties can fund are also affected by the different modes of administration and enforcement of finance laws. When enforcement agencies promulgate rules and regulations concerning how to raise qualifying money, what are allowable party in-kind contributions, and how to define legitimate campaign expenses, the party's activities are shaped accordingly. In New Jersey, where the law specifies that public funds are to be used by the candidates only for specific communication-related expenditures, "the effect of providing public funding and imposing prescribed uses for those public funds was to increase the percentage of total campaign expenditures spent for communication purposes."[12] The fact that the New Jersey Election Law Enforcement Commission played an active role in the 1977 campaign through its rulings related to the use of public funds clearly affected the behavior of both the candidate and the party regarding this aspect of the statute.

States in which a reasonably large budget and staff are allocated to a new agency mandated to oversee the campaign finance law tend to have more rigorous, active administration and enforcement of finance laws; a comparable level of activity is more difficult for states where public finance has simply been added to the responsibilities of an existing agency without a corresponding increase to its resources. The more active the agency, the more salient it is likely to be to the day-to-day campaign operations of parties.

Depending on the agency, of course, compliance with finance regulations could become a most time-consuming duty of the party's staff;

---

[12] Ibid., p. 22.

consequently, the amount of attention they have to give to other party matters would be diminished. As regulation over campaign money intensifies, the attention and accountability of party officials may shift from the traditional contributors, constituents, and party elite to a governmental regulatory agency. It is conceivable, moreover, that even the types of people who are selected to serve as state party officials and staff will change. Experienced grass-roots activists whose political expertise is in person-to-person contact, internal party organizational work, and fund raising may be replaced by attorney/accountants whose professional expertise enables them to steer the party through areas of debits and credits, legal interpretations, and compliance mandates.

When a totally new agency is created, there is always an incunabular period in which the new personnel act so as to establish legitimacy and to institutionalize rules and procedures. Because new agencies are centralized in scope and function, it may be easier for party leaders to work with a single agency that centralizes all aspects of campaign finance than to deal directly with the multiple of existing state agencies (departments of Revenue, Treasury, Secretary of State) that are necessarily involved in public financing policies. When established agencies take on the responsibility, however, the actors are not always new and the rules and norms of the office are more likely to follow established patterns. In the latter case party leaders report that they are spared time and effort in learning to deal with a new bureaucracy. But established state agencies are often headed by partisan officials, whereas new agencies are usually created in the spirit of neutrality and bipartisanship. For minority parties, the new agency may be psychologically, if not politically, more acceptable. Thus far we have seen no evidence to support the fear that new agencies will "become a political boondoggle as soon as one political party manages to obtain control of the Commission."[13] Special agencies certainly do not please all the politicos all of the time, but they apparently have not yet been coopted and used for partisan gain.

Concluding Comments

The total impact of public financing is, of course, far from clear, but our inquiries suggest that campaign subsidies provide additional political money from new sources. For the parties, the impact of public financing is largely determined by provisions for who shall receive funds and under what conditions. The more control parties have over publicly generated funds, the more influence they have in recruiting and coordinating cam-

---

[13] "Should Tax Dollars Pay for Politics," *U.S. News and World Report,* August 20, 1973, p. 34.

paigns. The more funds to which they have access, the more parties extend the scope of their electoral activities.

Based on our limited experience it would be tempting to conclude that political parties, as political institutions, can be revived and/or strengthened with publicly generated and administered campaign subsidies to political parties. However, such a conclusion is undoubtedly premature because many important questions about the relationship between public campaign financing and political parties remain unanswered. The preceding discussion should merely whet the appetite. For example:

- In states where funds go directly to candidates, will the parties become less centralized organizations with less elaborate bureaucratic infrastructures?
- What happens to the autonomy of county and local party units when the state organization exercises more budget control over, for example, state legislative races?
- Does increased money to parties mean a more professionalized and stable party staff? Does this in turn lead to a more open or closed party organization?
- When party resources increase, do parties begin to rely more on modern technology for assistance in political campaigning and less on grass roots volunteer involvement that traditionally has given the party legitimacy and popular support?
- Does public financing increase or decrease equity in the political process? In campaign contributions and expenditures? Between parties?
- Candidate participation in public campaign financing programs is thus far voluntary. Do some types of candidates utilize these funding opportunities more than others? To what effect? When candidates refuse public money, does the party become more important to the electoral campaign? Do incumbents gain or lose?
- When public money goes to one candidate (usually governor) but not others, does the party become more important to the campaigns of the nonfunded candidates?
- When only one office is eligible for public funding, do the private resources that traditionally would go to that election campaign get diverted to the party? Or to other candidates? Or to neither?
- What is the impact of having expenditure ceilings on some campaigns but not others? Do nonfunded campaign expenditures increase disproportionately to expenditures in publicly funded campaigns?
- Are incumbents protected by public subsidies for political campaigns? Under what conditions?

- When public money is available to candidates, do third parties fare better than when allocations are made to political parties?

There are unanswered questions not only about the impact of public money on political parties, but also about the causes of variation in state statutes that relate to this impact. It may be that some of the relationships between parties and public financing are, in a sense, spurious and that antecedents of public financing legislation formulation are responsible for the differences we have found. For example, the politics of the decision to allocate money to parties rather than to candidates is obviously important to understanding public subsidy and party relationships. One might expect that states in which parties have traditionally been strong would allocate money to parties, and states in which parties have been weak would allocate money directly to candidates. A preliminary look at the evidence, however, suggests otherwise. The candidate states tend to be the states with traditionally strong party systems, and many of the party states are generally considered to have weak party systems.[14] But why? Whatever the reason, understanding *why* some states give public money to parties and some to candidates may be as important to the understanding of public campaign financing as recognizing that states *do differ* on this dimension.

For the proponents and opponents of public campaign financing, these questions may identify strengths or weaknesses in existing policies; for the practicing politician and political analyst, they may provide a framework for structuring future experiences and observations; and for scholars, they may provide a research agenda. For everyone interested in campaign finance reform, they are reminders of how little we know about public campaign financing. Given the incremental nature of change in the American political system, we expect that the jury on the impact of public financing of state election campaigns will probably be out for quite a while.

During this time, examination of the evidence will continue: some will view public campaign subsidies as a cancerous growth in the electoral process that unless stopped will eventually destroy the traditional electoral party campaign process; others will continue to see it as an experiment that will have its day, make a few modest changes, and ultimately fade into political oblivion; and yet others will perceive it as an established part of the electoral process to be accepted and allowed to flourish—for better or worse. Any attempt to reach a verdict today would undoubtedly result in a hung jury.

---

[14] Malcolm E. Jewell and David M. Olson, *American State Political Parties and Elections* (Homewood, Ill.: Dorsey Press, 1978), chap. 2.

Only two very general conclusions about state political parties and public financing of election campaigns seem in order at this time: (1) political parties are indeed influenced by state public campaign financing policies, both directly and indirectly; and (2) the direction and magnitude of the impact of these policies is determined, in large part, by the specific methods states choose to raise, allocate, and oversee public campaign funds.

Commentaries

David Broder

I found the essential argument of both papers quite persuasive. Xandra Kayden makes the case that technological changes and structural changes have had a nationalizing tendency, which is particularly evident in the fairly sophisticated bureaucracy of service organizations that the Republican party has developed. We will probably see some further evolution of that trend on the Republican side as the organizational self-confidence is carried over into the programmatic area. Already the Republican national chairman and the congressional campaign committee chairmen, after studying the operations of the British Conservative party, are formulating a kind of strategic approach rarely seen in an American opposition political party; they are trying to shape a legislative issue—in this case budget and tax policy—into a tool explicitly for public education or for propaganda leading up to a campaign that is still some distance away. We would not have had that kind of strategic thinking unless there was first the centralization, particularly the staff resources, that Xandra Kayden describes in her paper.

In addition, her cautionary remarks about the ideological components of this kind of fund raising and the short time that we have had to observe these phenomena are important. Chairman Bill Brock of the Republican National Committee has already been in several battles with the direct mail fund-raising people. Some of these battles have centered on the competition for money. A particularly interesting one in terms of Ms. Kayden's argument concerned the money raised from a letter on the Panama Canal issue that Ronald Reagan signed. The question was whether the money should be used to fight the Panama Canal issue or whether it should be used for projects that seemed to have a higher utility from the point of view of the political professionals. Brock may have won that battle, but it remains to be seen whether he won the war.

That leads to another point that I would raise just by way of underlining the caution expressed by Ms. Kayden. All the trends that she has identified—and they are accurate in terms of national parties—may change and decline in importance when a party's candidate becomes president. We still do not know whether an organization as sophisticated and self-confident as the Republican National Committee and its congressional adjuncts would immediately become a secondary operation if a Republican were sitting in the White House; whether such an organization would become once again a personal vehicle for the president; or whether it would become simply a factional organization, whose fund-raising efforts might be cut off by other factions in the party that did not support that particular president and his particular policies. The relative weakness of the Democratic party at the present time in all the respects that Ms. Kayden talks about at least suggests that the president's agenda for his party may still be in conflict with the trend that she describes.

My other point is really the same question that Ruth Jones's paper implies. If I understand Ms. Kayden's argument correctly, nationalization trends will inevitably erode the state and local parties. Is that inevitable either logically or practically? Ruth Jones makes at least a preliminary case that public financing has tended to strengthen state party organizations. As one who is very fond of the federalized nature of our party system, I must say just on a wholly subjective basis, that her description of the invigoration of state parties through this new source of funds is the best news that I have heard about party organization in a long time.

Morley Winograd

I do not regard campaign finance laws as inherently evil or automatically beneficial for political parties. It may be my "professional" upbringing, but I think of them as simply another piece of the political equation, a dependent variable subject to manipulation. This is not a good attitude for policy makers or political scientists to take, and certainly should not be the focus of this bipartisan discussion, but it is the way people of my ilk tend to approach the making of campaign finance laws, and this makes the prediction of their future impact or the analysis of their origins shaky at best.

Nevertheless, I do believe that this discussion and the general debate on campaign finance laws can be of great value. These laws should be evaluated on the basis of some set of political values and with some regard for their consequences. This is particularly true because the short-term, selfish political advantage my fellow professionals are always seeking in the process of changing these laws is rarely gained and, if achieved, extremely short-lived.

305

For instance, the Michigan law that publicly funded the 1978 gubernatorial primary was passed because it simultaneously limited those public expenditures for an uncontested primary, which the incumbent Republican governor was sure to have. We Democrats were counting on an increased exposure during the primary for whomever won to help defeat the theoretically ham-strung incumbent. It helped, but not nearly enough. After the defeat of our candidate, we recognized the potential electoral mischief such a system encourages. Now moves are afoot to do away with this portion of our law. I am not saying that an intelligent discussion of the provision's impact would have stopped us from pressing our advantage originally, but it would have at least helped to prepare the public for our subsequent retreat!

The other reason I welcome this discussion is that underneath my veneer of tough professionalism, I must confess, beats the heart of a political scientist. I have a deeply held conviction on the criterion that should be used to judge the wisdom of a particular campaign finance law or amendment. Unlike Ms. Jones, I am ready to defend publicly "the position that political parties are essential to responsible democratic government." To the degree that changes in the law increase the institutional strength of our political parties at any level, I am prepared to support and encourage them out of concern for the future of American democracy. I will try to illustrate here the practical implications of adhering to this criterion.

First, it leads me to disagree with those who are opposed to public funding in any form. As Ms. Jones has correctly pointed out, such laws can be beneficial to political parties. Her paper represents a first attempt to document the nature of this strengthening process when public funds are channeled through the political parties. The effects should continue to be monitored and analyzed, but there is an even more important aspect of this activity at the state level to which she barely alludes.

She finds that somewhat paradoxically those states that have a tradition of relatively weak political parties have adopted "party" as opposed to "candidate" systems of public funding. This can be explained if one thinks about the threat an elected official may perceive in giving money to the Oregon Democratic Party as compared with the threat in giving the same kind of money to the Cook County Democratic Party. Where elected officials have been exposed to the limits that strong parties can impose upon the official's independent decision making, they are naturally reluctant to impose additional restriction upon their ability to make policy. Still by encouraging the adoption of such party-oriented laws in these weak-party states, we can repair the two-party system at its weakest link. It is essential for all who believe in the importance of revitalizing our two-party system to advocate the adoption of party-oriented public funding laws at the state level.

The national level is a little trickier. My own association has attempted to win congressional support for partial public funding for state parties checkoff. Our efforts were blocked by those Democratic committee members who came from states with a history of strong state parties. Of course the defeat was helped along by the short-sighted opposition of the Republican National Committee—but I shall restrain my partisanship. In any case, the alternative public-funding proposal for congressional elections then died a quick and deserved death. Once again the two-party system escaped further harm from its worst enemy: the well-meaning nonpartisan reformer. Still, the difficulties of getting Congress to do anything right gives one pause before advocating the continued pursuit of party-oriented public funding at the federal level.

If you accept my criterion about increasing the institutional strength of parties, you can find yourself saddened by the defeat of the federal checkoff system for political parties and simultaneously gladdened by the defeat of the attempt to extend the "matching-fund" theory of political clout. I am not ready to accept the overwhelming influence that Ms. Kayden ascribes to direct mail in the future development of our national political parties. However, I am prepared to holler "Stop!" to the spread of the insidious notion that causes supported by many individual small contributors are somehow more entitled to the public's subsidy than those whose support comes from a few large contributors or a collection of like-minded citizens who have taken the time to associate themselves into a group. Nothing has contributed more to the atomization of our political process than the requirements of matching funds in our public funding laws, most notably the presidential one. Why shouldn't parties be given the role of qualifying the candidates for public funds? It is the activists within each party who are best able to judge the capabilities of their potential candidates. Their decision for the general election is widely respected and acknowledged in most of the campaign laws, why can't a similar screening mechanism be developed for the primary process? I argue this not because I accept Ms. Kayden's suggestion that Bill Brock (chairman of the Republican National Committee) is my future, but because I think public funding laws offer one of the best hopes for strengthening our parties as well as one of the greatest potential dangers for weakening them.

There are other aspects of campaign laws which can negatively or positively affect political parties. Most provisions of the current federal law have negative effects. Contrary to Ms. Kayden's statements, the current contribution and expenditure limits put more restrictions on political parties than any other player in the political game. Only political parties are restricted in the amount of their independent expenditures. In fact, state parties are theoretically prohibited from making any such expenditures for their presidential and vice-presidential nominees. As political action committees (PACs) gain greater familiarity with this kind of campaign activity, the disadvantage for political parties will increase.

Campaign expenditure is not the only area of the current law which puts parties at a disadvantage. Only some adroit reading of the law by the Federal Election Commission has prevented the full negative impact from being felt by the political parties. The Iowa decision Ms. Kayden mentions is only one of several such key decisions. Hope for reversing this situation now rests with H.R. 5010, adopted just prior to recess by the House Administration Committee, which has the effect of increasing the importance of state parties in federal elections by increasing their freedom to operate in the campaign without undue restrictions and regulations. In addition, it frees most local party committees from any reporting requirements at all, thereby eliminating the chilling effect, which Ms. Kayden correctly identifies, upon local party participation in federal campaigns.

In fact, many of these changes will reverse some of the tendencies in party development described by both papers. And therein lies a very important lesson. As one of the leading "rules freaks" in my party, I am constantly on guard against overrating the real impact of rules or, for that matter, laws upon the final electoral outcome. Both rules and laws are made, if not to be broken, at least to be changed. Usually those changes will occur when the faction or party in control of the process perceives an advantage that can be gained from such a change, and usually the excessive zeal with which such changes are made will create a sufficient backlash to rally the other side to neutralize the advantage by changing the rules or laws again. Right now, the backlash is against direct mail consultants and PAC contributions; before it was political organizations or groupings, particularly political parties. In the future, if Ms. Kayden's predictions come true, it may be against technologically proficient but overcentralized national parties. In any case, none of these changes are likely to effect who is elected president or even how Congress votes. The tinkering may be fun, but its political impact is minimal. And above all it should be recognized in making predictions about impact that the only constant is change.

For that very reason, I believe it is important to rally around one standard and hold that standard high. If we can tinker with the laws to increase the freedom of action of political parties and in some small way strengthen them, we will have increased five-fold the *perception* of their power. It will then be up to us, the small band of issue-oriented, responsible party advocates, to demonstrate how our technologically proficient state and national parties can provide critical services to candidates, and thereby earn our right to be a part of the governing process, not just the campaign. With a little help from the academic community the cause of strengthening one of democracy's most essential volunteer associations, the political parties, can become a rallying cry for reformers of all types across the country. If our elected officials can be properly persuaded, then we can use this "mass movement" to reach the day when the power will be, if not in our hands, then at least in the eyes of the beholder. For American democracy, that day cannot come too soon.

Steven F. Stockmeyer

The current federal election law has had minimal effects on the structure and approach of our two major political parties, although its consequences do vary between the parties and among the various levels of party organization. Of course, any current assessment must not fail to consider that important elements of the law have been changed almost every year of its brief history. In my opinion, the law is mainly a constant nuisance and frequently an unnecessary hindrance to legitimate and effective party action. Of course, nuisances and hindrances can develop into something much worse over time, and that potential accounts for most of my concern.

The effects on the parties of the law itself, and particularly its creation, the Federal Election Commission, might best be compared to the old medical practice of leeching. If someone had a malady, real or imagined, a leech was applied to drain the bad blood. Of course, medical science ultimately discovered that the leech, no matter how well intentioned, could not differentiate between the good and bad blood. So, both the good and the bad blood flowed; not enough to inflict a lot of damage, but probably enough to hamper recovery.

The decline of party influence in our society over the last few decades has been well documented. Many explanations for this decline have been offered, but underlying all of them is the ever decreasing public support for and confidence in the parties—a development that appears to be outside the control of the party organizations or their elected officials. From time to time, however, we apply a force—a leech if you will—of our own which tends to accelerate the decline. The federal election law is clearly one such force.

Within this framework, I would like to discuss a few of the many thoughts which have been stimulated by Ms. Kayden's excellent paper. I do not wish to ignore the fine presentation by Ms. Jones on state party financing, but the other area is where I have the most experience and concern. I will concentrate on four general subjects: regulation and bureaucracy, financing the national party committee, building the party, and nationalization and professionalism in campaigns, which Ms. Kayden has so appropriately discussed.

Regulation and Bureaucracy

Just as politicians are beginning to respond to what appears to be a national mood favoring deregulation in our society, these same politicians feel a need to subject themselves and their supporting organizations to ever increasing regulation. It is astounding, but true, that only once in this decade has an election been operated under the same federal ground rules as the previous election. What started out with the relatively simple goal of campaign finance disclosure and limitations has become a maze of complex and sometimes conflicting requirements levied by an impossible structure with six heads. What took the Interstate Commerce Commission, the Environmental Protection Agency, and the Occupation Safety and Health Administration years to do, the Federal Election Commission has done almost overnight.

To respond to these new demands, the parties have had to commit significant resources from their already limited treasuries. In our own case, the National Republican Congressional Committee estimates our annual cost of compliance at close to $150,000. This is after start-up costs approaching $250,000. We employ five individuals who spend almost all their time keeping us in compliance, answering numerous nitpicking requests from the commission, and helping our candidates do the same. Incidentally, we do the latter largely because information from the commission staff is often nonexistent or unreliable. Multiply this type of commitment by the five other national party committees according to their relative size, and it is not difficult to imagine the thousands of man hours and hundreds of thousands of dollars involved —all valuable resources that could be utilized to rescue and build the parties, rather than defend and justify them before an overly suspicious and hostile commission staff.

At the national level, we can probably survive this type of bureaucratic regulation no matter how senseless and depleting it becomes, but state and local party committees, as Ms. Kayden points out, have a much more difficult time. Without the resources or the patience to put up with the FEC bureaucracy and with their highest priorities placed on state and local races, these party committees might find it much easier to stay out of federal races altogether. Such would be, of course, a consequence of more serious proportions than those of the nuisance variety we have experienced to date. We have not yet noticed any great deterioration in the degree of involvement of state committees in federal races. It should be noted, however, that there was not very much direct activity even before the current law was adopted. This is particularly true of races for the U.S. House, where there is little or no return for state party organizations. We have no real way to quantify local committee involvement before and after the law's implementation. It is generally agreed, however, that the local party committee is much less likely to pitch in and do something for their good old congressman when it learns that it will be walking into a whole new regulatory maze in order to do so.

Financing the National Party Committee

This is an area where the law is probably given too much credit for change, and where the Republican party, through which the most change has taken place, is given too little credit for what it has done on its own. The Republican party nationally began in 1975 to expand greatly its direct mail fund-raising activities. While direct mail had already accounted for a not insignificant portion of party income, this new effort built a base of a few thousand small donors into one that today approaches 1.5 million contributors. In 1978, these contributors financed over three-quarters of the national committee budgets with donations of under $100.

Of course the current law provided some encouragement for us to move in this direction, but there were a number of other reasons we chose this course as well. Included among these, as Ms. Kayden points out, was the desire to eliminate the fat-cat, big-business image of the party. Even more important was the need to eliminate the roller-coaster nature of party funding, so we could develop and maintain a year-round professional effort without having to worry constantly about how we were going to meet the next payroll. We gambled that direct mail could offer this kind of stability, and the gamble has paid off beyond our most optimistic expectations. I submit that this development would have occurred with or without the influence of the current law.

If the law were the main reason for the change among the Republicans, it would also be a catalyst for change among the Democrats. But this has not been the case; Democratic national committees still depend on big contributors, those giving over $500, for almost half their income. With or without the law, the Democrats have yet to make a substantial, long-range commitment and gather the technological expertise to build a broad-based network of contributors such as the Republicans have already established. They appear to be gradually moving in this direction, but they still have a long way to go.

There is still a debate in the Democratic party and elsewhere over the efficacy of direct mail fund raising. One school of thought, which seems to have been somewhat convincing to Ms. Kayden, holds that it only works for the conservatives or when single-issue, negative, and rather extreme appeals are employed. Of course, besides forgetting the experience of George McGovern in 1972, this view misrepresents what the Republicans have been doing. While I concede that our direct mail sometimes employs a somewhat negative tone, we have not used more than two or three single-issue appeals out of the ten or twelve mailings we have done each year for the past five years. Our most successful mailings this year have concerned themselves with a poll of choices for the Republican presidential nomination and a rather bland appeal for our contributors to renew their membership in the committee.

We have found that utilizing professional techniques, going after proven supporters, having party luminaries sign the appeals, and similar tactics have as much, if not more, to do with the success or failure of a direct mail appeal than does the flavor of the content. I have to reject the suggestion in the paper we are discussing here, that direct mail is somehow narrowing the philosophical base of the party. I also have to reject the notion that our direct mail success is somehow due to the Democrats' occupancy of the White House, especially because most of the spectacular growth of our contributor base occurred when Gerald Ford was in the White House.

Party Building

In an effort to help the parties, the Congress gave both the national and state committees certain advantages over any other political committees. These advantages are not without merit, but what the law or the commission gives with one hand, it often takes away with the other. Let me cite some examples:

The law allows an individual to give $20,000 a year to a national party committee. This sounds good until one discovers that the grand total this individual can give to all federal races is $25,000 per year. If this individual has the will and ability to give his full annual limit, it is unlikely to expect that he or she will give 80 percent to a party committee.

The law also was supposed to discourage CREEP-type operations, by suggesting that the national committees could become the campaign committees for their presidential nominees. The lawyers tell me this will never happen, however, because if it did, the national committee could lose its authority to accept the large contributions to which I just referred.

In addition, the law, now with the help of the Supreme Court, contains provisions for independent expenditures, which in theory allow anyone to spend any amount independently as an exercise of his free-speech rights. Yet, the FEC, without any direct authority in the law, has seen fit by regulation to deny this right to party committees.

With this exception, the few special advantages the law gives to party committees actually result in making the party like a large political action committee, with a few times the normal potential for income and expenditures. But, when you think about the magnitude of the tasks facing the parties to build organizations, to tell their stories to the American people, and to help finance their candidates, the law really only throws us a few small crumbs. If Congress and the commission are serious about wanting to help to rebuild the parties, then they will have to look at us as something much more than just super-PACs, and grant us major new authority and maneuvering room.

Nationalization and Professionalism

It is difficult to imagine that any political party controlling the majority of a legislative body would not attempt to tilt election law in its own favor. We have seen it for years in state legislatures and, more recently, in the Congress, since the federal government has gotten into detailed regulation of the election process. There are traces of it in the basic act passed in 1974, and there are blatant examples to be found in every attempt to amend it. Fortunately, most of these efforts have been defeated, and in the process Republicans have learned to beware of Democrats bearing election reform.

Generally what happens is that a proposal emerges under the guise of reform, which in practice will tend to decrease the impact of those forces favoring the "outs" and increase or maintain those forces favoring the "ins." This is true particularly as the laws and proposals relate to the party organizations. Because Republicans have always relied heavily on their party committees and Democrats have not, we find very little support in the majority party for measures favoring a strong party role. In fact, we often find efforts to minimize or eliminate it. If Ms. Kayden is right, and I think she is, that the Democrats will be less able to fall back on labor to do for them what party committees do for Republicans, and if they follow our lead in building strong and professional party organizations, then perhaps we will begin to find more suppport for the party committees among Democrats in the Congress.

But missing in this scenario and absent from most analysis of election law, is the supporting role played by the government—that is, the ever growing and awesome power of incumbency. While, as Ms. Kayden points out, Republicans are building strong professional expertise within their national committees, Democrats are doing the same through the government. To ignore the several-fold increase in professional staff, expense accounts, newsletter allowances, computer access, radio and television availability, and the like is to ignore the single most important current factor in congressional elections. Any half-way intelligent Democratic member of Congress will be practically unbeatable if he strategically utilizes these official allowances and listens to the professional campaign expertise available to him from the government-funded Democratic Study Group or from key leadership staff. He certainly has far, far more available to him—we estimate the value at about $1.2 million—than his Republican challenger can receive under the law from his highly professionalized national party committees or from any other sources for that matter.

If labor support is undependable and party resources insufficient, then the Democrats will, and indeed have, discovered government as the best resource to fill the void. Government support above all else is the strongest force in congressional elections today. As long as that remains true, nothing the law does for the parties will ever allow them to compete effectively or to assume the leading role in federal elections.

David W. Adamany

There has been more than a little commentary arguing that recent changes in political finance laws will have an adverse impact on the vitality of American political parties. It is surprising and quite refreshing, therefore, to find both Professor Jones and Ms. Kayden suggesting that in at least some circumstances political parties are being strengthened by recent reforms. Although I will express some reservations about the propositions advanced in these papers, I applaud Professor Jones and Ms. Kayden for inviting us to reappraise a wisdom which, though rapidly becoming conventional, is not yet proved.

It would be unfair to tax either Professor Jones or Ms. Kayden in a forum devoted primarily to the implications of political finance practices and laws, with an obligation to analyze more broadly the reasons why American political parties have become enfeebled. Jeane Kirkpatrick has suggested that reform rules and legislation have accelerated the trend toward party decline;[1] but I believe there is general agreement that these structural changes—whether rules for nominating candidates, procedures for internal governance of political parties, or methods for financing politics—may be at best only marginal causes and, indeed, perhaps only dependent variables. Our tendency to say, as Ms. Kayden does, that "a consequence of reform has been a decline in whatever strength the parties as organizations may once have held" may reflect a wishfulness that Humpty Dumpty could be put back together again by changing statutes, which in the scheme of things is a much easier task than reversing basic changes in society. Let me confess at the outset that I have no objection to the principle or practice of strong parties that are capable of performing both electoral and governmental activities. To analyze political finance reforms, however, one must distinguish between the aspiration for strong parties and the contemporary environment which has sapped the vitality of party organizations.

A better educated, highly transient, and middle-class population, relatively homogeneous and becoming increasingly so, is not likely to need the short-term material benefits once produced by party organizations and not likely to accept guidance in politics from traditional institutions—such as churches and labor unions—which in concert with grass-roots party organizations encouraged party allegiance and mustered the party vote. The messages of politics now tend to reach voters directly through pervasive electronic media or, if indirectly, through opinion leaders who are more attentive to media messages than to communications generated from traditional institutional sources.

The decline in the party allegiance of voters is matched, of course, by the erosion of incentives for party activism. The availability of material incentives for party work has declined markedly; and such incentives are not, in any case, very important to the dominant middle classes. The nature of social life has changed so dramatically in two generations that party clubs scarcely can lure activists with social incentives, formerly important, in both clubhouse and reform politics. Purposive or issue-oriented activism is now largely directed through single-issue organizations, narrowly focused interest groups, or campaigns of ideological candidates.

These trends are unlikely to be undone by more intellectually satisfying, comprehensive, and consistent political programs advanced under the labels of competing political parties, which will strongly influence candidates and office holders to support and enact such plat-

---

[1] Jeane Kirkpatrick, *Dismantling the Parties: Reflections on Party Reform and Decomposition* (Washington, D.C.: American Enterprise Institute, 1978).

forms. Not only does this argument ignore changes in the population and in the incentive structure for political activism, but it also wishes away the pervasive influence of the media and the emerging revision in the practical operation of the separation of powers, which has gone beyond strengthening Congress as an institution to lavishing important political and governmental resources on each congressman individually.

Let me turn, now, to several of the more thoughtful and provocative claims advanced by Professor Jones and Ms. Kayden. First, it is useful to underscore the point that some deference to the special status of political parties is embedded in our political finance laws. Ms. Kayden specifically identifies four aspects in federal law that recognize the role of parties.

Professor Jones points out that eight states allocate public subsidies to parties, eight to candidates, and one to both parties and candidates. The party-oriented nature of state public financing provisions is accentuated when one realizes that three of the states that fund candidates obtain public subsidies through the tax surcharge, which has failed to raise even minimal amounts. Only one state which funds parties uses the surcharge. The most generous subsidy plans have therefore been targeted to parties rather than to candidates in a majority of the states with public financing.

Second, it is appropriate to register skepticism about Ms. Kayden's argument that changes in technology and in the complexity of regulation will centralize national political parties. Temporarily, this may be true. National party committees have usually adapted to technological change more readily than either state and local party committees or the committees of political candidates, especially those for the House of Representatives and state legislatures. But public opinion polling, computer mailing, and complex legal requirements have rapidly enough found their way from Washington to the hinterlands, probably to the detriment of the latter. And there is no reason to believe that present changes in technology or laws will produce a different, centralizing dynamic.

Third, Ms. Kayden, observing recent successes scored by the Republican National Committee in fund raising by mail, suggests that this might signal the financial revitalization of party organizations. She postulates, as an alternative, that parties will be driven from traditional coalition-building activities to more diverse ideological advocacy if such appeals succeed only when they are pitched to "expressive moral issues" and when they tap "strongly-felt, often hostile, views."

Laid bare, the evidence suggests two different and largely unrelated circumstances in which mass fund raising by mail succeeds. The first is ideological, issue-specific, and frequently candidate-oriented. The Goldwater, McCarthy, McGovern, and Wallace campaigns are examples. So are the recent successes of Richard Viguerie and his imitators in raising funds for certain right-wing interest groups and candidates. As a caveat to claims of success for these fund-raising techniques, we should note that they do not genuinely broaden the citizen base for financing politics. The 600,000 contributors to George McGovern's 1972 protest campaign constituted only one-half of 1 percent of the eligible electorate. But the main point is that ideological fund raising destroys political parties by strengthening their least moderate elements and by destroying their capacity to set a governmental agenda by building coalitions on behalf of programs acceptable to national majorities.

A second, quite distinct style of fund raising is associated with the Republican party's successes in raising medium-sized contributions. The GOP has done this by mail in both the mid-1960s and in the late 1970s; and it has also raised money in modest contributions by face-to-face solicitation. These party-oriented successes ought not to be confused, as Ms. Kayden tends to do, with the fund-raising programs of ideological candidates and groups. Although mail techniques characterize both, they are not the same. The Republican fund-raising successes have been possible because the GOP was a more narrowly class-based party than was the Democratic party, and it encompassed the nation's professional and managerial classes. Hence, it was able to project a clearer, though moderate, issue posture that appealed to persons with the education, motivation, and means to make contributions. Moreover, the structures of corporations and professional associations constituted preexisting networks through which Republican fund solicitations could be made.

None of those conditions prevail in the Democratic party, a loosely joined coalition, which has raised its funds from unions, from businesses whose fortunes were particularly linked either to the Democrats or to governments controlled by the Democrats, from wealthy and middle-class apostates from class and caste, and from patronage employees. These groups are not susceptible to national, party-oriented appeals, by mail or otherwise. It is only when Democrats—such as George McGovern or Tom Hayden—assume the role of ideological leaders of polar factions within the Democratic party that they can emulate Republican fund-raising techniques.

Ms. Kayden's analysis of past and present Republican fund-raising successes not only combines quite different phenomena but also does not support her prediction of similar opportunities for financial centralization in the Democratic party, when next it loses the White House.

Professor Jones may unintentionally call our attention to the improbability that party-centered fund raising will play a major role either in revitalizing or in centralizing American parties when she reports: first, that the checkoff does less well in states that allocate public funds to parties than in states that make allocations to candidates; and, second, that in states that include both party and nonparty checkoff options on tax forms, the nonparty designations exceed the party checkoffs.

Fourth, Professor Jones's proposition that "when [public] monies are given to the political parties, . . . the party appears to become a stronger political organization and a more significant force in campaigns" —while undoubtedly true—must be read in light of other propositions. One forgoes the philosophical question whether political party organizations ought to be strengthened artificially and given additional influence over public officials at a time when public trust in parties is certainly lower than is confidence in elected officials. That question will become even more troublesome if the parties of the future are likely, as Ms. Kayden suggests, to be narrowly based, bureaucratic cadre parties in which specialists play a dominant role rather than broadly based membership parties drawn widely from partisan segments of the population.

A less lofty question probes the presumed trade-offs involved in financing parties rather than candidates. To the extent that parties use public subsidies to finance campaigns, they will distribute their funds unevenly, focusing on marginal districts which promise a reasonably good opportunity for victory. But party strategy may not be the same as democratic strategy. Candidates and parties already show a capacity to raise substantial sums in marginal districts. The real stagnation in American politics occurs in one-party electoral districts. Here the party organization shrivels so badly that it cannot recruit respectable candidates or sustain even a modest campaign. Without vigorous opposition, incumbents become more and more independent of public scrutiny.

The argument is not that incumbents are very likely to be defeated by vigorous opposition in such districts. Rather, it is that energetic opposition raises the salience of their stands on issues, requires them to pay more attention to their constituents both during and between campaigns, and in election after election exposes their weakest points, always posing the threat that under unforeseen circumstances the accumulated criticism may give a primary rival or an unusually skilled minority-party opponent an opening.

If one adheres to the Madisonian vision that we are safe from tyranny only as long as the people can find means to keep control of government, then vigorous opposition, which presses incumbents even though it might not defeat them, is essential in every district. Public subsidy plans which distribute money to candidates assure at least a financial base for opposition in one-party districts. Plans that allocate money to parties, however, will usually have the effect of increasing the funding in marginal districts at the expense of maintaining opposition in electorally noncompetitive constituencies.

Also, before conceding Professor Jones's proposition that party strength and public subsidies are related, one wishes to ask the question what is done with public subsidies to parties. Professor Jones indicates that in many states the funds are used to support staff, permit long-range planning, and conduct other party operations. I have no objection to such activities in principle. But one might argue that citizens are better served if scarce financial resources are used directly to stimulate competition in election campaigns than to affect those campaigns only indirectly by strengthening party organizations, which may or may not heighten the intensity of competition. As one who served a long apprenticeship in politics, I have seen many, many party organizations whose resources were diverted from the priority business of winning elections to the social activities necessary for organizational maintenance.

Even this might not be an unproductive use of resources. In a candidate-centered political system, the absence of opposition except during election seasons is a serious weakness. Investment in political parties would be justifiable to ensure interelection watchfulness over elected officials. But party organizations, even where strong, have shown little taste for such activities. The opposition press (if any), interest groups, and visible individuals have assumed this function, albeit weakly, in most American constituencies.

Fifth, one must quarrel with the premise of a party official, quoted by Professor Jones, that "the party doesn't mean much anymore; they don't raise the money so they can't control the candidate." There is little evidence that political parties, except for a few old-style machines, have been major sources of funds for candidates. As a result of factors previously mentioned, the Republican party has played a larger role in financing candidates than have their Democratic counterparts. But Alexander Heard's classic analysis reveals that even a quarter-century ago, party support of candidates varied widely among locales and various levels of the party organizations.[2] My own studies of Connecticut, a strong party-organization state, and Wisconsin, a citizen-party state, suggested that in the 1960s the Republican candidates received as much as 77 percent and as little as 15 percent of their funds from party organizations, while Democratic aspirants obtained only between

---

[2] Alexander Heard, *The Costs of Democracy* (Chapel Hill: University of North Carolina Press, 1960), chap. 11.

319

1 and 23 percent of their money from party treasuries.[3] Roland McDevitt has pointed out that party organizations provided a maximum of 11 percent of funds in House campaigns from 1972 to 1976.[4] Some nostalgia may be warranted for the passing of party activities actually performed, but public financing of campaigns should not be faulted for the displacement of activities that parties performed only fitfully, inadequately, and unevenly in the whole of the postwar period.

Sixth, Professor Jones comments that advocates of public financing of campaigns argue that "it will reduce the costs of elections." Those, like myself, who have been on every side of the question whether public subsidies to candidates should be conditioned by expenditure limits, can seize such an opening to forsake all of our previously clear, but contradictory, positions in favor of a carefully qualified middle ground. Professor Jacobson has very effectively shown that, in races for the House of Representatives, challengers gain greater marginal electoral advantage from each additional dollar expended than do incumbents.[5] He therefore argues that low expenditure limits disadvantage challengers. Expenditure limits generous enough not to interfere with vigorous opposition presumably allow so much spending that they undermine a policy of curbing campaign costs.

Jacobson also points out that expenditure limits disadvantage Republicans in congressional campaigns because they have fewer incumbents and because, as the minority party, they have a heavier burden in building election-day majorities. These observations do not, of course, apply to each specific circumstance. In any particular district or state, it is the challenger, regardless of party, who is disadvantaged; and there remain some states and regions where the Republicans are the dominant party electorally and are therefore advantaged by low expenditure limits.

Professor Jacobson's findings only indirectly take into account the fund-raising advantages of incumbents. Their fund-raising ability might outdistance that of their challengers by more than the marginal advantage the challenger gains from the expenditure of each additional dollar

[3] David Adamany, *Financing Politics* (Madison, Wis.: University of Wisconsin Press, 1969), pp. 221–229; David Adamany, *Campaign Funds as an Intraparty Political Resource: Connecticut, 1966-1968* (Princeton, N.J.: Citizens' Research Foundation, 1972), pp. 22–25.

[4] Roland McDevitt, "The Changing Dynamics of Fund Raising in House Campaigns," in Herbert Alexander, ed., *Political Finance: Sage Electoral Studies Yearbook*, vol. 5 (Beverly Hills, Calif.: Sage Publishing Co., 1979), p. 144.

[5] Gary Jacobson, "The Effects of Campaign Spending in Congressional Elections," *American Political Science Review*, vol. 72 (June 1978), pp. 469–492. Also, Gary Jacobson, "Public Funds for Congressional Campaigns: Who Would Benefit?" in Alexander, *Political Finance*, pp. 99-127.

he can raise. In such cases, the incumbent might be advantaged by the absence of spending limits if the smaller marginal return on each dollar he spends is offset because he raises—and spends—vastly more money than his opponent.

In so uncertain a world, it may be wise simply to abandon the notion of spending limits because their effects are too uncertain to warrant any curtailment they might impose on levels of political involvement, which is usually a "good thing" in a free society.

Finally, one must take careful note of Professor Jones's concern that where public funds are spread too broadly—to primary as well as general elections and to legislative as well as executive offices—"the amount . . . available to each campaign is diminished and the significance of public financing reduced." That important warning is not, however, without counterbalancing considerations. Public financing may alternatively be envisioned as start-up or seed money, permitting a candidate to gain the initial visibility for his candidacy that will allow the public to decide whether to make contributions that will support a more elaborate campaign.

Even if public financing is intended to support a large percentage of campaign activities, the allocation of funds only to executive or to legislative campaigns raises sensitive questions about the separation of powers. A gubernatorial candidate largely freed from raising private funds for his own campaign may devote substantial efforts to raising funds for privately funded legislative races, thus extending his influence over the coordinate branch. Richard Nixon's activities in 1970 are a prototype, although they were additionally shrouded in the paranoid secrecy that marked so many of his political maneuvers. Also, if candidates for one branch are publicly financed while aspirants for the other are not, public confidence may tend subtly to shift toward officials perceived as being free from the taint of special-interest campaign funds.

Both these papers remind us that the velocity of change in public-finance regulations and practices has scarcely abated since Watergate. Moreover, the diversity of these changes tends to fly in the face of predictions that federal political financing laws and certain reform rules adopted by the national parties will significantly curb the longstanding adaptation of politics to the divergent settings of the states. Indeed, it might be argued that, unlike earlier waves of reform, campaign financing laws—especially their public financing provisions—reflect a great concern for stimulating both party and candidate activity. But these reforms cannot be expected to bear the burden—and indeed do not attempt to do so—of revitalizing party politics in the face of strong currents of fundamental change in American society which tend further to weaken already emaciated party structures.

Authors' Replies

Xandra Kayden

First, I will give you my defensive reactions. I think I say in the paper that I agree with Mr. Adamany that the decline of parties is not just the result of party reform, that other factors are involved, and that one view holds that the parties do have, as I think someone on the other side mentioned, a dependent rather than an independent variable effect. The parties are the results of lots of factors going on in the society. In the long run, there is not that much difference between the strength of the Democratic and the Republican parties if you include the elected officials. And I was struck by some of Steve Stockmeyer's reactions, since much of my data comes from talking to him.

The only other remark I would like to make is that it is curious to me, if maybe not to you, that I neglected to say that public financing would be a good thing for the parties, although I do believe that. I happen to be very fond of bureaucracy. I consider it the last frontier.

I think we ought to have strong parties, although I agree with Mr. Adamany that there are probably reasons why we don't that go deeper than campaign finance. My suggestion that the parties may have stronger national organizations is based largely on the view that there will probably be a separation of federal candidates from state and local candidates, and that local parties will not participate in federal elections very much, which is not to say that they won't participate in state and local elections.

Ruth S. Jones

I just want to comment on Mr. Winograd's point that, in fact, all these laws are terribly political. They are ideological, they are partisan, but above all, they are political. We can see this in states when a party comes into power—the whole ball game shifts. And so just underscore that. My lack of discussion of that point was not from naivete but from acceptance. Those are the rules of the game, and we will go from there.

322

To Professor Adamany, I would say that I may be more patient than he seems to be, for I am not trying to make a silk purse out of a sow's ear in one conference, in one paper, overnight. Although politicians do the right things for the wrong reasons sometimes, things they do in a sense help to strengthen parties. My concern with some of his remarks is that he is equating party system and party strength with increase and development of mass parties. At the state level, however, we seem to be shoring up the cadre party, and it will function and will be involved, and it will not be the grass-roots mass party that we think of in terms of mass participation.

In some places the states probably do target public money for marginal races that they think they can win. But they also have been willing to use public money to put forth a candidate in the state legislative race where they have not had a candidate before. This may be token opposition, but maybe that is the way to get it started. In my state, parties are putting ads in the newspaper to try to generate candidates for the state legislature! If we can help to fund some of that effort, maybe it is a way to operate in the safe as well as the marginal districts.

Discussion

AUSTIN RANNEY, American Enterprise Institute, and a former member of the Winograd Commission: Insofar as this discussion has implied that our society is developing an elaborate new technology, which is really just above and beyond the ordinary politicians, I would like to mention that the Winograd Commission, under Morley Winograd's leadership, developed something known as a sliding window with a triggering threshold.

Second, just to boggle your minds in terms of cruel and unusual punishment, double jeopardy, and all that, this is my ninth straight day of discussions of party reform. Throughout the discussions of the usefulness of past reforms and future reforms, I have been struck by the fact that people—and they can be easily divided into two classes—talk about these things past each other. There is a little bit of that here today, although I think you are predominantly what I will call Group 2.

Group 1 dominates the discussion of reforms in political science and in newspapers, and it certainly dominates discussion of who actually has the power to adopt or to reject reforms. This group, believing that reform has made politics more fair, more honest, more open, more democratic, might have as its motto, "Virtue is its own reward." If Group 1 is asked for what purpose or with what consequence politics should be more fair, it responds that isn't really the point; it's just that it *is* more open and more fair. A fitting motto for Group 2, on the other hand, might be "By their fruits ye shall know them." This group believes that the reforms are good or bad not for themselves, but for their impact on what political groups become powerful, and for the kinds of presidential candidates that get produced, and the like.

As we study the whole situation—past, present, and possible future reforms—most people like you will always be a little baffled by the difference in the two basic responses to reform. One of the reasons that political scientists read David Broder's work and think it is terrific, and why the world nonetheless keeps following the same wrong-headed way is because you belong to Group 2, which believes that by their fruits ye shall know them, whereas most of your readers belong to Group 1, which believes that virtue is its own reward. As long as Group 1 is dominant, any change that isn't going to make things even worse than they are now will be exceedingly difficult to secure. With regard to any changes we make in federal campaign financing now, the old physician's approach to treatment, that is, first do no harm (which in the case of campaign finance laws has to be "Do no more harm") is not a bad place to start. After that, if we can do a little good, that is great.

However, the view that virtue is its own reward is widely shared. I think it permeates our society, for it represents a basic hostility to almost all intermediary organizations—that is to say, political parties are bad, PACs are bad, and anything that intervenes between the sovereign people and their government is somehow or other bad. The polls tell us that between 70 and 75 percent of the American people want to abolish the electoral college. Why this desire? Because it is thought that the college as a "funny collection of people" intervenes between the sovereign voter and the president. Almost the same percentage favor a national presidential primary, which will probably be adopted sometime in the 1980s. There again, it is because our strange conventions are said to intervene between the sovereign people and the selection of their candidates. This argument is already proving successful in the states. Until the contrary can be shown by events, can be argued in even more eloquent and convincing columns by David Broder, in books by David Adamany, and in wisecracks by Morley Winograd, and can be expressed in wringing of the hands by me, it will be difficult to convince people that intermediary organizations, including PACs and certainly including political parties, are the very lifeblood of democratic government in any kind of a modern society. Until that point is made, whatever reforms we consider are much more likely to do further harm rather than undo harm, let alone do any good.

Jeane Kirkpatrick, Georgetown University and AEI, and another member of the Winograd Commission: The first point that I want to make is that I agree that laws have not alone been responsible for the decline of the parties. Reform laws and party rules, largely adopted since 1968, have merely accelerated and contributed to a process of party decline that has been assisted by many social, political, and economic forces in the society with which we are all familiar. Legislators, when confronted with such social processes, either go with them, if you will, trying to help history on its way, or they attempt to intervene judiciously and to counteract developing trends. In other words, historical outcomes are not inevitable and human intelligence, intelligently applied, may make a difference.

Second, on the point of parties as intermediary institutions or mediating structures, to the extent that political parties have become, and will become, objects of legalization, thereby being regulated and incorporated into the government structure—our parties are already the most highly regulated of any parties in democratic societies in the world— they are incapacitated vis-à-vis their role as mediating structures. In the future, as long as we have not separated the government from the society, there will probably arise in the free society new mediating structures that will express social forces and seek their translation into political power, which is what Sigmund Neumann once described as the function of political parties. Single-issue groups are a hint of the shape of this future and the shape of these new mediating institutions. Since no one knows how they will work out or what their long-term consequences may be, we are unsettled by them.

THOMAS MANN, Chairman: I am wondering whether David Adamany wanted to respond. Austin Ranney has put you in Group 2, and yet you seemed to disagree with the rest of the panel.

MR. ADAMANY: I like Group 2 and feel very comfortable there. I would just add this. If the argument is that ultimately we will have cadre-style parties rather than mass parties, then we have to ask whether or not we hope they will perform the same functions as the traditional political parties, which so many of us are interested in preserving. That is, will the new cadres build coalitions, will they mediate, will they compromise, and will they hold back the worst instincts in society? Maybe the cadre parties can do that, but in the past they have done so only when they have been able to control the candidates. That does not seem to be the pattern today. If in the future cadre parties will be dominant but will not control the candidates, then why are we busy rushing to their defense?

I would like to see Neil Staebler's mass citizen party of the 1950s and early 1960s in Michigan become the prototype that we would hope for. That will show you how up to date I really am, since, of course, that school of thought is affiliated with people in the distant past of political science. But short of that, in a candidate-centered political system, I cannot become excited about saving political parties.

MS. KAYDEN: I would like to react to that last statement. Both Ms. Jones and I, and all of us, seem to be saying that we are moving toward cadre parties, certainly. However, we at the same time may be moving toward greater party control of candidates, of nominations, and that is what intervention in primaries implies.

MR. BRODER: I would like to strike a note of modified, limited optimism, unusual for a journalist. For individual human beings, especially younger people, it is possible in one lifetime to move from Group 1 to Group 2 because a learning process is taking place among these younger people, who by and large were the instigators of the changes whose effects we have been discussing. Unless I misread them, the thinking of at least some of them seems to be shifting from the notion that virtue is its own reward to a concern for the consequences. And some of the consequences are now becoming fairly unpleasant for them.

For the activists now, particularly the elected officials who have done so many of these wonderful things to us or for us, the world of the special-interest group is not a very happy world in which to live. Up until recently, it was pleasant to be a political entrepreneur, to be one's own political party, to raise one's own funds, to hire one's own campaign manager, pollster, media advisor, and so forth. Now the officials are finding that the issue-oriented people, who tend to be somewhat extremist from the officials' point of view, are playing the same games. On Capitol Hill or anywhere else that elected officials now congregate, they are complaining about being whipsawed around by people for whom only one issue is of consequence at any given moment. They are looking for a more stable base of support, for people who will stick with them because of their general position and their general tendencies. And whether they realize it or not, they are reinventing or rediscovering the utility of having a political party.

Second, a dynamic is developing, described by Xandra Kayden, in which one party begins to pull its act together and, as a result, the other party is forced to examine the things that hold it together. This dynamic is also now evident in Congress. (I wish I knew more about what is happening in the state legislatures, whether similar developments are occurring there or not.) The fact that the Republicans are now organizing to present an alternative budget is forcing the Democrats in Congress to determine what budget they would draft if only Democrats were voting, because they may have to pass a budget just that way. In other words, they are being forced to discover the things that hold them together as a party.

Third, although I may sound like Pollyanna, we should consider the motives of these people. Most of them did not push these changes or reforms in order to deliberately weaken institutions. They were striking out against elements in the political world that seemed to them unjust in a basic way, such as the possibility that some old guy, just because he had been there for 40 years, could sit on a bill and kill it even if the whole country, as they thought, wanted that bill. They thought that type of political behavior was wrong, and they wanted it to change. They did not consider whether or not their changes would decentralize decision making in the Congress of the United States to the point that Congress was unable to function. However, it is a mistake to assume that they do not care about that other question now that it is before them. Therefore, I think they are changing.

My final, entirely personal argument is that when the young people on Jimmy Carter's White House staff say, with their characteristic intensity and frequency, that fragmentation is making government impossible in this country, and yet acknowledge that if it were not for that fragmentation they would not be there any more than Carter would be there, then you have to believe that a learning process is possible.

NEIL STAEBLER, former commissioner, FEC: I would like to build on Dave Broder's optimism, starting with both a great hope and respect for parties and considerably more respect for the Federal Election Act than has been expressed here today. There is reason for being optimistic. Let me preface that, however, by saying that two important points omitted from today's discussion explain why we got the Federal Election Act. It was due to the great decline in confidence in practically all our public institutions, especially in parties and in the political process. Money played a very great role. Although its importance was probably overestimated, it became the symbol of what was wrong. People really wanted to clean up the process, but as many of the papers here have pointed out, their efforts led to side effects. If no effort had been made to clean it up, further devolution of confidence would have occurred. It has continued to dissolve, I might say.

The second factor that led to the act was the great increase in expenditures for political activity. Notice what happened to the expenditures for the presidential elections from 1964 to 1972: each election approximately doubled the expenditures of the preceding one. The rate of increase was frightful, and obviously we could not sustain that rate. Certainly we could not sustain it honestly. A somewhat parallel change is going on in congressional and senatorial elections, the cost of which has been rising spectacularly. In consequence, as Dave Adamany and the others have pointed out, the relative importance of the political parties has diminished. However, we take too short a view of this whole process and tend to think that political parties were pretty good sometime in the past. Relatively, they seemed effective because there wasn't much else that purported to do the things that political parties did, but in fact they were terribly ineffective, terribly dishonest, and therefore they dug their own grave. We are rising from that grave, however, for we now have a handle on the situation. If we can avoid a national primary, which would mean the demise of the national parties because it really is the one grip that the national parties have on any credibility—that is, nomination through party channels of the candidates —we can find a way to rebuild the parties.

DAVID COHEN, president of Common Cause: I think there is a tendency on the part of Austin Ranney's Group 2 or school of thought to make an absolutely irrebuttable presumption against change. There is a constant tendency to make proposed changes meet an impossible burden of proof.

I would suggest that there is much more mixture between Group 1 and Group 2, accompanied by a tension between representation and participation. We can have extreme forms of what might be participation, such as the national initiative or the national primary. And yet, we can have the kind of situation we had in 1968, during which many people felt shut out of the presidential selection process at a time when the country was in tremendous turbulence, at least among those who opposed the war.

Dave Broder hit on something that I think is right: many of us are not only questioning old assumptions, but we are also trying to be sensitized to how things actually work out. Many congressional reforms, even the one that unfortunately created all those subcommittees, came about because of attempts to correct abuses of power and to strengthen the institution and the leadership. One question we have to address now is a point that Morley Winograd touched on but did not have the chance to develop: How do you make political parties part of the governing process both in advance of the election and after the election? We all go through the business of party platforms, which we know are long wish lists that are not taken seriously. At the risk of being taken for a well-meaning reformer, I want to suggest that some thought be given to allowing political parties to set the priorities of a legislative body after the election. For example, after the election in an even-numbered year or after every four years, no matter who was in control of the party, we could have a type of plenary session that would involve the state party chairholders, the chief executives in states, and the legislative people in the various political parties who would go through the process of determining their minimal priorities and who could make sure that the institutions of which they are a part—in this instance, the Congress—deal with those priorities. No matter what one thinks of public financing of congressional elections, the way it was defeated in the House by the Democratic chief deputy whip's efforts to derail it was not healthy for the institutions. It was not healthy in terms of what

329

parties are supposed to stand for. To make certain that an institution deals with public priorities, we need to find approaches, ways, and mechanisms by which the parties themselves can take responsibility for translating that long wish list of the platform into some priorities, without dictating how a legislator votes.

EDWARD ROEDER, free-lance journalist: Everybody seems to be suggesting that the demise of parties is due to campaign finance regulations and the parties' lack of money. I am concerned about the possibility that giving the parties money might weaken them further by turning them into mere competitive brokers of money, just as PACs are, and nothing more.

MR. MANN: My impression is that you have built a bit of a straw man. None of the authors have really argued that changes in federal law are responsible for the demise of party. They say that the changes are one small, modest factor in a very hostile environment.

MR. ROEDER: But the idea of giving parties more money or allowing them to raise money and spend pushes them toward their weak turf, toward the idea of becoming money brokers instead of political organizations that encourage communication from the bottom, up.

MS. KAYDEN: My mother always told me that it was just as easy to fall in love with a rich man as a poor man, and—more money is more, and less is less—it's better to have it.

Part Five

Campaign Finance Regulation
in International Perspective

Political Finance Regulation in International Perspective

Herbert E. Alexander

In democratic societies it is natural that individuals and groups with abundant economic resources will try to use their wealth to influence the course of government. While money is a common denominator in shaping political power, other ingredients are vital as well: leadership, skill, information, public office, votes, public opinion, legal maneuvers. Many philosophers from Aristotle on have regarded property or economic power as the fundamental element in political power. The attempt to reconcile economic inequalities lies at the base of the problem of money in politics. In a sense, broadly based political power, as effected through universal suffrage, was conceived and has been used to help equalize inequalities in economic resources. The wealth of one group thus may be matched by the human resources or voting power of another.

Representative government is built upon three constituencies: the electoral, the financial, and the organizational; these in turn are composed of three basic sources of political power: numbers of people, resources, and social organizations.[1] Thus, numbers of persons, situated in electoral constituencies, find political expression through their elected representatives who are grouped according to political party. The power of social organizations, or interest groups, stems from the combination of two factors: people and resources. Resources are brought to bear upon the political process in many ways, through many available channels.

When wealthy persons seek to translate their economic power into political power, one of their tools may be monetary contributions. The translation of individual or group demands into public policy occurs in various ways, mediated in part by ideological references and by group or class alignment. Since policy preferences are in competition with conflicting claims for political action, individuals or groups with wealth

---

[1] Robert Bierstedt, "An Analysis of Social Power," *American Sociological Review,* vol. 15 (December 1950), p. 737.

use it to achieve policy goals by promoting nominations or elections of candidates and parties with views congenial to their own. Between and during election campaigns they cultivate the sympathies of public officials and the public through lobbying and other means, and through party activity.

Coincident with the extension of the franchise and the democratization of the institutional framework, the economic element that makes for political power—wealth—has been increasingly concentrated. The great industrial, financial, labor, and other interests not only vie to dominate economic life, but also seek to master the political environment. They do this in many direct and indirect ways—directly through lobbies and the contribution of money, indirectly through access to the public in both election and nonelection activities.

In modern societies the interests of various segments of industry, finance, labor, and agriculture vary widely. Monied interests need to enlist the support of other constituencies and to temper their demands into politically and electorally viable claims. The fact that a minority representing wealth must get a majority on its side by constitutional means also implies that this minority can lose to the majority in the same way, as it often does despite high levels of political expenditures.

Thus, money is but one element in the equation of power. In the broadest sense, government is legitimized, and its course largely determined, at the ballot box. People, not dollars, vote. But dollars help shape both voter behavior and governmental decisions, and hence are subject to various forms of regulation. This is particularly true when high levels of support are perceived as increasingly necessary to pay for the advanced technology often employed in political campaigns.

Adamany and Agree have identified five goals associated with the regulation of elections:

• To enable a nation with a private property economy and, consequently, a massive inequality of individual and institutional means to preserve opportunities for all its citizens to participate equally or nearly equally in financing politics.

• To structure a system that will provide enough money for vigorous, competitive campaigns for public office.

• To ensure that each candidate is entitled to a fair share of the financial resources through a formula flexible enough to acknowledge newly emerging, as well as established, movements without rewarding frivolous candidates or propping up decaying political organizations.

• To free candidates and elected officials from undesirable or disproportionate pressure and influence from contributors and to free citizens from pressure by politicians to give financial support to candidates or parties.

• To prevent corruption—that is, where explicit understandings accompany either solicitation or giving.[2]

While this is essentially an American perspective, the American way has led to recognition of six basic forms of regulation which can be used to measure various political systems comparatively.

Limitations on Expenditures. To meet the problems of the disproportion of funds among candidates and of rising costs, limitations on expenditures have been imposed. In the United States, the Supreme Court, in *Buckley* v. *Valeo,* found spending ceilings to be unconstitutional except when imposed as a condition of acceptance by the candidate of public funding. Elsewhere, except in Canada, Israel, and a few other countries, and at the constituency level in Great Britain and Australia, spending ceilings are not favored.

Restrictions on Donations. To prevent candidates from obligating themselves to private interests, prohibitions against contributions from certain sources have been enacted and ceilings imposed on individual contributions. For example, in the United States, corporations, national banks, and labor unions are prohibited from contributing funds. Corporate executives and union officials may contribute out of their own pockets. Labor unions, corporations, and trade associations may establish political action committees (PACs) to solicit and collect voluntary contributions from rank-and-file members, and from corporate employees and stockholders, for political purposes.

For certain purposes, such as registration and get-out-the-vote activities, which are considered nonpartisan, corporate and union funds can be used despite the ban; unions particularly spend considerable amounts on such activities from dues money. Moreover, federal law limits individuals from contributing more than $1,000 or political action committees from contributing more than $5,000 to any federal candidate per election. At the U.S. state level, prohibitions of individual, corporate, and labor contributions are not uniformly imposed.

Elsewhere in the world, prohibitions and limitations on the vested economic interests are fewer; business associations flourish as political

---

[2] David W. Adamany and George E. Agree, *Political Money: A Strategy for Campaign Financing in America* (Baltimore: John Hopkins University Press, 1975), pp. 8–12; this format was suggested by *A Comparative Survey of Election Finance Legislation 1978* (Toronto: Commission on Elections and Expenses, 1979), pp. 1–2.

givers; labor unions form the basis of socialist, communist, and leftist parties; and church and other groups participate directly in politics through parties they may control.

Prohibitions against Government Employee Contributions. To prevent government power from being used to solicit contributions, regulations protecting government employees have been legislated. All but top policy-making positions are protected, thus reducing the effects of the "spoils system" and patronage and making illegal the assessment of government employees. With variations, this principle is widely followed in other countries, precluding many rewards to contributors, making the raising of money more difficult, and conditioning the acceptance of limitations.

Disclosure of Contributions. Laws have been enacted to require disclosure of sources and amounts of campaign contributions and expenditures. These laws serve to provide the public, both during and after campaigns, with knowledge of monetary influences upon its elected officials, to increase financial accountability by making secret funds illegal, to increase public confidence in the electoral processes, and to help curb excesses and abuses by increasing political risk for those who would undertake sharp practices.

In the United States, at the federal level and in most states, disclosure is required of candidates and both party and nonparty political committees on a periodic basis, before and after primary and general election campaigns. The right of the public to know, or to judge the candidate's sources of support as well as his qualifications and programs, is considered essential to a voter's rational choice on election day. No country has as elaborate a disclosure agency, with administrative and enforcement functions, as the Federal Election Commission (FEC) and certain state agencies.

The keystone of American regulation is disclosure, which is used more sparingly or not at all in other democracies. A Swedish committee concluded in 1952 that the disclosure of the names of contributors violated the principle of secrecy of the ballot.[3] That position continues to be widely held in Scandinavian countries. No country has put as great an emphasis upon preelection reporting as has the United States, and disclosure in many democracies occurs annually or after elections, not before.

---

[3] *The Commercial and Financial Chronicle,* January 24, 1952, cited in Alexander Heard, *The Costs of Democracy* (Chapel Hill: University of North Carolina Press, 1960), p. 355.

Equality of Media Exposure. To prevent domination of the airwaves for partisan purposes, U.S. federal law regulating radio and television requires stations to make available equal amounts of free or paid time to rival candidates or parties, but other candidates for the same office must be afforded equal opportunity to receive free or buy the same amount of time. The so-called equal time provision applies to candidates of different parties for any office, federal or not, and it applies to candidates of the same party for nomination to any public office. The United States added a provision in 1971 that broadcasters must sell political time at the lowest unit rates, thus seeking to control excessive charges for candidates who use the media.

Most other nations with state control of television and radio provide free time to parties on government stations; most also broadcast simultaneously on all channels, including privately operated ones, and prohibit private purchase of time by candidates or parties. In Italy, radio and television make safer platforms in an age of terrorism than does street campaigning.

Public Financing of Campaigns. Public funding has been instituted in order to give candidates or political parties alternative sources of funds, to reduce financial pressures upon them, and to increase voters' access to and awareness of information about candidates. (See "Public Financing Abroad: Contrasts and Effects," by Khayyam Zev Paltiel, in this volume for a more complete discussion of this issue.)

Alexander Heard informed us two decades ago that the United States sought to do more by way of regulation than did other countries. He wrote:

> It is *not* correct to conclude, as is the fashion, that satisfactory legal regulation has been achieved, by American standards, in Great Britain, or elsewhere. American ambitions far exceed anything attempted in Great Britain and in most of the world. In foreign eyes, American legislative regulation falls short because it attempts the impossible.
>
> . . . At any rate, all attempts at legal control in the United States have *not* been futile. Much has been accomplished that was intended by those who passed the laws, as well as much that was not.[4]

These comments were perceptive when written in 1960, and apply equally to the reforms adopted in the United States in the 1970s. They apply, too, to any current comparative assessment of regulatory patterns in mature democracies across the world.

---

[4] Heard, *The Costs,* p. 6.

CAMPAIGN FINANCING IN INTERNATIONAL PERSPECTIVE

Two Basic Models

Two basic models for election financing regulation can be suggested, with variations of each. The American model derives from our candidate-centered culture in which political parties play a subordinate and diminishing role, and interest groups increasingly, through their PAC and lobbying activity, have a direct relationship with many candidates and elected officials. The parliamentary model differs in reflecting a party-oriented political system in which interest groups often are the basis of the parties, and candidates are subordinated to the interests of the parties. The Canadian regulatory system is a cross-breed modeled substantially on the American, although Canada's political system is parliamentary. Numerous other systems are essentially variations of each, although because the American system is unique it requires extensive treatment.

The American Model. Until the Revenue Act of 1971, "political party" was not even defined in federal law. Now election law is burgeoning, and parties are frequently mentioned in the 1974 and 1976 amendments to the Federal Election Campaign Act, mainly with reference to limitations and public funding.

The American electoral process tends to encourage loyalty to the candidate, not to the party and its programs. This undermines the party and leads to emphasis on the candidate's own organization. For an incumbent president, the view of his party's role in his reelection campaign has been a relatively uncluttered one—the White House traditionally runs the campaign. The party in power normally belongs to the president—to use, abuse, or ignore as he sees fit. The president usually puts the campaign in the hands of loyalists, and the national committee is relegated to a supplemental role. The results can be bruising to the party when inordinate focus is on the top of the ticket and not on the rest of the party's candidates.

The nonincumbent has a more difficult problem with using his party's national committee once he has won the nomination. He can either run a divided command, hoping that the trusted lieutenants of his prenomination battles can operate on one track with the party professionals at national headquarters on a parallel one, or he can seek to bring the national committee completely under his control through wholesale replacement of its top officials. Either route is hazardous, leading to uncoordinated efforts, confusion over goals, and spending of campaign funds on party projects which rarely receive full support from the candidate, and triggering resentment among the party regulars who are dislodged from functions which they feel they could perform better than the "amateurs" replacing them.

The Republican and Democratic national committees seek to remain neutral during the intraparty nomination struggle, but that is a difficult posture, particularly when an incumbent president is running for renomination and is being challenged for nomination. Then party newsletters and efforts boost the president's administration.

The candidate's committee, focusing attention wholly on him, sets the stage for a presidency independent of party. Power resides in the incumbent, subject to his idiosyncrasies and character, and need not necessarily be shared with his party, cabinet, or even a responsible White House staff, not to mention the Congress.

In 1976, for the first time, public funding was provided for presidential candidates.[5] The government supplied $21.8 million to each major party candidate in the general election, and private contributions were prohibited excepting for those of the candidate's political party, whose national committee could spend up to two cents per voting age population, or a total of $3.2 million in addition. Private contributions could be made to the parties for this purpose, but not directly to the candidates' committees.

This role for the parties in presidential elections has been variously assessed. On the one hand, the parties were given a role, albeit a supplemental one, in the presidential campaigns. On the other hand, the party limits were low, as was the public funding ceiling, thus not permitting significant grass roots or organizational efforts—the areas the parties are best equipped to handle. Because of the limits, the parties were only junior partners, not integral elements of the campaigns, and achieved little leverage from the relationships.

With or without public funding, essentially the same characteristics are found in the relationships between governors and their state parties, and mayors and their local parties. Members of Congress and of state legislatures are usually quite independent of the national, state, and local parties; they remain very much their own person, whether running for office or in office. At the federal level, the senatorial and congressional campaign committees provide some funding and services to candidates, but these are not unifying instruments; there is no public funding, hence no limitations on spending. Interest groups and PACs operate at all levels, although in some states corporate and labor contributions are not prohibited, and treasury money can be contributed directly to candidates and parties.

---

[5] For full treatment of the 1976 election and legislative developments throughout this paper, see Herbert E. Alexander, *Financing the 1976 Election* (Washington, D.C.: Congressional Quarterly Press, 1979).

Corporate and labor union political action committees contribute to presidential candidates' prenomination campaigns, although no private contributions are allowed in the general election if the candidate accepts public funding. Corporations and unions also engage in parallel activities on behalf of presidential and other candidates through various means: independent expenditures,[6] communications expenses, and registration and get-out-the-vote activities.[7] Labor's main advantage is its ability to generate manpower, not money, but labor can sustain large amounts of communication expenses, using treasury and nonvoluntary funds, in dealing with its members and their families on electoral issues and candidates. While corporations have been more restrained in making communications expenditures, and relatively few corporations have solicited stockholder contributions to their PACs, these activities are increasingly being undertaken. Labor's registration and get-out-the-vote activities are generally more extensive and more effective than are those of business.

Watergate disclosures provided a view of the ways a few businesses funneled money into federal campaigns. A total of twenty-one corporations and/or their executives were indicted in 1973 and 1974 for illegally contributing corporate funds to political campaigns.[8] Much of the money went to the Nixon reelection campaign before the 1971 reform legislation took effect in April 1972, but other contributions were made by some of those companies to Democratic candidates as well.

No one knows how widespread the corporate practices exposed by the investigations were, but of the thousands of publicly owned corporations, relatively few, perhaps 100, had subsequent exposure of secret slush funds. The involvement of these companies and their officers in the illegal use of corporate money unquestionably increased public suspicion of business involvement in politics and helped to trigger some provisions of the 1974 and 1976 amendments. Their problem was compounded when it was disclosed that certain American-based multinational corporations had made larger political contributions abroad than at home, to selected parties in Canada, Italy, Korea, and other countries. This, too, led to a restraining law, the Foreign Corrupt Practices Act.

Public policy seldom develops in precisely the way reformers want. Ironically, the political financing reforms of the 1970s are leading to the development, through business political action committees and lobbying techniques, of even greater business and special-interest influence in poli-

---

6 Maxwell Glen, "How to Get around the Campaign Spending Limits," *National Journal,* vol. 11, no. 25 (June 23, 1979), pp. 1044–1046.
7 Michael J. Malbin, "Labor, Business and Money—A Post-Election Analysis," *National Journal,* vol. 9, no. 12 (March 19, 1977), pp. 412–417.
8 Herbert E. Alexander, *Financing the 1972 Election* (Lexington, Mass.: D.C. Heath and Co., 1976), pp. 513-530 and Appendix X, pp. 707-710.

tics.[9] As the role of political parties continues to decline in the United States, interest-group politics appears to be on the rise. Most special-interest groups now have offices in Washington, and many have established political action committees. It is difficult to determine whether the volume or aggregate of political contributions is so much greater, or whether more activity that previously was secret has now surfaced.[10] In recent years there have been no election-related labor cases of the magnitude of the corporate experiences, and in fact, labor seems frozen in its size and potential relative to business sources.

There are more definable groups than ever before seeking attention —business, labor, professional, public interest—and each has its subgroups dealing with a specific industry or issue. Larger groupings are fragmented, so the voices heard most effectively seem to be those with large resources or those achieving dramatic appeal. Pluralism may be more extensive than ever but what is heard is a vast clamor. The fragmentation is evident in independent voting, and few groups can deliver voters with diverse interests. Single-issue candidates such as Ellen Mc-Cormack can survive in the maelstrom, and her 1976 pro-life presidential candidacy is only the first instance of many such single-issue candidates successfully tying into an organized group for electoral support. In any case, lobbying and electoral activity are more intensive, focused, and sophisticated than ever before, utilizing more professionalism and advanced technology than previously.

The Parliamentary Model. In contrast to the American system is the parliamentary model. Whether an ideal forum—perhaps a party responsibility variety that some political scientists might cherish[11]—or a more fluid and interactive variation, the parliamentary model is based on relationships between the party and its candidates that are relatively unfettered by legal restrictions. The party is free either to set fully the terms of the candidate's campaign (because it nominates him), or to help the candidate to the extent needed within the party's available resources. Neither an ideal nor a loose parliamentary model is possible with statutory limitations on what the party can contribute to the candidate or can spend directly on his behalf in parallel campaigning.[12] The

9 Edwin M. Epstein, "An Irony of Electoral Reform," *Regulation* (May/June 1979), pp. 35–41.
10 Michael J. Malbin, "Neither a Mountain nor a Molehill," *Regulation* (May/June 1979), pp. 41–43.
11 See *Toward a More Responsible Two-Party System,* a report of the Committee on Political Parties, American Political Science Association, Supplement to *American Political Science Review,* vol. 44, no. 3, pt. 2 (September 1950), pp. 1–96.
12 Some variations, such as the British system, which limits candidates but not parties, will be noted below.

parliamentary model is also not possible with government funding of political campaigns if the money is provided directly to the candidate and is not channeled through the party machinery, which has some discretion in allocation, and hence some leverage with the candidate. The unique characteristics of the American system stand out in comparison.

The parliamentary model is most viable in mature democracies where the government funds the parties, which in turn fund and in varying degrees control the candidates' campaigns. Subsidies in most such countries, with the exception of Canada, France, and Japan, are made to political parties, not to candidates. Parties control the campaigns, and candidates mobilize only limited and local supplemental support to that provided by the party at the national or constituency level. Primaries in which party candidates can be challenged do not exist, and the parties choose the candidates without cost to the one seeking nomination. In most of the nations with subsidies, governments fund the parties, or their research functions, or their newspapers, annually, not only at election time.

Political parties in parliamentary systems tend to be permanent organizations with many full-time employees, and most of them barely increase their size during their relatively depersonalized national campaign periods. In contrast, the U.S. system finds expansive candidate staffs supplemented by bloated party organizations which disintegrate or deflate once the election is held. In West Germany and Israel, on the other hand, intense party competition has led to well-staffed party bureaucracies complemented by extensive short-term campaign efforts.[13]

Business federations play an informal role in financing center and conservative parties in many countries, but they are especially significant in Austria, West Germany, the Low Countries, and Japan. Conservative, centrist, and agrarian parties are usually highly organized and well-staffed, whereas liberal parties tend to reflect a low propensity for formal party membership. Union affiliation provides special advantages and relatively large memberships to socialist and leftist parties. Mass membership parties often levy a tax on salaries and honoraria their elected officials receive; some derive income from business activities operative outside their party memberships, as, for example, in Finland. The parties in Italy receive funding from their representation in state enterprises.

In parliamentary systems, funding is usually supplemented by free broadcast time, again made mainly to the parties, and not to candidates.

---

[13] Arnold J. Heidenheimer, "Major Modes of Raising, Spending and Controlling Political Funds during and between Election Campaigns," in Arnold J. Heidenheimer, ed., *Comparative Political Finance: The Financing of Party Organizations and Election Campaigns* (Lexington, Mass.: D.C. Heath and Co., 1970), p. 11.

In Austria, time is provided not only to the parties but also to interest groups, mainly associations of labor and industry which play a considerable role in Austrian politics. In Canada, stations are required to make available six-and-a-half hours of prime time for sale to the parties on a proportional basis, but the parties are then reimbursed by the government for 50 percent of the cost; additionally, candidates can purchase time within their spending limits. In Australia, free party time is provided by the government, but time also can be privately purchased. In the United States, little free time is provided and most time is purchased. Major campaigns are well-covered in news and interview programs. Debates among candidates have been designated as news events, thus exempting them from equal opportunity provisions and permitting free time.

The British variation. No national officials are elected in the British and some other parliamentary systems.[14] Rather, candidates for the House of Commons are elected at the constituency level, and the national leadership is chosen in an "apprenticeship" system,[15] whereby party leaders are selected by the parliamentary party to advance to the front bench after serving in secondary cabinet posts.

Candidates at the constituency level must file statements called Returns of Expenditures: these are submitted after the election to the returning officers, who send them on to the home office where a nationwide compilation is made and published.[16]

The filings verify that the candidate did not exceed the expenditure limit. The expenses a candidate may incur are limited and any infringement may involve penalties, including the annulment of the election for the winning candidate. The maximum expenditure which may be incurred by a candidate is: (1) in borough constituencies, £1,075, plus 6p. for every eight entries in the register of electors; (2) in county constituencies, £1,075, plus 6p. for every six entries in the register.[17]

A candidate may mail one communication not weighing more than two ounces, free of charge, to every elector in the constituency. All other expenses, apart from the candidate's personal ones, including fees to the

[14] Some, however, do elect a president, as, for example, in France and West Germany.
[15] Hugh Heclo and Aaron Wildavsky, *The Private Government of Public Money: Community and Policy inside British Politics* (Berkeley and Los Angeles: University of California Press, 1974), p. 6.
[16] See, for example, *Election Expenses,* Home office and Scottish office (London: Her Majesty's Stationery Office, August 8, 1966).
[17] Michael Pinto-Duschinsky, *Britain: The Problem of Non-Campaign Finance,* paper presented at the Conference on Political Money and Election Reform, University of Southern California, December 1977, p. 31.

election agent, printing and stationery, advertising and bill posting, the hire of rooms for committee and public meetings, and the employment of a secretary, must be covered within the statutory limits. No expenses for the election of a candidate may be incurred by anyone other than the candidate himself, the election agent, or a person authorized by the agent. Local constituency parties abstain from participating in candidates' campaigns so as to avoid activities that might be construed as on behalf of a candidate.

The candidate, or someone on his behalf, has to deposit the sum of £150 with the returning officer when delivering the nomination papers. If the candidate receives at least 12.5 percent of the votes cast, his deposit is returned; if not, it is forfeited. The deposit is intended to discourage candidates who are not serious contestants.

There are no spending ceilings on the parties at either the national or constituency levels, nor any limit on support from voluntary sources. Yet campaign costs remain under control, despite some leakage that occurs at the constituency level when candidates nurse their constituencies heavily before the anticipated election call, and some agents are known to have gone off the payroll by ostensibly taking their vacations during the campaign period. The national parties are not limited, but they generally fear impinging upon candidate constituency limits, since specific national spending might be considered to be promoting local candidates who are subject to the limits. According to Michael Pinto-Duschinsky, British parties welcome the imposed and voluntary limits, which mask their inability to raise more money.[18]

One reason for expenditure control is the arrangements for party election broadcasts, which are made by a committee comprising political parties, the British Broadcasting Corporation (BBC), and the Independent Broadcasting Authority (IBA). Election broadcasts are relayed simultaneously on all channels. The allocation of broadcasts for the May 1979 general election gave the Labour and Conservative parties five television broadcasts of ten minutes each, and seven radio broadcasts (four of ten minutes and three of five minutes); the Liberal party had three television broadcasts of ten minutes, and five radio broadcasts (three of ten minutes and two of five minutes). The Scottish National party had three television and three radio broadcasts, lasting ten minutes each. Plaid Cymru (Welsh Nationalists) had one television and one radio broadcast, each lasting ten minutes. Other parties with more than fifty candidates also may receive some television and radio time: during the 1979 election, the National Front, the Workers' Revolutionary party, and the Ecology party each had one five-minute broadcast on television

---

[18] Pinto-Duschinsky, *Britain,* pp. 27–28.

and radio. The broadcasting authorities also arrange regional programs which include, on a basis of parity, representatives of parties with candidates in at least 20 percent of the constituencies within the region. Under the Representation of the People Act, a candidate cannot take part in a program about his constituency during an election campaign unless each of his rivals either takes part or consents to its being broadcast.

In Great Britain, the national parties need not disclose their funding, although in recent years the Conservative and Labour parties have done so voluntarily. The Companies Act of 1967, however, requires a corporation to declare in its accounts any money given for political purposes if it exceeds £50. Companies disclose gifts and the recipients in their annual reports; the Labour Party Research Department collects these and compiles a list of such corporate contributions to the Conservative party, which is the only centralized, if partial, listing available.[19] Only a portion of the corporate funds go directly to the central headquarters of the Conservative party. The rest goes to constituency parties or propaganda organizations such as British United Industrialists, the Economic League, and Aims of Industry. These organizations also contribute to the party, but they operate parallel campaigns promoting Conservative views.[20]

Under the Trade Union Act of 1913, unions wishing to use funds for "political objects" must obtain members' approval by ballot in order to establish a political fund. Once set up, individual union members may "contract out" of payments to the fund, but this requires an overt act; otherwise political payments are automatically collected along with dues. Unions provide income on a regular basis to the Labour party, at both the national and the constituency party levels. They must make annual financial statements, including overall income, expenditures, and reserves of the political funds, but the expenditures are not presented in detail.[21]

Local unions provide manpower and services, as in the United States, in parallel campaigning carefully avoiding specific candidate support. Constituency party income for both parties comes from members' dues, contributions from supporters, and voluntary activities of supporters, including various social events, lotteries, and games. Michael Pinto-Duschinsky claims that, nationally, union contributions seem to be as

---

[19] See, for example, Labour Party Research Department, *Company Donations to the Tory Party and Their Allies,* Information Paper no. 4 (London, September 1978).

[20] William V. Shannon, "Money and Politics" (New York: Alicia Patterson Fund, February 1970), p. 4.

[21] Pinto-Duschinsky, *Britain,* p. 34.

large in the aggregate as is company giving.[22] The Conservative party, however, benefits from a larger and more generous membership than that of the Labour party, which accounts in part for the Conservative party income advantage.

The British method of control utilizes the law of agency; this is also true of Canada and other countries where candidates must appoint agents who centralize funding and are responsible for receiving contributions and making disbursements. In the United States, in contrast, agents need not be appointed, but principal campaign committees must be designated, other political committees must be authorized, and each committee must have a chairperson and a treasurer, who have statutory responsibilities which are enumerated in the law.

Other systems. Canada and its provinces combine systems of assistance to the parties with schemes of partial reimbursement of candidates' election expenses federally and in several provinces. Limited tax credits are provided for contributions at the federal and provincial levels. Gifts are unlimited at the federal level, but are limited in some provinces. Corporate and labor contributions are not prohibited at the federal level, but are in Quebec and elsewhere. Expenditure limits apply federally and in some provinces.[23] Because of spending limits and fund control by agents, advertising is limited in effect to parties, candidates, and their official agents, but issues can be discussed by interest groups as long as specific party and candidate references are not made.

In France, political parties enjoy no special status, and they cannot legally receive gifts or legacies, but are expected to be financed solely from contributions of members and the proceeds of appeals.[24] In practice, the parties have established links with industry providing support to ensure better funding. These relationships assume a more complex

---

[22] Pinto-Duschinsky, *Britain,* p. 13.

[23] *A Comparative Survey,* pp. 24–57.

[24] Information following derived from a variety of sources: *Report of the Committee on Financial Aid to Political Parties,* known as The Houghton Report (London: Her Majesty's Stationery Office, August 1976); U.S., Library of Congress, *Public Financing of National Elections in Foreign Countries,* June 1979; Adamany and Agree, *Political Money,* chap. 9, pp. 156–174; Dick Leonard, *Paying for Party Politics: The Case for Public Subsidies* (London: PEP, 1975); Dick Leonard, "Contrasts in Selected Western Democracies: Germany, Sweden, Britain," in Herbert E. Alexander, ed., *Political Finance* (Beverly Hills: Sage Publications, 1979), pp. 41–73; Khayyam Z. Paltiel, "The Impact of Election Expenses Legislation in Canada, Western Europe, and Israel," in Alexander, ed., *Political Finance,* pp. 15–39; Richard Crossman, Kurt Southeimer, and Liv Reay Geddes, "Financing Political Parties: A Symposium," *The Political Quarterly,* vol. 45, no. 3 (July–September 1974), pp. 333–345; and Harry Forsell, *Some Aspects of the Communal Party Subsidy in Sweden* (Princeton, N.J.: Citizens' Research Foundation, 1973).

form than in other countries because of the legal obstacles. The limited assistance provided by government goes to candidates, not to the parties. Laws in Japan, most of which have been influenced by American standards, control party contributions and place restrictions on campaign advertising. There are limits on donations by individuals and corporations to parties, political groups, and candidates. Corporations and trade unions are limited according to the amount of capitalization of the company or the size of the union membership. The restrictions, however, are not applicable to gifts from business associations, which play a large role in Japanese politics. Candidates receive a free car for electioneering, posters, and limited advertising. Restrictions are imposed on advertising by candidates' support organizations and on the free distribution of party newspapers.

Cross-National Comparison

Spending Limits. Apart from the U.S. system, which limits spending by some candidates, the election codes of Britain, Canada, Australia,[25] and Japan place ceilings on the amount which a candidate may spend during the brief campaign period permitted. Several of the Australian states and Canadian provinces have similar provisions.

Austria and Israel place ceilings on party spending,[26] Israel by placing a limit on outside sources and by prohibiting a party from exceeding its allocation by more than one-third through private funds. When public funding was adopted in Finland, agreement was reached to eliminate large quantities of outdoor posters in large cities, and to share fewer billboards instead.

Contribution Limits. Perhaps influenced by United States standards, four Canadian provinces (but not the federal government), and Japan limit individual or group contributions. Israel and Japan limit support group spending on behalf of a candidate.

Tax Provisions. Countries providing limited tax benefits to contributors, including corporate or association entities in some cases, are the United States, Canada, and West Germany. Austria did not directly permit tax deduction of donations, but that effect was achieved by gifts to profes-

---

[25] Colin A. Hughes, "Party Finance and Compulsory Voting: The Australian Experience," paper presented at the 11th World Congress of the International Political Science Association, Moscow, August 1979.

[26] Leon Boim, "The Financing of Elections," in Howard R. Penniman, ed., *Israel at the Polls: The Knesset Elections of 1977* (Washington, D.C.: American Enterprise Institute for Public Research, 1979), pp. 205–208.

sional associations which in turn gave to the parties. This was eliminated in 1975 by tightening the deductibility of contributions to professional associations, while simultaneously levying a 35 percent tax on contributions made by such associations to political parties.

Auditing. In Canada, each candidate must appoint an auditor who reports to the candidate's official agent on the election expenses filed on behalf of the candidate. In Austria, Costa Rica, Israel, and West Germany, audits of public funds are done by government or expenses must be validated before a government agency before public funds are provided. In the United States, audits by the Federal Election Commission have been a subject of controversy, and the scope and tardiness of some audits have led to considerable criticism of the FEC. Some presidential candidates have had to return public funds when audits have disputed certain uses.

Linkages. In the United States, spending limits are linked to public financing. The architects of the federal law based their arguments for government funding on two interrelated theories. One was that government funds should be provided within the framework of campaign expenditure limits, because Congress and state legislatures were thought unlikely to add tax dollars to whatever private funds could be raised, thus seeming to escalate campaign costs uncontrollably. The second theory was that government funding should be enacted to provide a necessary alternative source to make up for the reduction in funding caused by the contribution limits.

The American dialogue has only lately come to recognize the concept of floors without ceilings; this approach is accepted in such mature democracies as the Scandinavian countries and West Germany, where government subsidies are provided but there are no limits on private contributions. The notion is that partial public funding, or a floor, can be provided without simultaneously mandating a spending ceiling.

Recently, there have been mixed reactions to spending ceilings. In New Jersey, where expenditure limits in the publicly funded 1977 gubernatorial campaigns tended to rigidify the process, a majority of the New Jersey Election Law Enforcement Commission has since recommended repealing overall expenditure limits; however, a cap would be placed on the amount of public funds available, and limitations on contributions, on loans, and on candidates' personal funds would be continued.[27] In 1979, states (unlike the federal government) continue to adopt subsidies

---

[27] New Jersey Election Law Enforcement Commission, *Public Financing in New Jersey: The 1977 General Election for Governor,* August 1978, p. 35.

despite the Proposition 13 atmosphere of fiscal restraint. Oklahoma recently enacted such a law without imposing spending ceilings,[28] whereas Hawaii linked the two.[29] In Hawaii and Minnesota, efforts have been made to link expenditure limits to tax deductions.

In the United States, optional provisions that a presidential candidate can refuse the public money could produce a general election campaign with only one of the major candidates totally financed by public funds—an incongrous situation which could escalate accusations about the virtues of public or private funding into a major campaign issue. Of course, the candidate not accepting public funds is not subject to expenditure limits.

In the United States, public funding is generally linked to a tax checkoff or a surcharge. The latter permits a taxpayer to add a dollar or two onto one's tax liability, while the former earmarks a dollar or two, which would have to be paid anyway, to a special political fund. Only in New Jersey has money been appropriated for the purpose (before a state income tax was enacted).

While presidential public funding provides money directly to the candidates, nine states permit party designation, and in seven of them the money is not mandated for candidates but can be used by the state party committees at their discretion in general elections. By some standards, the states are truly "laboratories of reform," as Justice Brandeis once put it, in another context, and are experimenting by assisting political parties financially, even without linkages to spending ceilings.

In some countries, political parties must make disclosures, but often after elections or on an annual basis, not before elections. However, in Austria, campaign expenses are limited by a requirement that eight weeks before the election the parties must publish their anticipated expenditures for the campaign period, including the last five weeks preceding the election. If the parties exceed the published limit by more than 10 percent, 50 percent of the excess is deducted from the next payment of funds due under the law. Thus Austrian disclosure and limitation are both tied to public funding. One of the pressures for subsidies was to ensure that parties would publish their accounts. The same linkage occurred in Finland.[30]

---

[28] "Oklahoma Gets Public Financing for Statewide Elections," *Campaign Practices Reports,* vol. 6, no. 12 (June 11, 1979), pp. 7–8.
[29] "Hawaii Starts Limited Funding of State, Local Elections," *Campaign Practices Reports,* vol. 6, no. 14 (July 9, 1979), pp. 6–8.
[30] Pertti Pesonen, *Impact of Public Financing on Political Parties: The Finnish Experience* (Princeton, N.J.: Citizens' Research Foundation, 1973), pp. 12–14.

Commentary

Foreign custom is more tolerant than is U.S. custom of campaign spending generally—specifically of spending excesses, large contributions, group contributions, and split giving. Abroad, there is more recognition of the integral relationships between government, parties, citizens, groups, and institutions. American traditional patterns of giving were upset by the strict contribution limitations imposed by the Federal Election Campaign Act, as amended, and the mechanisms set up for their enforcement.

Growth of PACs. Ironically, the laws designed to reduce special-interest influence, especially individual contribution limits, have accelerated the growth of PACs. PACs are focusing increasingly on congressional campaigns, where there is no public funding and no consequent expenditure control. From 1972 to 1976, of all political dollars spent, the presidential portion fell from 33 percent to 30 percent, whereas the congressional rose from 23 percent to 26 percent. Larger portions of congressional campaign income comes from PACs than in the past. The combination of public and party funding provides almost all of presidential general election funding, while presidential prenomination financing is derived from individual contributions, minimal PAC assistance, and no legitimate party help at all. Parallel labor and corporate spending has been noted above.

In the United States, there are increasing levels of sophistication among PAC managers. Umbrella groups, such as the National Association of Business Political Action Committees (NABPAC), seek to share data, circulate candidate evaluations which include information on campaigns and their financing, and generally to keep members informed. Because each PAC decides individually which candidates to support, the degree of coordination falls short of the centralized character of business federations in foreign countries. Yet the exchange of information and the development of intelligence sources could lead to greater flows of money to favored candidates, particularly those in marginal races given a chance to win if adequate funding is available. The next step, taken in foreign countries, would involve PACs or their sponsors to a greater extent in the recruitment of candidates. Where labor or business interests do not have the power to nominate in the United States, as in open primary elections, they sometimes are able to exercise veto power, or they may discourage candidates from running by refusing financial support.

Split Giving. Split giving occurs most often in countries where parties are strong. In numerous countries, Canada, Denmark, and Japan, among others, business concerns often give to several parties simultaneously.[31] In many of these countries, including West Germany and the Low Countries, powerful industrial, commercial, and financial concerns have set up machinery for raising and supplying political funds.[32] Business associations are the favorite means and a continuing source of funds, although efforts have been made to control them in Austria, Japan, and West Germany, among others. Union financial support of labor parties is especially significant in Commonwealth countries, and is made more so where "contracting out" is not permitted.

In the United States, opposing candidates seldom receive money from the same source, although candidates of opposing parties at differing levels do receive contributions from the same source. More often, party committees receive funds from the same source, particularly when PACs support annual party dinners.

Declining Party Strength. Political parties formerly played some of the roles which interest and lobbying groups now perform. The erosion of party influence in the United States, particularly, has often been noted. American attitudes toward parties differ from those in other democracies, but there are signs of lessening party allegiances and diminishing party efforts even in countries noted for their party stability. In Britain, one activist calls the Labour party an "empty shell" and decries the "puny circulation" of *Labour Weekly*.[33] The party and the parliamentary party are sometimes at odds, and a Labour government could not control striking unions. The treasurer of the Labour party writes of "Labour's lamentable failure over the last twenty-five years to make much headway" and claims further—though without presenting evidence—that state aid in Germany and the Scandinavian countries "has stultified the socialist cause."[34] Others elsewhere feel similarly. In all free and democratic societies, propertied interests remain influential, even where socialist parties rule or are strongly competitive, or where efforts have been made to control business or federation activity. Compared with other groups, industry, finance, and business have few voters or direct political representation, yet they maintain power derived from their place in society

---

[31] Heard, *The Costs*, p. 67.

[32] Arnold J. Heidenheimer and Frank C. Langdon, *Business Association and the Financing of Political Parties* (The Hague: Martinus Nijhoff, 1968), pp. 1–13.

[33] Leslie Huckfield, "The Case for State Aid," *Tribune* (London), January 19, 1979, p. 12.

[34] Norman Atkinson, "Should the Labour Party Go for State Aid? Increase Membership Subscriptions? Appeal to the Unions?" *Tribune* (London), January 12, 1979, p. 5.

and the essential nature of their functions, in creating capital, employment, trade, and commerce.

Political parties in power, either singly or in coalition with others, find that national interests—however defined—cause them to modify business, labor, church, or other influences. Parties, in or out of power, factionalize, and even communist parties do not enjoy the solidarity and discipline that would make them monoliths within democratic societies.

Differing Regulatory Climates. Differing regulatory climates affect the roles of parties and interest groups in diverse ways. Spending control is relatively effective in some countries, such as Great Britain, even without restrictions on the parties themselves. In some countries, Canada, West Germany, Israel, Japan, and Venezuela, for example, advanced campaign technology and professional management have brought high costs despite highly developed party bureaucracies.

Nowhere is money so available as to appear to be excessive, unless Israel and Venezuela qualify for that distinction. Exhortations about the high cost of campaigning in the United States sound hollow in view of the lack of two-party competitiveness in many areas and the under-financing of many candidates and party organizations. America, particularly, fails to provide adequate funding for party research and media functions, and discretionary funds go for "nuts and bolts" organizational seminars rather than research and planning, which are important functions of the party foundations in West Germany. Of course, part of the gap is filled by executive and legislative personnel whose governmental salaries provide the means for extensive partisan issue development in the guise of staff work.

Implications for the United States. Election law in the United States and elsewhere does not always recognize the legitimate concern of labor, management, and other groups with public policy. There is nothing inherently immoral or corrupting about a corporate or labor dollar, any more than any other private dollar, apart from responsibilities to stockholders and members.

The reformer's ideal in the United States has been criticized for seeking "a direct dialogue between candidates and voters, both free of outside influences."[35] In mass society, however, politics without the influence of interest groups is not realistic. Politics can be improved, but it probably cannot be sterilized and purified to a degree that reformers seek. Eugene McCarthy has reminded us that water lilies do not grow

---

[35] Carleton W. Sterling, "Control of Campaign Spending: The Reformers' Paradox," *American Bar Association Journal,* vol. 59 (October 1973), p. 1153.

without a bacteria count. Moreover, when parties are treated as little more than super–interest groups, their historic role is not appreciated. Politics is about people and groups of people, their ideas, interests, and aspirations. Many people seek political fulfillment through groups and parties, which serve as reference points for atomized citizens in rudderless societies. Some groups and parties with few members participate mainly through their wealth. Since people and groups differ, conflict occurs, but it does so in a political arena in which government sets the rules and the players are expected to play by them. The government, however, is also a player, and the only fail-safe guarantee against its dominance lies in the ability of groups and interests in society to articulate their demands, to coalesce, and to oppose government with resources, including money resources, they command.

Citizen participation in politics, including pocketbook participation, is one way to baffle concentrated privilege. Politics is properly animated by the voluntary efforts of individuals, political parties, groups, and organizations. Election laws which restrict, prohibit, and subsidize have created environments that affect certain forms of political voluntarism: accordingly, the laws influence the roles of candidates, political committees, political parties, special interests, and political action groups, which all depend to some degree on the voluntary actions of citizens. In democracies, citizen actions combine with various types of resources to form the basis of political activity. But money and resources are only one part of a complex political ecology in which voting remains the single most important individual act, and politicians listen to voters regardless of contributions accepted from other sources. Strong competition among various individuals, interests, groups, and parties in society, each trying to generate widespread support, is essential to the vitality of systems of free elections.

Public Financing Abroad: Contrasts and Effects

Khayyam Zev Paltiel

The movement toward the public financing of parties, candidates, and election campaigns, which began in Puerto Rico in 1957 and has since spread throughout the democratic world, may be traced to socioeconomic developments and recent electoral experiences in the states concerned. Among the main causes of legislative action have been recurring scandals regarding the raising and spending of campaign funds; public revulsion against the intervention—often clandestine—of powerful economic interests, domestic and foreign, in the electoral process; shifts in public mores related to the erosion of traditional patterns of patronage and relationships between politicians and their "clients," or voters; cost inflation and new campaign styles; and the relative decline of the press and the rise of the electronic media and professional communicators involving heavy financial outlays. In turn these reforms have been shaped by the particular constitutional arrangements, executive and legislative structures, and electoral and party systems prevailing in each country.

Whether the motive for change was financial stringency, the reduction of the burden of rising election costs, or the desire to escape the taint of corruption, or a mixture of these, efforts were made to justify these reforms in terms of liberal democratic ideology. Democracy, it was argued, required a fair chance for competitors in the electoral process. The allocation of public funds to parties and candidates was necessary to assure equality of opportunity and access to the electorate whose support was being sought. Such assistance would further reinforce the voters' right to know and to be informed of the policy alternatives and the candidates and parties competing for their favor. Furthermore, public subsidies would reduce the dependence of parties and candidates on large contributions from powerful sectoral interests and free politicians from the temptation to resort to questionable sources of funds, thus rendering the electoral process more transparent and pure.

Campaign subsidy schemes have rarely been adopted in isolation from other regulatory measures. Such subsidies are never unconditional and have usually, but not invariably, been linked to a number of legal stipulations. These may require the reporting and disclosure of details of income and expenditures, and the audit of party and candidate records by public officials and publication of their findings. The provision of subsidies has frequently been accompanied by the imposition of total or segmental ceilings on contributions and expenditures. Limits may be imposed on particular types of expenses and restrictions or bans may be placed on certain sources of funds; some campaign activities may be completely prohibited. Public financing of parties and candidates operates within a network of regulations peculiar to each state, every element of which impinges upon the other and helps determine the impact of the subsidy scheme on the particular party system.

The question of the reform of party finance can be examined from various standpoints. One can investigate the motives of the legislators and the particular historical circumstances which precipitated the demand for change. Laws passed in the aftermath of scandal will differ markedly from those arising out of financial stringency or sharp rises in election costs. Subsidy schemes resulting from the constitutional invalidation of tax exemptions for party donations will reflect a reality other than one arising from a reform movement stressing the German liberal notion of *Chancengleichheit,* or equality of opportunity for all legitimate political parties. Although the forms of subsidy schemes derive from the circumstances of their origin, a formal analysis would stress their shape and content; the nature of the activities subject to control; the legal, contractual, or normative nature of the controls; and the control agencies and the activities benefiting from direct and indirect support of the public treasury. Not least, such an analysis would examine the points at which public support enters the party system, and the persons or groups subject to control.

Motive and form are of paramount interest to the political historian and legislator, but the practical politician and political scientist should pay particular attention to the structural impact of the subsidy system. The form and content of control schemes take on meaning in the light of their effects on internal party organization and the articulation of the party system. A study of form and content would indicate the impact of subsidy systems on the distribution of power within each party and the differential effect of the subsidy on the parliamentary leadership, backbenchers, candidates, the extraparliamentary organization, and professional staff. Such a study might further disclose the relative advantages or disadvantages of such schemes to incumbent governmental or opposition parties, to large and small political factions, to groups which have not yet achieved representation in elected representative bodies, and to independent candidates. The questions of the openness and accessibility of the party system and of whether public subsidies promote participation in the electoral process raise the related subject of the consequences of subsidies on the ties which bind elected officials, parties, and candidates to specific social, economic, and ideological interests. Finally one cannot ignore the fact that while subsidy systems have been adopted within particular formal legal frameworks, these reforms may have intended or unintended effects on the interaction between the constitutional levels of government, as in federal states, by concentrating or dispersing decision-making power and authority.

A brief selective review of the different kinds of public campaign finance laws will serve as a background to the analysis of the effect of subsidy schemes on incumbents, major and minor parties, central party organizations and paid party staff, federalism, and the issue of neo-corporatism.

Types of Public Financing

Three distinct methods of subsidizing campaign expenses and supporting party activities may be discerned: direct subventions, specific grants or services, and indirect subsidies. These commonly occur in combination. Direct subventions include grants of money to the parliamentary caucuses of recognized or registered parties, annual allocations for organizational expenses, and cash advances or reimbursements for a portion of the total campaign expenses of qualifying parties and candidates. Such direct subventions are made for general purposes. By contrast, specific grants or services are designed to cover part of the costs of distinct expenditures, such as broadcasting, mailing, billposting, paper (including the printing of ballots), press and information bureaus, nomination meetings, and operations of women's and youth groups, or party educational and research foundations. Included here might be the assumption by the state of such costs as voter registration and the free use of public facilities for meetings and other purposes. Indirect subsidies usually take the form of tax credits or tax deductions for contributions to parties and candidates. The rationale for indirect subsidies is to provide an incentive to parties to seek a broader participation of the electorate in the monetary aspects of the electoral process. In contrast to American law makers, most legislators abroad have opted for "objective" modes of allocation to electoral competitors and have avoided "subjective" methods, such as earmarking taxes for the benefit of designated political organizations or matching the sum of small donations deposited to the credit of particular candidates and parties.

Direct Subventions. Most of the legislatures in the democratic world provide some form of assistance to the parliamentary caucuses of the parties by way of funds for secretarial, research, and informational purposes. Although these funds are designed primarily for the legislative faction, in some countries such as Denmark they may be the principal source of help to the parties, especially when the application of these funds is unrestricted by legislative rules. The usual formula for the allocation of these funds takes into account the number of seats held by each recognized faction. Variants might provide a basic fixed sum for each group plus the size factor, or a somewhat reduced allocation for the government parties which are presumed to benefit from the public servants at the disposal of their ministers.

Similar formulas are used in those countries which make grants for the regular or annual organizational expenses of the parties. Argentina, Austria, Finland, Israel, Italy, Norway, Sweden, and the Canadian province of Quebec provide state support for these purposes on an annual basis. In every case the law requires that a party receiving organizational support have representation in the elected chamber of the legislature. Sweden makes such grants to parties without legislative seats that have received a certain percentage of support at a general election on the national or constituency level; Austria, on the other hand, restricts support to unrepresented parties to election years, provided such parties fulfill disclosure conditions and have received a minimum percentage of votes in the previous general election. In protest against the former requirement, the Austrian Communists refuse to accept such aid. Norway requires that beneficiary parties present candidates in at least 50 percent of the constituencies. Sweden also tries to mitigate violent fluctuations in party income by basing half the annual subsidy on each of the last two general elections. The Italian Organizational Fund follows the common pattern of a fixed sum plus a proportionate amount for national parties with seats in the Senate and Chamber of Deputies, but includes special provisions for the Valdaostan, Tyrolese, and other linguistic and minority parties.

The most significant direct subventions are the grants made in various countries to help meet the election expenses of parties and candidates. These payments may be made as post-campaign reimbursements of all or a portion of permitted expenditures, or as advances against the anticipated costs of a forthcoming election. Combinations of these schemes may be employed; advances may be based on the results of the previous election supplemented by reimbursements (and sometimes repayments) to accord with the results of the immediate voting outcome. In several cases, such as Puerto Rico and West Ger-

357

many, partial payments of the reimbursements are made annually, scaled and staggered over the period between elections to provide an ongoing organizational maintenance subsidy to the qualifying parties. The shape of the subsidy system varies not only with whether there is a fixed interval between election dates but also with the nature of the electoral system. A system with proportional representation may have a different type of subsidy scheme than a single-member first-past-the-post territorial constituency system. Still another approach might be needed in a situation such as that in Puerto Rico, which has a Commonwealth-wide constituency for the election of the chief executive, a system that permits a facsimile of the schemes in force in PR systems.

The issues raised here can perhaps best be illustrated by providing some details regarding the Puerto Rican, West German, and Canadian reimbursement systems. The pioneering subsidy system introduced in Puerto Rico with the Election Fund Act of 1957 was designed to remove the former dependence of the island's main political parties on the entrenched sugar interests and on the "macing" of civil servants, many of whom were pressured into donating as much as 2 percent of their salaries to the party in power. The act provided for the creation of an election fund in every four-year cycle from which registered "principal" political parties—those which had gained 10 percent of the votes cast for governor in the previous general election, presented candidates in every district, and won representation in the legislature—could withdraw up to $75,000 in nonelection years and $150,000 in election years to meet administrative, operational, and election costs. Limits were set on the size of contributions, public employees were protected against compulsion, and parties were required to maintain records and file reports of their finances. The act has been amended in 1958, 1960, and 1964 and periodically since then to make subsidies available to smaller parties by reducing the qualifying percentage of votes, to increase the sums available, and to link disbursements to the number of votes received in the gubernatorial elections.

The first West German direct subsidy scheme was introduced in 1959 as a budget allocation. The plan was enacted after the Federal Constitutional Court in 1958 declared tax exemptions for political donations to be unconstitutional because they violated the fundamental rights of political parties to equality of opportunity, of citizens to equality of treatment, and of corporation shareholders to their profits through the diversion of corporate funds to political parties. Crude pressure by private industry on the liberal Free Democrats also played a role. The initial public grants for party political education work were expanded in the next five years to cover the general activities of the parties. Fixed sums totalling 20 percent of the grant were allocated to each party represented in the Bundestag; the other 80 percent was divided according to each party's electoral strength. Several small parties—including the right-wing National Democrats, who lacked parliamentary representation because failure to attain the minimum "exclusion percentage" precluded them from receiving such grants—and a section of the Social Democrats who controlled the Länd Hesse government challenged the validity of these budget allocations. In 1966 the Karlsruhe Constitutional Court ruled the existing system of subsidies for the general activities of parties to be unconstitutional. However, the court moderated the implications of its judgment by indicating that it could accept the establishment of subsidies to cover the necessary costs of election campaigns. The court said that as long as such grants were linked to direct election costs and as long as the principles of equality of treatment and opportunity for parties and citizens were respected—by implication, as long as subsidies were not limited to groups with seats in the Bundestag—public financing of parties would be permissible. The lack of clear guidelines and the generality of the judgment paved the way for the present system.

The West German Parties Law of 1967 introduced a formula which linked direct subventions to actual campaign costs of the 1965 federal general election. The total sum of 95 million deutsche marks was divided by the number of eligible voters and the subsidy fixed at 2.5 deutsche marks per elector, payment of which was to be made over the following four-year inter-election period to parties which had received at least 2.5 percent of the total votes cast (this percentage was lowered to 0.5 percent in 1972). Receipt of the reimbursements was made conditional on annual reports of income at federal and länder levels to the president of the Bundestag, including the specific itemization of large contributions over 20,000 deutsche marks. The payments are scaled and spread over four years as follows: first year after the relevant election, 0 percent; second year after, 10 percent; third year, 15 percent; fourth year just before the next election, 35 percent; and immediately after the election, 40 percent. In 1974 the basic subsidy per eligible voter was raised to 3.5 deutsche marks. In the period 1972–1976 the federal parties had shared in the total of 142 million deutsche marks, or about $56 million. Similar subsidies are paid to the German parties at the provincial or länd level, albeit in different basic amounts and scales. One estimate places the total income of German parties from public sources in the period 1972–1976 at approximately $200 million in 1976 rates of exchange. It should be noted, however, that despite the German concern for constitutional niceties, the problem of independent candidates has not been resolved by the legislators or the courts. The electoral laws, with their stress on parties and their needs, have not provided for the reimbursement of the campaign costs of independents. The solution suggested by the courts would require that such persons achieve a qualifying percentage ten times as high as for parties.

By contrast, the Canadian system of federal and provincial campaign subventions is particularly concerned with the reimbursement of a portion of the election costs of qualifying candidates at the constituency level. All candidates conforming to other provisions of the electoral laws who have won or have gained at least 15 percent of the total votes cast in their ridings are eligible in the provinces of Alberta, Nova Scotia, and Saskatchewan and at the federal level. In Quebec, candidates must receive 20 percent of the vote or must have been the standard bearers of parties whose local nominees won the greatest or second greatest number of votes in the previous election. Depending on the number of eligible electors in the constituency, repayments are either of actual costs up to a ceiling, or on a flat rate or sliding scale. The federal act defines the subsidy in terms of the equivalent of the cost of first-class postage for a one-ounce item plus eight cents for each elector below 25,000 on the list, and plus six cents for every one over that number; currently those figures are twenty-five cents and twenty-three cents, respectively, and cover about one-third of the permitted expenses in the average riding. The system is clearly of greatest value to the two largest traditional parties.

The Italian election subsidies follow the pattern of the organizational subventions. Fifteen percent of a fixed election fund of 15 billion lire or $25 million for each campaign is divided equally among the largest parties which have presented candidates in at least two-thirds of the multimember constituencies and have received at least 2 percent of the vote; the remaining 85 percent is allocated among *all* parties proportionate to their share of the vote.

Variants of these schemes are in effect in a number of other countries, such as Costa Rica, Turkey, and Venezuela. Israel, for instance, links its direct subsidies for the organizational and election expenses of parties to the cost of living. A yearly *financing unit* based on the cost of living is determined periodically and is paid to parties in monthly shares depending on the number of seats each party holds in the Knesset. When a campaign is imminent, an advance of 60 percent of the unit is paid to each party or faction with seats in the outgoing Knesset presenting a list of candidates. The balance is paid after the election or used as repayment to the public treasury if the party fails to maintain its previous number of seats. For newly elected parties or those gaining additional seats, 85 percent of the financial unit per seat won is paid immediately after the election with the remaining 15 percent paid after the state comptroller has submitted a positive report on the party's finances to the speaker of the Knesset. Although Israeli law generally favors established parties, it differs from many others in that a party suffering a drastic loss in seats, as the Labor Alignment and its smaller allies did in 1977, may find the subsidy repayment provisions extremely onerous.

Specific Grants and Services. The oldest and most widespread forms of public assistance to political parties and candidates are the assumption by the state of certain costs and services which at one time were considered to be the obligation of those seeking political office. Although these must be considered a transfer rather than a reduction of total costs, the effect is a considerable saving to the participants in the electoral process. In contrast to the United States, the registration or enumeration of voters in most countries is a public charge carried out by civil servants or by specially hired staff. In Canada, this service provides an additional aid to the parties in that the enumerators are hired on nomination by the winning and runner-up candidates or their local organizations in each constituency. The payment of this small army of over 50,000 enumerators serves as a reward to the humblest of party workers who may later be expected to help in candidate committee rooms and as door-to-door canvassers during the campaign. Free election broadcasting time on radio and television is almost universal in the majority of countries with public broadcasting systems. Certain problems have emerged in states which have made such services available, such as the United Kingdom, the Scandinavian countries, France, Germany, Israel, Italy, Austria, Japan, and Canada. The greatest problem is the allocation of time. Granting equal amounts of time to each party might encourage the formation of splinter groups; on the other hand, the system favors the status quo where time is given in proportion to the number of seats won or votes received at the previous general election. A special problem arises in mixed public and private commercial broadcasting systems such as Canada's. There the problem is resolved by allocating a fixed amount of prime time on all networks and stations for all parties for a four-week period prior to polling day. This total is then divided among the registered parties roughly according to their strength at the previous general election; each small or newly registered party is assured at least one minimum period. The parties may purchase up to the maximum of the times alloted them on each outlet and are then reimbursed half the cost of the amount bought. Free time follows a similar principle of allocation by the Canadian Radio-Television and Telecommunications Commission.

Other services made available in some countries are the use of public buildings for political meetings and free mailings in the United Kingdom and France, the distribution of campaign pamphlets in France and Japan; free transportation for candidates in Japan and subsidized travel for delegates to nomination meetings in Norway; paper and free bill posting in France, Finland, and Japan; and the provision of ballots in France to each party. Most continental European countries provide generous assistance to the press and publications of the recognized parties in addition to the press and information bureaus maintained by their parliamentary factions. Not least among these specific grants are the budgetary provisions in aid of the women's organizations and youth groups affiliated to the main parties in the Scandinavian countries and West Germany. The most important form of assistance to the parapolitical affiliates of political parties in Europe are the public grants made to the political, educational, and research institutes and party foundations in Austria, the Netherlands, and West Germany.

The Austrian and Dutch institutes seem to restrict themselves to domestic educational and research functions, but the West German foundations do more. They not only supply skilled organizers, publicists, and communicators and perform a great number of important services for their backers on the German domestic scene, but also are actively involved abroad in development projects in the Third World and in sponsoring and financing sister parties in Europe and Latin America. The SPD's Friedrich Ebert Foundation dates back to the 1920s and the FDP's Friedrich Nauman Foundation and the CDU's Konrad Adenauer Foundation, to 1958 and 1964, respectively. The CSU's Hanns Seidel Foundation was founded only in 1967. It was the Constitutional Court decision of 1966 which brought these institutes to the fore as a means of continuing to supply the parties with public funds for nonelection research, political education, training, and other purposes. Some assistance is provided by individuals, business corporations, and party-controlled enterprises like the Socialist-managed Bank für Gemeinwirtschaft. The bulk of the institutes' funds come from the Federal Center for Political Education, the Ministry for Inner German Affairs, the Foreign Ministry, and the Ministry for Economic Cooperation. Other public funds are granted by some of the länder and communes; several foundations also exist on the länd level and are affiliated to the federal foundations. The Konrad Adenauer Foundation carries out activities in Ceylon and Latin America, helping to organize cooperatives, community development projects, and Christian trade unions where the situation is hospitable. The Friedrich Nauman Foundation carries out parallel activities and works closely with the Liberal International. The Friedrich

Ebert Foundation not only is involved in the developing world, but also has fostered the Portuguese Socialist party and been active in aid of fraternal parties in Spain and Italy. Indeed, the Konrad Adenauer and other foundations have set up offices in Italy and elsewhere, and it is known that the French Socialist and other parties have frequently been the beneficiaries of German largesse. The foundations try to coordinate their activities in order to avoid overlaps and duplication. Serious questions arise, first, as to the propriety of these international activities and, second, with regard to the identification of party and state as the foundations carry out projects using resources subject directly and indirectly to government control. (The usual exclusion percentage of 5 percent of the vote is imposed before a party foundation can qualify for such grants, underlining the preferred position of the established institutionalized parties.)

Indirect Subsidies. Tax incentives, which effectively are indirect public money subsidies to parties and candidates, may take the form of tax deductions or tax credits. Deductions tend to appeal to higher income groups, because the tax benefit increases with the size of the donation. On the other hand, a system of tax credits attempts to resolve the question of equity in one of two ways: (1) by having the taxpayer assign a part of his assessed income tax, up to a fixed maximum, to the support of a party or candidate; or (2) by establishing a staggered scale of tax credits which diminish with an increase in the size of the contribution and eliminate the tax advantages of deductions which accrue to wealthy persons under the progressive income tax system. It was this feature which prompted the German Constitutional Court to outlaw tax deductions for political purposes in 1958. Nevertheless, some jurisdictions still permit tax deductions under certain limited conditions. Examples are the Netherlands and West Germany for small donations. In the Canadian province of Ontario, corporations may take limited deductions for donations whereas individuals may only claim tax credits, as they may in the rest of the country.

The Canadian federal parliament and the provinces of Alberta, Ontario, and Quebec employ the tax credit approach. All except Quebec allow the following annual credits for donations to political parties or to candidates at election periods. Credits are allowed for 75 percent of the aggregate contribution if the aggregate does not exceed $100. If the contribution totals between $100 and $550, the donor can take a tax credit of $75 plus 50 percent of the amount by which the aggregate exceeds $100. If the total donation exceeds $550, the tax credit is either $500 or $300 plus 33.3 percent of the amount by which the aggregate exceeds $550, whichever is less. The maximum annual credit is $500 for a donation of $1,150 at the federal and provincial levels, respectively. Quebec's tax credit scheme permits a credit of 50 percent of the first $100 contributed and 25 percent of the second $100 to a maximum total annual provincial credit of $75. A significant feature of these schemes is that established registered parties can benefit from them on an annual basis, whereas local candidates are limited to the formal, legal campaign period.

A third form of indirect subsidies to political parties is the systematic kickback of parliamentary indemnities and public service salaries by parliamentarians and public officials to treasurers of the parties to which they owe their nominations or appointments. In most European and numerous other parliamentary regimes, deputies are expected to contribute generously to the party coffers; an increase in their annual salaries benefits their parties as well. This system is most systematic on the socialist left wing of the political and parliamentary spectrum. It reaches its most sophisticated form among the Communist parties of France and Italy, whose elected deputies are expected to rebate their entire monthly or annual idemnities to the party and who in return receive the salary of a first-class skilled metal worker. Nor are other officials spared. In Switzerland, for instance, high functionaries and even judges are expected to contribute generously to party funds. The principle appears to be that wherever the *proporz* or party-key system of appointment to public office prevails, beneficiaries are expected to acknowledge their obligations to their political sponsors.

Effects of Public Financing

On Federalism. In an earlier study, I indicated that the traditional pattern of financing Canadian political parties tended to counteract the fragmentation and centrifugal forces of Canadian federalism, in which rival centers of power are located in the provincial legislatures and party systems. This highly centralized mode of party finance was undermined by the expansion of provincial powers because of the increase in provincial functions and budgets based on the growth of the extractive industries. Provincial party organizations attracted the support of powerful economic interests in their search for contracts and concessions; in Quebec this process was abetted by the growing self-consciousness of a newly aroused modernizing nationalism. Provincial parties learned that the control of campaign finances and public subsidization could lessen their dependence on the federal parties, thus freeing them from the dominance of the national parties and the central government. Some provinces, such as Ontario and Quebec, adopted provisions which limited or banned interparty transfers from the federal level to the provincial level to reinforce provincial party autonomy. Only those poorer provinces and their parties which lacked resources remained dependent on the central party organizations for the wherewithal to finance their activities. To a not inconsiderable extent, coordinated nation-wide decision making has been weakened in a process that can be attributed in part to the changes in Canadian party finance.[1]

Geopolitical considerations have checked divisive tendencies on the European continent. Nevertheless, separate public financing at the provincial levels in Austria and West Germany have served to maintain powerful regional political organizations capable of challenging the central parties or serving as bases and springboards for strong local länd leaders to launch their careers at the central level. Although none of the Scandinavian countries has a true federal system, it should be noted that the impact of public funds varies with the point at which such money enters the party system. Sweden has a system of county and district communal subsidies paid by each level of government to the qualifying parties at that stratum. By contrast, Finland provides no direct subsidies to parties at the local level; the central party organizations do transfer about half the state funds they receive to their district groups, but the result, as one student of Finnish politics observes, is to give the national parties a powerful hold on the lower levels.[2] This differs sharply with the relative autonomy of local Swedish parties. Switzerland provides no direct public support to parties. One of the reasons, as I gathered in interviews conducted in 1976, is that the cantonal party organizations feared the effect of federal subsidies on their internal balance of power, which are centered in the cantons.

Clearly, public subventions are affected by federal structures and have a reciprocal effect on the articulation of these regimes. The distribution of legislative powers and the nature of the electoral system and the party system contribute to either the centralization or the peripheralization of federal states, but the types of subsidy and the points at which money enters the parties influence the direction of the process.

The Institutionalization of Existing Party Systems. In another place, I argued that one must add to the three motives usually advanced in favor

---

[1] Khayyam Z. Paltiel, "Federalism and Party Finance," in K. M. Gibbons and D. C. Rowat, eds., *Political Corruption in Canada* (Toronto: McClelland & Stewart, 1976), pp. 193–203.

[2] Pertti Pesonen, "Impact of Public Financing of Political Parties: The Finnish Experience," Paper delivered to the 9th World Congress of the International Political Science Association, Montreal, 1973.

of the regulation of campaign finances and public subsidies, namely the reduction or restraining of rising costs, the assurance of probity, and the pursuit of equity in the electoral process. I advanced the hypothesis that legislators sought to stabilize the party system and entrench their electoral positions "through the institution of a regular, reliable, and predictable source of funds."[3] A thorough investigation of this proposition would require an examination of other aspects of each of the regulatory systems as well as the subventions proper. Certain conclusions may be drawn, however, from the material presented in the foregoing pages, elaborated where necessary with further details from the respective regulatory schemes.

In every known instance, public subventions have been introduced by the parties in office. Given the nature of parliamentary regimes, this is inevitable, as only those parties commanding a majority in the legislature can assure the passage of the necessary legislation. It is scarcely to be expected, therefore, that incumbents will adopt measures to their own detriment. Allied with the governmental parties are their smaller coalition partners, like the Free Democrats in Germany or the Liberals in Austria, which, pressed for funds, are often the instigators of action in this field. The long-established historical minor opposition parties in Scandinavia, Italy, and Canada have also shown an eagerness to push for these reforms on grounds both of ideology and of necessity. Even major opposition parties like the skeptical German Social Democrats of 1958 and the Communist party of Italy have willingly accepted these proposals when they were shown that their positions would not be undermined. The gravest doubts and opposition have come from two sources: (1) conservative parties in such countries as the United Kingdom, which has yet to adopt the Houghton recommendations, and in Scandinavia and elsewhere where conservatives have access to wealthy private sources; and (2) from right- and left-of-center Liberals and Radicals, as in Italy, who oppose such grants on the grounds that the system favors large parties and that the state should not interfere with internal party autonomy. Also opposed are the extraparliamentary groups and small parties, which view subsidies as cementing the institutionalization of the established party systems.

A scrutiny of the regulations and the regulatory bodies administering the subventions tends to corroborate the impression that the major promoters and beneficiaries are the incumbents and the established

---

[3] Khayyam Z. Paltiel, "The Impact of Election Expenses Legislation in Canada, Western Europe, and Israel," in Herbert E. Alexander, ed., *Political Finance,* Sage Electoral Studies Yearbook, vol. 5 (Beverly Hills & London: Sage Publications, 1979), pp. 15–39.

parties. Direct grants are usually made only to those parties and candidates who have achieved a certain percentage of the vote, often fixed so as to exclude the "frivolous" or "nonserious"; this hampers the entry of new parties. Specific grants, such as broadcasting time, if allocated proportionately benefit the largest groups, or if made equally tend to favor those which have achieved at least some representation in the legislature. In either case, the established groups profit. Even tax incentives, which benefit recognized and registered parties on an annual basis and limit new parties and individual candidates to the formal campaign period, are biased toward the incumbents. More significant is the tendency to entrust the administration of these schemes to bodies made up, or subject to the overview, of representatives of the parliamentary parties. Examples are the Ontario Commission on Election Contributions and Expenses, and the informal advisory committee established by the chief electoral officer of Canada, consisting of the senior paid officials of the parliamentary parties plus the parliamentary secretary of the Government House Leader. The net result is a clear distinction between the established parliamentary parties and those outside parliament, rather than one of size. The grants tend to freeze the *status quo ante* except where new groups are able to muster new private resources and gain from an ideological surge such as a nationalist movement.

The biggest immediate beneficiaries of direct cash subsidies tend to be the central party organizations and the party staff professionals who serve them, except where federalism, law, or party statutes make special provision for regional and local party organs. Public subventions in Austria, Canada, Finland, Italy, Sweden, and West Germany have been accompanied by a vast expansion in the apparatuses of the party organizations. No one who has visited Sweden or West Germany can fail to be impressed by the lavish quarters and by the numbers and quality of the personnel employed by the parties. Public funds have provided access to the most sophisticated techniques of communications, publicity, and survey analysis. Increased dependence on professional expertise has led to the relative decline of middle-level party leaders and the restriction of party militants to routine tasks. Austrian and West German party spokesmen have told me that they are frequently embarrassed by the election activities of their member-volunteers and prefer to use the professional staff of the parties and their related foundations. In the process these parties have been transformed from closed membership groups to open voters' parties which stress the personalities of the top party leadership to the detriment of the cadres and policies in election campaigns.

A sharp critic of the Italian system[4] summarized the impact as follows: Public finance has reinforced and institutionalized the existing party system; it has preserved the small groups but has frozen the relationship between the parties. The Communists have never considered subventions as their main resource, while public finance has not eliminated the dependence of the Christian Democrats on questionable sources. With respect to party structure, subsidies have strengthened the central organs vis-à-vis the periphery and the parliamentary group within each party against the rest of the party. Public finance has reinforced the internal majorities in face of their factional minorities. The central majority is controlled by the parliamentary group which punishes those regional and local sections controlled by the minorities. Public finance has not led to more openness but rather to greater bureaucratization of Italian parties. The paid party secretariats and staff have close links and a solidarity of interests with the leadership of the parliamentary groups, which leads to pressure on internal minorities. The net effect is a crystallization of internal as well as external party relationships.

Canadian observers have noted a similar experience regarding the expansion of the role of paid party staffs following the introduction of subsidies. But, in addition, the ceilings and reporting procedures now required have obliged the parties and candidates to engage paid help and appoint hundreds of agents to comply with the various control provisions, thus stimulating the process of bureaucratization.

Canadian and British observers have recently made sharp attacks on public subsidies of parties and campaigns on the ground that they conduce to the emergence of liberal or neocorporatism.[5] As evidence, they point to the experience of Sweden, Austria, and West Germany, where there is close cooperation between the functional representatives of the peak employers and labor organizations and their respective states which exhibit variant forms of elite accommodation on the consociational, *proporz,* or *party-key* models. Arguing from social democratic and neo-Marxian viewpoints, these critics contend that subventions will promote political conformity and freeze the extremely limited available party choices.

---

[4] Author's interview with Professor Gian Franco Ciaurro, counsellor, Camera dei Deputati, Montecitorio, Roma, April 27, 1977.

[5] Anthony Howard, "Political Parties and Public Funds," *The New Statesman,* London, September 3, 1976, pp. 295–296; and Leo Panitch, "The Role and Nature of the Canadian State," in Panitch, ed., *The Canadian State: Political Economy and Political Power* (Toronto & Buffalo: University of Toronto Press, 1977), pp.3–27. See also, Khayyam Z. Paltiel and Clinton Archibald, "L'évolution de l'idée corporatiste au Canada," Communication préparée pour le colloque international sur La Vie Politique au Canada, à l'Université de Mons, Belgique, 24–25–26 avril, 1978 (forthcoming in Etudes Canadiennes, Bordeaux, France).

Writing from a different perspective, others have noted corporatist tendencies throughout the Western world, but can one contend that the process has been precipitated by subsidization? It is true that corporatist mechanisms are constitutionally embedded in Austria, but so are they in France and Switzerland which do not provide subventions. Indeed, Swiss party officials argued in personal interviews with the author that such assistance was necessary if Swiss parties were to counterbalance the influence of affluent interest groups which are able to exploit the Helvetic system of initiatives and referendums to veto or promote legislation.

Nor is there a necessary connection between public financing of political parties and candidates and the contemporary prominence of single-issue organizations and political action committees.[6] Traditional interest groups have always known how to exploit various avenues of access to executive and legislative decision makers, offering support and rewards of various kinds. The single-issue organization appears to have come to the fore in the aftermath of the decline of ideological politics, the failure of old parties to absorb new issues, and the emergence of consensual styles. Rootless parties and candidates lacking ideological ballast thus become subject to temporary tides of opinion, sometimes artificially stimulated. Here public assistance may actually free parties and candidates from the pressures of such movements.

British electoral law permits such organizations as Aims of Industry to conduct antinationalization campaigns during election periods so long as their publicity does not appear to be promoting a particular party or candidate. Similar provisos hold true in Canada, where the electoral law permits no one other than the parties, candidates, and their agents to promote or oppose the election of a particular party or candidate during the formal campaign period. The courts in Canada have to draw a fine line between the attempt to control and pinpoint the responsibility for election spending and interferences in legitimate free speech. Thus far, the judges have not spoken their final word.

Conclusion

There can be no doubt that campaign finance regulation has fostered increased probity, transparency, and a degree of equity in the monetary aspects of the campaign processes in most of the countries surveyed. The financial operations of parties are increasingly subject to public scrutiny and review. But significant reductions in the costs of campaigns

---

6 Edward Greenspon, "Single-issue Groups," unpublished paper prepared for the School of Journalism, Carleton University, Ottawa, March 27, 1979.

and party operations have yet to be achieved, in part because of the galloping inflation of the past decade and to changes in campaign style with the widening resort to professional communicators and the electronic media. The legitimizing of public subventions has also made it easy for parties to resort to the state treasury when threatened with shortfalls.

However, our review has indicated that despite the partial improvements in the nature of the campaign process, too little thought has been given to the secondary consequences of these reforms. Subsidy systems and their accompanying regulations have made it difficult for new groups and individuals to enter the competitive electoral struggle and may be promoting the ossification of the party systems in certain states. To the extent that these schemes limit entry of new competitors and parties, they may well promote alienation from democratic methods of change and may stimulate recourse to extraparliamentary opposition tactics of violent confrontation by those who may feel themselves rightly or wrongly excluded from the electoral process.

Commentaries

Howard R. Penniman, chairman

We are all, as they say in sociology, culturally bound. We tend to think almost exclusively in terms of the United States when we think of electoral laws. We sometimes think of state laws as well as national, but we do not go much beyond those. If, however, we consider campaign financing abroad, we find great variety. France, for example, would horrify some of us who are reformers because it is impossible to find out who spent a dime on what—and the French must spend a great deal more than a dime because they carry on pretty exciting campaigns. Yet no reporting of any kind, no legal requirements of any kind exist in France. At the other end of the range are numerous countries where the national government finances most campaign costs, but at the same time the parties are free to raise more money and spend more money if they possibly can. Spain is different again. Money comes in openly and freely from outside the country so that almost as much money from the outside as from the inside may be spent on the campaign for some parties.

As you know, originally three people were going to be the discussants but unfortunately, we have only one of those three with us, Mr. Agree who wrote *Political Money* with David Adamany and is now working on an important study for Freedom House that deals with international financing of campaigns.

Mr. Warnfried Dettling, who was to be here from the Christian Democratic union in the Federal Republic of Germany, wrote to us at the end of last week to say he could not come. I have asked Manfred von Nordheim, who is the director of the Konrad Adenauer Research Foundation here in Washington, if he would pick up a little slack during the question period and talk about foundations. I know the political foundations will be discussed here; in Germany they are of immense importance.

Unfortunately, F. Clifton White went to the hospital yesterday afternoon. We will miss hearing about his direct experience a year ago of a campaign in Venezuela in which an estimated $180 million was spent and in which the maximum number of voters was about 5.8 million. At that rate, the United States would spend about $5.5 billion in next year's campaign. Even our most imaginative campaigners might have difficulty handling that amount. Of course, Venezuela is not the only country to exceed U.S. campaign spending on a per voter basis. Recent publications of the American Enterprise Institute on elections in more than a dozen Western democracies suggest, where figures are available, that expenditures per voter in the United States are among the lowest in the world and that our campaigns are the most heavily regulated. (Figures are not available, of course, for countries such as France where there are not disclosure laws.)

At this point I will ask George Agree for his comments on the two papers.

George E. Agree

I want to start with an apology of a sort. Paltiel dates the beginning of the movement toward public financing of politics to 1957 in Puerto Rico. So did Adamany and I, in a passage written by me in *Political Money*. So, I believe, do all other references to that beginning in the English language literature.

All of us appear to have been mistaken. I was told by Cristina Guzmán, president of the bloc of the Federalist Alliance in the Argentine Congress, that public financing was introduced in her country in 1955 after the overthrow of Perón. If this information is correct, it merely indicates a certain factual imprecision in a discipline which nevertheless may be overly preoccupied with data.

National regulation of political finance tends to address particular and limited problems, growing out of circumstances that do not at first evoke fundamental scrutiny by lawmakers or political scientists. As indicated by Alexander and Paltiel, in some countries such as Germany and the United States, the courts have traditionally measured campaign laws against basic liberal democratic constitutional principles. Surely political scientists, no less than judges, have the intellectual equipment and also the responsibility to evaluate phenomena in the light of underlying democratic principles. Perhaps the most constructive effect of comparative studies like the two we just heard is precisely that they direct our attention to the more fundamental issues in political regulation.

Paltiel's distinction between foreign "objective" and American "subjective" modes of allocation of government subventions has especially important democratic implications. At issue is who, or what, should decide the distribution for partisan use of public money.

In all cases but one, legislatures either have been reluctant, or have felt it would be indefensible for them, to take that responsibility upon themselves. They have passed it on to the entire voting public, either by allocating funds directly according to the number of votes cast, or indirectly according to the number of parliamentary seats won. In each case, all electors participate, and, significantly, each elector has equal weight with every other. Some problems remain with respect to small parties and independent candidates, but the achievement of equity for both politicians and taxpayers is nonetheless considerable.

The exception, of course, is the United States. Here, instead of letting all voters decide allocations on an approximately "one man–one dollar" basis, we have diverged in two other and contradictory directions. On one hand, the Congress itself determines allocations for major party nominees for president. These are equal in amount, regardless of the relative support for the candidates and regardless of the possible presence of any other and conceivably more popular candidate. This approach may be defensible in the framework of what normally is a two-party system. However, it invites trouble when a serious third-party effort emerges. Theodore Roosevelt, the first national advocate of public campaign financing in America, would not have meekly tolerated the freezing out of his Bull-Moose party, as would happen under present law.

On the other hand, the provision for matching funds in presidential nomination contests is even more "subjective." Candidate allocations are made neither by Congress, which presumably represents the electorate, nor by any approximation of the electorate itself. They are made instead by the relatively small number of people who finance the candidates anyway. Moreover, even these contributors are not counted equally, as are voters in other systems; instead, they are weighted according to the size of their donations up to a generous $250 limit. Thus it was possible in 1976 for one candidate with 90,000 donors to receive $4 million of public money while an opponent, also with 90,000 donors, received only $2 million.

Because American politicians generally are not informed about foreign systems, their virtual obliviousness to the implications of such "subjective" allocation is understandable. It is the lack of attention to those implications by American scholars that remains puzzling. Foreign colleagues, who are in a position to examine American "subjectivity" with detachment, might find it an interesting exercise.

This "subjectivity" has another important consequence touching directly on the main theme of this conference, and on many of the problems aired in earlier panels. In stark contrast to the intent and effect of foreign modes of allocation, our matching system of triggering public subventions by private donations actually enhances the role of special-interest groups. Inevitably, when a special interest gives or mobilizes contributions, its value to a candidate, and therefore its clout, is doubled at taxpayer expense. The special-interest group's power in such situations would apply not only to single-issue candidacies, but also to most mainstream ones. In Europe, on the other hand, while public financing has not at all diminished the flow of special-interest money in politics, the subventions are totally neutral with respect to such interests and act to dilute their overall effect.

Paltiel's concern that "in every known instance public subventions have been introduced by the parties in office"—a statement that can be generalized to include every known instance of political regulation of whatever sort—is illuminated by Alexander's distinction between American and parliamentary models. Perhaps the outstanding difference between these models, one which substantially explains most of the other differences, is precisely the nature of "the parties in office." In the American system, the true party in office consists of incumbents, all with a greater interest in protecting their own seats than in enhancing the ability of their nominal parties to capture seats held by opposition incumbents. Thus campaign regulation is dictated by the mutual interests of what in effect is a single party of incumbents, and almost inevitably is framed to the detriment of nonincumbents.

Parliamentary parties, in contrast, are necessarily seeking to gain seats currently held by the opposition, and therefore have a continuing interest in preserving opportunities for electoral change. For this reason, despite the centralizing effects their mode of public financing may have within parties, it has not inhibited competition between parties. And this, after all, is what affords most citizens their only chance to affect their governance.

Indeed, public financing in Germany clearly and decisively paved the way for Willy Brandt's Social Democrats to come to power in 1969—by enabling the Free Democratic party (FDP) to survive going into coalition with them. The FDP had been threatened with major defections whichever way it turned: with loss of many of its members if it reentered a coalition with the Christian Democratic union (CDU), and with loss of its most important financial backers if it "put the Socialists in power" by forming a coalition with the SPD. In choosing the latter course, it became dependent on public funds for 90 percent of its money during the following three years. Without public funding it would not have been free to make that choice. A comparable effect was evident in Sweden, where public subventions to opposition parties, and particularly to the relatively resource-poor Center party, were important in breaking the Socialists' forty-year hold on power.

Notwithstanding apparently beneficial effects of government subventions on political competition, the shift away from laissez faire in
elections, as in other areas of public life, makes continuous examination
of Paltiel's concerns a matter of high importance. As revealed in this
proceeding, the dangers of regulation to an open political process are
more than theoretical.

The international activities of political foundations call for particular attention by scholars in the next few years, in part because of their
relatively recent development, and in part because of the growing volume
and political effect of their operations. In 1978 alone, the four German
party foundations collectively spent upwards of $70 million on inter-
national activity (including the running of newly opened offices in
Washington, D.C., by the Konrad Adenauer and the Friedrich Ebert
foundations); and virtually all that money came from the German
government. Since this is almost as much annually as is spent every
four years to elect a president of the United States, there is relevance
to Paltiel's questions "first, as to the propriety of these activities and,
second, with regard to the identification of party and state. . . ."

Again acknowledging the need for close and continuing scrutiny
of these issues, it may be useful here to sketch a rationale for the
foundation activities. Democratic parties have real international interests, which more or less closely relate to their domestic imperatives.
At a minimum, parties need reliable information about those international issues that affect daily politics; and special efforts often are
required to obtain this information since, unlike domestic information,
it does not percolate up from their constituency. Some parties, such as
the Socialists and Christians, attempt to articulate a world view and
need visible international ties for domestic credibility. Moreover, party
interests frequently coincide with nonpartisan or multipartisan perceptions of national interests. There was broad partisan and governmental
interest in preventing a communist takeover and in helping the development of democracy in Portugal, which is both a NATO partner of the
northern European countries and a prospective member of the Common
Market. Finally, if political influence is exerted and resources are transferred more or less overtly, they create little or no problem for the
receiving institutions, even when governments are known to be the
ultimate source of the funding. On the contrary, such political assistance—when it is given as openly as economic and cultural aid, and
when it is subject to market forces, which affect ideas as much as they
do goods—appears to be widely acceptable where it is offered. Regarding the specter of neocorporatism, it may be pertinent that such private
American institutions as churches and labor unions conduct many of

375

the programs funded by the Agency for International Development (AID) with no suggestion that they are being influenced in either their dogmas or their political behavior.

The issue at bottom may depend not on the fact of a governmental connection, but on its dynamics. This, too, should be explored. At the moment, at least in Germany, it appears that the parties have more to say about how much their foundations receive from government, and for what purposes, than does the government itself. Appropriations are made consensually in parliament, always subject to the possibility of partisan criticism, and with a degree of participation by the opposition that would be impossible within the relevant ministries.

As for the Bundestag-authorized entry into the United States of the Adenauer and Ebert Foundations, far from being threatening, it may be testimony to the health of the impulse toward democratic community. Germans may or may not believe they are returning our favor of 1945, but it surely is true that we still have much to learn from and about each other, and that these foundations are helping.

Manfred von Nordheim

I was asked to contribute to this meeting on short notice, and so I have to try to improvise as much as I can.

In order to help you understand and better appreciate the role that German foundations play, perhaps it would be worthwhile to mention why these foundations were established. As Professor Paltiel pointed out, some impetus came from a decision of the Supreme Court of the Federal Republic of Germany. But a far deeper and more important reason had to do with the German experience: the war, the resulting devastation, the realization that political parties did not take root in the political culture of the Weimar Republic. Second, there was a great fear, understandably so, of excessive centralization as we experienced it during the Third Reich. Therefore, a constitution was framed that emphasizes the principles of federalism, especially the subsidiary principle, that is, to delegate as much power and responsibility to the lowest level—political and administrative—that is competent to do the job.

It has been stated that the foundations receive government money. Mr. Agree accurately pointed out that while this is technically correct, we should say that an act of parliament provides this money: that gives it a somewhat different emphasis. Parliament can reduce that amount, can take it away completely, or can increase it. Unfortunately, because of the recession in Germany during the past few years, we have not received as much money lately as we would have liked.

Although the money is allocated to the foundations through various ministries, these ministries cannot control how the foundations spend it. For example, when the foundations receive money to work in developing countries, this money comes directly from the appropriate ministry. Let us say, that the Konrad Adenauer Foundation has come up with a project to develop an adult education center in Indonesia. We work out the project, we submit it to the appropriate ministry, and if there is still money available within the total budget allocation for this particular foundation, we will get that money, and we will use it. Afterwards, we are audited and we have to make sure that the money is spent according to established principles, such as those set up in the U.S. with the General Accounting Office or other organizations.

To cite another example, when we take a group of high school students to Berlin—which we do frequently because we want them to see the divided city and we want them to go to East Berlin and to East Germany—that money may come from the Federal Information Center. But there is no direct connection between the ministry and the foundation, and we are certainly under no obligation to pursue a particular policy.

Even though we cannot spend the money directly on party activity, some of our activity does benefit the party. However, our effect is vastly overestimated. Out of a budget of about 19 million German marks, which we have in the current fiscal year—and we have about 300 employees in our headquarters near Bonn—only a small fraction of that money and of our manpower and technical resources benefits the party. In fact, the foundation people often complain that they do not have any access to the politicians.

Much of our money is used for completely innocent social science projects. For example, we do studies on the role of migrant workers in Germany, on leftist or right-wing movements among people under eighteen in Germany, and on the role of women in urban centers in Germany. This work has very little party-related impact. If the party wants to use the data that we collect or the dissertations that are written within the foundation, they are welcome to do so; but so is everyone else because at least 90 percent of our research activity is published in monographs and books that are openly accessible.

Mr. Paltiel questioned the propriety of international activities of the foundation. I have a number of problems with this because I do not see any improper activity. This is an open activity. Everyone knows about it. One should probably differentiate between our activities in underdeveloped countries, where we build—as Mr. Paltiel correctly pointed out—cooperatives or Christian trade unions or community centers, and our activities in Rome, Lisbon, Madrid, or Washington.

Washington is a special case, anyway, and I will be glad to go into this if there are any questions. The offices in Europe and Washington are very small offices, indeed. They consist of one person and a secretary. What we have done in Madrid, in Lisbon, and to some extent in Rome is to support fledgling democratic parties that have emerged there. And, frankly, I am rather proud of that. If you remember, Henry Kissinger's prediction was that Portugal and Spain would become communist within a short period of time. Well, the fact that they have not is, to a small degree, due to some of these activities that foundations have engaged in.

What have we done? Primarily, we have sponsored numerous seminars, workshops, and conferences in Portugal and Spain, or in Germany. It is true that we have tried to share our accumulated experience and our values with the Portuguese and Spanish, hoping to help them build a viable democratic party system in their countries. The fact that the two foundations and all major political parties in Germany cooperate along these lines is testimony to the consensus that has emerged there. As for the question of propriety, the Social Democratic party's Friedrich Ebert Foundation recently gained observer status at the United Nations. That is to say, the propriety of its international activities has been recognized officially.

The important question is not whether this money is being spent; rather, it is how it is being spent. If I had a choice between some government agency and a private or semiprivate organization, I would rather have the private organization conduct the job, not the government. This is what these political foundations are all about.

Mr. Agree mentioned that $70 million are spent abroad by German foundations, almost as much as in a presidential campaign. Although I have not calculated this, probably only $2 million or $3 million have been spent on the offices in southern Europe and in Washington, D.C. In other words, more than 90 percent of this money is aid to developing countries: establishing trade unions, community centers, and cooperatives, or setting up schools of journalism, TV stations, and radio stations —that is, things that normally the government would do, except that in this case, the work has been delegated to another organization such as ours. And I think we have done a darn good job.

Whenever diplomatic relations have been severed between an underdeveloped country and West Germany—and this has been happening with increasing frequency since we have become a medium-sized power—the foundations in almost every case have been allowed to stay, and have even been asked to stay, instead of being kicked out. This response suggests that the foundations have done a credible job. And so permit me to say that I am rather proud of what we have accomplished.

Discussion

MARY MEEHAN, Committee for a Constitutional Presidency: Mr. Alexander mentioned earlier that a court decision in Sweden has found disclosure of campaign contributions to be a violation of privacy. Have there been many debates in other countries over similar civil libertarian issues, such as infringements on free speech, on spending limits, or on contribution limits? Are these real issues elsewhere?

MR. ALEXANDER: The case in Sweden was not a judicial decision, incidentally, but that of a royal commission. The answer, briefly, is that the Swedish commission report was somewhat duplicated in Denmark. In other countries, disclosure has often been connected with the issue of civil liberty or invasion of privacy, so that in order to get a leverage for disclosure some countries have had to introduce public funding, because the parties or people would not accept disclosure without public funding. However, questions of limitations in issues of civil liberty generally have not been raised as much elsewhere as in the United States.

MR. PALTIEL: In Canada, the civil liberties question has arisen in connection with the system of controls that pinpoints responsibility and accountability for election spending. The law states that from the moment that the writ of dissolution of parliament is issued until the polling day, no one but candidates, parties, and their official agents may purchase advertising or may advertise during the period of the campaign. An exception in the law was made for newspaper editorials and legitimate organizations that discuss problems of public moment at any time.

A case arose during one election campaign of a union organizer whose union was affected by the anti-inflation program brought in by the Trudeau government. During a bi-election he hired a plane and flew it over a football field during a game the Sunday before the election. He was dragging an advertising slogan—this was one day before the election—that said, "Vote, but vote against the Liberals." The chief electoral officer took him to court on the charge that this was election advertising. The lower court judge threw the case out. It was taken to the county court, and the county court judge also threw it out on the grounds that the union discussion of anti-inflation programs was a legitimate interest, and therefore under the legal exception, it could not be prevented. Now, apparently the chief electoral officer is scanning the events of the last campaign for violations because he wants the courts to define the limits of this decision. Some discussion arose about question-naires, whether questionnaires deliberately stimulated by political parti-sans and published in order to embarrass candidates fell within this rubric. This has yet to be treated by the courts.

In Britain, of course, even though the campaigns do not involve public financing, and stringent limits have been put on the amount of spending by local candidates, the parties have to be very careful in their spending because their expenditures could be attributed to a candidate. This situation has stimulated the formation of parallel action groups, which represent the aims of industry or antinationalization campaigns, for example. These groups are allowed to discuss an issue as long as it is not identified with a particular party or candidate, or does not oppose a particular candidate or party—because the law says "promoting or opposing." There is, however, a very fine line.

MR. ALEXANDER: The "principal campaign committee" in U.S. election law, because of its responsibility for funding and for possible violations of law, is comparable to that of an agent under the Canadian or British system.

MR. PALTIEL: Remember the shortness of their campaigns, however. You have very long election campaigns. Election expenses under British or Canadian law are defined as expenses made from the moment of the issuance of a writ or made in anticipation of that. So that this is a very limited period of time, and a closely defined series of expenditures. For instance, nomination costs are not considered election expenses in Canadian law.

MR. McCOY: For all the reasons mentioned, it seems difficult to see the lessons to be learned from foreign systems, because they are based on such totally different concepts. For example, we choose our chief of government on a basis totally different from all parliamentary systems. What I found most informative in this afternoon's discussion is a remark made by Mr. Paltiel, who said that the systems in Canada and else-where have not brought about more active participation in the political system, as well as George Agree's statement that Teddy Roosevelt would not have tolerated the kind of treatment that Eugene McCarthy got from the Federal Election Commission. Gene McCarthy told us at lunch that he was writing a paper not on campaign financing, but on "zero-based thinking." That is where we ought to be, in regard to the regulation of campaigns and their financing in the United States. We ought to start at ground zero and ask ourselves what we are trying to accomplish through this regulation.

I propose that we should consider two principal goals. One is the improved access of the public to the contributions received by any candidate, so that the voter will be able to judge where the candidate's money comes from and whether or not he is compromised by that money. Having done that, we need not worry about equalizing the legislative influence of the General Motors Corporation and a porter at the General Motors dealership in Bethesda, or about protecting the American people from what Common Cause seems to believe is the inherent venality of all elected officials from which we have to be protected. The second aim of any campaign regulation probably should be an effort to make it easier—or at least not make it harder—for those who wish to participate in the system to do so. You can't do anything to help the person who doesn't want to play in the game. But if he does want to play in the game, either as a candidate or as an activist on behalf of a candidate, then we ought to make it easier for him, not more difficult. The current law does nothing for either of those goals. We do not have accurate information on a timely basis that can help the electorate make improved judgments before an election, and we have done nothing to facilitate participation.

RACHELLE HOROWITZ, American Federation of Teachers: I visited Spain and Portugal last year, and I was terribly impressed with the work, especially in Portugal, of German foundations in developing democratic trade unions and training trade unionists. This is in the face of much larger secret contributions from Moscow to the Communist-dominated unions, particularly in Portugal. As an American trade unionist, I wondered why our unionists were not playing the same kind of role in developing democratic trade unions in those two countries. However, it became evident that we could not do it that way, that the only way that American trade unionists could function was on a union-to-union basis. My union is now dealing with the counterpart unions in Spain and Portugal.

My question to George Agree is, given the ideological weakness of the American parties and the similar nonideological bent of American trade unions, how would you try to import lessons from the German

381

foundation system to the American system? I do not think that we can imitate the Germans in terms of developing trade unions, and I do not see where foundations would fit in the American political system, either.

MR. AGREE: There are two questions there. American trade unions might find a mechanism. Their nonideological approach will limit the numbers of people with whom they can deal abroad. However, they are working in Latin America, trying to promote nonideological unionism there, while the Germans are trying to promote Christian and Socialist unions. In this difference of opinion the German foundations may have the advantage both in terms of their resources and in terms of the climate that they find where they work. Although you cannot improve the climate, you can improve your resources, and with some adroit lobbying, you might even obtain government help in this, as they do.

The American parties, too, clearly have no particular interest in promoting ideological parties elsewhere. They may have a general interest in supporting the idea of democracy. Probably if they want to do it and want to learn about the devices used in other countries, they can find ways of doing so.

MR. EPSTEIN: Yesterday we spent two sessions talking directly and indirectly about "special interests," such as labor unions, trade associations, or trade federations, as important ingredients to parties in various developed and developing countries. I have been struck by the fact that the term has not come up once in this session. Is this concern with "special interests" an American idiosyncracy, growing out of our national culture? Why have we been so preoccupied in this way, whereas elsewhere there is less concern?

MR. PENNIMAN: If you visit any other country in the midst of an election, you are apt to hear exactly the same thing. In Australia, for example, the Australian Labor party would surely be beating as hard as it could on the heads of those business interests, and, likewise, the Liberal party would be beating on the heads of the labor special interests. Because we happen to be talking about other peoples' countries from this platform, the "special interests" become "political participants." It isn't that they ignore special interests in other countries, certainly.

MR. EPSTEIN: But isn't there something a little bit deeper in the sense that they are really structured into the way that the parties function?

MR. ALEXANDER: That's right.

DISCUSSION

MR. VON NORDHEIM: I am not a party specialist, but perhaps I can suggest some answers to Mr. Epstein's question. The papers and the oral remarks here have portrayed a very impressive German party system. It should be pointed out, however, that this picture can be misleading. The German political parties, for all practical purposes, are bankrupt today, precisely because, for various reasons, individual and organizational contributions have dwindled; every party is deep in the red. For example, one major party has accumulated debts of about 30 million marks. That is not much according to American standards, but it does worry the parties, and as a consequence they are trying to look for additional ways of financing their activities. Europeans and Germans are able to cope with this because they are more realistic, or you can say more cynical, about the connection of politics, parties, interest groups, and money. Without the public funding the situation would be worse.

Perhaps in an indirect way, what has happened in West Germany is that parties have relied too much on public funding and have overspent their resources. We have a party organization with a full-time staff and a couple of part-time people in each of the 248 electoral districts in West Germany, not to mention countless other organizations, as well as a strong organization in Bonn on the national level. Another influential factor was the recession. People just did not give as much money any more. Their disenchantment with the political process and the party system was reflected in dwindling contributions. This may change again.

BART DOYLE, political director of the Ripon Society: What about the public financing of European parliamentary elections? This ties into the whole question of transfers of funds across national lines, the cooperation of ideologically related parties, and the issue of the conservative bloc versus the socialist bloc versus the liberal bloc in the European parliament. Is this a new phase of campaign financing?

MR. PALTIEL: This presents a problem. I know that the Dutch do not have much public financing except in the specific areas that we have talked about. So far, however, the elections have taken place according to the rules set by each country.

MR. AGREE: The parties in some countries that have public financing, such as Germany, last June received full election allocations for the conduct of the campaigns for the seats in the European parliament. That is to say, in order to conduct their campaigns for seats in the European parliament, the Christian Democratic Union and the Social Democratic party in Germany received from their federal government financial support comparable to what they would receive for a general election campaign for the Bundestag. This happened in some other countries to varying degrees.

However, you may be referring to another development. The European parliament gives funds to the party groups within the parliament. The parliamentarians do not sit in national blocs; they sit in party blocs, the Socialists, the Christians, and so on. Within the parliament, they have party groups whose staffs are funded out of common market funds appropriated by the parliament. In anticipation of the common market elections, party federations were formed that differ from the parliamentary party groups. These are quartered in Brussels to coordinate the campaign activities of the various member parties in the separate countries—which they did to varying degrees. There was some attempt to coordinate the campaigns throughout the common market. These party federations received public funding, in a sense, from the parliamentary groups, that is, the common market parliamentary groups. Enough money was voted to the parliamentary groups in order to permit them—and it may have been an unofficial contribution—to give some money to the party federations for their coordinating activities.

MR. MALBIN: When Dick Leonard from the *Economist* visited the American Enterprise Institute, he made a point that was pertinent to Mr. Doyle's and Mr. Epstein's questions. Regarding the prospects for public financing in Britain, he noted that with the forthcoming general election, the European parliamentary elections, and the prospect of one or two referenda—there was one on devolution and there might be others—the traditional methods of financing the parties in Britain are proving to be inadequate. The support from business for the Conservative party and from labor for the Labour party is simply not enough to handle so many campaigns. So, the role of the special interests, if you will, is not debated in the same terms in Britain as in the United States, because the real problem is perceived to be a shortage of funds. Public financing is not proposed as a way of eliminating the special interests but, rather, as a way of increasing participation and increasing the resources for conducting elections. Public financing, to borrow Mr. Alexander's formulation, is advocated in Britain—as in all other countries but the United States—as a floor for campaign financing and not a ceiling. That is, it is a supplement to and not a substitute for funds from private sources.

Date Due

11 · 197663 ILL			
DEC 1 4 '87 APR 2 3 '92			
		ᵇ	